Environmental Co-operation and Institutional Change

NEW HORIZONS IN ENVIRONMENTAL ECONOMICS

Series Editors: Wallace E. Oates, *Professor of Economics, University of Maryland, USA* and Henk Folmer, *Professor of General Economics, Wageningen University and Professor of Environmental Economics, Tilburg University, The Netherlands*

This important series is designed to make a significant contribution to the development of the principles and practices of environmental economics. It includes both theoretical and empirical work. International in scope, it addresses issues of current and future concern in both East and West and in developed and developing countries.

The main purpose of the series is to create a forum for the publication of high quality work and to show how economic analysis can make a contribution to understanding and resolving the environmental problems confronting the world in the twenty-first century.

Recent titles in the series include:

Environmental Co-operation and Institutional Change
Theories and Policies for European Agriculture
Edited by Konrad Hagedorn

Valuing Environmental and Natural Resources
The Econometrics of Non-Market Valuation
Timothy C. Haab and Kenneth E. McConnell

Controlling Global Warming
Perspectives from Economics, Game Theory and Public Choice
Edited by Christoph Böhringer, Michael Finus and Carsten Vogt

Environmental Regulation in a Federal System
Framing Environmental Policy in the European Union
Tim Jeppesen

The International Yearbook of Environmental and Resource Economics 2002/2003
A Survey of Current Issues
Edited by Tom Tietenberg and Henk Folmer

International Climate Policy to Combat Global Warming
An Analysis of the Ancillary Benefits of Reducing Carbon Emissions
Dirk T.G. Rübbelke

Pollution, Property and Prices
An Essay in Policy-making & Economics
J.H. Dales

The Contingent Valuation of Natural Parks
Assessing the Warmglow Propensity Factor
Paulo A.L.D. Nunes

Environmental Policy Making in Economics
with Prior Tax Distortions
Edited by Lawrence H. Goulder

Recent Advances in Environmental Economics
Edited by Aart de Zeeuw and John A. List

Sustainability and Endogenous Growth
Karen Pittel

Environmental Co-operation and Institutional Change

Theories and Policies for European Agriculture

Edited by

Konrad Hagedorn

Professor of Resource Economics, Humboldt University of Berlin, Germany

NEW HORIZONS IN ENVIRONMENTAL ECONOMICS

Edward Elgar

Cheltenham, UK • Northampton, MA, USA

Published by
Edward Elgar Publishing Limited
Glensanda House
Montpellier Parade
Cheltenham
Glos GL50 1UA
UK

Edward Elgar Publishing, Inc.
136 West Street
Suite 202
Northampton
Massachusetts 01060
USA

A catalogue record for this book
is available from the British Library

ISBN 1 84064 841 4

Printed and bound in Great Britain by MPG Books Ltd, Bodmin, Cornwall

Contents

Figures

Tables

Contributors

Mieczysław Adamowicz, Professor of Agricultural Economics, Warsaw Agricultural University, Department of Agricultural Policy and Marketing, Nowoursunowska 166, PL-02-787 Warsaw, Poland, Email: adamowicz@alpha.sggw.waw.pl

Katja Arzt, Ph.D. Student, Humboldt University of Berlin, Department of Agricultural Economics and Social Sciences, Resource Economics, Luisenstraße 56, D-10099 Berlin, Germany, Email: katja.arzt@agrar.hu-berlin.de

Regina Birner, Research Associate and Lecturer, Göttingen University, Institute of Rural Development, Waldweg 26, D-37073 Göttingen, Germany, Email: rbirner@gwdg.de

Jacques Brossier, Professor of Rural Economics and Management, Institut National de la Recherche Agronomique, 17 Rue Sully, BP 86510, F-21065 Dijon, France, Email: jacques.brossier@dijon.inra.fr

Floor Brouwer, Head of the Research Unit, Agricultural Economics Research Institute (LEI), Management of Natural Resources, P.O. Box 29703, NL-2502 LS The Hague, The Netherlands, Email: f.m.brouwer@lei.wag-ur.nl

Denis Claude, Ph.D. Student, Institut National de la Recherche Agronomique, 2 place Viala, F-34090 Montpellier Cedex 2, France, Email: claude@ensam.inra.fr

Gert van Dijk, Professor of Cooperative Science, Wageningen University, Department of Social Sciences, Marketing and Consumer Behaviour Group, Hollandseweg 1, NL-6706KN Wageningen, The Netherlands, Email: g.vandijk@cooperatie.nl

Erik Fahlbeck, Senior Lecturer of Agricultural Economics, Swedish University of Agricultural Sciences, Department of Economics, P.O. Box 7013, S-750 07 Uppsala, Sweden, Email: erik.fahlbeck@ekon.slu.se

Katherine Falconer, Economist, Scottish Executive Environment and Rural Affairs Department (SEERAD), Pentland House, 47 Robb's Loan Edinburgh, EH14 1TY, Scotland, Email: katherine.falconer@scotland.gsi.gov.uk

Mohamed Gafsi, Professor of Management Science, Ecole Nationale de Formation Agronomique, B.P. 87, F-31326 Castanet-Tolosan, France, Email: mohamed.gafsi@educagri.fr

Marie-Béatrice Galan, Ingenieur Agronom, Agrotransfert, Domaine de Brunehaut, F-80 200 Estrée-Mons, France, Email: galan@worldnet.fr

Michael Getzner, Associate Professor of Economics, University of Klagenfurt, Department of Economics, Universitätsstrasse 65-67, A-9020 Klagenfurt, Austria, Email: michael.getzner@uni-klu.ac.at

Arkadiusz Gralak, Lecturer, Warsaw Agricultural University, Department of Agricultural Policy and Marketing, Nowoursunowska 166, PL-02-787 Warsaw, Poland, Email: ekr_kpaim@alpha.sggw.waw.pl

Konrad Hagedorn, Professor of Resource Economics, Humboldt University of Berlin, Department of Agricultural Economics and Social Sciences, Chair of Resource Economics, Luisenstraße 56, D-10099 Berlin, Germany, Email: k.hagedorn@agrar.hu-berlin.de

Niels Halberg, Senior Researcher, Danish Institute of Agricultural Sciences, P.O. Box 50, DK-8830 Tjele, Denmark, Email: niels.halberg@agrsci.dk

Ingo Heinz, Environmental Economist, University of Dortmund, Institute of Environmental Research, D-44221 Dortmund, Germany, Email: i.heinz@infu.uni-dortmund.de

Guido Van Huylenbroeck, Professor of Agricultural and Rural Environmental Economics, Ghent University, Department of Agricultural Economics, Coupure links 653, B-9000 Gent, Belgium, Email: guido.vanhuylenbroeck@rug.ac.be

Britta Jell, Project Manager, Richthofenstraße 5, D-86899 Landsberg am Lech, Germany, Email: bjell@t-online.de

Andrea Knierim, Consultant, Tempelberger Weg 43, D-15374 Müncheberg, Germany, Email: knierim@web.de

Christian Lippert, Research Associate, Technical University of Munich, Weihenstephan Centre of Life and Food Sciences, D-85350 Freising-Weihenstephan, Germany, Email: lippert@weihenstephan.de

Armelle Mazé, Economist, Institut National de la Recherche Agronomique, 16 Rue Claude Bernard, F-75231 Paris cedex O5, France, Email: maze@inapg.inra.fr

Klaus Müller, Research Associate, University of Potsdam, Faculty of Economics and Social Sciences, August-Bebel-Str. 89, D-14482 Potsdam, Germany, Email: klausmue@rz.uni-potsdam.de

Jerker Nilsson, Professor of Co-operative Business, Swedish University of Agricultural Sciences, Department of Economics, P.O. Box 7013, S-750 07 Uppsala, Sweden, Email: jerker.nilsson@ekon.slu.se

Egon Noe, Ph.D. Student, Danish Institute of Agricultural Sciences, Department of Agricultural Systems, P.O. Box 50, DK-8830 Tjele, Denmark, Email: egon.noe@agscri.dk

Ernst-August Nuppenau, Professor of Rural and Environmental Policy, Justus Liebig University Giessen, Institute of Rural Policy and Market Research, Senckenberg Str. 3, D-35390 Giessen, Germany, E-mail: ernst-august.nuppenau@agrar.uni-giessen.de

Francois Papy, Research Director, Institute National de la Recherche Agronomique, 16 Rue Claude Bernard, F-75231 Paris cedex O5, France, Email: papy@grignon.inra.fr

Ursula Peters, Senior Researcher, Humboldt University of Berlin, Department of Agricultural Economics and Social Sciences, Resource Economics, Luisenstraße 56, D-10099 Berlin, Germany, Email: u.peters@agrar.hu-berlin.de

Nico B.P. Polman, Ph.D. Student, Wageningen University, Agricultural Economics and Rural Policy Group, Hollandseweg 1, NL-6706 KN Wageningen, The Netherlands, Email: nico.polmann@alg.aae.wau.nl

Louis H.G. Slangen, Associate Professor, Wageningen University, Agricultural Economics and Rural Policy Group, Hollandseweg 1, NL-6706 KN Wageningen, The Netherlands, Email: louis.slangen@alg.aae.wau.nl

Jifke Sol, Senior Researcher, Nyenrode University, The Netherlands Institute for Cooperative Entrepreneurship, Straatweg 25, NL-3621 Breukelen, The Netherlands, Email: j.sol@nyenrode.nl

Ingrid Verhaegen, Ph.D. Student, Ghent University, Department of Agricultural Economics, Coupure links 653, B-9000 Gent, Belgium, Email: guido.vanhuylenbroeck@rug.ac.be

Hans-Peter Weikard, Associate Professor, Wageningen University, Department of Social Sciences, Hollandseweg 1, NL-6706 KN Wageningen, The Netherlands, Email: hans-peter.weikard@alg.shhk.wau.nl

Heidi Wittmer, Research Associate, University of Göttingen, Institute of Rural Development, Waldweg 26, D-37073 Göttingen, Germany, Email: hwittmer@gwdg.de

Thomas Zabel, Consultant, Water Research Centre WRc plc, Henley Road, Medmenham, Marlow, Bucks, SL7 2HD, England, Email: zabel@wrcplc.co.uk

Preface

The history of the Common Agricultural Policy (CAP) is dominated by a process of centralisation as regards the mechanisms and instruments by which the farming sectors are regulated. Admittedly, this concept has been rather successful if we consider the progress in European integration to which it has contributed significantly. However, the CAP has also produced many negative effects such as the introduction of milk quotas and set-aside schemes, the McSharry Reform and the Agenda 2000, creating problems with which EU politicians have had to cope in the last decades, problems they are still trying to solve through permanent reforms. In particular, the mounting political pressure to integrate agri-environmental policies into the CAP have increasingly revealed the necessity of combining centralised and decentralised approaches in a way that leads to an efficient federal structure of decision making.

There is, in likelihood, an additional reason why EU development is at a turning point: it seems no longer necessary to shift competencies from the national level of the member states to the EU level primarily for the purpose of providing the Union with additional tasks and, through this, strengthening the process of integration. Instead, EU politicians can now afford to think about concepts of differentiation which obviously follow the initial phase of centralisation. At what level of the federal system should the various tasks be allocated, for example what should be left to regional and local decision makers? What should be done by government agencies and what should be the domain of other actors or organisations, for instance co-operatives or networks?

The principle of subsidiarity which has been strongly emphasised by the European Commission in the discussion about the Agenda 2000 can be taken as an indicator of this change in attitude. Simultaneously, environmental issues related to agriculture represent a good example of this new orientation. There are two main policy areas which show that agri-environmental strategies will be less successful in the future if decentralisation and increased co-operation and participation of land users are not properly considered. This applies to the agri-environmental programmes introduced by the McSharry Reform within the framework of accompanying measures, and secondly, to the attempt to implement the principle of 'cross compliance' as an element of the Agenda 2000.

As far as the agri-environmental programmes are concerned, both farmers and the administrative units at the community level usually complain that these measures are not adjusted to the heterogeneity of ecological conditions and environmental problems which differ significantly between regions and locations. In addition, monitoring and supervising these measures has turned out to be more difficult than expected. Most of the people involved in these programmes agree that more competencies should be shifted to the regional and local level. They also demand more flexibility in implementation and administration.

Regarding the introduction of cross compliance, the Agenda 2000 has made transfer payments conditional upon compliance with ecological standards. The European Commission has not solved this problem by defining these standards itself, but has delegated this task to national governments of the member states. However, the latter recognise more and more that such a general link between compensation payments and ecological standards can only be achieved by means of extreme simplification. Again, the resulting environmental impact will be rather ineffective given the differences, the complexity and the variability of ecological issues, and of the economic and social implications of these issues at the local and regional level.

These cases demonstrate that agricultural economists should improve their capacity to advise politicians as to how to design agri-environmental institutions and policies that can be adjusted to the varying nature of agri-environmental problems. Unfortunately, our knowledge in this field is still very incomplete, and we particularly have to look for adequate theoretical concepts, empirical studies and research results which deal with strategies of co-operation and participation. For this purpose, the 64th Seminar of the European Association of Agricultural Economists (EAAE) was organised at Humboldt University of Berlin in Autumn 1999, focusing on 'Co-operative Strategies to Cope with Agri-environmental Problems'. Support from the Wissenschaftsfonds der DG Bank (DG Bank Science Fund) for exploring the research topic and from the Deutsche Forschungsgemeinschaft (German Research Foundation) for conference funding is gratefully acknowledged. The chapters in this volume are based on contributions to the Seminar.

The chapters deal with a variety of topics. First, theoretical approaches and institutional foundations of environmental co-operation, participation and co-management are discussed. After this introduction, the Dutch experience in designing and managing environmental co-operatives which have been established in past years in The Netherlands is presented in Part II. Part III focuses on the farm level and discusses governance structures and learning processes which aim at changing agricultural practices. Applicability of property rights, auction and political economy concepts of agri-environmental problems, and programmes in rural communities are analysed in Part IV.

Then, co-operative arrangements and voluntary approaches in implementing environmental policies are described in Part V. Part VI deals with knowledge systems, stakeholders' interests and conflict resolution in protected areas. The final Part shows how environmental protection can be supported by the co-operative marketing of food products.

Many persons have contributed to this book. First of all, I want to express my gratitude to all authors for their careful and innovative work, and to the participants of the 64th EAAE Seminar for their ideas and discussions. Numerous people at the Chair of Resource Economics and at the Institute of Co-operative Studies of Humboldt University of Berlin have promoted this project. In particular, I am grateful to Dr Ursula Peters who, aside from her research input, devoted much effort to the organisation of the Seminar, to Elizabeth Birmingham who did the English editing, and to Sigrid Heilmann for technical support. Last but not least, I want to thank Marlis Werner and Georg Ruhm from the Berlin Institute for Co-operative Studies for their intensive work in designing and completing the manuscript.

Konrad Hagedorn
Berlin, November 2001

PART I

Theoretical Approaches and Institutional Foundations of Environmental Co-operation

1. Institutional Arrangements for Environmental Co-operatives: a Conceptual Framework

Konrad Hagedorn, Katja Arzt and Ursula Peters

1 INTRODUCTION

The chapters in this volume address a variety of topics which refer to co-operative strategies to cope with agri-environmental problems. Some of them deal directly with environmental co-operatives of farmers (Slangen and Polman, Chapter 4; Polman and Slangen, Chapter 5; van Dijk and Sol, Chapter 6; Falconer, Chapter 13), or with important features and pre-requisites of such co-operatives like participation, co-management with bureaucracies and common property and management of common property (Claude, Chapter 2; Birner, Jell and Wittmer, Chapter 3) or with co-operative agreements and arrangements aiming at particular tasks and objectives (Brouwer, Heinz and Zabel, Chapter 14; Adamowicz and Gralak, Chapter 15). Other chapters provide important conceptual and theoretical contributions to these topics (Lippert, Chapter 10; Müller and Weikard, Chapter 11; Nuppenau, Chapter 12), show how co-operatives, co-operation and participation help to change farming practices (Gafsi and Brossier, Chapter 7; Noe and Halberg, Chapter 8; Mazé, Galan and Papy, Chapter 9) to support nature conservation (Knierim, Chapter 16; Getzner, Chapter 17), and to improve marketing (Fahlbeck and Nilsson, Chapter 18; van Huylenbroeck and Verhaegen, Chapter 19).

This chapter differs from these approaches: it provides less answers as to how agri-environmental co-operatives and co-operation should actually be developed in order to solve agri-environmental problems. Instead, it tries to ask the theoretical and methodological questions we have to deal with to achieve this goal. In this way, we try to find tools and procedures to conceptualise and to implement environmental co-operatives and co-operation in agriculture and rural areas. Although the concept presented is incomplete and far from providing reliable guidelines for research steps towards environmental co-operation in general, and environmental co-operatives in particular, it may be instrumental in finding a systematic approach for organising into research institutions in this area.

The chapter is organised as follows: first, the main determinants of agri-environmental co-ordination mechanisms will be structured in four categories. Then, these groups of relevant factors will be described in more detail in the following sections by discussing properties of transactions in agriculture linked to ecological effects, features of the actors involved in these transactions, property rights to nature components and ecological attributes, and governance structures on a regional and local level. The last section will try to identify combinations of transactions and actors, and choices of property rights and governance structures that call for co-operative arrangements.

2 TOWARDS AN INSTITUTIONAL APPROACH TO AGRI-ENVIRONMENTAL CO-ORDINATION

Institutional change in the area of agri-environmental co-ordination, that is mainly property rights regimes and governance structures, can be understood as a response to technological (or biological) and economic factors, on the one hand, and societal and political influences, on the other. To structure and to analyse the relationships and the interplay between these factors, an explorative concept is necessary (see also Hagedorn 2000). For this purpose, it seems to be useful to distinguish between the following four groups of determinants:

1. Which institutional arrangements arise, that depend on the features and implications of the transactions related to nature and the ecosystem (for example leaching of nitrates into the groundwater on sandy soils). This is mainly influenced by the physical properties and material transformations with which environmental positives and negatives, benefits and damages are associated. Technological innovation and structural change lead to permanent changes of these properties and transformations.
2. Simultaneously, institutional change depends on the characteristics and objectives of the actors involved in those transactions (for example farmers who reinforce nitrate leaching by high nitrogen fertilisation and unfavourable crop rotation without catch crops). This is not only true for individual actors whose values, interests and resources to exert influence (power) are very different, but also for groups of individuals like

communities using organisations and networks to shape institutions according to their objectives.

3. The changes in institutional arrangements, which result from the two main categories of driving forces mentioned above, affect the design and distribution of property rights on nature components, or, more precisely, on those cost and benefit streams which can be attributed to natural capital and ecosystem services (for example trade-offs between reducing nitrogen balances by means of lower fertilisation and intercropping and decline in gross margins). The property rights tend to become more and more differentiated, for example they apply not only to physical goods like land, but also to various dimensions and many details of land use relevant to environmental protection and sustainable agriculture, for example the right to decide on catch crops as an element of crop rotation.
4. Necessarily, such changes in property rights to nature components are accompanied by corresponding changes in governance structures, mainly for two reasons: first, property rights to nature components, like other property rights, must be supervised and sanctioned to become effective instead of being only formal in nature; and secondly, the actors can only make use of their rights and entitlements and will only fulfil their duties and obligations if transactions are organised and co-ordinated (for example farmers will only comply with fertilising restrictions and cropping prescriptions if an adequately working system of measuring and monitoring activities, information and administration, positive and/or negative incentives, that is of subsidies and/or penalties, exists). Similar to the property rights regimes mentioned above, governance structures are also very differentiated. They include self-organised co-ordination (for example environmental co-operatives) and governmental regulations (for example environmental bureaucracies), and they are not only related to the implementation of environmental instruments, but also to decision making on environmental policies which takes place on the different levels of co-operative federalism (community, region, province, national, EU, international). Last but not least, the political economy behind the process of joint implementation and decision making in a federal system has to be taken into account.

Figure 1.1 provides a visual representation of these four groups. We now try to describe and explain these four groups of determinants in more detail, referring to approaches of New Institutional Economics and Institutional Analysis of Natural Resources (for example, Richter and Furobotn 1996; North 1992; Williamson 1996; Ostrom 1990, 1998, 1999; Bromley 1991, 1996, 1997; Loehmann and Kilgour 1998). Studies available on environmental co-operation and participation are used as an additional source

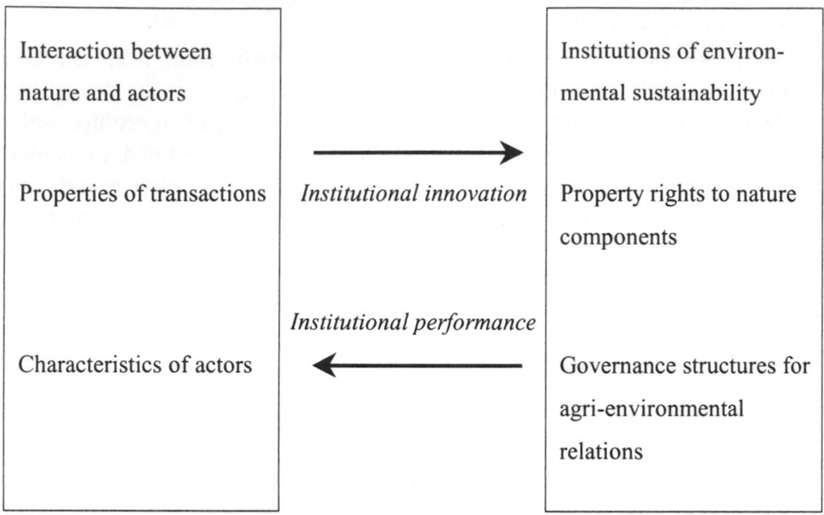

Figure 1.1 The logic of institutional arrangements for agri-environmental co-ordination

of theoretical concepts and empirical information (see OECD 1998; Bahner 1996; Zimmer 1991, 1994a,b; Campbell 1998; Fisk, Hesterman and Thorborn 1998; van Woerkum and Aarts 1998; Woodhill and Röling 1998; and the contributions to the 64th EAAE Seminar published in this volume). After having dealt with these four groups of determinants, some ideas on the scope for co-operative arrangements will be developed at the end of the chapter.

3 PROPERTIES OF TRANSACTIONS AFFECTING THE NATURAL ENVIRONMENT AND ECOLOGICAL SYSTEMS

Transactions which are relevant to the impact of agriculture on nature and ecosystems can be considered from two (opposite) points of view:

(a) Producing or increasing an environmental problem by production or consumption activities (for example, excessive nitrogen leaching) is a transaction between the farmer and the public or community concerned.

(b) Solving or diminishing an environmental problem by self-organised or government policies (for example, introducing limits to nitrogen surpluses) is a transaction between the regulator and the farmer.

Not surprisingly, these views are more or less reciprocal. We will primarily concentrate on the first one. Simultaneously, transactions at the regional level will be investigated, excluding transactions originating from higher policy levels of the federal system in the EU.

Environmental problems caused by agricultural activities can usually be considered as being a result of (often impure) public goods (or club goods and common-pool resources) whose legal transformation, defined as their transfer between different actors or groups of actors, shows particular difficulties. Some of these problematic features of transactions are specific to public goods, others can also be found with private goods but lead to similar problems when they are combined with the characteristics of public goods. The main properties are:

1. Excludability of actors from access to environmental goods, closely related to the mechanisms and costs of exclusion that have to be covered. Both mechanisms and costs of exclusion differ considerably among different natural resources and environmental goods. If exclusion of actors who are not entitled to use the goods or resources (or are only eligible to use a limited amount of it or to use it in a certain well-defined way) do not work properly, free riding will result in depletion of natural resources or undesirable environmental damage.
2. Rivalry among the users of environmental goods is also not equally distributed, if we compare the resources and goods that are of interest when dealing with agri-environmental co-ordination. Using pure public goods, like viewing a beautiful landscape, does not cause any competition among the users, because the benefits from the landscape are not reduced when the number of users increases. However, if an impure public good, like the limited amount of fish in a lake, is used by one additional actor, the amount available to all other actors will be reduced correspondingly. Between this case of complete 'subtractability', as it is called in the literature on common-pool resources (Ostrom 1998), and the other extreme situation of pure public goods, we find a continuum with different degrees of rivalry.
3. Asset specificity and the resulting co-ordination problems to be solved by adequate institutional arrangements can be observed if durable investments have been made by the supplier in order to prepare for a long-term relationship between the parties involved. As pointed out in the fixed-asset theory (Johnson and Pasour 1981), such assets will lose much of their value if the contract is voided earlier than expected. This enables the purchaser to lower the price of the goods or services provided by means of durable investments and calls for adequate governance structures to avoid this sort of strategic behaviour (lock-in and hold-up

situations). In the case of agri-environmental goods, asset specificity plays a major role in at least three cases (see also Slangen and Polman, Chapter 4, this volume): (a) site specificity, for example if a specific biotope or species that a farmer takes care of by means of adequate agricultural practices, is located in a certain area or plot, (b) capital specificity, for example if a farmer has invested sunk costs in nature conservation (planting hedges, and so on), and (c) specific knowledge which land users and inhabitants have collected and developed on nature and the environment where they live and work, representing group-specific human capital.

4. Separability is often low due to joint production of the environmental goods provided by the farmers. This is a widespread and important feature, for example with regard to landscape and habitats, a fact that is particularly emphasised by Falconer (Chapter 13, this volume). This requires a governance structure which is able to co-ordinate the activities of the group of landowners participating in the production of the common good. If this involves incentives provided by political agencies, for example agri-environmental policy payments, it is often inadequate to orient these monetary supports only to individuals.
5. Frequency of transactions may differ considerably, for example if we compare single resource utilisation like deforestation with seasonal utilisation patterns, like wheat cropping. Recurrent transactions make it easier to invest in specialised governance structures, because the costs can be distributed over many transactions, economies of scale can be made use of and learning by doing over time helps to find more efficient solutions. Most of the transactions which are relevant to the impact of agriculture on the ecological system and the natural environment show high frequency, for example fertilising with nitrogen. However, if long-term agreements are made, this implies a much lower frequency of decision making.
6. Uncertainty plays a major role in the demand and supply of agri-environmental goods and services, because farmers and regulators do not know very precisely either whether certain environmental problems will arise, and when they will occur, or what the nature of these problems will be, and to what extent they will have serious impacts and who will be affected. The same is true for the policies and activities aimed at preventing these problems. Reduction of these uncertainties causes transaction costs, for example for measuring and monitoring environmental degradation and gathering adequate information. This property of agri-environmental transactions is closely connected with the following feature, and its relevance is considerably reinforced by the facts mentioned in the next paragraph.

7. Complexity of the causal relationship of ecological systems, particularly as it is combined with the still insufficient availability of well-established scientific knowledge, invites actors to practice opportunistic behaviour. For operationalising transactions, the complex ecological phenomena have to be described by means of simplifying criteria. If even scientists do not know what is the right thing to do for the environment, individual demanders will find it difficult to form reliable and reasonable preferences. In addition, as public goods are at stake, these preferences have to be channelled and aggregated by complicated organisational procedures. In this process, simplification is indispensable, particularly if government bureaucracies are involved. This is even more necessary if they have to collaborate across several policy levels in a federal system like the EU. While for private goods, like bread or sausages, consumers are quite well able to reveal their true preferences, preferences for environmental protection in the agricultural sector are likely to be distorted when they finally arrive at the supplier, for example at the land user. The latter and his political representatives, for example farmers' unions, may consider this as an opportunity to influence the process in a way that makes it easier for farmers to comply with the environmental requirements, for example by choosing a favourable indicator and monitoring system and producing plausible justifications for compensation payments. The tendency of CAP to instrumentalise environmental aspects for legitimating income policies is obviously a strategy of this kind.
8. Heterogeneity and variability are typical attributes of 'many environmental problems, especially those to which agriculture contributes, (which) are heavily influenced by stochastic phenomena, such as the weather' (OECD 1998, p. 17). The same applies to other differences between vegetation periods or plots of land, for example regarding soil quality. It is difficult to design strategies and measures that are adjusted to the manifold phenomena of heterogeneity and variability which could also be termed 'site and situation specificity'.
9. Legitimacy refers to the question of whether or not transactions are compatible with the normative views of the actors and groups concerned by or even involved in both decision making and implementation activities. Penalising farmers who pollute the groundwater may appear to be much more legitimate than distributing pollution rights to them, even if the latter strategy may yield better ecological as well as economic effects.

4 CHARACTERISTICS OF ACTORS INVOLVED IN AGRI-ENVIRONMENTAL CO-ORDINATION

Before turning to the differences and particularities of the actors involved, it should be mentioned that the distinction between properties of the transactions and characteristics of the actors sometimes appears to be rather artificial. This is because the actors certainly shape and arrange the transactions related to physical and natural elements of the environment, but they, in turn, are simultaneously influenced, or even formed, by what they are doing. For example, by cultivating his land using modern farming technologies, a farmer gains practical knowledge and detailed local information about the response of nature to the applied technologies, and it is difficult to decide whether this feature should be attributed to the transaction or to the actor.

Furthermore, we have to be aware of the fact that we could think of numerous categories of actors which might also include policy makers and administrators at the national and EU levels. However, we restrict our considerations to land users and regulators or co-ordinators on the regional level, for example administrators of a government agency or managers of a self-organised environmental co-operative. Of course, the ability to mobilise their political entrepreneurs and, in this way, to exert political pressure can be an important attribute of these actors, like the following attributes:

1. The values and beliefs of the actors and their particular attitudes and perceptions of agri-environmental issues are relevant to their readiness to collaborate with other actors and to comply with rules of co-operation and also with policy measures. Admittedly, if farmers are purely self-interested, they can still be motivated towards environmental goals by economic incentives. But if they are convinced that sustainable agriculture is an objective worth working for, they will be prepared to be systematically involved in such activities. Their values have an influence on how they evaluate situations which require (often collective) decisions in favour of sustainability.
2. It is equally important, particularly for contractual and co-operative arrangements, how actors are evaluated by other actors. This refers to their reputations for reliability and trustworthiness which are decisive factors for the credibility of their commitments. Polman and Slangen (Chapter 5, this volume) have particularly emphasised the importance of credible commitments for the emergence and stability of co-operative arrangements.
3. Resources for influencing agri-environmental strategies like self-organised co-ordination of agri-environmental activities or administrative

implementation of agri-environmental policies at the regional and local levels, that is by direct participation in these processes. This refers to resources, like time and capacities to collect information, access to networks and bargaining power, which are necessary or instrumental to establish and maintain relationships and to achieve acceptance of own interests. Actors who are involved in processes of communication usually have advantages and groups whose members can communicate with each other can more easily find common rules (Ostrom 1999).

4. Resources for influencing processes of political decision making and policy implementation at higher than the regional level, that is mechanisms of interest representation in decision-making processes in which land users cannot participate directly. Farmers can use well-established channels for delegating the enforcement of their political demands to political entrepreneurs. The Political Economy of Agricultural Policies is based on intensive political preferences of farmers; electoral control and party competition; interpretation systems for justifying farmer-supporting policies; farmers' unions as efficient organisations for collective action; friendly relations with bureaucracies, ministries and parliamentary committees; an agrarian policy network; joint decision making of agricultural experts across all levels of the federal system; and so on (see, for a more detailed theory, Hagedorn 1996a,b; 1998).
5. Information and knowledge, and capacities for acquiring and processing, retaining and using knowledge and information represent a resource that has to be mentioned separately. Above all, asymmetric information of actors, well known from the principal–agent theory, is a widespread phenomenon in agri-environmental decision making. Farmers who know a lot about their land and the vegetation on it and are at the same time well aware of the fact that administrators find it difficult to obtain such detailed information, may not be able to resist the temptation of opportunism. For example, they may accept extensification subsidies for plots they could not use intensively anyhow.
6. The 'actor's method of action selection' (Ostrom 1998, p. 70) may also be very different between the persons involved. These persons can be assumed to be maximising homines oeconomici, as constrained maximisers with bounded rationality, or fallible learners who make mistakes but are able to learn from them. For explorative and innovative tasks like forming institutions dealing with new problems which arise from changes in agricultural technology and structures, the latter two assumptions seem to be appropriate.
7. In addition, the social environment and embeddedness of actors affect their behaviour. 'Community attributes relevant to the structure of an

> action arena include behavioural norms, the level and nature of the common understanding shared by potential participants, the extent to which those living in the community have homogeneous preferences, and the distribution of resources. The term culture is frequently applied to this bundle of variables. When all appropriators of a common-pool resource share a common set of values and interact within a complex set of arrangements, there is a much greater probability that they will develop adequate rules and norms to manage resources . . . If keeping one's word is important in such a community, the need for costly monitoring and sanctioning mechanisms is reduced. Conversely, if the appropriators of a resource represent different communities, or are distrustful, then the task of devising and sustaining effective rules is substantially more difficult' (Ostrom 1998, p. 71).

What mechanisms will arise or could be chosen to co-ordinate the transactions between the actors are both described in the preceding sections. It has already been pointed out that these co-ordination mechanisms can be conceived of as an interplay between property rights regimes and governance structures. Therefore, the next two sections structure these two areas of institutional arrangements.

5 PROPERTY RIGHTS TO NATURE COMPONENTS RELATED TO AGRICULTURE

Property rights theory is often misunderstood as an approach explaining the definition and distribution of disposition rights focusing on physical entities (that is, material goods). This view needs to be modified as regards the following aspects:

1. Strictly speaking, actors only attribute (positive or negative) values to a physical good because the right holder is favoured by benefit streams or in case of a duty is burdened by cost components which are connected with the physical good. Bromley (1991, p. 189) calls these nature components 'countryside and community attributes' (CCA), de Groot (1992, p. 13) environmental functions (regulating, carrier, production and information function). These ecological properties that are linked to costs and benefits which can be derived from a physically defined piece of nature can be further differentiated according to results (that is, impacts of pieces of nature on costs and benefits) or according to actions (that is, ecologically relevant activities when dealing with nature).

2. A natural good, like soil, is usually considered to carry only one homogeneous property title. However, such rights cannot only be classified according to the conventional division into (a) the right to use, (b) the right to alter and (c) the right of alienation. What is more, categories of property rights can be separately defined for numerous ecological properties of the physical piece of nature, each of them related to particular costs and benefits. For each of these differentiated rights components, the institutional design of the right or duty can differ: private, collective and state property regimes are imaginable, and also the absence of property rights definition and delineation in the sense of open access (Bromley 1991, 1997; Ostrom 1990).
3. However, creating and using property rights will not take place without transaction costs, which are, for example, caused by defining and establishing these rights and also by measuring the environmental attributes they apply to and supervising that these attributes are properly provided. Since these transaction costs can be prohibitively high and may exceed the benefits, property rights for some or even many components of nature may not be established. This may change when the valuation of an environmental attribute increases or when the distribution of the benefits changes or when the transaction costs of enforcement of the single rights or of measuring and supervising the nature components decrease, for example, as a consequence of technological progress (Barzel 1989).
4. The resulting structure of property rights is usually supposed to be reasonable if the rights related to the differentiated attributes accrue to those actors who can influence their design in the most efficient way. Since it seems legitimate in this case, too, that he or she may obtain the surplus value, that actor also becomes a 'residual claimant' (see also Lippert, Chapter 10, this volume). In this context, low transaction costs are an argument for bundling the rights on all nature components of a physical object in the hand of one actor, whereas the advantages of specialisation and economies of scale may favour distribution of the single rights to different actors ('divided property'). This raises the question whether particular (partial) rights, for example the right to organise ecological networks of biotopes and habitats, which is a control right, should be given to special actors, for example to environmental co-operatives or regional agencies (Hodge 1991; Lippert, Chapter10, this volume).
5. Bundling property rights on the manifold components and attributes of a physical piece of nature, that is giving it to one land user, usually means at the same time that the distribution of rights is rather decentralised (at least, if there are many land users like farmers). Dividing those rights

between the land users and other specialised agents automatically results in a higher degree of centralisation of those rights that the former holders are deprived of. This has, of course, social and political consequences. It may affect the motivation and participation of the land users, precipitate moral dilemmas and lead to less identification with the local and regional natural environment.

6. The term 'property rights to nature components or ecological attributes' certainly is useful on the one hand, because it reflects the fact that there are manifold claims on agricultural production and that land and other natural assets used by agriculture are related to a variety of cost and benefit streams, many of them being public positives or negatives. On the other hand, it could support the notion that each of those fragmented rights could be used, and each of the single duties could be fulfilled, in an isolated way. As we are dealing with ecological systems, this will neither be possible nor reasonable. Perhaps it might be more appropriate to talk about rights and duties which are conditional upon the use and fulfilment of other rights and duties respectively.

6 GOVERNANCE STRUCTURES FOR REGIONAL OR LOCAL AGRI-ENVIRONMENTAL CO-ORDINATION

In New Institutional Economics, usually three categories of governance structures (see Williamson 1996) are distinguished: markets, hierarchies – or, more generally, considered as 'organisations' – and so-called 'hybrid forms', sometimes termed as contractual relations. Slangen and Polman (Chapter 4, this volume) try to put more emphasis on this 'third way of co-ordination' and call it 'horizontal non-market co-ordination' where also co-operation can find its place. The scope for reasonable applications is extended to a type of governance structure which plays an important role in reality.

Another extension of the concept can be derived from the following reasoning: First the categories of governance structures mentioned above predominantly reflect the relationship between actors involved in a transaction. Secondly, action selection is obviously considered the relevant subject of this relationship. In markets, selection of action is based on voluntary bilateral agreements between individuals, in hierarchies action is compulsorily selected by an authority on a higher level, and contractual relations contain both voluntary action before the contract has been finalised and compulsory action when the contract is in force. However, transactions which are relevant for agri-environmental phenomena are not limited to the question of whether action selection is voluntary or compulsory, and they are even not restricted to selecting action, but include many other activities which represent either prerequisites or consequences of action selection. This refers to gathering and processing knowledge and information, measuring and monitoring, bargaining and conflict resolution, organising adjustments and regulating liabilities, and so on.

How can we conceive of this extended range and more comprehensive meaning of governance structures? The Enquête Commission of the German Bundestag: 'Protection of Man and the Environment' has recently published two books on the institutional interpretation of sustainability. In its works previously published, the Commission had mainly concentrated on the question: what is sustainable development? Objectives of environmental quality and activities were defined, for example for the area of soil protection, and management rules as well as policy instruments for the implementation of sustainable development were developed. However, sustainable development has to be conceived of as a comprehensive process of searching, learning and gaining experience. For that reason, it is not only the question of what might be sustainable development but also the question of how and by means of what organisational principles applied to learning processes in society sustainable development can be achieved. As a consequence, environmental goals and their implementation by means of policy instruments is not the only task. In addition, sustainable development has to be interpreted as a regulative idea which requires adequate institutions to become effective in the various areas of society.

For this purpose, the Commission has defined four basic strategies (Minsch et al. 1998):

- Strategies to improve reflexivity: These strategies reinforce the sensitivity of all actors regarding the ecological, economic and social side effects of their behaviour. Such strategies can be seen as an answer to the increasing complexity and differentiation of societal and political processes. Strategies of reflexivity have to be implemented at all levels and in all phases of the political process. In many cases they serve as a starting point and as a basis for further institutional reforms of the processes of consensus building and policy making.
- Strategies to reinforce self-organisation and participation: These strategies can be considered as a response to the fact that political processes are increasingly isolated and separated from the citizens and the people concerned. Accordingly, self-organisation and participation are supposed to have an integrative impact by which politics are embedded again into society. People and groups concerned with political decisions are supposed to become political actors again, and poorly organised groups which are not able to express their interests in the political sphere, for example many social and ecological interests, may use such strategies to get a hearing in the political process.

- Strategies for interest harmonisation and conflict regulation: These strategies aim at balancing inequalities of power and control over resources. They may lead to constructive solutions regarding conflicts between different interests and conflicting values, for example between ecological, economic and social aspects of sustainability. Particularly in the agricultural sectors, ecologically motivated restrictions on property rights and new environmental policies cause winners and losers. The feasibility of such concepts may be lacking if mechanisms to deal with conflicts of distribution are underdeveloped.
- Strategies for innovation: These strategies create new options and capacities for action in society which may be societal, political, economic or technical in nature. They provide possibilities for creative processes of searching and learning in society during the process of achieving sustainable development. In this way, they may help to reduce or even to avoid conflicts between the different objectives which constitute sustainability. Co-operative approaches to cope with environmental problems on the regional level could be an example for such innovations.

The Commission stresses the point that the actors in a society should learn to interpret their position as a member of a network. They are supposed to take into account the framework conditions of other actors and the determinants and constraints guiding the development of society as a whole, and they are expected to include these aspects in their own decision making. A better understanding of mutual dependencies enables each actor to integrate long-term societal conditions into his or her reasoning and helps him or her to contribute to sustainable development.

In this way, society is moving towards a 'learning organisation'. Sustainability as a regulative idea requires such processes of searching within society because the design of institutions and of policy instruments cannot immediately be derived from this basic principle. As a consequence, discourses play a central role in this process of learning. Organising such discourses requires learning organisations which both provide signals for learning processes to and receive such signals from society. Learning organisations as well as the learning society as a whole can be conceived of as being both prerequisites and results of the processes of discourse.

In principle, all the aspects of governance structures supporting sustainability also apply to agri-environmental co-ordination on the regional and local level. Accordingly, the following elements play a role:

1. markets, for example tradable pollution quotas;
2. hierarchies (organisations) like environmental bureaucracies;

3. hybrid forms (contractual relations), for example stewardship contracts;
4. horizontal non-market co-ordination, that is co-operation and participation of farmers;
5. knowledge and information systems, formal and informal networks;
6. methods and infrastructure for measuring, monitoring and evaluating environmental damages and benefits, for example laboratories;
7. rules and procedures for conflict resolution, distribution of costs and benefits, regulation of liability;
8. incentives and opportunities to promote innovation and learning.

In reality, governance structures will consist of different combinations and complex arrangements of these elements.

7 THE SCOPE FOR AGRI-ENVIRONMENTAL CO-OPERATIVES AND CO-OPERATION AS AN INSTITUTIONAL INNOVATION

Of course, nobody will reasonably expect that co-operatives and co-operation can solve all agri-environmental co-ordination problems. In other words, this would mean that

(a) for all combinations and groupings of transactions and actors with the described properties and features, co-operative arrangements would be the most efficient institutional innovation, which would prove to be superior in a process of institutional competition with other institutional solutions.
(b) all institutional solutions designed in an optimal way to deal with the co-ordination problems originating from those combinations and groupings of transactions and actors with different properties and features and, hence, surviving institutional competition, would fall into the range of co-operative arrangements, leaving the other categories outlined above empty.

As a consequence, the question arises as to when co-operatives and co-operation will be competitive and when other institutional alternatives will be preferred. If we could find answers to this question, we simultaneously would have better knowledge of how we should orient our efforts to intentionally design institutional innovations in this area. However, since most of the answers are still lacking, we must restrict ourselves to a few arguments for identifying situations and solutions in which priority might be given to co-operative arrangements. According to the structure of groups of determinants developed in this chapter, we start by asking which transactions could be co-ordinated by co-operatives or co-operation:

1. Costs of administration, monitoring and enforcement, or generally speaking, the transaction costs of policy, can be lowered by co-operation and participation (see Hanna 1995). 'During the stages of problem identification and policy design, transaction costs are minimised by a top-down approach – that is one that avoids spending time and resources in co-ordination, information, dissemination and conflict resolution. However, such an approach creates uncertainty in the mind of the users as to the goals of the process, encouraging short-term actions at the expense of long-term sustainability. By contrast, the bottom-up approach, involving extensive participation by users, gives them a stake in the outcome and reduces uncertainty about the process goals. Users are more likely to comply with regulations, and to adopt a stewardship ethic, when they understand and endorse the policy goals, and have some assurance of control over outcomes' (OECD 1998, p. 16). In other words, when visibility and transparency are low and costs of monitoring and supervision are high, compliance with environmental rules and norms can be improved by participation and co-operation instead of using hierarchical instruments of enforcement. In addition, group leaders or co-operative managers can make use of tools for control and enforcement government agencies cannot access, like appealing to members' loyalties and applying peer pressure.
2. Economic approaches often try to attribute well-defined values and tasks of functions to components of nature and corresponding criteria to environmental problems that would enable them to find optimal and stable economic solutions. However, some authors criticise this view because it considers natural resources in the same way as 'commodities', as if goods derived from nature and ecosystems were separate and discrete elements (Berkes and Folke 1998; Holling, Berkes and Folke 1998). Additionally, natural systems are always dynamic and many of their changes are not predictable (see Hanna, Folke and Mäler 1996). As a consequence, institutions are necessary which account for the complexity and dynamics of such systems. Environmental co-operatives may be appropriate solutions for this, because they use local knowledge and adjust to local conditions.
3. Balance of power between farmers and government agencies may be a problem because of the opportunities to practice opportunism against farmers due to the above-mentioned reasons of site and capital specificity. Agri-environmental co-operatives can build countervailing power, and co-operative contracts between such co-operatives and

administrative units may avoid hold-up problems. In addition, the managers of the co-operatives can contribute to farmers' interest representation and develop procedures of conflict resolution regarding relations to external agents.

4. While some agri-environmental problems like soil compaction can be tackled by addressing single farms, many other environmental issues related to agriculture require participation of several or even many farms, for example reduction of habitat fragmentation and maintenance of ecological networks (see also Falconer, Chapter 13, this volume). Specifying and exploiting property rights which have remained in the public domain because they could not be separated and allocated to single land users due to high transaction costs (see, for this aspect, Slangen and Polman, Chapter 4, this volume) also belong to this point. The spatial distribution of ecological effects originating from the production activities of individual farmers is relevant for potential gains from joint action for capturing such externalities (see, for more details, OECD 1998, p. 20).
5. Due to the fact that transactions in agriculture which are ecologically relevant often show a high degree of heterogeneity, as mentioned above, 'uniform standards and charges that are non-targeted . . . are relatively inefficient instruments for dealing with such variability. On the other hand, any public law approach that involves frequent tinkering with constraints and penalties, besides requiring a considerable effort in order to communicate changes to those expected to comply with law, in general risks reducing their acceptance of it. . . . More generally, delegating greater responsibility of environmental and resource policy to social institutions may prove to be the only pragmatic way for governments to deal with the number and complexity of environmental issues that they are being asked to address' (OECD 1998, p. 17).

Similarly, the following features of actors play a role for the establishment of agri-environmental co-operatives:

1. The importance of trust and credible commitments has frequently been emphasised in the literature on co-operative management of natural resources (see, above all, Ostrom 1999). It has also been treated in some detail by Polman and Slangen (Chapter 5, this volume). One of the main insights of the literature available on this issue is that trust and credible commitment are not just an individual accomplishment of the persons involved, but can be systematically provided in a stable, long-lasting way by means of organisation and culture (Ostrom 1999, p. 46, p. 56) Here we can find another opportunity for environmental co-operatives which

may be better able to fulfil these conditions than other institutional options.

2. Conflicts about environmental problems and natural resources increase in the countryside leading to polarisation of stakeholders and contradicting interests. The 'fundamental strength of co-operative approaches to resolving natural resource disputes is that they encourage the various stakeholders to identify with the particular place, environment, resource and to take responsibility for it' (OECD 1998, p. 18). The co-operative-conflict model used as a conceptual basis for a co-management approach by Birner, Jell and Wittmer (Chapter 3, this volume) aims at similar goals.
3. Mutual learning among practitioners is another advantage of co-operation, particularly if the farmers and other land users have frequent contact in an atmosphere of trust. They may exchange experiences and ideas which stimulate them to find solutions to their problems and to introduce technological and organisational innovations.
4. Whether or not an environmental co-operative is stable and successful depends not only on the members and the management of the co-operative itself. It is important that other actors and organisations recognise the co-operative as a legitimate partner. Ostrom (1999, p. 131) mentions that those fishing co-operatives that were recognised by the regional governments and to which the tasks of co-ordination were delegated, proved to be more stable than other ones.

8 CONCLUDING REMARKS

As far as the selection of a reasonable property rights regime for environmental co-operatives for farmers is concerned, an important question is whether or not farmers should keep their rights to nature components and ecological attributes or whether these rights should rather be transferred to the co-operative. As has been pointed out above, one of the main arguments for environmental co-operation is the opportunity to use local and detailed knowledge of the land users and to reduce the transaction costs of implementation by increased participation. Taking away property rights, and the corresponding duties, to nature components from the members of environmental co-operatives counteracts these objectives. In contrast, responsibilities and motivation for sustainable agriculture should remain with the land users, for example farmers, and the co-operative should rather be understood as a governance structure co-ordinating the members' activities by working rules and management procedures.

For the same reason, that is asymmetric information and motivation of producers, property rights are divided in other areas of the economy. This refers to producers of wrappings, used motor oil and solvents and, in the future, even to cars which have to be taken back by their producers because they know best about the contents and composition of their commodities. Leaving these property rights components with the producer saves and even creates information about causal connections of environmentally relevant side effects of production processes and adequate techniques to avoid or to reduce these impacts. This can be considered as a 'transparency-creating institutional arrangement' (Haberer 1996, p. 186) because every transfer of that duty to actors others than the producer would be connected with a loss of information. The same applies to motivation, because being explicitly responsible for the negative environmental effects of his production processes, as well as being entitled to appropriate positive results, will make the producer interested in environmentally friendly production.

For finding adequate governance structures for environmental co-operatives we can learn from the design principles applied to the co-operative management of common-pool resources (see, for a comprehensive description, Ostrom 1999). Another source could be the economic theory of collective action which emphasises selective incentives as a tool to avoid free riding (see Olson 1965) which may be attainable by 'mixing public and private goods' when defining the concrete tasks of the co-operative.

In the case of public goods, co-operative management of natural resources or environmental pollution abatement can increase allocative efficiency if it allows the participating individuals or farms to decide on different levels of effort according to their abatement costs and possibilities. If the amount of greenhouse gases originating from agriculture were to be reduced on a regional basis, which might be a reasonable strategy, an environmental co-operative could allow its members to make different reductions based on their different abilities to carry the abatement costs, accept income losses and to find ways of adjustment. For this purpose, the management of the co-operative could economise on the cost of negotiation and the costs of opportunistic behaviour, and it could also use compensating mechanisms or establish an internal system of tradable certificates or greenhouse gas banking.

In the case of private goods, members of agri-environmental co-operatives could benefit from economies of scale when purchasing inputs like big amounts of plants and seeds or investing in equipment or infrastructure. Furthermore, agri-environmental co-operatives 'can generate positive external economies for group members. These economies relate to the collection and sharing of information and expertise, the formation and reinforcement of expectations, the promotion of a climate of innovation, and the exploitation of economies of scale' (OECD 1998, p. 15). Collecting, processing and evaluating information can be achieved more economically by a group which can also hire specialists than separately by individuals, and the same is true for administrative tasks, solutions to legal questions, and bargaining with others. In this way, agri-environmental co-operatives can become an additional element in the institutional environment of farms and in the networks existing within rural areas.

REFERENCES

Bahner, T. (1996), *Landwirtschaft und Naturschutz: Vom Konflikt zur Kooperation. Eine institutionenökonomische Analyse*, Europäische Hochschulschriften, Reihe V, Volks- und Betriebswirtschaften, Bd. 2005, Frankfurt am Main: Peter Lang.

Barzel, Y. (1989), *Economic Analysis of Property Rights*, Cambridge: Cambridge University Press.

Berkes, F. and C. Folke (1998), *Linking Social and Ecological Systems. Management Practices and Social Mechanisms for Building Resilience*, Cambridge: Cambridge University Press.

Bromley, D.W. (1991), *Environment and Economy: Property Rights and Public Policy*, Cambridge Massachusetts: Blackwell.

Bromley, D.W. (1996), 'The Social Construction of Land', in Hagedorn, K. (ed.), *Institutioneller Wandel und Politische Ökonomie von Landwirtschaft und Agrarpolitik*, Festschrift zum 65. Geburtstag von Prof. Dr. Günther Schmitt, Frankfurt: Campus, pp. 21–45.

Bromley, D.W. (1997), 'Property Regimes in Environmental Economics', in Folmer, H. and T. Tietenberg (eds), *The International Yearbook of Environmental and Resource Economics: A Survey of Current Issues*, Cheltenham, UK and Lyme, US: Edward Elgar.

Campbell, A. (1998), 'Formatting Synergy: Experiences with Facilitating Landcare in Australia', in Röling, N.G. and E. Wagemakers (eds), *Facilitating Sustainable Agriculture*, Cambridge: Cambridge University Press, pp. 232–49.

De Groot, R.S. (1992), *Functions of Nature. Evaluation of Nature in Environmental Planning, Management and Decision Making*, Groningen, The Netherlands: Walters-Nordhoff BV.

Fisk, J.W., O.B. Hesterman and T.L. Thorborn (1998), 'Integrated Farming Systems: A Sustainable Agricultural Learning Community in the USA', in Röling, N.G. and E. Wagemakers (eds), *Facilitating Sustainable Agriculture*, Cambridge: Cambridge University Press, pp. 217–31.

Haberer, A.F. (1996), *Umweltbezogene Informationssymmetrien und transparenzschaffende Institutionen*, Hochschulschriften, Bd. 31, Marburg.

Hagedorn, K. (ed.) (1996a), *Institutioneller Wandel und Politische Ökonomie von Landwirtschaft und Agrarpolitik*, Festschrift zum 65. Geburtstag von Prof. Dr. Günther Schmitt, Frankfurt: Campus.

Hagedorn, K. (1996b), *Das Institutionenproblem in der agrarökonomischen Politikforschung*, Schriften zur Angewandten Wirtschaftsforschung, Bd. 72, Tübingen: J.C.B. Mohr (Paul Siebeck).

Hagedorn, K. (1998), 'Reasons and Options for Analyzing Political Institutions and Processes', in Frohberg, K. and P. Weingarten (eds), *The Significance of Politics and Institutions for the Design and Formation of Agricultural Policy. Studies about the Agri-Food Sector in Central and Eastern Europe*, Institut für Agrarentwicklung in Mittel- und Osteuropa (IAMO), Kiel: Vauk, pp. 14–33.

Hagedorn, K. (2000), 'Umweltgenossenschaften aus institutionen-ökonomischer Sicht', in Kirk, M., J.W. Kramer und R. Steding (eds), *Genossenschaften und Kooperation in einer sich wandelnden Welt*, Festschrift zum 65. Geburtstag von Prof. Dr. Hans-H. Münkner, Münster: LIT, pp. 267–91.

Hanna, S. (1995), 'Efficiencies of User Participation in Natural Resource Management', in Hanna, S. and M. Munasinghe (eds), *Property Rights in a Social and Ecological Context. Case Study and Design Applications*, Washington DC: The Beijer International Institute of Ecological Economics and the World Bank.

Hanna, S., C. Folke and K.-G. Mäler (eds) (1996), *Rights to Nature*, Washington DC: Island Press.

Hodge, I.D. (1991), 'The Provision of Public Goods in the Countryside: How Should it be Arranged?', in Hanley, H. (ed.), *Farming and the Countryside: An Economic Analysis of External Costs and Benefits*, Oxford: CAB International, pp. 179–96.

Holling, C.S., F. Berkes and C. Folke (1998), 'Science, Sustainability and Resource Management', in Röling, N.G. and E. Wagemakers (eds), *Facilitating Sustainable Agriculture*, Cambridge: Cambridge University Press, pp. 342–61.

Johnson, M.A. and E.C. Pasour Jr. (1981), 'An Opportunity Cost View of Fixed Asset Theory and the Overproduction Trap', *American Journal of Agricultural Economics*, **63** (1), pp. 1–7.

Loehmann, E.T. and D.M. Kilgour (eds) (1998), *Designing Institutions for Environmental and Resource Management*, Cheltenham, UK and Northampton MA, USA: Edward Elgar.

Minsch, J., P.-H. Feindt, H.-P. Meister, U. Schneidewind and T. Schulz (1998), *Institutionelle Reformen für eine Politik der Nachhaltigkeit*,

Enquête-Kommission: Schutz des Menschen und der Umwelt des 13. Deutschen Bundestages, Konzept Nachhaltigkeit, Studienprogramm, Berlin et al.: Springer.

North, D.C. (1992), *Institutions, Institutional Change and Economic Performance*, Cambridge (deutsch: *Institutionen, institutioneller Wandel und Wirtschaftsleistung*), Tübingen: J.C.B. Mohr (Paul Siebeck).

OECD (1998), *Co-operative Approaches to Sustainable Agriculture*, Paris: OECD Publications.

Olson, M. (1965), *The Logic of Collective Action*, Cambridge, MA: Harvard University Press.

Ostrom, E. (1990), *Governing the Commons*, Cambridge: Cambridge University Press.

Ostrom, E. (1998), 'The Institutional Analysis and Development Approach', in Tusak-Loehman, E. and D.M. Kilgur (eds), *Designing Institutions for Environmental and Resource Management*, Cheltenham UK and Northampton MA, USA: Edward Elgar, pp. 68–90.

Ostrom, E. (1999), *Die Verfassung der Allmende, Die Einheit der Gesellschaftswissenschaften*, Bd. 104, Tübingen: J.C.B. Mohr (Paul Siebeck).

Richter, R. and E. Furobotn (1996), *Neue Institutionenökonomik. Eine Einführung und kritische Würdigung*, Tübingen: J.C.B. Mohr (Paul Siebeck).

Van Woerkum and N. Aarts (1998), 'Communication between Farmers and Government about Nature: A New Approach to Policy Development', in Röling, N.G. and E. Wagemakers (eds), *Facilitating Sustainable Agriculture*, Cambridge: Cambridge University Press, pp. 272–80.

Williamson, O.E. (1996), *The Mechanisms of Governance*, Oxford: Oxford University Press.

Woodhill, J. and N.G. Röling (1998), 'The Second Wing of the Eagle: The Human Dimension in Learning our Way to More Sustainable Futures', in Röling, N.G. and E. Wagemakers (eds), *Facilitating Sustainable Agriculture*, Cambridge: Cambridge University Press, pp. 46–77.

Zimmer, Y. (1991), 'Überlegungen zur nicht-staatlichen Bereitstellung des beschränkt öffentlichen Gutes "bäuerliche Kulturlandschaft"', *Zeitschrift für Umweltpolitik und Umweltrecht*, **14** (3).

Zimmer, Y. (1994a), *Naturschutz und Landschaftspflege – Allokationsmechanismen, Präferenzanalyse, Entwicklungspotentiale*, Kiel: Vauk.

Zimmer, Y. (1994b), 'Zur institutionellen Regelung von Naturschutz und Landschaftspflege im Bereich der Landwirtschaft – private Güter, öffentliche Güter und Club-Güter?', in Hagedorn, K., F. Isermeyer, D. Rost and A. Weber (eds), *Gesellschaftliche Forderungen an die Landwirtschaft. Schriften der Gesellschaft für Wirtschafts- und*

Sozialwissenschaften des Landbaus e.V., Bd. 30, Münster-Hiltrup: Landwirtschaftsverlag.

2. Valuing Co-operation and Participation: a Challenge to Standard Normative Economics*

Denis Claude

1 INTRODUCTION

The idea that this book intends to promote – namely, that co-operation and participation are two key concepts when dealing with agri-environmental problems – contrasts sharply with views commonly held on the subject just twenty years ago. At that time, economic and environmental issues were thought to be resolved thanks to either a 'command and control' or the 'laissez-faire' system. This belief, substantiated by the well-known fundamental theorem of welfare economics, left no room for a discussion of other conceivable policies and especially co-operative strategies. Furthermore, the force of utilitarian arguments led economists to disregard compelling arguments belonging to the other realm of human motivation, morality. As a result, they believed, and will probably believe for a long time to come, that selfishness can save the environment. However, it is widely acknowledged that the utilitarian stance of welfare economics is ill-equipped to handle policy issues in this area, and there is increasing evidence that its traditional recipes have failed. I shall argue that traditional welfare economics is unable to recognise the virtues of co-operation as an alternative to command and control or laissez-faire. Moreover, the principle of selfishness has revealed itself to be counterproductive. In contrast, it is widely thought that it threatens the integrity of our social fabric. In this chapter, I shall not argue that an appeal to the morality of individuals is a more appropriate response to environmental issues than an appeal to their egoism. I do not subscribe to the view that human nature should be changed. Neither do I believe that economists should replace their selfish model of human behaviour with an altruist one. However, I argue that this model of human behaviour should be extended in order to take into account moral motives along with selfish ones. I argue that such an extension would be necessary to bear out our intuitions regarding the ability of co-operative strategies to cope with environmental issues.

2 UTILITARIANISM AND BEYOND[1]

Utilitarianism[2] was originally designed and most successfully proposed as a guide to policy makers.[3] For that reason, following the lines of Kymlicka (1999), I shall interpret it as a 'standard of rightness'.

Definition 1: Utilitarianism as a standard of rightness. An act (or policy) is right if it maximises utility.

Economists have found in utilitarianism a ready-made, highly-sophisticated and convenient form of assessing public policies. It relentlessly endorsed the view, initiated by J. Bentham, that governments should promote 'the greatest good for the greatest number'. As a result, economics is biased in favour of a specific conception of governments and public regulators' tasks: the command and control view. Following this view, the government should specify an objective for society, which is usually to maximise a social welfare function. Then, alternative policies should be evaluated on the basis of the overall amount of social welfare predicted in consequent states of affairs. That is to say, the government or the public regulator should predict the consequences of alternative policies on social welfare, rank alternative policies given their consequences, select that which ranks higher and implement it. This particular conception has dominated debates for the past thirty years. However, it has been increasingly questioned in recent years as opinions have become increasingly aware of the limited ability of governments to plan for the social good. Contractualist and Libertarian schools of thought have benefited from this shift and gained a wider audience (Sugden 1993, p. 1948). Both of these schools advance alternative views with regards to which policies are acceptable.

Definition 2: Contractualism. 'An act is wrong if its performance under the circumstances would be disallowed by any system of rules for the general regulation of behaviour which no one could reasonably reject as a basis for informed, unforced general agreement.[4]

Loosely speaking, contractualism means that a public policy is acceptable if it does not offend the particular system of rules that has been hypothetically agreed upon by the members of the community. It is important to note that this system will differ across communities according to prevailing social norms (see Scanlon 1982).

Definition 3: Libertarianism. 'Everyone has the general right to liberty' (Narveson 1998, p. 4). An act (or policy) is wrong if it infringes upon this general right.[5]

Libertarian thinkers believe that liberty is closely related to property rights. More precisely, they hold that people naturally possess themselves and that individuals cannot be regarded as authentically free if they are denied this essential right to self-ownership. Therefore, a public policy is right if it does not infringe upon an individual's property rights (see Narveson 1998). However, both contractualism and libertarianism rely on a similar conception of society. Sugden (1993) summarised it as follows: 'Society is seen as a system of co-operation among individuals for their mutual advantage. According to this view, the primary role of government is not to maximise the social good, but rather to maintain a framework of rules within which individuals are left free to pursue their own ends.'[6]

As a result, utilitarianism, contractualism and libertarianism offer different accounts of what is valuable. While utilitarianism is focused on the well-being facet of morality, libertarianism promotes values which belong to the action facet, liberty and individual accomplishments.[7,8]

In contrast, contractualism is not a substantive moral theory. Rather, contractualism advances an ingenious method to identify and legitimate a particular moral view for a society.[9] The conception advocated will differ according to the values held by individuals. If it cannot be denied that utility consequences of social policies are highly relevant to the evaluation of such policies, it can still be argued that a social state is not fully described if only the utility of agents is provided. Consequently, we should be concerned with how policies score with regards to other values (efficiency, freedom, equality, safety, community and co-operation, to mention a few). Moreover, it has been argued that the very process through which outcomes are reached should fall under the scope of the assessment.[10] Hahn (1982, p. 188), for example, contends that 'my utility may not only depend on what I (or others) get but on the manner in which I get it. That is, my utility may not only depend on the consequences of policy but on the policy itself.'

In order to take outcomes along with procedures into account, the traditional informational framework of welfare economics should be extended. Indeed, several routes have been proposed. However, most policy discussions rely on the narrow framework of traditional normative economics. Therefore, values embedded into co-operation and participation are usually not properly taken into account and co-operative strategies are denied effectiveness. As a result, command and control, or as we shall see a disguised form of command and control, is still widely advocated.

3 COMMANDS, CONTROLS AND MARKET

For many years, all policy discussions have been relying, more or less implicitly, upon what is called the Fundamental Theorem of Welfare Economics (FTWE). No doubt, this result has been one of the most appealing and meaningful of mainstream economics. The theorem divides in two parts.

Theorem 1: Fundamental Theorem of Welfare Economics.

Part 1 *Under certain conditions and if markets are complete, a competitive equilibrium is Pareto optimal.*

Part 2 *Under more restrictive conditions (households' preferences and firms' production possibility sets are convex) and if markets are complete, any Pareto optimum can be sustained as a competitive equilibrium.*

The first part of the theorem provides what is regarded as a definitive proof of the commonplace belief in market efficiency. This point needs no further elaboration. Therefore, let us focus our attention on the second part of the theorem. Consider an economy of complete information. Suppose that, in this economy, agents possess an initial endowment of commodities. Then, we know from FTWE part 2 that the state can pick out any Pareto optimal allocation and implement it by means of a decentralised procedure. The procedure goes as follows:

1. the State announces a set of prices; one for each and every commodity;
2. the State imposes lump-sum taxes and subsidies in order to rearrange the initial endowments;
3. finally, it allows individuals to trade at these prices under their budget constraint.

However, it may be noted that if, as is usually assumed, the State has all the necessary information, it can do without the mediation of markets. That is, by means of direct expropriation and redistribution, the State may enforce the chosen optimal allocation. Are these two mechanisms equally effective? It is widely acknowledged that the answer is negative: 'for the set of "messages" the state must transmit under the command mode of planning will far exceed the set of messages it must transmit under the price mechanism' (Hammond 1982, p. 205); the command and control mechanism is judged costly.

In the world we know, part of the information is held privately and concealed by individual agents. Consequently, the information necessary for public policies appraisal is usually wanting. This point was emphasised by F.V. Hayek more than fifty years ago in the course of the socialist calculation debate. Hayek's early critique of the command and control mechanism was articulated around his own theory of knowledge. He contended that the information embedded in price is richer than that usually available to the policy maker. For that reason, he advocated the market mechanism as an alternative to command and control. Modern microeconomics, and especially the economics of information, emphasises that information is asymmetrically allocated and as a consequence may be used strategically. These asymmetries impose additional constraints on policy makers' choices. Moreover, it has been shown that market mechanisms might be used in order to reveal information. This collection of arguments has contributed to shifting the attention from command and control policies to market-based policies. However, it is noteworthy that both these mechanisms are outcome-driven. Consequently, they stand against a hierarchical conception of society.[11]

This conception is at variance with the one that libertarians advocate. Indeed, libertarian thinkers regard markets as intrinsically valuable. A clear illustration of this view is provided by Susumura (1999, p. 26):

> In addition to these instrumental values, competition allegedly has an intrinsic value of its own. It is the unique mechanism through which an economic agent can try out his/her own initiative and responsibility. It is true that the mechanism of competition can be very cruel and wasteful in weeding out the winners from the losers. It is also true that the freedom rendered by this mechanism is crucially conditioned by the initial distribution of assets and capabilities. However, these valid reservations do not change one iota of the fact that competition is a process which provides each agent with an equal and free opportunity to pursue his/her own aspirations in life.

By contrast, standard welfare economics disregards the intrinsic value of markets. According to this view, market processes are valuable only insofar as they provide an efficient way to reach good outcomes. Their value is, thus, derivative. As we shall see later in the chapter, this attitude is a feature of consequential ethics. To get at the heart of the matter, let us consider the commonplace prescriptions of standard welfare economics with reference to environmental issues. The scholar most responsible for highlighting the potential merits of the market mechanism when externalities are widespread is, no doubt, Charles Pigou. The arguments he advanced have provided a sound underpinning to economists' advocacy of a market-based environmentalism (MBE).

Environmental issues are difficult to handle. The difficulty stems from the existence of widespread externalities. As a consequence of these externalities, markets are incomplete and therefore the FTWE is no longer true. Proponents of MBE believe that market failures might be overcome by using markets against themselves (Cordato 1997).[12] The suggested process is somewhat similar to the one described earlier. In short, it requires the policy maker to select an (second-best) outcome and impose lump-sum taxes and subsidies. It aims at altering individual incentives so that the market system implements the selected outcome. An attractive feature of MBE-based policies is their pragmatism. MBE policies rely on selfishness. They do not appeal to people's morality in order to cope with environmental problems; they do not require a change in human nature, either. Rather, they acknowledge our selfish motives and retain them as a basis for the design of new policies. These policies aim at inducing selfish agents to interact in a way that promotes the common good.

4 UTILITARIANISM AS AN EVALUATIVE SYSTEM

I introduced utilitarianism as a standard of rightness at the beginning of this chapter. Now, the time has come to define the premises of utilitarianism. I argue that utilitarianism as an evaluative system deeply restricts the kind of arguments that can be advanced in favour of co-operative or participative policies. Utilitarianism is usually broken into three components: consequentialism, welfarism and utility maximisation.[13] Each of these components, when added, further restricts the kind of information that is available for the assessment of public policies.[14]

4.1 Consequentialism[15]

Utilitarianism requires a consequentialist form of assessing public policies. Loosely speaking, consequentialism has it that the rightness of an action should be judged by the goodness of its consequences. Under this view, a public policy derives its value from its effectiveness in promoting some kind of good. The particular kind of good referred to by utilitarianism is utility. Various competing environmental ethics are expressed in similar (consequentialist) terms. Leopold's Ecocentrism is such an example. It asserts that a 'thing is right when it tends to preserve the integrity, stability and beauty of the biotic community'.[16] It is important to note that these two positions differ according to who or what (for instance, non-sentient life) is regarded as morally significant. Mainstream environmentalism[17] usually rejects the atomistic conception of society in favour of holism.

Furthermore, mainstream environmental ethics are usually expressed in deontological (or non-consequential) terms. Deontologists believe that 'acts are wrong because of the sort of act they are' (Davis 1991). For that reason, they argue that 'we need not speculate about the projected consequences of our acts, or attempt to calculate their value' (Davis 1991). The debate over global warming and pollution trading has underlined the contrast between mainstream economics and mainstream environmentalism. This contrast is usually understood as one between consequential and deontological ethics.

The idea of pollution trading has been endorsed and promoted by most mainstream economists. Also, at the insistence of the United States, a provision was introduced in the global climate treaty signed in Kyoto in 1997. The idea of emissions trading is quite simple: The case for a trading of emissions permits stems from extensive evidence that a reduction of emissions could be achieved at a lower cost in the developing world. Nordhaus (in Sagoff 1999), for example, contends that a 50 per cent reduction in pollution from the dirtiest industries in Russia or India would be less costly to achieve than a 20 per cent reduction in European or US industries. Yet, substantial emissions reductions are not conceivable in the near future for at least two reasons. First, developing countries alone cannot bear the cost of such reductions. Second, they have not sufficiently acquired skill in environmentally friendly technologies. Pollution trading proponents argue that there is room for a mutually advantageous bargain. On the one hand, developed countries could assist less advanced ones to convert to cleaner technologies. On the other hand, developed countries could credit themselves with such reduction with regards to their own goals. However, this consequential 'gibberish' is hardly comprehensible from an environmentalist's viewpoint and the idea that emissions credits could be traded has been vigorously fought. Michael J. Sandel, among others, contended that 'it turns pollution into a commodity to be bought and sold' and removes 'the moral stigma that is properly associated with it'.[18] That is, he asserts that emissions permits trading is morally wrong not by virtue of its consequences but because it violates deontological constraints.

Pettit (1991, p. 231) has advanced an original elucidation of the distinction between consequential and deontological ethics. He suggests that we rephrase their definitions as specific views regarding the relations between agents and values:

> Consequentialists see the relation between values and agents as an instrumental one: agents are required to produce whatever actions have the property of promoting a designated value, even actions that fail to honour it. Opponents of consequentialism see the relation between values and agents as a non-instrumental one: agents are required or at least allowed to let their actions exemplify a designated value, even if it makes for a lesser realisation of the value overall.

These new formulations allow us to reformulate the positions held concerning the permit trading controversy by economists, on the one hand, and environmentalists, on the other hand. Economists believe that what is valuable is the reduction of global greenhouse emissions. According to this view, policies should be assessed solely on the basis of their consequences on global climate. Locally, emission permits trading may result in low reductions; however, it may be globally successful. From that standpoint, the spatial distribution of emission reductions is irrelevant. By contrast, environmentalists believe that emissions are intrinsically evil. Therefore, they require that we refrain from emitting greenhouse gases. Such a requirement applies to each (individual or institutional) moral agent and is to be met by each moral agent individually. Thus, it leaves no room for trade in emissions. Environmentalists would certainly recognise that this scheme is prone to be costly and economically inefficient. Yet, from their standpoint, the global level of greenhouse reduction and its associated global cost are irrelevant. What counts is that we refrain from emitting greenhouse gases.

Consequently, economists and environmentalists advance contrasting views regarding the function of public regulation and law. As Hirschman[19] puts it, 'economists often propose to deal with unethical or antisocial behaviour by raising the cost of that behaviour rather than by proclaiming standards and imposing prohibitions and sanctions . . .'. In so doing, they disregard a basic function of law which is: to 'stigmatise antisocial behaviour and thereby to influence citizens' values and behaviour codes. This educational, value moulding function of the law is as important as its deterrent and repressive functions.'[20]

Environmentalists and philosophers like M.J. Sandel certainly have this function in mind when they condemn pollution trading policies. They emphasise that public policies and laws contribute to shaping individual preferences – a position that utilitarianism is ill-equipped to understand in that it assumes that preferences are exogenous; that is, are fixed attributes of individuals.[21] I shall return to this point at the end of the chapter.

However, if I understand them correctly, environmentalists seem to assert their position against an implicitly consequential argument, the value moulding function of law. This point illustrates a general difficulty with deontological theories. On the one hand, most of them seem to be motivated by an implicit concern for consequences. On the other hand, most of them require a 'catastrophe clause' in order to deal with extreme or dire situations (see Sen 1995 or Nozick and Davis 1991). For that reason, Honderich (1996) has challenged the usual distinction between consequential and deontological motives. Actually, it is doubtful that one could design a convincing theory of public morality that would not take the consequences of policies as meaningful; that is, a purely non-consequential theory of public morality. Therefore, consequentialism seems to be an attractive feature of utilitarianism.

4.2 Welfarist Consequentialism

The specific kind of good that utilitarians intend to promote is well-being, or should I say a distinctive understanding of what well-being is. In reality, they usually do not distinguish the well-being experienced by an individual agent in a given social state from his utility level (in that social state). This view is usually referred to as 'welfarism'.

Definition 4: Welfarism. 'The goodness of a state of affairs must be judged exclusively by the individual utilities in the respective states' (see Sen 1977, 1979, 1993).

Welfarism takes individual utilities as the fabric of social welfare. The combination of consequentialism and welfarism imposes severe and clear-cut constraints on the information available in view of policy discussions. It is quite difficult to substantiate this restriction within the consequentialist framework. The particular kind of consequentialism it produces, welfarist consequentialism, prohibits the use of all non-utility information. This exclusive focus on well-being conflicts with our understanding of what is valuable in our daily life. Because we value freedom, equality and safety but also friendship, landscapes, or nature and so on, we cannot subscribe to such a restricted picture of our morality. Our values are manifold,[22] and a minimal requirement that the evaluative system should meet is to acknowledge this fact. Therefore, the range of values that is taken into account in both consequential and deontological ways should be enlarged. This observation has motivated several contemporary developments in political philosophy such as Rawls's theory of justice or Sen's theory of 'capabilities' and 'functionings'.[23]

4.3 Maximisation of Utility

Once we have agreed that the evaluative system should be consequential and should promote well-being, we still have to specify what our concern for consequences requires us to do. Utilitarianists believe that the appropriate reading of consequentialism is a requirement to maximise well-being. Kymlicka (1999) has questioned this point. This issue falls beyond the scope of this chapter. However, the usual philosophical justification that utilitarianists provide for welfare maximisation is directly relevant. The more convincing and appealing argument relies on an interpretation of utilitarianism as a principle of preference aggregation. Following this line, utility maximisation is the best way to guarantee a fair treatment to individuals. The argument goes as follows:

1. 'individuals count, and they count equally; therefore
2. each individual's interest should receive a similar weight; thus
3. morally good actions will maximise utility' (Kymlicka 1999, my translation).[24]

However paradoxical this justification might seem to be for a reader fed with critical accounts of utilitarianism that highlights its insensitivity to inequality, it is consistent with old utilitarian concerns and especially the liberal conception of society they defended. In this respect, it can be noted that if human rights originated 'as normative responses to experiences of oppression' (Winston 1999), this has also been the case with utilitarianism. However, a window of escape has been offered. It has been argued that the 'utilitarian calculus' is not to blame for the inequalitarian conclusions. The fault is to be found elsewhere; in the collection of interests and desires taken into account. Some of these are illegitimate, especially 'external preferences', and thus morally meaningless and should, therefore, be excluded. When illegitimate preferences are excluded, utilitarianism gains in attractiveness.

5 WHAT'S WRONG WITH THE UTILITARIAN STANCE OF ECONOMICS?

The usual justification for utilitarianism seems rather convincing and its motives, generous. However, its practical recommendations offend our intuitions with regards to what is valuable. We have seen that this problem stems from its narrow informational basis. We illustrate the inadequacy of utilitarianism with two examples. First, we consider the treatment of individual rights in standard welfare economics. Welfare economics value participation and individual rights only insofar as they promote utility. In contrast, we usually regard them as valuable in their own right (or intrinsically valuable). Whether or not individual rights will be respected and participation required depends on the particular procedure that the social planner has designed to implement the selected outcome. Therefore, means as well as ends matter and our assessment should take into account procedures along with outcomes. Second, we consider the potential conflicts between communities' values and incentive-based politics. We have already noted that utilitarian policies might break socially beneficial moral taboos and social norms,[25] as in the case of tradable permits. Moreover, it is plausible that policies affect preferences. Most economists neglect these two effects. However, they may weaken social ties and be detrimental to social co-operation. Therefore, economic analysis should be concerned with the consequences of policies on communities and prevailing social norms that sustain them. Both these points emphasise that the traditional framework of normative economics should be extended.

5.1 Utilitarianism, Rights and the Environment

The question of rights is a challenging issue for utilitarianism. Contrary to what is thought, it is simply not true that utilitarianism is unable to recognise rights as valuable. In reality, it is their intrinsic value that utilitarianism fails to take into account; their instrumental value is fully acknowledged. This attitude towards rights is the fruit of the adhesion to welfarist consequentialism. In this framework, only well-being is intrinsically valuable; values such as freedom, equality or safety, for example, may be acknowledged but only as derivative values. Textbooks are filled with instances of conflict between these values and utilitarianism. Modern welfare economics has endorsed a mild form of utilitarianism. It relies exclusively on the Pareto criterion. However, despite this departure from utilitarianism it is well known from Sen's theorem that such conflicts still arise.[26]

Environmental economics is a setting prone to give rise to such conflicts because of widespread externalities. Hammond has offered a straightforward illustration of this issue. He argues that 'one may feel in certain circumstances that a landowner has the right to cut down all trees on his land in order to grow crops, construct a house or a tennis court or a swimming pool, or whatever' (Hammond 1982, p. 89). Yet, he notes that 'if everybody cuts down all their trees, this may create problems of soil erosion and landslides as well as having adverse effects on the local climate' and that 'it would be Pareto superior to institute some tree conservation measures in the community as a whole, by taxing any individual landowner for each tree he fell beyond a certain acceptable level which maintains the stock of tree constant' (ibid.).

Such a scheme would be supported by most mainstream economists. However, libertarians would contend that it infringes the landowner's property rights. Libertarian thinkers, such as Narveson (1998), believe that 'everyone has a general right to liberty' (Narveson 1998, p. 3); that is, 'to the absence of imposed costs at the hands of others' (ibid., p. 4). According to this view, property rights are deontological constraints that must be respected by the regulator. Hammond (1982) endorses this attitude. He contends that

> in such a case, ... one simply has to recognise that there is an extra constraint on the social welfare maximising choices, arising because conservation measures are not really possible. The chosen social outcome is only Pareto efficient subject to such a constraint: conservation measures would produce a superior outcome but are unfeasible. The social outcome is constrained by the requirement that it must not infringe these rights. (Hammond 1982, p. 89)

Our concern for rights, thus, should lead us to restrict the range of policies that we regard as conceivable. This first difficulty has its origin in consequentialism. Now, I shall point to a second problem that stems from the symmetric (or impartial) treatment that agents enjoy under traditional welfare economics.[27] Consider a world of complete information and costless bargaining. That particular world is inhabited by two economic agents, P and V. P's activities result in an externality that affects V's well-being. In such a situation, the Coase Theorem asserts that the two agents will strike a mutually advantageous (Pareto efficient) bargain for the level of external activity. That is to say, agent P will have to pay a certain amount of money to V in exchange of the right to pollute. However, we can dissent from this understanding of the situation. One could argue that the polluter's interests, P, and his victim's interest, V, should enjoy different moral status. For example, we could entitle the agent V to the right to live in an unpolluted environment. As a result, Society would be required to protect by all available means agent V from P's nuisances. This example illustrates a potentially serious defect of utilitarianism as a guide to policy makers. Utilitarianism may induce us to illegitimately disregard the difference in moral status that the victim enjoys from an ethical standpoint.

5.2 Communities, Selfish Incentives and the Environment

As we have seen earlier, a utilitarian government or regulator depends on the selfishness of its citizens. And the view that selfishness is the answer to environmental issues is commonplace.[28] However, Mann and Plummer (1995) challenge this view. They argue that conservation should be promoted in ways more compatible with local (American) values and culture. This assertion might be puzzling for a classical economist. Why should the conservation measures adopted differ? In order to substantiate this question, and to answer it, economists must give up their prejudices and confront the real world. Then, he or she will realise that non-utilitarian motivations are often accountable for our behaviour. Consider the following example provided to illustrate this point. The state of Wisconsin has created an Endangered Species Trust Fund which covers seven species on the federal endangered list. Under this programme, 'landowners agree to a non-binding protection plan, and are rewarded with a picture of the species, a certificate of appreciation, ongoing management help, and, most important, the belief that they are voluntarily doing the right thing' (Mann and Plummer 1995). From an economic standpoint, this policy has not much merit. It is doubtful that valueless pictures, certificates of appreciation and so on will substantially change people's incentives. However, this programme is a success. Actually, it is true that this programme is not intended 'to deter big development plans but it serves its own, more restricted, purposes' (ibid.). The success of this programme indicates that people assign a non-utilitarian value to such items which is not accounted for by economists' evaluations. Therefore, we should rely on an extended conception of human motivation.

Drawing on both historical and contemporary experimental evidence, Gintis and Romer (1998, p. 1) propose a broader account of human motives and conduct. They assert that

> people are motivated by duty and obligation as well as by utility, they have preferences concerning the well-being of others (they are both altruistic and vengeful), they are concerned with issues of equity and dignity in interpersonal relations, their preferences are determined in part by the character of the economic institutions within which they operate, and their well-being depends on the quality of their social relations and the extent to which they have developed their personal capacities, not only the quantity of goods and services at their disposal.

Consequently, Bowles and Gintis (1998) invite us to consider a new persona christened Homo reciprocans. Homo reciprocans differs from Homo economicus in that it takes into account the ambivalence of human morality. His or her behaviour follows precepts of the Strong Reciprocity Norm. Bowles and Gintis (1998) define Strong Reciprocity as a 'propensity to co-operate and share with others similarly disposed, even at personal cost, and a willingness to punish those that violate co-operative and social norms, even when punishing is personally costly'.

Strong reciprocity motives differ from weak ones (for example, those which underlie tit-for-tat strategies) in that co-operative or punishing behaviours are not motivated by the prospect of subsequent repayments. They are, in a way, altruistic. The adoption of this or another extended conception of human nature which acknowledges altruistic as well as other motives should lead us to challenge our traditional views concerning which policies are good. Indeed, the substitution of homo economicus by homo reciprocans reflects a new understanding of people's needs and aspirations. As a result, and because of our liberal belief that governments or regulators ought to serve their subjects, we should rephrase the problem of institutional design as follows:

> The problem of institutional design is not as the classical economists thought, that selfish individuals be induced to interact in ways producing desirable aggregate outcomes, but rather that a mix of motives – selfish, reciprocal, altruistic and spiteful – interact in ways that prevent the selfish from exploiting the generous and hence unravelling co-operation when it is beneficial. (Bowles and Gintis 1998)

This view of institutional design agrees with the contractualist and libertarian conceptions of society as defined by Sugden (1993). Contrary to the utilitarian conception of society, it does not involve the existence of a transcendental value that individuals must pursue even if it is contrary to what they believe is good for themselves. Rather, this understanding of society as a system of co-operation emphasises that individuals are their own source of value. Thus the problem of institutional design amounts to inducing people to interact in ways that are not detrimental to social ties and co-operation. This account requires three remarks:

First, it should be noted that this role is usually partly played by social norms.[29] Social norms contribute to the overall regulation of society. They prohibit behaviours detrimental to the community and reward altruistic and co-operative behaviours. Moreover, they provide reasons for behaviours that are not exclusively outcome-oriented.[30] Thus a conflict may arise between utilitarian-based policies and social norms. Economists should acknowledge this point. Such conflicts may render their policies at best ineffective and certainly counterproductive.[31]

Second, environmental issues would certainly be better understood as collective choice problems; that is to say, as problems essentially about advancing common ways of understanding what the pertinent issues are about (Vatn and Bromley 1995). Since civil society is the place where ideas regarding what is valuable are formed (see Scn 1995, pp. 16–17), it would seem natural to rely on it in order to advance solutions to environmental issues, especially at the local level. For instance, co-operative management of natural resources may be effective in inducing people to understand the issue at hand and to find appropriate solutions.

Finally, it may be acknowledged that preferences and institutions affect one another. As Gintis and Romer (1998) put it: ‘Preferences determine the kind of institutions that arc viable, and institutions influence the kinds of preferences that people develop and express.’ There is little indisputable evidence to support this statement; however, it is highly plausible. Thus we should treat preferences as endogenous data. This last point underlies Puttman's theory of ‘the erosion of social capital’ and several other ‘communitarian’[32] critics of liberalism: ‘to the extent that economic policies weaken communities, they weaken personal development *as well*’ (Gintis and Romer 1998, my emphasis).

6 CONCLUSION

Economics relies on a uni-dimensional evaluative system, utilitarianism. This evaluative system assesses consequential states of affairs along a single dimension, utility. Therefore, it requires that we evaluate the various attributes of a social state in utility terms. Thus, freedom, safety, community links and so on are valuable only insofar as they contribute to a greater production of utility; their value is derivative. This view conflicts with our understanding of what is valuable in everyday life. We usually regard our ability to choose our health and our social relations as intrinsically valuable. For that reason, utilitarianism may be the only predictor of our well-being. However, in practice, economic scholars tend to measure our well-being from our consumption of goods and services and disregard our manifold values. As a result they systematically undervalue co-operative and participative strategies that appeal to the morality of individuals. By contrast, they advocate a disguised form of command and control policies, MBE policies, which rely on individuals' selfishness. I have emphasised that in practice these policies may conflict with prevailing social conventions. Moreover, I have stressed that these policies may weaken social ties and be detrimental to social communities. Co-operative and participative policies are intrinsically valuable. Economic scholars usually miss this point. Therefore, in order to acknowledge their intrinsic value, the traditional framework of welfare economics should be extended to take into account the value of procedures along with that of outcomes. Such an extension has already been advocated by Moulin (1997) and Susumura (1999) with regard to freedom and individual rights. It has also been the purpose of Rawl's Theory of Justice. I believe that it should be done with regards to the values embedded in co-operation and participation. Sen's theory of 'functionings' and 'capabilities' is perhaps a first step in this direction.

NOTES

* The author thanks Patrick Rio, Mabel Tidball and Sophie Thoyer for helpful comments. The usual disclaimer applies. Research supported by the Région Nord-Pas-de-Calais and the ISA (Lille). Part of this chapter was written while I was staying at the ISA (Lille) and the INRA-ESR (Montpellier); I would like to acknowledge their hospitality.

1. See Sen and Williams (1982).
2. Kymlicka (1999) provides an excellent introduction to political philosophy in general and utilitarianism in particular. See also Rawls (1997), Hare (1982) and Goodin (1991) for examples. Utilitarianism has been extensively debated among economic scholars; see articles by Dasgupta, Hammond, Harsanyi and Mirlees in Sen and Williams (1982). Also, see Hausman and McPherson (1993) and Roemer (1996).
3. Utilitarianism has also been interpreted as a theory of individual deliberation. According to this view, 'each individual act must be judged directly in terms of the utilitarian criterion. Thus a morally right act is one that, in the situation the actor is actually in, will maximise social utility' (Harsanyi 1982). However, this specific form of utilitarianism, known as 'act utilitarianism' (this term has been coined by Brandt), is hardly convincing. On this point, see Harsanyi (1982), Goodin (1991) and Kymlicka (1999), for example.
4. As defined by Scanlon (1982).
5. This definition is adapted from Narveson (1998). This review article contains an outstanding clarification of libertarian philosophy.
6. See also Sen's reply to Sugden, in Sen (1995).
7. On the distinction between the 'well-being' facet and the 'action' facets, see Sen (1993).

8. However, this point should certainly be qualified as follows: 'libertarians would like it to be the case that protecting freedom also makes people better' (Hausman and McPherson 1993, p. 704).
9. See Hausman and McPherson (1993, p. 708). See also Scanlon (1982).
10. On this issue see Hahn (1982), Moulin (1997) and Susumura (1999), for instance.
11. Namely, they imply that a central agent choose a particular outcome.
12. For a general critique of MBE policies, and especially of tradable permits and green taxes, see Cordato (1997).
13. On the factorisation of utilitarianism, see also Sen (1977, 1979) and Sen (1993, chapt. 2).
14. However, this is neither the time nor the place for an examination of comparability assumptions. On this issue, see Sen (1977, 1995) and Blackorby, Donaldson and Weymark (1984).
15. On the distinction between consequential and non-consequential ethics see Davis (1991) and Pettit (1991). Throughout this chapter I shall make no difference between non-consequential and deontological concerns.
16. Leopold (1968), cited in The Internet Encyclopedia to Philosophy.
17. For an elucidation of several environmental ethics see Brook (1993). See also, Elliot (1991) and Pearce and Turner (1990, chapt. 15).
18. Sandel, M.J., 'It's immoral to buy the right to pollute', *The New York Times*, December 15, 1997 cited in Sagoff (1999).
19. Hirschman (1985) cited in Gintis and Romer (1998).
20. Hirschman (1985) cited in Gintis and Romer (1998).
21. A classical illustration of this position is Thomas Hobbes' 'mushrooms metaphor'. Hobbes suggested that we 'consider men as if but even now sprung out of the earth, and suddenly (like mushrooms), come to full maturity, without any kind of engagement with each other' [Thomas Hobbes] (Bowles 1998).
22. Indeed, many environmental ethics that compete with utilitarianism have espoused distinct values. For an elucidation of the ethical structure of various environmental ethics, see Brook (1993). Also, see Elliot (1991) and Pearce and Turner (1990, chapt. 15).
23. For an outstanding elucidation of Sen's theory of justice, see Sugden (1993). Sen's list of intrinsically valuable functionings acknowledges our manifold values; Sugden notes that it includes among other things 'being happy', 'acting freely', 'being able to choose' but also 'appearing in public without shame' and 'taking part in the life of the community' (Sugden 1993, p. 1952). Also, see Roemer (1996).
24. See also Scanlon (1982): 'If all that counts morally is the well-being of individuals, no one of whom is singled out as counting for more than the others, and if all that matters in the case of each individual is the degree to which his or her well-being is affected, then it would seem to follow that the basis of moral appraisal is the goal of maximising the sum of individual well-being'.
25. I am well aware that social norms are not necessarily efficient nor beneficial.
26. See Sen (1970). Sen's theorem shows that a tension exists between individual rights and the very weak version of welfarism embedded in the weak Pareto criterion. Under Sen's formulation, an individual's right entails 'decisiveness'. An individual i enjoys rights for at least one pair of distinct alternatives (x; y) which differ only with respect to some aspects of i's personal life, if i strictly prefers x to y then y cannot be socially chosen from an issue that contains x. Under this formulation of individual rights, society should respect the choices of the individual as long as these choices are private (that is, as long as the choice has no consequence on other individuals' well-being). This first formulation is usually referred to as the social choice approach to rights. Sen's theorem asserts that no social decision rule with unrestricted domain can simultaneously respect rights as previously defined and satisfy the weak Pareto criterion. In recent years, the

appropriateness of Sen's modelling of individual rights has been challenged and new routes have been advanced, in particular the Game Form Approach to individual rights; see Gaertner et al. (1992), Deb et al. (1997), Deb (1994), Pattanaik and Susumura (1996), Sen (1992), Sen (1995), Sen (1999). However, it is widely acknowledged that this tension 'persists under virtually every plausible concept of individual rights' (Gaertner, Pattanaik and Susumura 1992).

27. This example is borrowed from Goodstein (1995).
28. See, for example, Ridley and Low's article: 'Can Selfishness Save the Environment?' (1993).
29. Elster (1989) provides a non-exhaustive account of social norms, it includes: consumption norms, norms against behaviour 'contrary to nature', norms regulating the use of money, norms of reciprocity, norms of retribution, works norms, norms of co-operation and norms of distribution.
30. Examples of these norms with regards to co-operation include the previously cited norm of Strong Reciprocity introduced by Bowles and Gintis (1998) but also related norms such as 'everyday Kantism', 'co-operate if and only if it would be better for all if all co-operated than if nobody did' or 'norm of fairness', 'co-operate if and only if most other people co-operate' (Elster 1989).
31. See Bowles and Gintis (1998). They argue that egalitarian welfare policies offend people's 'deeply held notions of fairness'.
32. The communitarian critique of liberalism, and the ensuing debate, has been of great moment in recent political philosophy. The influence of communitarian ideas now exceeds the boundaries of philosophy and is easily perceived in sociology and economics, where it gave rise to the so-called 'new socio-economics'. I suspect that in the course of the transposition of communitarian philosophy into economic theory a dose of anti-pluralism and conservatism has been introduced. I regret these additions that, in my view, render this new paradigm less attractive.

REFERENCES

Blackorby, C., D. Donaldson and J. Weymark (1984), 'Social Choice with Interpersonal Utility Comparisons: A Diagrammatic Introduction', *International Economic Review*, **25** (2), pp. 327–56.

Bowles, S. (1998), 'Endogenous Preferences: The Cultural Consequences of Markets and other Economic Institutions', *Journal of Economic Literature*, **XXXVI**, pp. 75–111.

Bowles, S. and H. Gintis (1998), 'Is Equality Passé? Homo Reciprocans and the Future of Egalitarian Politics', Technical Report, Department of Economics, University of Massachusetts.

Brook, A. (1993), 'The Structure of Ethical Positions on the Environment', in Cragg, W. (ed.), *Research Methods and Ethical Issues Associated with Resource Extraction and Resource Management in Forestry and Mining*, York: Laurentian, pp. 41–59.

Cordato, R.E. (1997), 'Market-Based Environmentalism and the Free Market, They Are Not the Same', *The Independent Review*, **1** (3), pp. 371–86.

Davis, N.A. (1991), 'Contemporary Deontology', in Singer, P. (ed.), *A Companion to Ethics*, Cambrigde, MA: Blackwell, pp. 205–18.

Deb, R. (1994), 'Waiver, Effectivity and Rights as Game Forms', *Economica*, **61**, pp. 167–78.

Deb, R., P.K. Pattanaik and L. Razzolini (1997), 'Game Forms, Rights, and the Efficiency of Social Outcomes', *Journal of Economic Theory*, **72**, pp. 74–95.

Elliot, R. (1991), 'Environmental Ethics', in Singer, P. (ed.), *A Companion to Ethics*, Cambridge, MA: Blackwell, pp. 284–93.

Elster, J. (1989), 'Social Norms and Economic Theory', *Journal of Economic Perspectives*, **3** (4), pp. 99–117.

Gaertner, W., P.K. Pattanaik and K. Susumura (1992), 'Individual Rights Revised', *Economica*, **59**, pp. 161–77.

Gintis, H. and P. Romer (1998), 'The Human Side of Economic Analysis: Economic Environments and the Evolution of Norms and Preferences', Technical Report, Department of Economics, University of Massachusetts.

Goodin, R.E. (1991), 'Utility and the Good', in Singer, P. (ed.), *A Companion to Ethics*, Cambridge, MA: Blackwell, pp. 241–48.

Goodstein, E.S. (1995), *Economics and the Environment*, Englewood Cliffs, NJ: Prentice-Hall.

Hahn, F. (1982), 'On Some Difficulties of the Utilitarian Economist', in Sen, A. and B. Williams (eds), *Utilitarianism and Beyond*, Cambridge: Cambridge University Press, pp. 187–98.

Hammond, P.J. (1982), 'Utilitarianism, Uncertainty and Information', in Sen, A. and B. Williams (eds), *Utilitarianism and Beyond*, Cambridge: Cambridge University Press, pp. 85–102.

Hare, R.M. (1982), 'Ethical Theory and Utilitarianism', in Sen, A. and B. Williams (eds), *Utilitarianism and Beyond*, Cambridge: Cambridge University Press, pp. 23–38.

Harsanyi, J.C. (1982), 'Morality and the Theory of Rational Behaviour', in Sen, A. and B. Williams (eds), *Utilitarianism and Beyond*, Cambridge: Cambridge University Press, pp. 39–62.

Hausman, D. and M.S. McPherson (1993), 'Taking Ethics Seriously: Economics and Contemporary Moral Philosophy', *Journal of Economic Literature*, **XXXI**, pp. 671–731.

Hirschman, A. (1985), 'Against Parsimony: Three Easy Ways of Complicating some Categories of Economic Discourse', *Economics and Philosophy*, **1**, pp. 7–21.

Honderich, T. (1996), 'Consequentialism, Moralities of Concern, and Selfishness', *Philosophy*, **71** (278).

Kymlicka, W. (1999), *Les Theories de la Justice: Une Introduction* (La Decouverte), French translation of *Contemporary Political Philosophy: An Introduction*, Oxford: Oxford University Press, 1990.

Leopold, A. (1968), *A Sand County Almanac*, New York: Oxford University Press.

Mann, C.C. and M.L. Plummer (1995), 'Empowering Species', *The Atlantic Monthly*, **2**, pp. 22–26.

Moulin, H. (1997), 'Procedural cum Endstate Justice: An Implementation Viewpoint', Discussion Paper, Department of Economics, Duke University, March.

Narveson, J. (1998), 'Libertarianism vs. Marxism: Reflections on G.A. Cohen's Self-ownership, Freedom and Equality', *Journal of Ethics*, **2**, pp. 1–26.

Pattanaik, P. and K. Susumura (1996), 'Individual Rights and Social Evaluation: A Conceptual Framework', *Oxford Economic Papers*, **48**, pp. 194–212.

Pearce, D.W. and R.K. Turner (1990), *Economics of Natural Resources and the Environment*, Baltimore: The Johns Hopkins University Press.

Pettit, P. (1991), 'Consequentialism', in Singer, P. (ed.), *A Companion to Ethics*, Cambridge, MA: Blackwell, pp. 230–40.

Rawls, J. (1997), *Theorie de la Justice*, Point Essais (Le Seuil), French translation of *A Theory of Justice* (1971), London: Oxford University Press.

Ridley, M. and B.S. Low (1993), 'Can Selfishness Save the Environment?', *The Atlantic Monthly*, **3**, pp. 76–86.

Roemer, J.E. (1996), *Theories of Distributive Justice*, Cambridge, MA: Harvard University Press.

Sagoff, M. (1999), 'Controlling Global Climate: The Debate over Pollution Trading', Report from The Institute for Philosophy and Public Policy, School of Public Affairs, University of Maryland.

Scanlon, Th.M. (1982), 'Contractualism and Utilitarianism', in Sen, A. and B. Williams (eds), *Utilitarianism and Beyond*, Cambridge: Cambridge University Press, pp. 103–28.

Sen, A.K. (1970), 'The Impossibility of a Paretian Liberal', *Journal of Political Economy*, **72**, pp. 152–57.

Sen, A.K. (1977), 'On Weights and Measures: Informational Constraints in Social Welfare Analysis', *Econometrica*, **45 (7)**, pp. 1539–71.

Sen, A.K. (1979), 'Personal Utilities and Public Judgements: Or What's Wrong with Welfare Economics?', *The Economic Journal*, **89**, pp. 537–58.

Sen, A.K. (1992), 'Minimal Liberty', *Economica*, **59**, pp. 139–59.

Sen, A.K. (1993), *Ethique et Economie* (French translation: On Ethics and Economics), Philosophie Morale, Presses Universitares de France (PUF).

Sen, A.K. (1995), 'Rationality and Social Choice', *American Economic Review*, **85**, pp. 1–24.

Sen, A.K. (1999), 'Welfare Economics and Two Approaches to Rights', in Pardo, J.C. and F. Schneider (eds), *Current Issues in Public Choice*, Cheltenham, UK and Northampton, MA, USA: Edward Elgar, pp. 21–39.

Sen, A.K. and B. Williams (eds) (1982), *Utilitarianism and Beyond*, Cambridge: Cambridge University Press.

Sugden, R. (1993), 'Welfare, Resources and Capabilities: A Review of Inequality Reexamined', *Journal of Economic Literature*, **XXXI**, pp. 1947–62.

Susumura, K. (1999), 'Consequences, Opportunities and Procedures', *Social Choice and Welfare*, **16**, pp. 17–40.

Vatn, A. and D.W. Bromley (1995), 'Choices without Prices without Apologies', in Bromley, D.W. (ed.), *The Handbook of Environmental Economics*, Cambridge, MA: Blackwell, pp. 3–25.

Winston, M. (1999), 'On the Indivisibility and Interdependence of Human Rights', Technical Report, The College of New Jersey.

3. Coping with Co-management: a Framework for Analysing the Co-operation between State and Farmers' Organisations in Protected Area Management

Regina Birner, Britta Jell and Heidi Wittmer

1 INTRODUCTION

In developing countries a wide range of co-operative institutional arrangements has been applied to cope with agro-environmental problems. A focus on participatory approaches has, in general, a long tradition in rural development in developing countries (World Bank 1996). In resource and nature conservation, the need for an approach which actively involves the rural communities has been particularly pronounced since other approaches have largely failed (Wells and Brandon 1992). A variety of terms is used to describe the diverse co-operative institutional solutions which have been tested, for example community-based resource management, collaborative management (co-management), adaptive co-management, participatory natural resource management, social forestry, and so on. These approaches require the organisation of the resource users (farmers) in a type of co-operative arrangement (co-operative, committee, association, and so on). The ample empirical experience with such co-operative institutional arrangements in the developing world allows one to derive valuable implications, both for theory and for practice. These co-operative approaches have attracted considerable scientific interest from different disciplines, as is documented by the activities of the International Association for the Study of Common Property (IASCP).[1]

Economic approaches have mostly used the concepts of the New Institutional Economics (NIE), especially the property rights approach, transaction costs economics and the theory of collective action (Meinzen-

Dick and Knox 2001; Hanna and Munasinghe 1995). From an NIE perspective, the challenge of studying such arrangements – which has still not been met – can be seen in analysing a governance structure which involves a complex interaction between co-operatively organised users' organisations involving collective action problems on the one hand, and hierarchically organised state agencies, on the other hand. Different types of instruments can be used to govern the interaction between users' groups and state agencies to cope with environmental problems, such as voluntary contracts, imposed regulations, change of the prevailing property rights structure, devolution of decision-making authority, and so on.

Against this background, this chapter proposes an analytical framework based on NIE concepts which allows one to classify and analyse such complex governance structures. To limit the scope of the agri-environmental problems to be considered, the focus is placed on nature conservation and protected area management, which typically involves serious conflicts of interests with farmers, both in developed and in developing countries.

The chapter is organised as follows: Section 2 clarifies the concept of co-management and suggests a structure for analysis. Section 3 introduces an empirical case study from Cameroon (Jell 1999) which will be used to illustrate the proposed analytical framework. Section 4 develops the framework for a normative analysis and section 5, the framework for a positive analysis of co-management. Conclusions are drawn in section 6.

2 THE CONCEPT OF CO-MANAGEMENT

2.1 Defining Co-management

According to Townsend and Pooley (1995), collaborative management, or – in short – co-management, refers to any set of institutional arrangements that structure an external relationship for resource governance between relevant stakeholders. As such, it has to be distinguished from an internal structure which is found, for instance, in a pure common property regime. Meinzen-Dick and Knox (2001) place co-management in the context of devolution and distinguish collaborative management, where the state retains a role in resource management, from community-based resource management, where control over resources is transferred more or less completely to local user groups. Borrini-Feyerabend (1996, pp. 3, 12) defines collaborative management as a partnership by which various stakeholders agree on sharing among themselves the management functions, rights and responsibilities for a territory or a set of natural resources under protected or non-protected status; the stakeholders primarily include the agency in charge (usually a state agency) and various associations of local residents and resource users. However, co-management can also involve non-governmental organisations, local administrations, traditional authorities, research institutions, business, and others. Vira et al. (1998) mention power sharing and joint responsibility as defining criteria of collaborative management. Drawing on Gray's ideas, they assert that 'collaboration implies a joint decision-making approach to problem resolution where power is shared, and stakeholders take collective responsibility for their actions and subsequent outcomes from those actions'. Borrini-Feyerabend (1996, pp. 3, 12) points out that the term co-management is not tightly defined and can be used for a variety of institutional arrangements ranging from mere consultation to the devolution of decision-making authority. Terms often used interchangeably with co-management include participatory management, joint management, shared management, multi-stakeholder management and round-table agreement (Borrini-Feyerabend 1996, p. 12).

2.2 Analysis of Co-management: Criteria and Objectives

Two types of institutional analysis of co-management arrangements are distinguished here: (1) normative analysis: identifying how the terms of a co-management agreement in the situation under study should be framed in order to meet defined objectives; (2) positive analysis: explaining why the terms of a particular co-management arrangement are as they are, as a result of different influencing factors.

The normative analysis is confronted with the problem of identifying the objectives according to which co-management arrangements are to be evaluated. Here we suggest deriving the criteria for a normative analysis of co-management arrangements from the concept of sustainable development as it is manifested in the documents of the UNCED Conference in Rio 1992.[2] Accordingly, three types of criteria can be distinguished: ecological, economic and social.

1. Ecological criteria can be derived from the ecological objectives on which the declaration of a protected area is based. Problems with the use of ecological criteria arise when the ecological objectives for the declaration of a protected area are not clearly specified and when appropriate ecological data for this area are not available. This is often the case in protected areas of developing countries.
2. Economic criteria can be derived from generally accepted economic goals of developing countries, especially economic growth and poverty alleviation. Criteria derived from these objectives are, for example, the impact of a co-management arrangement on the level and growth of the

household income of different groups of local residents. Depending on the size of the protected area and the value of its alternative uses, the impacts on economic growth at the regional and national level are also economic criteria to be considered. As an economic criterion, transaction costs, both private and public, have to be taken into account.

3. Social criteria can be derived from the goal of equity, justice or fairness. The distribution of the costs and benefits arising from the protection of an area which results from a particular co-management arrangement can be seen as a major social criterion. In protected area management, the question of fairness arises at different levels: between different groups of local residents, between local residents and the national and international community, and between present and future generations.[3]

There are – obviously – trade-offs between the different ecological, economic and social objectives from which the above criteria are derived, at least in a short-term perspective. To judge the efficiency of a co-management arrangement, one would have to know the society's preferences with regard to these objectives and the trade-offs. Stated differently, one would have to know the social welfare function of a society.[4] However, as Arrow's Impossibility Theorem (1950) implies, there is no social choice rule that would allow passing from individual preferences to social preferences, if some very reasonable and basic conditions are to be met. Acknowledging that it is, thus, not possible to determine 'the most efficient co-management arrangement', the objective of the analytical framework presented here is to make comparative evaluations of different co-management arrangements with regard to specified objectives.

2.3 Structuring Co-management for the Purpose of Analysis

For the purpose of analysis, a co-management arrangement is considered here as a relational contract, which structures the relationship between the contracting parties in a long-term perspective. In line with the above definitions of co-management, the contracting parties typically include (1) the local residents living adjacent to or in the protected area, and (2) the government agency or agencies responsible for the protected area. Depending on the framework conditions, the local residents may form one or more contracting parties to a co-management arrangement. In developing countries, most of the local residents are typically farmers, but in the following we use the term local residents. Other stakeholders, such as NGOs, business enterprises or eco-tourism agencies, may also be contracting parties. As already mentioned in the introduction, a specific feature of co-management is the fact that the contracting parties are organisations with different internal organisational structures. State agencies are typically organised hierarchically and have to cope with principal–agent problems. The local residents require some type of co-operative organisation to be able to become a contracting party to a co-management agreement. This implies collective action problems or free-rider problems. In addition, the local residents also face principal–agent problems if they have to select members to represent them in the bargaining process or in institutions created by a co-management contract such as monitoring committees. Applying the concept of contracting as analytical device does not imply that there is necessarily a formal contract on a legal basis. Informal agreements can also be analysed within this framework. Applying the concept of contracting allows for two types of analysis:

(1) *Normative analysis*: Structuring co-management arrangements as relational contracts makes it possible to apply Williamson's (1985) concept of governance and contractual relations, which is based on transaction cost economics. The character of this analysis is normative and comparative-static, as it allows us to compare the efficiency of different contractual arrangements for given transactions. Accordingly, the contents of the co-management contracts have to be analysed as referring to different types of transactions such as harvesting forest resources, bio-monitoring, and so on.
(2) *Positive analysis*: Conceptualising co-management arrangements as relational contracts allows one to apply Sen's (1990) bargaining model of 'co-operative conflict'. The contents of the co-management contract are considered as being determined by the bargaining power of the contracting parties and the factors influencing their bargaining power. Accordingly, the character of this analysis is positive: the objective is not to explain what the ideal co-management arrangement in a given situation should look like, but to explain why a particular co-management arrangement is as it is. This perspective also helps to identify which co-management arrangements are feasible under the given circumstances. Policy recommendations for 'second-best' solutions can be derived on this basis. The character of this analysis is, however, also comparative-static as it focuses on the bargaining power of the contracting parties and the factors influencing it, but not on the bargaining process. Even though it is fully acknowledged that the analysis of the process leading to a co-management agreement is important, this type of analysis is beyond the scope of this chapter.

3 THE CASE OF THE PROPOSED PROTECTED AREA OF LOBÉKÉ IN SOUTH-EAST CAMEROON

For the purpose of illustrating the proposed analytical framework, the case of the planned protected area of Lobéké in South-East Cameroon (Jell 1999) is introduced here. The proposed protected area covers, at present, approximately 212 500 ha of moist forest. Within its boundaries, there are no permanent settlements, and at present all hunting and timber logging is forbidden. The future gazettement as a protected area seems to be assured (Davenport and Usongo 1997), but so far neither the protection category (for example Wildlife Reserve, National Park, Forest Reserve) nor the final boundaries or internal zoning system have been decided.

The population density in the case study area of less than five persons per km² is comparatively low. The local population comprises the Bangando, an ethnic group of Bantu origin, and the Baka Pygmies. Both the Bangando and Baka engage in subsistence and commercial agriculture as well as in hunting, gathering of forest products and fishing. Rotational shifting cultivation is the predominant form of land use. The fauna of the region is known for its high diversity and its unusually high densities of large forest mammals which are internationally recognised as endangered, such as forest elephants and lowland gorillas. Hunting and the consumption of bushmeat is not only important for the local people with regard to food security and income generation, but also has a value of cultural and social dimension, especially for the Baka. During the past decade, people of various ethnic groups from other areas of Cameroon and the bordering countries have migrated to the area for commercial hunting (poaching), employment in logging companies and trading. The commercial hunters settle mainly in hidden temporary camps in the forest along the logging roads, which are also within the boundaries of the proposed protected area. Illegal marketing facilities for bushmeat are well developed as logging trucks can be used to transport the meat from the rather remote area to urban centres.

The government agency in charge of the proposed protected area is the Department of Wildlife and Protected Areas, one of the five departments of the Ministry of the Environment and Forests (MINEF). In the case study area, the Department is represented on a district level. By law, the control and monitoring of the activities concerning wildlife are tasks of the personnel of the administration in charge of wildlife affairs. The proposed protected area is situated within the project area of a Biodiversity Project funded by the Global Environmental Facility (GEF). In the entire GEF/Biodiversity Project site (23 000 km²) there were, in 1997, only about ten MINEF agents, distributed in three 'forestry posts', who were responsible for the control and monitoring of the forestry and wildlife activities (Mimbang 1998). Referring to this lack of personnel, and their lack of equipment and infrastructure to execute their deployments, Mimbang (1998) concludes that the administration of wildlife affairs does not have adequate means to implement its conservation policies.

The legal framework conditions in Cameroon allow the setting up of formally recognised ‘Committees for Development and Conservation of the Environment’. The committees are entitled to manage the funds which the local communities receive from the taxes of the logging companies in their area. The GEF/Biodiversity Project promotes the establishment of these committees and their participation in the elaboration of proposals for a regional land use and development plan and management plans for the proposed protected area of Lobéké. Two such committees, which had been formally registered in October 1997, were included in the case study (Jell 1999). The goals of the two committees laid down in their bylaws are quite similar and can be summarised as follows: (1) economic, social and cultural development of the community (including socio-economic organisation in working groups for economic activities such as agriculture, animal husbandry, and sensitisation of the villagers for an improvement of their housing and sanitary infrastructure), and (2) active participation in the conservation and management of their forest (including denunciation of overexploitation and destruction of forest resources *vis-à-vis* the project or the local administration as well as indiscriminate use of natural resources with specific attention on fish poisoning and hunting).

The case of the proposed protected area of Lobéké can be analysed within the framework of co-management because the local population is clearly entitled and encouraged to participate in the delineation and zoning of the protected area and its management. The land use and development plan and the management plan of the proposed protected area can be considered as the relational contract constituting the co-management arrangement. The contracting parties in this case comprise the Committees for Development and Conservation of the Environment, as representatives of the local residents, and the Department of Wildlife and Protected Areas, as representative of the state.

4 NORMATIVE ANALYSIS: EFFICIENCY CONSIDERATIONS

4.1 From Williamson’s Efficient Boundaries of the Firm to the Efficient Boundaries of the State

The search for efficient governance structures, as developed by Williamson (1985), starts from defined transactions and aims at identifying adequate institutional arrangements to carry out these transactions. Two behavioural assumptions of 'contractual man' are central to Williamson's approach: (1) bounded rationality and (2) opportunism. On this basis, Williamson (1985, p. 33) formulates an 'organisational imperative' as follows: 'Organise transactions so as to economise on bounded rationality while simultaneously safeguarding against the hazards of opportunism.' For the analysis of co-management, it is suggested that one applies the behavioural assumptions of opportunism and limited rationality to the individuals within the organisations of local residents and the state agencies which form the contracting parties. It is assumed that the internal organisation of the contracting parties determines the extent to which they, as entities, display characteristics of opportunistic behaviour.

Williamson (1985) argues that three dimensions of transactions favour relational contracting: asset specificity, uncertainty and frequency. Asset specificity may lead to 'lock-in' situations. Uncertainty is important because governance structures differ in their capacities to respond effectively to disturbances. Frequency is relevant because the cost of specialised governance structures will be easier to recover for large transactions of a recurring kind. Williamson analyses the organisation of transactions from the perspective of a business enterprise. Identifying the most efficient type of organisation for the different transactions of production, input supply and marketing allows Williamson (1985, p. 96) to analyse vertical integration and determine the 'efficient boundaries of the firm'. To apply Williamson's approach to the case of co-management, it is useful to take the perspective of the political decision maker who wants to achieve sustainable use and conservation of the natural resources in the area under consideration most efficiently.[5] Applying Williamson's three dimensions of transactions, one can derive that relational contracts have comparative advantage in protected area management: (1) protected areas can be considered as highly site-specific investments which involve idiosyncratic knowledge (specificity criterion), (2) management activities are recurrent (frequency criterion), and (3) threats, such as poaching, logging or encroachment, are inherent (uncertainty criterion). As the following sections will show, it is possible to extend Williamson's approach in order to obtain richer insights into the contract choice in protected area management. Analogous to Williamson's efficient boundaries of the firm, this perspective allows one to derive hypotheses on the 'efficient boundaries of the state'.[6]

4.2 Transaction Costs and Contract Choice in Protected Area Management

To derive hypotheses on contract choice, protected area management is conceptualised here as involving four types of management decisions:[7]

1. conservation decisions (determining restrictions on the extraction and use of resources, identifying and preventing hazards such as forest fires),
2. investment decisions (determining level and types of investments such as replanting of trees in degraded areas),
3. allocation decisions (determining how the benefits of using the resources shall be distributed),
4. regulation decisions (determining how the conservation and investment decisions are to be enforced).

For the purpose of analysis, it is further suggested here to consider as transactions both

- making these decisions, and

  the activities necessary to enforce the decisions (patrolling to prevent resource use which contradicts the conservation decisions, harvesting of resources in line with the conservation and allocation decisions, carrying out investment activities such as planting trees, preventing forest fires, and so on). In the following, these activities are called management activities.

Accordingly, one can distinguish the transaction costs of making management decisions and of carrying out management activities. The transaction costs arising from making management decisions include

- the costs for collecting the information necessary to make management decisions,
- the costs arising from making sub-optimal decisions,
- the costs for bargaining over the decisions and settling conflicts concerning these decisions (if they are not made by a single decision maker).

Transaction costs for the execution of management activities include the costs of

- making arrangements necessary to carry out the management activities (if they are not carried out by the decision makers themselves; for example hiring a park guard to control boundaries),
- monitoring the management activities,
- enforcing execution of management activities according to the management decisions, if necessary.

Costs for management activities which are typically taken into account in production economics are not considered as transaction costs. Examples are the labour and material used for tree planting, labour and transport costs of harvesting resources, and so on. Note that production costs and transaction costs have to be taken into account simultaneously when deriving hypotheses concerning the efficiency of organising the respective transaction. This is important because with increasing scale production costs often decrease while transaction costs increase (Coase 1937; North and Wallis 1994).

Different types of co-management contracts involving state agencies and local residents can be distinguished according to the following interrelated criteria:

1. organisation of making management decisions,
2. organisation of carrying out management activities, and
3. distribution of property rights between state agencies and local residents, which forms the basis of a co-management contract.

By definition, only those contracts will be considered here as co-management contracts where communities are not only involved in carrying out management activities, but also in making management decisions. In the theory of contract choice, the distribution of property rights, as the basis of contracting, is taken as given. However, from the perspective of the political decision maker, the distribution of property rights is – in principle – a choice variable as well. Therefore, it is included as a third criterion here.

(1) Hypotheses on the efficient organisation of decision making can be made by taking different dimensions of the decision-process into account:

Asymmetrical information: Participation of communities can reduce the transaction costs of making management decisions by providing relevant knowledge (site-specific, idiosyncratic knowledge, 'local knowledge'). This reduces the transaction costs of collecting necessary information and the costs of making sub-optimal decisions. The more remote the area, the more refined the local knowledge, the less staff and knowledge are available on the part of the responsible state agencies, and so on, the greater the effect on transition costs.[8] The advantage of idiosyncratic knowledge on the part of the local population can only be used if the persons or groups having this knowledge are involved in the decision-making process. In the Lobéké case, the Baka had probably more idiosyncratic knowledge of wildlife, but they were underrepresented in the Committees on Development and Conservation of the Environment which were supposed to be the contracting party for co-management arrangements.

Conflicts of interests: Participation of communities can increase the transaction costs of making management decisions by increasing the costs of bargaining, settling conflicts, and so on. The larger the potential conflicts of interests between state agencies and local residents and between local residents, the higher the costs. The costs can be reduced by establishing procedures of conflict resolution, developing a 'culture' of co-operation between state agencies and community representatives, and so on.[9]

Creation of legitimacy: Participation of communities can reduce the transaction costs involved in enforcing management activities by creating legitimacy and incentives for compliance with management decisions (Hanna 1995). The more difficult it is to monitor management activities (see below), the more important is this effect.

(2) To formulate hypotheses on efficient organisation management activities, it is useful to consider, in addition to Williamson's dimensions of frequency, asset specificity and uncertainty, the following dimensions of management transactions:

Care intensity versus effort intensity: Care-intensive activities are more difficult to monitor than effort-intensive activities (Fenoaltea 1984). Note that management activities in protected areas, such as controlling of poaching, protection from forest fires, and so on, are often rather care-intensive. Assuming opportunistic behaviour, incentives have to be created for such activities in order to reduce the transaction costs of monitoring. A typical economic incentive is to let the local residents either share or fully enjoy benefits from protected areas such as, for example, income from eco-tourism. Zimbabwe's CAMPFIRE project is a prominent example of this type of economic incentive (Furze et al. 1996). However, for eco-tourism, the necessary investment both in physical infrastructure and in human resources is often high and organisational arrangements have to be made to ensure the sharing of benefits with the local residents. In the Cameroon case, the eco-tourism option as economic incentive for the local residents was – in addition to these constraints – limited by the presence of 'well connected' commercial safari enterprises. Another typical benefit of local residents from protected areas is the collection of non-timber forest products. In the Lobéké case, non-timber forest products played an important role in the household economy of the local residents (Jell 1999). However, this benefit does not create an incentive for management activities which are not directly related, such as the prevention of poaching.

Type of threats to protected areas: The transaction costs involved in preventing damage from protected areas depend on the type of 'threat'. If the major threat is encroachment by the local residents, this group, as contracting party, may have lower transaction costs of preventing encroachment than state agencies, if they have functioning mechanisms of social control and sufficient incentives to use these mechanisms. In sparsely populated areas, such as in the Lobéké case, the major threat is typically not encroachment by local residents, but illegal poaching or logging by outsiders, who may use means of physical violence. In the Lobéké case, logging was not so relevant as most of the area had already been logged during the last 30 years. However, poaching by outsiders was a major problem, and the poachers were considered to be dangerous as they used guns. In such cases, the transaction costs of the local residents for preventing this type of damage are prohibitively high. In theory, the transaction costs of enforcement in such cases should be lower for state agencies because the state can, by definition, use coercive power. However, in practice, the state agencies concerned have to be organised in such a way that they have sufficient incentives for enforcement. As in the case of Lobéké, state agencies are often able to capture large rents from illegal activities. Obviously, co-management contracts cannot solve this enforcement problem if the internal organisations of the respective state agencies are not reformed. In the Cameroon case, the political pressure on a reform of the state agencies appeared to be insufficient.

(3) From the perspective of the policy maker, the allocation of property rights has to be compared with alternative policy instruments. For example, allocating communal property rights in a buffer zone is an alternative instrument to leasing out state land in this zone on a co-management contract. Collecting a tax after allocating property rights can be considered as the alternative to collecting a rent according to a lease contract. Passing regulations on land use after allocating property rights is an alternative instrument to including regulations in a co-management contract. Criteria for making these choices under efficiency considerations include

- incentives created for the local residents and transaction costs to be borne by them, and
- incentives created for state agencies as well as transaction costs arising for the state from the implementation of the different policy instruments.

Allocation of property rights to local residents may create additional incentives, based on the psychology of ownership. This appears especially relevant if it allows the formalisation of customary rights already held by the local residents (see below).

5 POSITIVE ANALYSIS: CO-OPERATIVE CONFLICT AND BARGAINING POWER

5.1 Co-operative Conflict in Co-management

As has been mentioned above, Sen's (1990) model of co-operative conflict will be applied to provide a framework for the positive analysis of co-management. The model is applicable if two conditions are met:

- Both contracting parties can improve their position by co-operation, this means by entering into a co-management contract, as compared to a situation without such a contract (non-co-operation).
- The second feature of the co-operative conflict model is that the contracting parties have conflicting interests concerning the contents of the contract.

The second condition, conflicting interests, is likely to prevail in protected area management. Conservation versus use represents the classical case of these conflicting interests. In the Lobéké case, conflicting interests concern mostly wildlife, while in cases of higher population density, land for cultivation is often a more important issue of conflict. The fact that co-management has become such an important policy instrument for protected areas of developing countries worldwide is an indicator of the relevance of the first condition. In general, both potential contracting parties – the local communities and the state – can improve their position as compared to the earlier non-co-operative approach of protected area management, namely 'fencing people out'. In particular cases, however, there may be groups of local residents who can reasonably assume that state agencies do not have adequate means or incentives to enforce protection regulations affecting them if no co-management agreement is reached. According to the co-operative conflict model, such groups will have a low incentive to engage in co-management.

5.2 Factors Influencing the Bargaining Power of the Contracting Parties

Following Sen's approach, the position of a contracting party in the relationship established by the relational contract depends on the 'break-down position' of this party, that is, its situation in the case that no co-management agreement is reached. The more unfavourable the break-down position, the more disadvantaged is the position of the contracting party within the relation established by the contract.[10] This points to a general problem of co-management. By the very nature of the state, which by definition has the legal monopoly to use coercive power, state agencies are principally the more powerful contracting party in a co-management agreement. It depends on the political, administrative and legal system of the respective country, to what extent the power of the state agency as contracting partner in a co-management agreement is regulated and limited. The problem of unequal break-down positions is especially pronounced in countries where the forest administration often has paramilitary protection units. The superior bargaining power of the responsible state agency is especially critical when the agency is organised in such a way that it represents special group-interests or self-interests of the agency members instead of the society's ecological, economic and social objectives. The case of Guatemala indicates how such problems can be avoided if a reform of the relevant state agencies is difficult to achieve. The legislature in Guatemala has leased out the entire management responsibility of one of the most important protected areas, the Sierra de las Minas, to a national conservation NGO, the Defensores de la Naturaleza. This NGO, which is nationally and internationally recognised for its management capacity and its commitment to combine conservation goals with socio-economic development, now acts on behalf of a state agency as contracting party to co-management agreements with the local population.

The internal organisation of the local residents as contracting party also has a major influence both on their bargaining power and on the interests they represent. The organisational capacity of potential interest groups depends on factors such as the number of potential members, their socio-cultural homogeneity, the risk aversion and time discounting rate of potential members, their access to communication and transportation infrastructure, political leadership and the possibility of using already existing organisations (Davis and North 1971). In the Lobéké case, the legal framework conditions required an organisation of the local population as one contracting party, represented by the Committees for Development and Conservation of the Environment. The social structure of the local population, however, was not conducive to such an organisation. The local residents consisted of two ethnic groups which traditionally had a non-hierarchical social organisation with dispersed decision making. The local village chiefs usually were not political leaders who, personally or as an institution, could increase the organisational capacity of the local population or enforce management regulations more effectively. While the social structure within the ethnic groups was non-hierarchical, there existed a traditional hierarchical structure between both groups, with the Bangando in the dominating position. This made equal participation of both ethnic groups rather difficult. The customary institution of the village court was dominated by the Bangando people and no Baka were included. The Committees for Conservation and Development which were created in the villages with support of the GEF/Biodiversity Project were dominated by the Bangando, too; they included only one Baka each. Likewise, women were underrepresented. These conditions represent a danger with regard to equity goals as the Baka will continue to be marginalised. To create better conditions for a collaborative approach, the supporting agencies (project, NGO) would have to invest in the empowerment and the organisational capacity of the Baka first. This involves not only transaction costs but also potential social conflicts with the Bangando.

5.3 Legitimacy, Discourse and Perception Bias

The break-down position is not the only factor influencing the bargaining power of the contracting parties. To gain more insights into bargaining power, it is useful to consider the co-management contract, in line with Sen's model, as an exchange of 'initial' entitlements or property rights of the contracting parties. Similar to the case of Sen's intra-household contract, the terms of exchange in co-management contracts are not usually determined by a market mechanism. Rather they depend on

- the perceived value and legitimacy of the initial property rights held by the contracting parties,
- the perceived legitimacy and importance of their objectives, and
- the perceived fairness[11] of the terms of exchange.

Conflicting claims concerning the initial property rights of the contracting parties are an important problem in bargaining for co-management contracts. Local residents who have used the resources in and around the protected area for generations claim traditional property rights to these resources. At the same time, state agencies claim formal state ownership of these resources on the basis of formal legislation, often dating back to the colonial era. Moreover, state agencies claim the legitimacy of state ownership in protected areas on the basis of the value of biodiversity for the society as a whole, including future generations. By the same account, local residents may claim that, taking into consideration their culturally based traditional management institutions, they have a greater interest and capacity to conserve and manage biodiversity effectively than state agencies prone to corruption problems. Use of biological resources for home consumption, especially in a situation characterised by widespread poverty and malnutrition, is generally considered as more legitimate than use of resources such as wildlife for marketing. Groups which cannot claim any legitimacy of their resource use, such as the non-local poachers in the Lobéké case, cannot usually be included in a co-management contract at all. The relevance of this type of problem should not be underestimated, since continuous poaching by non-locals will destroy any incentive by local residents to reduce their current use of wildlife resources.

Prevailing ideologies and the public discourse in the country under consideration have a decisive influence on the perceived legitimacy of the claims and objectives of the contracting parties. International donor organisations and international conventions, especially the Convention on Biological Diversity, have a marked influence on the national discourse. The legitimacy of conservation goals in the public discourse of developing countries has certainly increased due to such influences. This also applies to Cameroon, which has signed the Convention on Biological Diversity and receives funds from the GEF, as in the case of the Lobéké area. Besides influencing public opinion, national or international conservation NGOs such as the WWF or donor-funded projects may play an important role as facilitators of the bargaining process which leads to a co-management agreement. This was the role of the GEF project and the WWF envisaged in the Lobéké case.

Applying another feature of Sen's co-operative conflict model, one can introduce the concept of the 'perception bias' in analysing the role of the public discourse and legitimacy. The local populations living in or adjoining National Parks often consist of ethnic minorities. The legitimacy of their customary property rights, the value of their local knowledge as opposed to scientific knowledge, and their capacity to manage biological resources in a sustainable way are often underestimated in public opinion. Therefore, one can speak of a perception bias which weakens the bargaining power of indigenous local residents as a contracting party. Efforts by international organisations, including UN organisations, to stress the legitimacy of indigenous rights can be seen as a means to reduce this perception bias. Likewise, cultural anthropologists who produce scientific knowledge to prove the value of 'local knowledge' for sustainable resource management may also reduce this perception bias. However, scientific knowledge, especially the use of powerful – but simplifying – explanatory models may also increase the perception bias against indigenous populations. The perceived damaging role of shifting cultivation under increased population pressure, a legacy of Boserup's (1965) seminal work, can lead to an underestimation of the adaptive potential of such systems (Forsyth 1999).

6 CONCLUSIONS

The proposed analytical framework shows that the concepts of the New Institutional Economics are useful both for a normative and a positive analysis of co-management contracts. In a normative perspective, the application of transaction costs economics supports the claim that co-management, as a relational contract, is usually more efficient than other arrangements of protected area management. The application of transaction costs economics allows one to derive hypotheses on the 'efficient boundaries' of the state and helps to identify the factors which influence these boundaries. Major factors influencing the optimal choice of institutional arrangements in protected area management are asymmetrical information, the characteristics of the necessary management activities and the type of 'threats' to the protected area.

Switching from normative to positive analysis of co-management, it has been shown that Sen's bargaining model of co-operative conflict can be applied usefully to the case of co-management. The model shows that the fall-back position of the contracting parties and their internal organisation has a crucial influence on the extent to which ecological, economic and social goals of co-management can be met.

A limitation of the concepts used in this framework is that they do not allow the analysis of the process which leads to the establishment of co-management arrangements. This process, if it is well managed, may lead to a change in the position and perception of contracting parties, to a reduction of conflicts of interests and to the building of trust – as a form of 'social capital' – not only among the local residents, but also between the local residents and state agencies. This may reduce enforcement problems and the transaction costs and, therefore, change the optimal structure of co-management arrangements. The contribution of other disciplines such as political sciences and sociology is required to better understand the dynamic process of establishing co-management contracts.

NOTES

1. See the extensive bibliography of IASCP at http://www.indiana.edu/~iascp/.

2. Especially relevant in this context are the Convention on Biological Diversity, Agenda 21 and the Rio Principles.
3. Adopting a biocentric ethical perspective, one can include equity considerations among human and non-human beings, as well. With regard to the extinction of species, this question is relevant in protected area management.
4. See Bromley (1989), who suggests using the social welfare function in order to judge the efficiency of institutional change.
5. In this section, the conservation goals are considered as given. The problems involved in determining the conservation goals are discussed in the next section.
6. In accordance with this concept, the devolution of resource management which leads to co-management and community-based resource management has been described as 'the rolling back of the boundaries of the state'.
7. See Hanna (1995), who distinguishes conservation, allocation and regulation. With regard to natural resources such as forests and soil, it appears useful to include investment decisions, as well.
8. The asymmetry of information between state agency and local communities may depend on the type of management decision. For example, local communities may have more idiosyncratic information concerning regulation and allocation decisions while state agencies may have more relevant information on investment decisions.
9. See Sah and Stiglitz (1988) on the optimal design of decision making procedures in view of asymmetrical information (decision making in committees, hierarchies and polyarchies).
10. Sen (1990) uses this model to explain the disadvantaged position of women in intra-household relations.
11. It is beyond the scope of this chapter to discuss the problems of the concept of fairness here in detail. One needs a theory of distributive justice to deal with this concept. Rawls (1971) proposed a hypothetical procedure (decision making under a 'veil of ignorance') to solve the problem. See Cullity (1995) for a discussion of different theories of justice advanced by moral and political philosophers. Roemer (1994), in a paper on 'The Mismarriage of Bargaining Theory and Distributive Justice', argues that bargaining theory is 'too impoverished to capture the important issues of distributive justice. Bargaining theory admits information only with respect to the utilities of the agents once the threat point has been determined, while distributive justice is concerned with issues of rights, needs, and preferences as well' (Roemer 1994, p. 203).

REFERENCES

Arrow, K.J. (1950), 'A Difficulty in the Concept of Social Welfare', *Journal of Political Economy*, **58**, pp. 328–46, reprinted in K.J. Arrow (1984), *Social Choice and Justice*, Oxford: Basil Blackwell, pp. 1–29.

Borrini-Feyerabend, G. (1996), *Collaborative Management of Protected Areas: Tailoring the Approach to the Context*, Gland: IUCN, Switzerland.

Boserup, E. (1965), *The Conditions of Agricultural Growth – The Economics of Agrarian Change under Population Pressure*, London: George Allen & Unwin Ltd.

Bromley, D.W. (1989), 'Institutional Change and Economic Efficiency', *Journal of Economic Issues*, **23**, pp. 735–59.

Coase, R.C. (1937), 'The Nature of the Firm', *Economica*, **4**, pp. 386–405.

Cullity, G. (1995), 'Moral Free Riding', *Philosophy and Public Affairs*, **24** (1), pp. 3–34.

Davenport, T. and L. Usongo (1997), 'Justification and Recommendations for the Gazettement of a "Protected Area" in Lobéké Forest, South East Cameroon, Report for the Ministry of Environment and Forests, Yaoundé', WWF, Yaoundé, Cameroon.

Davis, L.E. and D.C. North (1971), *Institutional Change and American Economic Growth*, London: Cambridge University Press.

Fenoaltea, S. (1984), 'Slavery and Supervision in Comparative Perspective – A Model', *Journal of Economic History*, **3** (44), pp. 635–68.

Forsyth, T. (1999), 'Questioning the Impacts of Shifting Cultivation', *Watershed,* **5** (1), pp. 23–29.

Furze, B. et al. (1996), *Culture, Conservation and Biodiversity – The Social Dimension of Linking Local Level Development and Conservation Through Protected Areas*, Chichester: John Wiley & Sons.

Hanna, S. (1995), 'Efficiencies of User Participation in Natural Resources Management', in Hanna, S. and M. Munasinghe (eds), *Property Rights and the Environment: Social and Ecological Issues*, The Beijer Institute of Ecological Economics and The World Bank, pp. 59–67.

Hanna, S. and M. Munasinghe (1995), *Property Rights and the Environment: Social and Ecological Issues*, The Beijer Institute of Ecological Economics and The World Bank.

Jell, B. (1999), 'Collaborative Management of Wildlife Resources in the Lobéké Area of South-East Cameroon – An Institutional Analysis of Potential and Constraints', M.Sc. thesis, Göttingen University, Faculty of Forest Sciences and Forest Ecology.

Meinzen-Dick, R. and A. Knox (2001), 'Collective Action, Property Rights and Devolution of Natural Resource Management – A Conceptual Framework', in Meinzen-Dick, R., A. Knox and M. Di Gregorio (eds), *Collective Action, Property Rights and Devolution of Natural Resource Management – Exchange of Knowledge and Implications for Policy*, Eurasburg: CAPRi, ICLARM, ZEL/DSE, pp. 75-109.

Mimbang, L. (1998), *Les circuits de commercialisation des produits de chassée dans les sur-est de Cameroun*, Yaoundé, Cameroon: GTZ-MINEF (Gesellschaft für Technische Zusammenarbeit – Ministere de l' Environnement et de Forets).

North, D. and J.J. Wallis (1994), 'Integrating Institutional Change and Technical Change in Economic History – A Transaction Cost Approach', *Journal of Institutional and Theoretical Economics*, **150** (4), pp. 609–24.

Rawls, J. (1971), *A Theory of Justice*, Cambridge, MA: Harvard University Press.

Roemer, J.E. (1994), 'The Mismarriage of Bargaining Theory and Distributive Justice', in Roemer, J. (ed.), *Egalitarian Perspectives – Essays in Philosophical Economics*, Cambridge: Cambridge University Press, pp. 202–18.

Sah, R.K. and J.E. Stiglitz (1988), 'Committees, Hierarchies and Polyarchies', *Economic Journal*, **98**, pp. 451–70.

Sen, A. (1990), 'Gender and Co-operative Conflicts', in Tinker, I. (ed.), *Persistent Inequalities – Women and World Development*, New York, Oxford: Oxford University Press, pp. 123–49.

Townsend, R.E. and S.G. Pooley (1995), 'Distributed Governance in Fisheries', in Hanna, S. and M. Munasinghe (eds), *Property Rights and the Environment: Social and Ecological Issues*, The Beijer Institute of Ecological Economics and The World Bank, pp. 47–58.

Vira, B., O. Dubois, S.E. Daniels and G.B. Walker (1998), 'Institutional Pluralism in Forestry: Considerations of Analytical and Operational Tools', *Unasylva*, **194** (49), pp. 35–42.

Wells, M. and K. Brandon (1992), *People and Parks – Linking Protected Area Management with Local Communities*, World Bank, World Wildlife Fund, Washington: USAID.

Williamson, O.E. (1985), *The Economic Institutions of Capitalism – Firms, Markets, Relational Contracting*, New York: The Free Press.

World Bank (1996), *The World Bank Participation Sourcebook*, Washington, DC: The World Bank.

PART II

Designing and Managing Environmental Co-operatives: the Dutch Experience

4. Environmental Co-operatives: a New Institutional Arrangement of Farmers

Louis H.G. Slangen and Nico B.P. Polman

1 INTRODUCTION

In addition to marketable goods such as food, raw materials and ornamental plants, the agricultural sector also produces 'non-marketable' goods like wildlife and landscape. These are called external effects. They are the result of a specific way of using agricultural land. Agricultural landscapes such as 'small-scale landscapes' – characterised by small fields surrounded by hedges or wooded bank, or peatland areas with narrow plots and wide ditches – were a by-product (or joint production) of farming when land use was relatively capital-poor, small-scale and labour-intensive.

After 1950, the rise in wages induced labour-saving and production-enhancing techniques in agriculture, which increased agricultural output and helped the dwindling number of farmers to achieve income comparable to those outside the sector. A high level of mechanisation, intensification of land use and specialisation at the farm and at the regional level accompanied the changes in agriculture. As a result, there was a deterioration of wildlife and landscape and in the quality of soil, water and air. While agriculture experienced these developments, higher incomes increased the demand for wildlife and landscape, for leisure and outdoor recreation. Thus, during the time when the supply of wildlife and landscape decreased, the demand for these amenities actually increased. The changes on the demand side are a result of changes in the institutional environment. This implies that the rules of the game for the agricultural sector are changing.

The agricultural sector has to develop new institutional arrangements to meet these changes in the institutional environment. One of them is the environmental co-operative for farmers as a supporting structure to implement and operationalise the changes of the demand side. First, in this chapter we will apply New Institutional Economics (NIE) to analyse the theoretical background, the reasons and tasks of environmental co-operatives. Second, we will investigate the state of the art regarding environmental co-operatives in the Netherlands.

Section 2 deals with the question of why we need environmental co-operatives. The reasons include market failure, the need for a new institutional arrangement to countervail opportunistic behaviour and hold-up problems, the need for developing countervailing power, and reducing transaction costs. In section 3 we start with a short overview of the concepts of institutional arrangements and governance structures from the perspective of NIE. Both are different terms for the same concept: supporting structures to facilitate transactions. In section 4 we typify the institutional arrangement/governance structure of environmental co-operatives for farmers. Environmental co-operatives are on the one hand an organisation, and on the other they have a relationship with their members who maintain their private property rights, and remain mainly independent farmers. Important questions to be considered are: What is the nature of the contractual relationship and how is the contractual relationship determined? What are the characteristics of the contracts between members and the organisation? How are the property rights of the organisation and of the members specified? Who has the power of control or the right to the residual incomes? Section 5 deals with the results of a mail survey. This survey is the first and most intensive survey concerning environmental co-operatives for farmers in the Netherlands. Section 6 gives a summary and conclusions.

2 REASONS FOR ENVIRONMENTAL CO-OPERATIVES: MARKET FAILURE, LACK OF PROPERTY RIGHTS AND ASSET SPECIFICITY

Farmers often produce, in addition to marketable goods such as food, raw materials and ornamental plants, non-marketable goods like wildlife and landscape. Wildlife and landscape could be seen as a 'by-product' of land use by farmers or as a result of the joint production of agricultural land use. Because of the character of these goods as non-marketable goods, the market fails as a co-ordination and price-setting mechanism. We have two important criteria to characterise goods and to investigate the reasons for market failure: exclusiveness and rivalry.

The non-marketable attributes of land like wildlife and landscape have the properties of non-rivalry and (to some extent) non-excludability. Wildlife and landscape are non-rival (or indivisible) and (partially) non-excludable goods. Non-rivalry in consumption and in production characterises the benefits derived from wildlife and landscape. Non-rivalry in consumption means indivisibility of the benefits. A good is non-rival or indivisible when a unit of the good can be consumed by one individual without detracting, in the slightest, from the consumption opportunities still available to others from the same unit (Cornes and Sandler 1996, p. 8). Non-rivalry in production is often a result of joint production (see Boadway and Bruce 1989, pp. 112–13).

Non-excludability is the property of a good such that the benefits of that good not only can be, but also in fact are, made available to all. Non-excludability is – because it refers to a lack of property rights – the crucial factor in determining which goods must be publicly provided. Exclusion may not be feasible for technological reasons, as in the case of national defence, or for an institutional reason, as in the case where property rights cannot be assigned. When exclusion is impossible, the free rider problem and the associated prisoner's dilemma arise (Boadway and Bruce 1989, pp. 129–30).

When the characteristics of rivalry and excludability of goods are defined, the so-called spectrum of goods can be distinguished. Pure public goods have the two properties of non-rivalry and non-excludability. Pure private goods are fully rival and excludable. Impure public goods, whose benefits are partially rival and/or partially excludable, occupy the in-between points along this spectrum. An important subclass of such goods comprises those where the benefits are excludable but partially non-rival; these goods are club goods (Cornes and Sandler 1996, p. 9). The essential difference between club goods and pure public goods depends on the existence of an exclusion mechanism. A club is a voluntary group deriving mutual benefits from sharing one or more of the following: production costs, the members' characteristics (for example, members have land, are farmers) or a good characterised by excludable benefits (Cornes and Sandler 1996, pp. 33–34).

Land, as an asset with valuable wildlife and landscapes, has many attributes. The question is who has the property rights over these attributes? Ownership of all these attributes is often divided between two or more persons rather than being assigned to a single person. The costs of determining, capturing and retaining the attributes of an asset are defined as transaction costs. The presence of transaction costs means that asset attributes cannot be fully known to (prospective) owners. The result is that the rights to the assets – or more specially, the asset attributes – are not fully delineated (see Barzel 1997, p. 4). Farmers could say: It is my land, and therefore I have the property rights. But because of the properties of non-rivalry and (to some extent) non-excludability, wildlife and landscape are not pure private goods.

The consequences of assets possessing many attributes and also the relatively high transaction costs involved in determining these attributes thus are twofold. First, divided property rights emerge, with two or more individuals having rights to distinct attributes of the same asset. Second, the incomplete separation of property rights means that some attributes cannot be specified or allocated to the property rights holders. As a result of these effects, some of the attributes remain part of the 'public domain' or form what Barzel (1997, p. 5) calls common property. This gives rise to the problem of specification of the property rights. To govern the common property we need a specific institutional arrangement or governance structure. This could be an environmental co-operative.

According to Barzel (1997, p. 5) a commodity lies in the public domain when the resources needed to acquire it accrue to no one. Once attributes are in the public domain, individuals will spend resources to 'capture' it. This is characterised as capture because here, in contrast to a market sale, the original owner does not receive what the recipient spends. For example, the travel cost and waiting time that people spend in line to acquire a 'free' good accrue to no one, therefore such a good lies in the public domain (Barzel 1997, p. 5).

People tend to delineate their property rights more carefully as the value of these rights increases and less so as their value declines. Imperfect delineation of property rights is sometimes a result of the choice of the owners not to exercise all of their rights. Owners find or deem some of their rights too expensive to exercise and choose to place them in the public domain (Barzel 1997, p. 93). In the past, farmers have left (or placed) the gain from the attribute wildlife and landscape in the public domain. They did not claim the property rights over this attribute.

Based on the criteria rivalry and excludability, the benefits of wildlife and landscape are impure public goods. Technically, it is possible to exclude people from the (or a part of the) benefits, for example by fencing off. Geographical exclusion is also possible. However, technical exclusion can involve considerable costs. Under the assumption of no congestion the benefits will be non-rival.

The first reason why we need a new institutional arrangement such as an environmental co-operative is due to the problems of non-rivalry and non-excludability. Both are reasons for market failure. Typical for wildlife and landscape are non-rivalry (in consumption and in production, the latter because of the joint production) and to some extent non-excludability because of incomplete property rights. An environmental co-operative for farmers is an institutional arrangement to reduce the cost of delineating the property rights and to extract some income from the asset. Market failure creates an incentive for producers to react collectively. They need an institutional arrangement as a supporting structure for co-ordination and motivation. The increase in the income potential of an asset has another effect/incentive on the behaviour of its owners. It increases the aggregate gains from co-operation among them, which in return is expected to lead to better delineation of the asset (Barzel 1997, p. 95). Hence an environmental co-operative for farmers is not only an important institutional arrangement but it is also an important incentive for better delineation of property rights, to generate income, and visa versa.

A second reason that justifies an environmental co-operative (as an institutional arrangement) is that individual farmers need an institutional mechanism to countervail opportunistic behaviour and hold-up problems. The core of the hold-up problem consists of asset specificity together with incomplete contracting. The problem arises in a situation in which each contracting party worries about being forced to accept disadvantageous terms later, after it has made an investment, or worries that its investment may be devalued by the actions of others. The party that is forced to accept a worsening of the effective terms of the relationship once it has made an investment has been 'held up' (Milgrom and Roberts 1992, p. 136).

Asset specificity refers to the degree to which an asset is committed to a specific task, and thus cannot be redeployed to alternative uses without sacrificing the majority of its value. Williamson (1996, pp. 59–60) distinguishes between six types of asset specificity. For our purpose the following are relevant:

1. Site specificity, which refers to an asset that becomes committed to a particular use owing to its location. The land used for preserving wildlife and landscape, because of its 'use' but also because of its 'site', is asset specific. Valuable areas for wildlife and landscape are immobile and local (that is tied to a particular area).
2. Physical asset specificity, such as an investment in machinery, equipment or land, and one that has a narrowly defined purpose. Investments in land or in machines used for wildlife and landscape preservation have a narrowly defined purpose, and are sunken investments.
3. Human asset specificity that arises through learning-by-doing. Preserving wildlife and landscape is a process of learning-by-doing; it requires an investment in human capital and time.

A third reason that justifies environmental co-operatives is that such an institutional arrangement could be used to develop countervailing power of control, building up oligopolistic or spatial monopolistic market power. If farmers pay more attention to wildlife and landscape they will sacrifice gains, on the one hand, from specialising in more regular or prevailing agriculture. On the other hand, the attribute wildlife and landscape is an impure public good or common good. It lies, according to Barzel (1997, p. 5), in the public domain. The (opportunity) cost for the farmer to produce wildlife and landscape is a private cost and the benefits of the attribute wildlife and landscape are an impure public good. This means that the property rights are different and vaguely defined, which leads to conflicts over the residual claims and decision control.

The fourth reason is transaction costs. The environmental co-operative for farmers is an institutional arrangement to reduce the transaction cost of delineating property rights and to extract some income from the asset wildlife and landscape. According to transaction cost theory, there are three critical dimensions involved in a transaction which are important for the level of the transaction cost: asset specificity, uncertainty and frequency (see Williamson 1998, pp. 30–31, p. 36). The first and most influential dimension is asset specificity, which has already been discussed above. The second dimension is that transaction cost theory assumes that human agents are subject to bounded rationality and are given to opportunism and strategic behaviour. Uncertainty reveals itself in the assumption of bounded rationality. The third dimension, frequency, involves the repetition of the same transaction. It is much easier to learn about prices, quality of products, and so on, if there are a large number of people in the market and a large number of exchanges are taking place.

Transaction costs are high when an exchange depends on a specific person, a specific location or specific physical assets. Under these conditions, the ability to bargain is low and the chances for opportunism are high. Rules or institutional arrangements like environmental co-operatives, which also make the activities of others more predictable, can reduce transaction costs. Because of asset specificity, uncertainty, and frequency, transactions with the impure public goods, wildlife and landscape, involve high transaction costs. Asset specificity and uncertainty are high. The frequency of concluding agreements in an environmental co-operative is low because agreements generally have a long duration. An organised form of co-operation in the form of an environmental co-operative can reduce the transaction costs of the supply of the impure public goods wildlife and landscape.

The last reason that justifies environmental co-operatives is also connected with market failure. Traditionally, market failure forms an argument for government intervention. Even if there is a justification for government intervention, an analysis of this interference is necessary. Such analysis casts light on the functioning of the government itself; after all the government can also fail (for an overview of non-market failure, see for example Wolf 1993). The reason for government failure can be lack of information, the character of the political decision making process, the bureaucratic way of production, or disincentives arising from taxes, regulation, levies and subsidies (Schram et al. 1991, p. 95). For impure public goods, an environmental co-operative as a *club* (see section 5) could be an alternative to government provision. This possibility has been investigated in Slangen (1994, pp. 42–59).

3 NEW INSTITUTIONAL ECONOMICS: INSTITUTIONAL ARRANGEMENTS

Over the past several decades, economists have given increasing attention to the role of institutions in the operation of economic systems. The term New Institutional Economics originates from Williamson. According to Williamson (1998, p. 24) NIE comes in two parts. One part deals with the institutional environment – the rules of the game. The other deals with the institutions of governance – the play of the game. One of the salient differences between the institutional environment and the institutions of governance are that the former mainly defines (or acts as a constraint on) the environment of the latter (Williamson 1996, p. 5). According to Ménard (1995, p. 175) a governance structure is a way to implement and operationalise the 'rules of the game' as they are defined by the institutional environment. Governance structures or institutional arrangements are supporting structures for transactions.

A second difference is that the institutional environment operates at a higher level of generalisation than do markets and organisations: it delineates the rules of the game within which such 'governance structures' actually operate. For example, the legal system, which most economists would agree on calling an institution, is a framework which defines the ways in which property rights can be implemented and enforced (Ménard 1995, p. 164). Thus the level of analysis is different. The institutions of governance operate at the level of individual transactions, whereas the institutional environment is more concerned with the composed levels of activity.

Important contributions in the recent literature on institutions of governance focus on the polar cases and the 'hybrid forms'. According to Williamson (1987, p. 16), the polar cases are markets and hierarchies. In the case of markets, co-ordination is based on prices, while in the case of hierarchies it is based on authority. Hierarchy involves the capacity to supervise and to control: it includes the right to make decisions (see Ménard 1994, p. 237). Many economists subscribe to Williamson's bipolar distinction between market and 'something else', but for 'something else' they prefer the term organisations instead of hierarchies. They argue that Williamson has taken an extremely narrow view of non-market co-ordination. Organisations cannot operate exclusively through command: they also require co-operation by their members. Such co-operation involves their commitment to specific goals, their willingness to endorse or transform existing routines, and their responsiveness to incentives deliberately designed to maintain or improve their participation.

The two governance structures 'markets' and 'organisations' are both embedded in an 'institutional environment'. However, there are areas of overlap, which give rise to hybrid forms (Ménard 1995, pp. 163, 173). A major contribution of the recent literature on transactions is the demonstration of the fundamental importance of 'hybrid forms' between the two polar cases of markets and organisations. Hybrid forms are characterised by specific combinations of market incentives and modalities of co-ordination involving some forms of hierarchical relationship (Ménard 1995, p. 175). The three main governance structures: markets, hybrids and organisations (sometimes referred to as hierarchies) are called institutional arrangements.

Williamson's original formulation of the markets and hierarchies paradigm has been criticised as a too narrow approach to modern organisations (see Milgrom and Roberts 1992, p. 291; Hart 1995, pp. 29–30; Douma and Schreuder 1998, p. 140). The criticism pertains to two related points:

- it is too simple to view markets and hierarchies as the only two governance structures for transactions: there is a third way of transacting;
- markets and hierarchies should not be viewed as two mutually exclusive governance structures: hybrid forms exist as well.

In contrast to hierarchical co-ordination – that is mostly vertical – the third way of co-ordination consists of forms of horizontal non-market co-ordination. The third way consists of more or less equal members who have informal communication with each other. Important basic elements of these relationships are motivation, trust and commitment. The co-ordination mechanisms that are used within such an organisation are mutual adjustments and the standardisation of values and norms. Mutual adjustment refers to the co-ordination achieved by informal horizontal communication. Standardisation of norms and values means shared codes of conduct usually for the entire organisation, so that everyone functions according to the same norms of behaviour. The motivation, trust and commitment underlying the operation of this organisation can be understood as evolving from the standardisation of values and norms or shared codes of conduct through selection (see Douma and Schreuder 1998, pp. 140–43). To work effectively, such a horizontal organisation could be partly based on formal rules, but they must be complemented by informal rules (sanctions, conventions, norms or codes of behaviour) that supplement them and reduce enforcing costs (see North 1993, p. 20).

Standardisation of values and norms leads to common values and norms. Common values and norms pertain to a congruent set of preferences within a group of people. Common values and norms form guiding co-ordination principles among a group or community. Various types of groups exist, ranging from a family to a club, a church and a volunteer group or a team of people working towards a common goal. Repeated interaction promotes solidarity, consensus, trust, and common values and norms in a group. Dasgupta (1991, pp. 75, 79) interprets social norms as implicit social contracts to co-operate, embedded in customs and rituals and resulting from repeated interactions. If people are not extremely myopic, it is the self-interest of each member of the group to keep to the norms, in other words the norms are self-enforcing. Common values and norms diminish the incidence of opportunistic behaviour between the members of the group. Effective co-ordination based on common values and norms coincides with strong motivation and high commitment of individual members of a group to achieve their common goal (CPB 1997, p. 55).

Nooteboom (1999, pp. 24–25) emphasises the role and meaning of trust. This has the effect of lowering the cost of search and monitoring, because trusting people are less secretive and more readily supply information. Trust reduces the costs of contracting and control because it lowers fears of opportunism and leads to the acceptance of more influence from the partner. In the case of trust, people will deliberate and renegotiate on the basis of give and take ('voice') rather than walk out ('exit') when conflicts arise.

Most people work in an organisation of some kind. Almost everyone grows up in an organisation called the family. There is a variety of groupings in which people interact for various reasons. The most important characteristic of such an organisation is that the members co-operate under some forms of agreements. This agreement may be based on a formal contract, on a quite informal contract, mutual expectation, or just on bonds of kinship as in a (possible extended) family. Co-operation or interaction inside an organisation is often more important than a market exchange, though an organisation (like a firm) also has to interact with markets, as when inputs are purchased and outputs are sold (FitzRoy et al. 1998, p. 1).

The question is, how can we typify the institutional arrangement or governance structure environmental co-operative for farmers? On the one hand, environmental co-operatives are an organisation. On the other hand, they have a relationship with their members, who maintain their private property rights and who remain mainly as independent farmers. A number of questions arise regarding these contractual relationships. What are the characteristics of the contracts between members and the organisation? How are the property rights of the 'organisation' and the 'members' specified? What is the co-ordination mechanism? Who has the power of control or the right over the residual income?

4 ENVIRONMENTAL CO-OPERATIVES AS GOVERNANCE STRUCTURES AND CONTRACTUAL RELATIONSHIPS

Contracts and the contracting process play central roles in modern institutional economics. The approaches to contractual arrangements can be structured along different lines. One is the agency-contract theory, which is concerned particularly with the problem of asymmetric information possessed by the parties to the contract. Types of asymmetric information are hidden information, hidden action and shirking (the latter is a form of hidden action in team production). The other approach focuses on the incompleteness and complexity of most contractual arrangements. Incomplete contracts are contracts that do not try to take into account all future contingencies, because of incomplete foresight into what the future will bring. Incomplete foresight makes it impossible to take all future contingencies into account when writing a contract. Furubotn and Richter (1997, p. 146) call (long-term) incomplete contracts relational contracts. The complexity of most contractual arrangements has to do with specification and implementation of the property rights in contractual relationships. To typify the governance structure of the environmental co-operative and to analyse the institutional setting of environmental co-operatives, we focus our attention on the incompleteness and complexity of most contractual arrangements.

Since the beginning of the 1980s there has been a growing interest in contract theories of various kinds. According to Hart and Holmström (1987, p. 71), this development is partly a reaction to our rather thorough understanding of the standard theory of perfect competition under complete markets, but more importantly a reaction to the resulting realisation that this paradigm is insufficient to accommodate a number of important economic phenomena (like environmental co-operatives). Contracts provide the foundation for a large part of economic analysis. Any trade – as a quid pro quo – must be mediated by some form of contracts, whether it be explicit or implicit. In the case of spot trades, where the two sides of the transaction occur almost simultaneously, the contractual element is usually downplayed, presumably because it is regarded as trivial. In recent years, economists have become much more interested in long-term relationships where a considerable amount of time may elapse between 'quid' and the 'quo'. In these circumstances, a contract becomes an essential part of the (trading) relationships. The question that arises is how can these different types of contract be characterised?

Lyons and Mehta (1997, pp. 48–49) distinguish, based on five key elements, between three types of contracts: classical, neoclassical and relational. The first element is related to the identity of the parties to the contracts. This is unimportant for a classical contract, but crucial for a relational contract. Second, the duration of the relationship is fixed in a classical contract, while it is open-ended in relational contracts. The third element relates to how the contract is expected to deal with contingencies, and the fourth, to the role of written documentation. The final element is the dispute procedure in anticipation of problems in dealing with changing circumstances.

The diversity of contractual arrangements, although limited, explains the necessity of providing adequate frameworks for transactions that have diverse characteristics. A better understanding of the attributes of the transactions considered allows us to predict the most adapted type of contract, that is the contract that can be drawn and implemented at the lowest possible cost, with the easiest enforcement procedures (see Ménard 1997, p. 8). Different contractual arrangements are related to different governance structures for implementing, co-ordinating and monitoring of different kinds of transactions. The differences among contracts correspond to the characteristics of the governance structures in which they are embedded (Ménard 1997, p. 13).

Governance structures correspond to classes of contracts. Selection of a governance structure must take into account the mutual interdependency between the governance structure and the characteristics of the contracts. Ménard (1997, p. 24) distinguishes between three types of governance structures or institutional arrangements: markets, organisations and hybrids. They are given in Table 4.1 with the numbers I, II and IV. Which governance structure corresponds with which contract depends on the completeness and complexity of the contracts. Incompleteness results from bounded rationality, particularly if the environment is uncertain, and from opportunistic behaviour of the partners. Complexity has to do with the writing of contracts and, even more importantly, with their implementation, mainly as a result of unclear distribution of the residual control rights between contracting parties. An important point is that ownership is a source of power when contracts are incomplete. According to the property rights approach, it is the owner of the asset in question who has the residual control rights (Hart 1995, p. 30). Under this approach, the residual control rights are the separating factor between 'not complex' and 'complex'.

The fifth category (agency) represents no specific governance structure. According to Ménard (1997, pp. 25–26) it is typically the territory of agency theory, which considers all forms of contractual arrangements as a continuum. Contracts tend to be complete, even though they may be very complex. Agency theory is continuously looking for an optimal contract, which includes built-in mechanisms that are self-enforcing. In that case there is no need for an enforcement procedure other than the built-in mechanisms.

Table 4.1 *Contracts, governance structures and agent theory*

Residual control rights	Complete contract	
	No	Yes
Clear	*Organisations* with mainly vertical co-ordination Neoclassical and relational contracts (I)	*Markets* Classical contracts (II)
Unclear	*Organisations* with mainly horizontal co-ordination (such as clubs) Relational contracts (III)	*Agency* Principal/ agent contracts (V)
	Hybrid forms Neoclassical contracts (IV)	

Source: Based on Ménard (1997, p. 24).

Owing to bounded rationality and the associated transaction costs, most agreements framing behaviour are incomplete and, as such, fail to determine future actions exactly (see FitzRoy et al. 1997, p. 234). Contractual incompleteness has important economic implications. Under complete contracting, the division of income in each eventuality would be specified contractually, and there would be no returns that could be considered as residual. If contracts are incomplete the ex post allocation of power of control matters. The party that has power of control has also the residual rights of control, and the one who is entitled to receive the residual income is the residual claimant (see Milgrom and Roberts 1992, p. 291).

The organisation type in the first cell (I) of Table 4.1 is partly based on Ménard (1997) and Williamson (1987). The latter is a direct descendant of Coase (1937; see Putterman and Kroszner 1996, pp. 89–104). In the standard approach of organisations based on Coase and Williamson, organisations are primarily characterised by authority or 'fiat', the capacity of some agents to give orders. The most important co-ordination mechanism is command and control. According to this notion the owner of a firm (= organisation) has the power of control, or the residual rights of control, and receives the residual income as the residual claimant. This implies that the allocation of the property rights over the residual income is simple and clear. Contracts are incomplete, but not complex.

In cell (III) we have to deal with more or less equal members who work together in an organisation which makes use particularly of forms of horizontal (non-price) co-ordination. The basic elements of the co-ordination mechanism are commitment, trust, reputation, standardisation of norms or beliefs, and shared codes of conduct. Of course, in some cases there is vertical co-ordination but this is not so important as in cell (I). Members largely maintain the property rights over their assets, but some of the attributes of the assets are or become common property. This implies that the residual control rights are not clear. Contracts between the members and the organisation itself are largely relational. In activities with unclear residual control rights, neoclassical contracts can be used. Environmental co-operatives belong to cell (III). In neoclassical contracts, parties maintain their property rights over their assets (cell IV). These types of contracts are therefore incomplete and complex because of the property rights. It implies that the residual control rights are the separating factor between 'not complex' and 'complex'.

According to the property rights approach, it is the owner of the asset in question who has the residual control rights (Hart 1995, p. 30). Residual income and residual control rights are highly complementary and it makes sense to allocate them to the same person. However, according to Hart (1995, p. 64) residual income and residual control are not always bundled together on a one-to-one basis. In some cases it may not be possible to measure or to verify all the aspects of an asset's return. The property rights view does not consider employees to be part of the firm because given that employees cannot be owned, there is no sense in which they are any different from agents who contract with the firm at arm's length (see Rajan and Zingales 1998, p. 388). In the case of environmental co-operatives we have a similar ownership situation. Farmers are not owned by the environmental co-operative. They maintain their property rights over capital goods, like cattle, buildings and land.

Organisations are situated in cell (I) or cell (III) of Table 4.1. Cell (I) consists of organisations based on hierarchies (that is vertical co-ordination based on authority). On the other hand, cell (III) consists of organisations with a rather horizontal organisational form (that is non-hierarchical co-ordination based on commitment, motivation, communication and information). Environmental co-operatives are mainly horizontal organisations. They belong to cell (III). The column of cell (III) indicates that we have to deal with incomplete contracts. However, an important question is, are these contracts complex or not? The answer depends on the distribution of the residual control rights between the parties.

An important characteristic of organisations – such as environmental co-operatives – in cell (III) is that the members of such organisations maintain (for a major part) their private property rights over their land and other marketable assets. On the other hand, the attribute wildlife and landscape is an impure public good or common good. It lies, according to Barzel (1997, p. 5), in the 'public domain'. Both forms of property rights indicate that we have to deal with complex contracts. The employees of the environmental co-operative do not have power of control. They have no property rights or, in this case, control rights over the residual income. The internal contracts with the employees of the environmental co-operative are therefore 'not complex'.

Because members of environmental co-operatives maintain the property rights over their land and other marketable assets, they retain the power of control over the residual income earned with marketable products. The farmers are the complete residual claimants over these products. For the impure public goods wildlife and landscape, the property rights are defined differently by farmers and the interest groups for wildlife and landscape. On the one hand farmers would say 'it is my land', and on the other hand interest groups or users would say it is 'our wildlife and landscape'. It means farmers lose the right to develop land when it leads to loss of certain public good characteristics (for example loss of wildlife habitat or scenic amenities). These vaguely and differently defined property rights lead to conflicts over the residual claims and decision control. If these goods lie in the public domain, the question that arises is: who has the power of control over these goods? There is a difference of opinion regarding the property rights regimes between the society and the farmers. This creates uncertainty, which is an important dimension for the level of transaction costs.

5 ENVIRONMENTAL CO-OPERATIVES IN THE NETHERLANDS

This section deals with the results of a mail survey. This survey is the first and most intensive survey concerning environmental co-operatives for farmers in the Netherlands. The mailed questionnaire was addressed to the organisation, hence the chairman or secretary probably filled in the questionnaire. We did not intend to survey individual farmers.

Our design was to a large extent descriptive. The reason was that there are no good sources available for characteristics about these organisations, the number of people involved, the way they are organised, and so on. Our survey is a cross-section of the total number of environmental co-operatives. In the middle of 1999 we had traced the addresses of 81 environmental co-operatives of farmers by using information from the government and other organisations. However, a number of addresses were not correct and some co-operatives replied that their organisation was not really active so that they were not able to fill in the questionnaire. Fourteen organisations were not mailed because they had recently been visited by another organisation. Our mailing list consisted of 67 co-operatives.

The total number of environmental co-operatives in the Netherlands is about 81 organisations. These organisations have about 6600 members who are farmers. The total area in use by environmental co-operatives in the Netherlands is about 134 thousand ha. The regional distribution of co-operatives and the importance of environmental co-operatives in the Netherlands are given in Table 4.2.

Table 4.2 Regional distribution of environmental co-operatives in the Netherlands[1]

Province	Area in use (1000 ha)	Area in use in % of total agricultural area	Number of co-operatives	Number of farmer-members	Members in % of total number of farms
Groningen	7	4	6	200	1
Friesland	23	8	16	590	8
Drenthe	4	2	2	70	1
Overijssel	–	–	2	130	1
Gelderland	4	1	12	330	2
Limburg	15	11	6	3030[2]	40
Utrecht	17	19	10	590	13
North-Holland	27	15	12	530	6
South-Holland	34	18	12	1060	9
Zeeland	3	1	4	70	1
Total	134	7	81	6600	6

Notes:

1. We did not get questionnaires back from Flevoland and Noord-Brabant.
2. This figure can be biased because it depends on an outlier.

Source: Survey on environmental co-operatives and LEI-DLO/CBS (1998).

If we look at the total agricultural land in use in the Netherlands, North-Holland, South-Holland and Friesland count for more than 60 per cent of the total area. The most important provinces for the environmental co-operatives in the Netherlands are Friesland, North- and South-Holland (and Gelderland). However, when we look at the number of members, Limburg seems to be very important, followed by South-Holland. The figure for Limburg is biased because of one organisation, all the members of the farmers' organisation in that area are indirect members of the co-operative. On an average 7 per cent of the total agricultural area is in use by environmental co-operatives. With regard to the land use, environmental co-operatives are most important for provinces in the western part of the Netherlands (North-Holland and South-Holland). This area is also a densely populated area. The participation of farmers is largest in Limburg and South-Holland. Table 4.3 gives an overview of land use, size and corresponding numbers of environmental co-operatives aggregated for the Netherlands.

Table 4.3 Size characteristics of environmental co-operatives in the Netherlands

	Land use (*1000 ha)	Land use in % of land use agricultural sector	Number of co-operatives	Average land use of co-operatives (ha)
Grassland	109	11	58	1901
Maize land	5	2	36	143
Arable land	16	2	15	1041
Non-agricultural land	2	–	13	137
Rest land	2	–	8	297
Total	134	7	81	1654

Source: Survey on environmental co-operatives and LEI-DLO/CBS (1998).

The largest part of the land in use by the co-operatives is grassland, followed by arable land. On 11 per cent of the total area of grassland in the Netherlands, co-operatives are active, whereas on arable land environmental co-operatives are not that important. The average area per co-operative is also very large for grassland.[1] The total average size of environmental co-operatives is about 1600 ha. The data from the survey shows that in a region where a co-operative is located, an average of 50 per cent of the area is in use by the co-operative.

About 10 per cent of the grassland of farmers who are members of a environmental co-operative is used under the 'Regulation Management Agreement and Nature Development'. Management agreements are private contracts between individual farmers and the Dutch government. In this case the Dutch government is the principal and the farmers are agents. The 'Regulation Management Agreement and Nature Development' identifies six management goals, each with a limited number of packages of management practices (Ministerie van Landbouw Natuurbeheer en Visserij 1997). The packages can be classified as follows: (a) maintaining natural handicaps; (b) maintenance agreements as management agreements; and (c) management agreements. The most important under (c) is that farmers must eschew certain treatments, and land use is restricted. (The totality of the management obligation to which the contractor binds him and the compensation to which he is entitled are referred to as the management package.)

About 75 per cent of thc environmental co-operatives contract individual farmers. These contracts range from maintaining hedges and farmland margin management to tolerating meadow birds or geese. This means that the co-operative serves as a principal for the farmers. If farmers get financial compensation for these contracts, funding will be originating from resources other than the 'Regulation Management Agreement and Nature Development'. This could be the environmental co-operative itself (by selling products or membership fees), the local government or other organisations (like the EU). In the latter cases the environmental co-operatives function as an intermediary. It is remarkable to see the non-agricultural area in use by the co-operatives, which has no official function as agricultural farmland and indicates that not all the co-operatives restrict their attention to agricultural areas exclusively. According to the answers in the questionnaire, many environmental co-operatives are developing new activities (for example about 25 per cent are developing regional and recreational products).

The availability of funding is of major importance for carrying out activities. The environmental co-operatives see funding as one of the most important bottlenecks for bringing ideas to activities like wildlife and landscape preservation contracting. Other bottlenecks are the time available to develop ideas and the adaptation to government regulations. Table 4.4 gives an overview of the most important financial sources. The difference in the financial sources for organisational activities like monitoring and meetings and other activities like preserving wildlife and landscape is interesting.

Table 4.4 Financial source of co-operatives for different activities (in percentage)

	Organisational activities	Other activities
Members	40	5
Non-government	7	6
Central government	16	36
Local government	24	43
Activities	13	10

Source: Survey on environmental co-operatives.

According to the results of the questionnaire the most important reasons for starting a co-operative are:

- contribution to conservation of wildlife and landscape;
- wishes of the society;
- being an interest group;
- generating an income from wildlife and landscape management.

Ranked in importance, the income goal is the fourth goal of a co-operative. It can be expected that there is a difference between the stated goals of the organisation and the goals of the individual farmers. Acting as an interest group of the farmers is also seen as an important task for a co-operative.

Recreation and regional products are clearly less important for these organisations. About a quarter of the organisations produce recreational or regional products. About 60 per cent of the organisations in our sample are involved in wildlife and landscape preservation on their own land. They value this activity also as the most important activity for their daily business. The reasons for starting an environmental co-operative, which are formally put down in the foundation acts, are:

- contribution to conservation of wildlife and landscape;
- continuity of the farms of the members;
- consultation with government on behalf of members.

These objectives stated in the foundation act are also the reasons for farmers to become a member of a co-operative. The organisation thinks that enthusiasm about the activities and objectives also plays an important role in becoming a member.

6 SUMMARY AND CONCLUSIONS

The agricultural sector has to evolve new institutional arrangements to meet changes in the institutional environment. One response has been the development of environmental co-operatives for farmers as a supporting structure to implement, operationalise and channel changes on the demand side. In this chapter, we use NIE to explore the properties, possibilities, limitations and design principles for environmental co-operatives. This should contribute to the development of an empirically supported theory of self-organising and self-governing forms of co-operation for the preservation of wildlife and landscape. There are several reasons for developing new institutional arrangements such as environmental co-operatives, including market failure. A new institutional mechanism is needed to countervail opportunistic behaviour and hold-up problems. Environmental co-operatives can create countervailing power and reduce transaction costs.

Our empirical research shows that the total number of environmental co-operatives in the first half of 1999 in the Netherlands is about 81 organisations. These organisations have about 6600 farmer members/participants and 1600 non-farmer members/participants. On an average, 6 per cent of the total agricultural area is in use by environmental co-operatives. The total average size of environmental co-operatives is about 1600 ha. In regions where a co-operative is located, about 50 per cent of the farmers are members of an environmental co-operative. About 75 per cent of the environmental co-operatives contract individual farmers. These contracts range from maintaining hedges and farmland margin management, to tolerating meadow birds or geese. The majority of environmental co-operatives in the Netherlands is of the formal association type (67 per cent) while a smaller part is organised as a foundation (25 per cent). The main activities of an environmental co-operative are producing impure public goods like wildlife and landscape. Important services are consultation with others on behalf of the members or being a pressure group.

We have to distinguish between the characteristics of the impure public good 'wildlife and landscape' and the activities and services of the organisation 'environmental co-operative'. Wildlife and landscape are in practice partially non-excludable goods. Regarding the property of rivalry, these are also non-rival goods. On the other hand, the activities and services of the governance structure environmental co-operatives as a club are excludable (and on a certain level rivalrous) public goods. Examples of these types of activities and services, based on our empirical research, are being an interest group and offering contracts for the preservation of wildlife and landscape.

Environmental co-operatives are not only a supporting structure for facilitating transactions, but also organisations which consist of contractual relationships. The members of an environmental co-operative mostly maintain the power of control (=ownership) over their assets, such as land and other marketable goods. In these cases the farmers have the residual control rights: the owner of the asset has the right to decide all uses of the asset in any way not inconsistent with a prior contract, custom or law. However, the distribution of the property rights between the parties is unclear because wildlife and landscape are common property. The property rights cannot be delineated completely. Because of these partial rights the residual rights control rights are not completely in the hands of the farmers. So they are not the only owners of wildlife and landscape and therefore they do not have complete power of control over the wildlife and landscape.

NOTE

1. The averages are calculated for co-operatives that use that type of land for their organisation.

REFERENCES

Barzel, Y. (1997), *Economic Analysis of Property Rights*, Second edition, Cambridge: Cambridge University Press.

Boadway, R.W. and N. Bruce (1989), *Welfare Economics*, Cambridge, MA: Basil Blackwell.

Coase, R.C. (1937), 'The Nature of the Firm', *Economica* **4**, pp. 386–405.

Cornes, R. and T. Sandler (1996), *The Theory of Externalities. Public Goods and Club Goods*, Second edition, Cambridge: Cambridge University Press.

CPB (Centraal Planbureau) (1997), *Challenging Neighbours: Rethinking German and Dutch Economic Institutions*, Berlin: Springer.

Dasgupta, P. (1991), 'The Environment as a Commodity', in Vines, D. and A.A. Stevenson (eds), *Information, Strategy and Public Policy*, Oxford: Basil Blackwell, pp. 71–103.

Douma, S.W. and H. Schreuder (1998), *Economic Approaches to Organisations*, London: Prentice Hall International.

FitzRoy, F.R., Z.J. Acs and D.A. Gerlowski (1998), *Management and Economics of Organisation*, London: Prentice Hall Europe.

Furubotn, E.G. and R. Richter (1997), *Institutional and Economic Theory: The Contribution of the New Institutional Economics*, Ann Arbor: The University of Michigan Press.

Hart, O. (1995), *Firms, Contracts, and Financial Structure*, Oxford: Oxford University Press.

Hart, O. and B. Holmström (1987), 'Theory of Contracts', in Bewley, T.F. (ed.), *Advances in Economic Theory; Fifth World Congress*, Econometric Society Monographs, 12, Cambridge, pp. 71–155.

LEI-DLO (Landbouw-Economisch Instituut)/CBS (Centraal Bureau voor de Statistiek) (1998), *Land- en Tuinbouwcijfers 1998*, Den Haag/Voorburg/Heerlen.

Lyons, B. and J. Mehta (1997), 'Private Sector Business Contracts: The Text between the Lines', in Deakin, S. and J. Michie (eds), *Contracts, Co-operation and Competition. Studies in Economics, Management and Law*, Oxford: Oxford University Press, pp. 43–66.

Ménard, C. (1994), 'Organizations as Co-ordinating Devices', *Metroeconomica*, **45**, pp. 224–47.

Ménard, C. (1995), 'Markets as Institutions versus Organisations as Markets? Disentangling some Fundamental Concepts', *Journal of Economic Behaviour and Organisation*, **28**, pp. 161–82.

Ménard, C. (1997), 'The Enforcement of Contractual Arrangements', Paper presented at the first Conference of the International Society for New Institutional Economics, Meeting, Saint-Louis, September 19–21, 1997, Centre ATOM University Paris.

Milgrom, P. and J. Roberts (1992), *Economics, Organization and Management*, Englewood Cliffs, NJ: Prentice Hall International.

Ministerie van Landbouw, Natuurbeheer en Visserij (1997), *Regeling Beheersovereenkomsten en Natuurontwikkeling*, Utrecht: Dienst Landelijke Gebied.

Nooteboom, B. (1999), *Inter-firm Alliances: Analysis and Design*, London: Routledge.

North, C.D. (1993), 'Institutions and Credible Commitment', *Journal of Institutional Economics*, **149**, pp. 11–23.

Putterman, L. and R.S. Kroszner (eds) (1996), *The Economic Nature of the Firm*, Cambridge: Cambridge University Press.

Rajan, R.G. and L. Zingales (1998), 'Power in a Theory of the Firm', *The Quarterly Journal of Economics*, **113**, pp. 387–432.

Schram, A.J.H.C., H.A.A. Verbon and F.A.A.M. van Winden (1991), *Economie van de Overheid*, Schoonhoven: Academic Service.

Slangen, L.H.G. (1994), 'The Economic Aspects of Environmental Co-operatives for Farmers', *International Journal of Social Economics*, **21** (9), pp. 42–59.

Williamson, O.E. (1987), *The Economic Institutions of Capitalism*, New York: The Free Press.

Williamson, O.E. (1996), *The Mechanisms of Governance*, New York: Oxford University Press.
Williamson, O.E. (1998), 'Transaction Cost Economics: How it Works; Where it is Headed', *The Economist*, **146**, pp. 23–58.
Wolf, C. Jr. (1993), *Markets or Governments; Choosing between Imperfect Alternatives*, Second edition, Cambridge, MA: The MIT Press.

5. Self-organising and Self-governing of Environmental Co-operatives: Design Principles

Nico B.P. Polman and Louis H.G. Slangen

1 INTRODUCTION

In this chapter we will analyse the factors which determine the effectiveness and efficiency in the self-organising and self-governing of environmental co-operatives. We will focus on environmental co-operatives of farmers and contracts used for preserving wildlife and landscape. The contractual relationships in wildlife and landscape preservation in the Netherlands are illustrated in Figure 5.1. We are mainly interested in contractual relationships in which environmental co-operatives participate: A_4 and C. These co-operatives have, on the one hand, (formal or informal) agreements with the government (or others) to achieve certain targets (case A_4), and on the other hand, relations with individual farmers to meet certain objectives (case C).

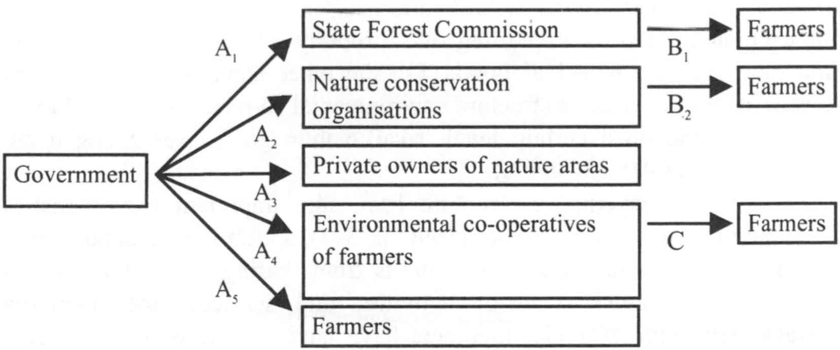

Note: The different arrows refer to sets of relationships.

Figure 5.1 Contractual relationships in wildlife and landscape preservation

We will make use of the New Institutional Economics (NIE) to explore ways (or design principles) to reduce the problems resulting from incomplete information and imperfect foresight. The goal of this chapter is to contribute to the development of a theoretical framework of self-organising and self-governing forms of co-operation for the preservation of wildlife and landscape by farmers.

Since environmental co-operatives can be viewed as clubs, we will investigate some theoretical aspects of clubs in section 2. Section 3 deals with possibilities (in the form of design principles) for reducing/limiting the problems resulting from asymmetric information, like hidden information, shirking in teams and hidden action, and from the lack of credible commitment and trust. These factors modify the quality of self-organising and self-governing. In section 4 we will analyse whether principles from the club theory and property rights view are used in practice. Further, we pay attention to ways of trying to overcome the problems of information asymmetries, and the lack of credible commitment and trust. Section 5 gives the summary and the conclusions.

2 THEORETICAL CONCEPT OF AN ENVIRONMENTAL CO-OPERATIVE: CLUB THEORY

We have to distinguish between the characteristics of the impure public good 'wildlife and landscape' and the activities and services of the organisation 'environmental co-operative'. The main difference is the possibility of excluding persons to make use (benefit) of the good. On the basis of the criteria: specification (= type of property rights) and establishing and enforcing of property rights, wildlife and landscape are, in practice, partially non-excludable goods. Regarding the property of rivalry, wildlife and landscape are also non-rival goods. On the other hand, the activities and services of the governance structure environmental co-operatives as a club are excludable (and on a certain level, rival) public goods (see Slangen and Polman, Chapter 4, this volume).

The club as governance structure has some important characteristics. According to Cornes and Sandler (1996, p. 347), a club is a voluntary group of individuals who derive mutual benefits from sharing one or more of the following: production costs of activities and services, the members' characteristics (for example, members have land, are farmers), or a good characterised by excludable benefits. When production costs are shared and the good is purely private, the structure of a private club is under consideration. The focus of our analysis, however, is the sharing of partly excludable (rivalrous) public goods. A number of aspects of such a club deserve attention.

- First, members choose to belong to the club voluntarily, because they anticipate a net benefit from membership. The utility or expected income jointly derived from membership and from the use of other goods must exceed the utility associated with non-membership status. Furthermore, the net gain in utility or expected income from membership exceeds or equals membership fees or toll payments (Cornes and Sandler 1996, p. 347).
- Second, clubs involve sharing, in the use of an impure public good, the use of the service of the club such as an environmental co-operative, and sharing in the benefits. Sharing often leads to a partial rivalry of benefits as membership increases, detracting from the quality of the service received. Crowding and congestion imply that one user's utilisation of the club good decreases the benefit or quality of service still available to the remaining users. As such, crowding or congestion depends on the measure of utilisation, which could include the number of members, the total number of members who use the club's facilities, or the number of visitors to the areas or provisions of the club (see Cornes and Sandler 1996, p. 348). A club can ration use effectively by means of internal institutions as long as the club is small, and the people meet sufficiently frequently and can therefore exercise mutual internal controls over property use. Internal institutions evolve from human experience and incorporate solutions that have tended to serve people best in the past. Examples are customs and good manners. Violations of internal institutions are normally sanctioned informally (Kasper and Streit 1998, p. 31). The internal institutions are more important for co-operatives that are relatively young and small. When clubs grow, there are increasing problems of internal information and informal control. Organisational costs rise as more formal institutions have to be implemented (Kasper and Streit 1998, p. 182).
- Club congestion may assume diverse forms: long files, long waits, slower and less service, and in the case of wildlife and landscape, lower quality. As membership size expands, both costs and benefits rise: costs involve increased congestion, while benefits result from cost reduction owing to the sharing of the provision expense associated with the club good. By adding a cost offset to the benefits derived from expanding the membership size, crowding leads to finite membership. This is a second characteristic serving to distinguish club

goods from pure public goods. For the latter, crowding costs are zero (Cornes and Sandler 1996, p. 348).

- A third distinguishing characteristic of club goods is the existence of non-members. For pure public goods, all individuals can be members without crowding taking place, so that non-members do not exist. For club goods, non-members to a given club have two options: they can join another club providing the same good, or they may not join any club offering the club good. If all individuals in the entire population are allocated among a set of clubs with no overlapping or non-assigned individuals, the population is partitioned into a set of clubs. The number of clubs then becomes an important choice variable. When, however, some individuals do not belong to any club supplying the club good, then the population is not partitioned (Cornes and Sandler 1996, p. 349).
- A fourth distinguishing feature of club goods is the presence of an exclusion mechanism, whereby non-members and/or non-payers can be barred. Without such a mechanism, there would be no incentives for members to join and to pay dues and other fees. The associated cost of operation and provision of an exclusion mechanism must be less than the benefits gained from allocating the shared good within a club arrangement. An analysis of the costs for the erection, operation and provision of an exclusion mechanism is important. If, for example, exclusion is not perfect owing to cost considerations, then free riders may utilise the club good. The design of the exclusion mechanism in terms of penalties and fees, needs to account for providing the proper incentive to both members and free riders. An important question would be if – based on exclusion cost arguments – an exclusion mechanism should include monitoring. The institutional form of a club may be tied to exclusion cost considerations (Cornes and Sandler 1996, p. 350).
- A fifth distinguishing attribute of club goods concerns a dual decision. Since exclusion is practised, members with user privileges must be distinguished from non-members. Moreover, the provision quantity of the shared good must be determined. Insofar as the membership decision affects the provision choice, and vice versa, neither can be determined independently. For pure public goods, however, only the provision decision needs to be considered – the membership is the entire population (Cornes and Sandler 1996, p. 350). So we have to distinguish between the membership decision and the provision decision.
- A final feature that differentiates club goods from pure public goods concerns optimality. Voluntary provision of pure public goods is

> typically associated with a Nash equilibrium that is sub-optimal; thus government provision may be required. In the case of club goods, members or firms can form clubs that collect tolls through an exclusion mechanism. Under a wide variety of circumstances, these clubs can achieve Pareto-optimal results without resorting to government provision (Cornes and Sandler 1996, p. 350). When the club decisions are represented as a co-operative action, the resulting outcome will be a Pareto optimum for the members. As noted earlier, members belong to a club because they perceive a net benefit from membership.

We can also analyse environmental co-operatives from a property rights point of view. This theory takes the view that, first, a firm is defined by its non-human assets; and, second, in the absence of comprehensive contracts decisions need to be taken over how these assets are used. The theory argues that the authority to make such decisions ultimately rests with the owner(s) of the co-operative (see Hart and Moore 1998, p. 2). In an ownership structure, there are both allocated residual control rights as well as rights to residual income, or profit. Provided that profit is well defined, the allocation of residual income can also be specified in an ex ante contract without reference to the issue to be decided ex post. Thus there are two ingredients to a constitution of a co-operative: the allocation of control rights, or votes; and the allocation of income rights, or shares (see Hart and Moore 1998, p. 37). Under outside ownership the outsider holds all shares and votes. In a co-operative, votes are allocated equally across the membership; and in a non-profit co-operative, the allocation of shares is irrelevant.

Typical for a co-operative is that it takes decisions by voting. Depending on the voting rule, a co-operative decides on a certain strategy. Often the median member's wishes will be decisive in a vote, rather than the average member's, and this typically leads to inefficiency. Also, in the case of outside ownership there are possibilities for inefficiencies. If the firm is owned by an outsider (who possesses all the residual income rights as well as all the residual control rights), there can be an inefficiency: the owner, who faces a distribution of consumers with different willingness to pay and has some monopoly power, extracts maximum surplus by charging a price above cost. As a result, some individuals are excluded who would consume in the first best case (see Hart and Moore 1998, p. 3).

It is difficult to rank co-operative and outside ownership in general, however Hart and Moore (1998, p. 42) arrive at the result that in the case of perfect competition, an outside owner achieves the first best solution; a co-operative typically does not. The reason for this result is that the rent from any cost advantage relative to the market issued to shield members from competitive pressure, and the median voter's preferences may not reflect average preferences. Further Hart and Moore (1998, p. 7) state that homogeneity of opinion across the membership is good for co-operatives, relative to outside ownership. An implication of this is that environmental co-operatives work well if their activities are narrowly defined, in which case presumably members' interests are aligned.

3 COMPLETE AND INCOMPLETE CONTRACTING: HOW TO LIMIT THE PROBLEMS OF INFORMATION ASYMMETRIES AND LACK OF COMMITMENT AND TRUST

Contracts and the contracting process play central roles in NIE. The different approaches to contractual arrangements can be observed to follow two broad trends. One, which is predominant in recent literature, emphasises the formal analysis of contracts, and focuses on conditions that would determine an optimal contract, that is, a contract that could fundamentally be self-enforcing (see Ménard, 1997, p. 1). The principal–agent theory belongs to this branch of research. In the standard principal–agent model, the parties negotiate only once and on a once-and-for-all basis. Under certain assumptions the principal can determine a remuneration plan for the agent that depends on results. Moreover, the situation created is one in which the agent maximises not only his own, but also the principal's utility. The assumption is that, after the contract is concluded, both parties fulfil their obligations without problems. This approach is also called the theory of complete principal–agent contracts (Furubotn and Richter 1991, pp. 18–19).

The other approach focuses on the incompleteness of most contractual arrangements. Incomplete contracts are contracts that do not try to take into account all future contingencies, because of incomplete foresight into what the future will bring (Slangen and Polman 2002). We will use insights from the principal–agent approach and incomplete contracting to analyse self-governing and self-organising environmental co-operatives.

The general framework of this chapter is given in Figure 5.2. As stated earlier, we will focus on the internal relations of the institutional arrangement 'co-operative' (arrow C in Figure 5.2). We will only refer to external relations (arrow A_4 in Figure 5.1) when it is important for this relation. Our objective is to develop design principles that are connected with the efficiency and effectiveness of the organisation.

The first row of Figure 5.2 relates to four different types of design principles. Ex ante refers to asymmetries of information that exist between

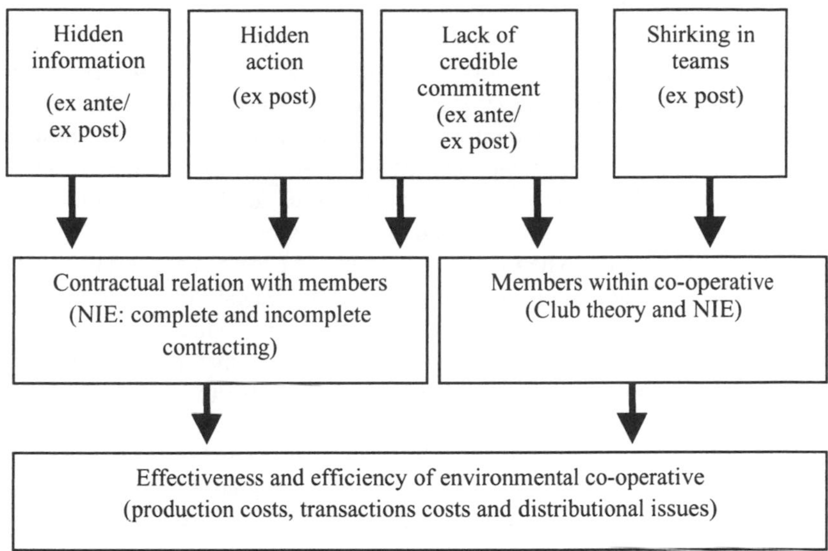

Figure 5.2 Efficiency and design principles for institutional arrangements in which farmers co-operate

individuals at the time of contracting. Ex post information problems are asymmetries of information that develop subsequent to the signing of the contract. These design principles are derived from contracting theory. They discipline the members and are relevant to the quality of the self-organising and self-governing mechanism of environmental co-operatives. The notion of design principles we use is: design principles are essential elements or conditions that help to account for the success of environmental co-operatives in producing goods and gaining compliance of generation after generation of farmers to the rules in use (see Ostrom 1990, p. 90). The care taken in designing these principles is important for the effectiveness and efficiency of the environmental co-operative. We will pay attention to the design principles which are meant for structuring the organisation of the co-operative. In this section we will also analyse the design principles important for the environmental co-operatives of the farmers. Information asymmetries are important for the contractual relationship. Shirking in teams plays a role in the level of organisation. Finally, we pay attention to commitment and trust, which are of concern to both the contractual relations and the internal organisation.

3.1 Information Asymmetries

The possibility of hidden information can lead to adverse selection. In this case, the environmental co-operative does not know if one of the (potential) members possesses private information which, if known to the environmental co-operative, would influence the attitude and conduct of the environmental co-operative. Ways in which the problem of hidden information can be reduced are signalling, screening and self-selection conditions.

Signalling occurs when the better-informed party makes certain verifiable facts known which, properly interpreted, may indicate the presence of other unobservable but desirable characteristics. In signalling, the privately informed party takes the lead in adopting behaviour that, properly interpreted, reveals their information. For signalling to be effective, the receiver must believe that the signal is credible. That is, the observable characteristic must clearly point to the unobservable, desirable characteristic (FitzRoy et al. 1998, p. 247). A signal for the qualification of a potential member could be his education. For example, did he follow a course in wildlife and habitats management? In another example, farmers may have to follow courses about wildlife management, or farmers may have to become, on a voluntary basis, a member of an environmental co-operative with membership dues.

Screening refers to activities undertaken by the party without private information (principal) in order to separate different types of informed parties (agents) along some dimension. It is the uninformed party who undertakes activities in order to make the informed parties group or sort themselves into separate types. Screening means that one of the contracting partners demands certain elements in the set of observed characteristics that are correlated with unobserved but desirable elements. According to FitzRoy et al. (1998, p. 247), screening is a strategy sometimes available to an uninformed party that, if successful, will get the better-informed party to reveal information. To effect the informed party revealing his private information voluntarily, we need an information-revealing mechanism.

Simply making what the organisation offers and what it expects known to the relevant group can induce some self-selection among potential candidate-members. This can be a by-product of other policies. Self-selection is usually a type of behaviour in response to some screening activity that causes workers to choose from a menu of contracts and sign the one they like best (see Kreps 1990, p. 638). To ensure that potential candidate-members choose the contracts intended, we need a particular form of the incentive compatibility condition, called the self-selection conditions (Slangen 1997, pp. 519–20). This means that the problem of hidden information can be reduced by the 'building-in' of self-selection conditions in the contract.

Hidden action is an ex post phenomenon. These problems could be resolved by monitoring and incentive contracts. An alternative solution is to require posting of bonds to guarantee performance, bonds which can be paid back if the performance is satisfactory or if the targets are reached. Using such solutions may still lead to incomplete contracts, but some self-enforcing elements will be incorporated. In homogeneous groups the incidence of hidden action can be reduced by common norms and values (CPB 1997, p. 74).

3.2 Commitment and Trust

An important element in co-ordinating and motivating members of an environmental co-operative is commitment of the members. However, the contracts within the governance structure 'environmental co-operative' are mostly incomplete and complex which gives rise to the problem of imperfect commitment.[1] Imperfect commitment refers to the inability of parties to bind themselves to follow through on threats and promises that they would like to make, but which, having been made, they would later like to renounce. This problem affects both market and non-market organisations, although their nature and impact may differ between organisational forms (Milgrom and Roberts 1992, p. 30). When contracts are incomplete and complex, they have only limited effectiveness for achieving commitment. Achieving commitment in an environmental co-operative is very important because it affects expectations of the members and thereby the behaviour they adopt.

Long-run relationships require commitment (Cooter and Ulen 1996, p. 195). There are different forms of commitment. Traditional forms of commitment include trust, friendship, kinship, ethnicity, religion, and so on. Traditional forms of commitment can facilitate economic co-operation without intervention or protection by the government. Consequently, traditional forms of commitment flourish in communities or in fields with weak government protection. Similarly, traditional forms of commitment are often important in communities or in fields where a conflict of interest with the government arises and the power of the government has to be faced (see Cooter and Ulen 1996, p. 196). Common values and norms support the commitment to keep agreements. They can reduce transaction costs and stabilise the underlying relationships.

Another form of commitment is used in the language of game theory. In game theory, a commitment forecloses an opportunity. To use a military analogy: burning the bridge behind you forecloses the opportunity to retreat. It is a signal that you are willing to fight. Commitment is achieved by foreclosing the opportunity to run away (Cooter and Ulen 1996, p. 170).

In general, communication facilitates co-operation. Organisations consist of more or less equal members who have informal communication with each other. Important basic elements of these relationships are motivation, trust and commitment. However, in situations that generate strong temptations to break mutual commitment or where there is a lack of common values and norms, an environmental co-operative cannot rely entirely on communication to sustain co-operation. More robust and long-lasting regimes involve clear mechanisms for monitoring rule conformance and graduated sanctions for enforcing compliance. Monitors – who may be the participants themselves – do not use strong sanctions for individuals who rarely break the rules. Modest sanctions indicate to rule breakers that others have observed their lack of conformance. By paying a modest fine, they rejoin the co-operation in good standing and learn that rule infractions are observed and sanctioned. Repeated rule breakers are severely sanctioned and eventually excluded from the group. Rules meeting these design principles reinforce contingent commitment and enhance the trust participants have that others are also keeping their commitment (Ostrom 1990, p. 10).

Commitment only is not enough. It should be credible. Burning the bridges behind you signals a credible commitment. External coercion is also a frequently cited theoretical solution to the problem of commitment. However, this solution does not address what motivates the external enforcer to monitor behaviour and impose sanctions. A self-organised group like an environmental co-operative must solve the commitment problem without an external enforcer. Members have to motivate themselves to monitor and be willing to impose graduated sanctions to keep conformance high (Ostrom 1990, p. 44).

The crux to bringing about credible commitment in an environmental co-operative is monitoring, graduated sanctions and conflict-resolving mechanisms (see Ostrom 1990, pp. 94–100). These activities should be carried out on a low cost level. Ostrom (1990, p. 45) emphasises monitoring: without mutual monitoring, there can be no credible commitment. Monitoring and graduated sanctions should be undertaken not by external authorities but by the participants themselves. Mutual monitoring or monitoring by volunteers reduces the costs. Farmers who violate the rules are likely to be assessed by graduated sanctions, depending on the seriousness and the context of the offence. If individuals are going to follow rules over a long period of time, there must be some mechanism for discussion and resolving what constitutes an infraction. The presence of a conflict-resolution mechanism does not guarantee that farmers will be able to maintain agreements. However, it is difficult to imagine how any complex system of rules could be maintained over time without such a mechanism. Such mechanisms could be at times quite informal. Those who are selected as the leaders could also be the basic resolvers of the conflict (see Ostrom 1990, pp. 94–101). To make promises trustworthy, credible commitments need to be established. This is unproblematic if agreements can be made binding by the courts, but such court-assured solutions are difficult to bring off in many relational contracts (Furubotn and Richter 1997, p. 276).

Building a reputation is one form of showing commitment. However, according to Ostrom (1990, pp. 93–94), it is clear from case studies that even in repeated settings where reputation is important and where individuals share the norm of keeping agreements, reputation and shared values and norms are insufficient by themselves to producing stable co-operative behaviour over the long run. Other ways to realise credible commitment are incentives contracts (with bonuses and penalties) and using posting of bonds to guarantee performance; bonds which can be paid back.

Nooteboom (1999, p. 25) emphasises – in a similar way to commitment – the role and meaning of trust. Trust lowers the cost of search and monitoring, because trusting people are less secretive and more readily supply information. Trust reduces the costs of contracting and control because it lowers fears of opportunism and accepts more influence from the partner. In the case of trust, people will deliberate and renegotiate on the basis of give and take ('voice') rather than walk out ('exit') when conflicts arise. According to Nooteboom (1999, pp. 25–28) there are different notions of trust: trust in people (behavioural trust, the object is individual people); trust in the institutional environment (confidence, the object is the social or natural system); and trust in organisations (the object is the intermediate level, the group or community). Organisational trust goes beyond a simple 'aggregate' of behaviour trust. It is a constellation of behavioural trust, with an organisational structure and culture acting as an institutional arrangement that guides the behaviour of the members and the staff.

In the approach of Nooteboom (1999, p. 29), the sources of trust are related to North's notion of 'institutional environment' (especially values, norms, codes of conduct) and related to 'institutional arrangements' (especially bonds of friendship or kinship and empathy). Trust can be produced or built up on shared norms of conduct, reputation, existing bonds of kinship or friendship, habitations and expectations. Some institutions, such as a system of certification, professional standards or rules, can be developed on the basis of some rational design. In the attempt to create conditions for trust to develop, detailed contracts can be destructive (cf. Nooteboom 1999, p. 33).

Often, trust based on friendship or kinship will not suffice as the basis for co-operation. Conversely, material self-interest and coercion are seldom sufficient as a basis for co-operation. According to Nooteboom (1999, p. 30) you 'really' trust someone when you are willing to forego guarantees on the basis of coercion or self-interest. Trust is nice and can work, but we have to take into account that trust may not always work (see Kreps 1990, p. 580). To make sure that co-operation works we can make use of the direct control that one may exercise over conduct by contract, monitoring or threat (coercion). This would also include motives of self-interest that restrain the partner in his opportunistic behaviour, such as preservation of reputation and expectations of future reward from co-operative conduct in the present (Nooteboom 1999, p. 29).

If we look to the sources of commitment and trust, there is some overlap. Trust is closely related to social norms for behaviour, which is also an important element for commitment. However, commitment can also be realised with more formal rules or foreclosing alternatives. Both can have the same effect: reducing hidden action.

3.3 Shirking in Teams

Shirking is a form of hidden action (in team production) which could easily arise in an environmental co-operative.[2] One method of reducing shirking is for someone to specialise as a monitor to check the input performance of team members. A second method is making use of incentives, which consist of penalties for low effort and bonuses for high effort. In both cases a principal is needed, either to enforce the penalties or finance the bonuses. A third method is to split the payments into fixed and variable parts. The principal offers all the agents a low fixed payment and a relatively high variable payment which depends on the ability and effort of the agent and his team-mates.

3.4 Design Principles

Figure 5.3 gives an overview of ways or design principles to reduce the effects of hidden action (adverse selection), hidden information (moral hazard), shirking, lack of credible commitment, and trust based on the literature and theory. We have already mentioned that shirking is a form of hidden action, but the term shirking is more connected with team production. There is some overlap in the various ways to reduce the effects, shown in the columns. Some methods can be used for different phenomena. Further, this list is not exhaustive but reflects important principles in setting up a co-operative.

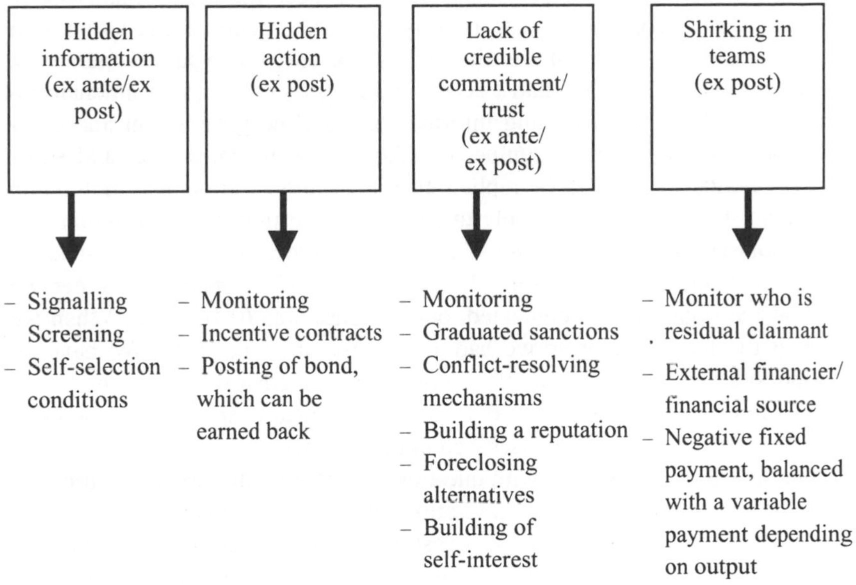

Figure 5.3 Design principles to reduce the effects of information asymmetries and the lack of credible commitment and trust

In section 4 we will analyse in which ways and on which levels environmental co-operatives in practice take into account the design principles to reduce information asymmetries and lack of credible commitment and trust. To what extent do they make use of the phenomena indicated in Figure 5.3 to reduce these effects?

4 ROLE AND FUNCTIONING OF ENVIRONMENTAL CO-OPERATIVES IN THE NETHERLANDS

This section deals with the results of the mail survey. Our survey is the first and most intensive survey concerning environmental co-operatives for farmers in the Netherlands. The mailed questionnaire was addressed to the organisation, hence the chairman or secretary probably filled in the questionnaire. We did not intend to survey individual farmers.

Our design was to a large extent descriptive. The reason was that there are no good sources available for characteristics concerning these organisations, the number of people involved, the way they are organised, and so on. Our survey is a cross-section of the total number of environmental co-operatives. In the middle of 1999 we had traced the addresses of 81 environmental co-operatives of farmers by using information from the government and other organisations. However, a number of addresses were not correct and some environmental co-operatives replied that their organisation was not really active so that they were not able to fill in the questionnaire. Questionnaires were not sent to 14 organisations because they recently had been visited by another organisation. Our mailing list consisted of 67 co-operatives. When we look at the organisations contacted, our response was 61 per cent. When we look at the total population we had a response of 51 per cent. We have no reason to assume that our sample is not a representative sample of the whole population. The questions asked in our questionnaire are based to a large extent on the theory already discussed in this chapter.

Our questionnaire started with questions concerning the reason for forming and the objectives of the organisation, the organisational structure, and activities of the organisation. Our questionnaire continued with questions on the motivation of the members and the help that the organisation gets from external sources. These questions allowed us to gather more insight into the problems with which an organisation has to cope. To examine activities and contracts we asked questions on monitoring and sanctions. Because financial sources are important we asked questions about the funding of the organisation and activities. Finally, we asked the organisations about their co-operation with the government and other organisations and how they see their own role in relation to their members and the government.

4.1 An Environmental Co-operative as a Club

In section 2 we argued that environmental co-operatives produce club goods. The presence of non-members who benefit from the club does spoil the effects of the club. In most environmental clubs farmers are members voluntarily. In areas with environmental co-operatives, on an average about 50 per cent of the farmers are members of a co-operative. This means there are non-members in such an area. Important activities of the environmental co-operatives are concluding contracts with individual farmers and being a pressure group. This kind of activity involves the sharing of cost and benefits. Sharing may give problems if the club shares the costs and the benefits are owned privately, such as in the case of marketable goods. In the case of marketable regional and recreational products, such a trade-off would be possible.

Non-members can be excluded from the benefits of the club arising from the contracting part. However, it is much more difficult to exclude non-members from activities like being a pressure group. Being a pressure group is seen as one of the most important tasks environmental co-operatives have. The dual decision is important because the provision of the contracts to the individual members is dependent on deciding to be a member. We did not find direct evidence for congestion in our questionnaire.

Exclusion within co-operatives is often carried out by excluding non-members from concluding wildlife and landscape management contracts with the environmental co-operative or producing regional products. In the case of a pressure group, exclusion is much more difficult. However, this also depends on the objectives of the pressure group. When the co-operative succeeds in decreasing the negative external effects of the production within an area, non-members will benefit from this reduction in the sense that they will have better opportunities in this area.

The members to a large degree finance the organisation and its activities, while the most important source for funding activities is the central, regional and local government. These funding relations make the relation with the government as a principal more complicated. The organisations also expect the government to fund their activities.

4.2 Property Rights and Voting

The juridical form of the organisation has consequences for the relationships within the organisation. Restricted accountability of the members is an advantage of organising like a formal organisation. The majority of environmental co-operatives in the Netherlands are formal associations (67 per cent) and some are organised as foundations (25 per cent). Formal associations and foundations are not allowed to make profits or to share profits among the members whereas legal co-operatives are allowed to do this. A formal association is an organisation which is laid down by a notary. In the articles of formal association the name, goals and obligations of members or the way obligations can be imposed are listed.

Foundations have no members. In the memorandum of a foundation the organisation has to lay down its name, goals, the way the board will be nominated, and the municipality where the organisation is located. The foundation is an institutional arrangement that is often used in the non-profit sector. Other, less important organisation forms are legal co-operatives and no legal form. Table 5.1 cites the characteristics of the ownership structures of the co-operatives.

Table 5.1 Membership characteristics for environmental co-operatives in the Netherlands (in number of organisations/persons)

Organisation type	Number	Farmer-members or participants	Other members or participants	Total area* (1000 ha)
Formal association	53	3000	1400	107
Foundation	18	900	200	18
Legal co-operative	4	2700	0	9
Rest	6	–	–	–
Total	81	6600	1600	134

Note: * This is the area in use by the co-operative and not by the members.

Source: Survey on environmental co-operatives.

In the Netherlands the total number of farmers participating in organisations of farmers with the objective of conserving wildlife and landscape is about 6600. About 3000 farmers are members of an environmental co-operative organised as a formal association. About 1400 civilians participate in formal associations. The 'Rest' category in Table 5.1 consists of co-operatives that have no legal status. The allocation of control rights, in the form of a voting system, within environmental co-operatives is organised in several ways. The control rights are not always the same for farmers and non-farmers. Often the voting right in a formal association is dependent on being a farmer or not. In about 50 per cent of the cases every member has one vote; 40 per cent of the associations have a voting system where every member with a farm has one vote. Voting as a possibility to use control rights is not important for foundations.

There are different reasons for farmers to become a member of a co-operative. The main reasons listed by the environmental co-operatives are: the enthusiasm to preserve the wildlife and landscape of the potential members, the extra income for the farmer, the negotiations of the co-operative with the government, and the function of the co-operative as a pressure group. The main reason for not taking part in the environmental co-operative is that the non-members do not agree with the aims and activities of the co-operative.

4.3 Information Asymmetries

Going back to the theoretical framework developed in the previous sections, we will discuss the internal relations of the institutional arrangement 'co-operative'. The boards of environmental co-operatives play an important role in the functioning of the organisation. Mostly they initiate and carry out new activities. Communication between co-operatives is also an important source for initiating new activities. For carrying out ideas, environmental co-operatives often use external bureaus. One of the main problems for translating new ideas into activities is the time constraint of farmers. Moreover, it is important to realise that many organisations are still thinking about issues like sanctions (also 25 per cent of the organisations are developing mechanisms).

The average fee is about 40 guilders per year. Only three formal associations have an entrance fee. It is questionable whether these fees are high enough to function as a screening device. Some organisations use courses as a screening device: farmers have to follow a specific course before they can become a member. A few organisations have a fee of about 100 guilders or a payment per hectare of about 2.50–5.00 guilders yearly. The incentive resulting from these fees will be higher. Signalling in the form of courses does not seem to play an important role.

Monitoring is important for the co-operatives: 85 per cent of the co-operatives have some form of monitoring activity. In 60 per cent of the cases in which monitoring takes place they use an external organisation and/or internal monitor. In 40 per cent of the cases both an internal and external enforcer are used. Often monitoring is carried out by measurement in the field by the farmers themselves (as members of the environmental co-operative) and by the judgement of external professionals. The most important form of monitoring is the collecting of data from and by the members concerning the numbers of clutches of eggs of meadow birds, numbers of rare plant species found in the field, and so on.

4.4 Commitment and Trust

Environmental co-operatives see the commitment and trust of their members as one of the most important factors for successful operation. It is considered to be the most important factor for success. External funding is ranked as the second factor for success, and activities that increase the opportunities of members as the third important factor. Increasing opportunities for the members is a source of building self-interest. A common vision with other groups or organisations like the government is less important for success. Ways to increase credible commitment that are used by the co-operatives are monitoring and sanctions. We have already discussed monitoring. Most of the co-operatives have the ability to use sanctions (75 per cent), although many organisations are still developing (new) sanctions. The most important options for sanctions are warning, followed by suspending members, excluding them from activities and imposing penalties. About 50 per cent of those organisations that have the opportunity to use sanctions have the possibility of using more than one type of sanction. The possibility of using more than one type of sanction suggests the presence of graduated sanctions. Whether the sanctions are actually imposed is also important to commitment. About 30 per cent of the organisations utilised sanctions. Several types of conflict-resolving mechanisms are used by environmental co-operatives. Often the board or the general memberships meeting decides on sanctions in the case of a conflict with the members. Other co-operatives have the possibility of establishing an arbitrage committee.

The average age of environmental co-operatives in the Netherlands is three years. About 30 per cent of the organisations are older than three years and about 20 per cent were founded in 1998. This means that the phenomenon of environmental co-operatives is relatively new for the Netherlands. Due to this short period of existence, many organisations and activities are still developing. Also, reputation building within this short period has not yet been possible for a large number of organisations.

5 SUMMARY AND CONCLUSIONS

Environmental co-operatives as a club are groups of individuals who derive mutual benefits from sharing the costs and benefits of activities and services which are characterised by excludable benefits. From our research, it appears that in most formal associations, members explicitly choose to become a member (voluntarily) because they anticipate a net benefit from membership. These benefits range from the protection of interests to extra income. The theory suggests that the utility or expected income jointly derived from membership and from the use of other activities and services should exceed the utility associated with non-membership status. Environmental co-operatives involve sharing, the use of the service of the club or environmental co-operative and sharing the benefits of an impure public good. Sharing often leads to a partial rivalry of benefits as larger numbers crowd one another, detracting from the quality of the service received. Crowding or congestion depends on the measure of utilisation, which in turn could depend on the number of members, the total number of members who use the club's facilities or the number of visitors to the areas or provisions of the club. Club congestion may lead to slower and less service, and may also result in a decline in the quality of wildlife and landscape. As membership size expands, both costs and benefits rise: costs involve increased congestion, while benefits result from cost reduction owing to the sharing of provision expenses associated with the club good. Environmental co-operatives use exclusion mechanisms, whereby non-members and/or non-payers can be barred from, for instance, wildlife and landscape management contracting. The allocation of control rights in environmental co-operatives mostly depends on the voting system. The allocation of income rights is not important.

We investigated design principles for limiting the problems resulting from asymmetric information, like hidden information, shirking in teams and hidden action, and from the lack of credible commitment and trust. These problems influence the efficiency and effectiveness of self-organising and self-governing forms of co-operation for the preservation of wildlife and landscape. In our research we found evidence for the application of design principles in the environmental co-operatives in the Netherlands for:

- *Hidden information*
  Design principles that can be used to reduce the problems of hidden information are signalling, screening and self-selection conditions. In our empirical research we found evidence for the presence of screening and signalling.
- *Hidden action*
  The problem of hidden action and hidden information could be resolved by monitoring and incentive contracts. An alternative solution is to require posting of bonds to guarantee performance, which can be paid back if the performance is satisfactory or if the targets are reached. As said before, monitoring plays an important role in environmental co-operatives, but less attention is paid to the other possibilities.
- *Commitment and trust*
  Credible commitment can be created in an environmental co-operative via monitoring, graduated sanctions and a conflict-resolution mechanism. Monitoring has already been discussed. We found evidence that most of the co-operatives have the possibility of using graduated sanctions. Our research suggests that credible commitment is available because in many organisations sanctions are actually used. The degree of commitment is not always clear. There are several types of conflict-resolving mechanisms in use. Since co-operatives have existed for only a short period, many organisations and activities are still developing. Also due to this short period, reputation building has not been possible for a large number of organisations.
- *Shirking in teams*
  In the literature we found three methods to reduce shirking. The first method to reduce shirking is for someone to specialise as a monitor to check the input performance of team members. A second method is to

make use of incentives which consist of penalties for low effort and bonuses for high effort. In both cases a principal is needed, either to enforce the penalties or to finance the bonuses. A third method is to split the payments into a fixed and variable part. The principal offers all the agents a low fixed payment and a relatively high variable payment, which depends on the ability and effort of the agent and his team-mates. Our empirical research indicates support for the first method (half of the organisations). The board plays the role of the monitor. Financial incentives play a minor role.

Information asymmetries and a lack of commitment and trust do harm to the effectiveness and efficiency of environmental co-operatives. Reduction of the effects of hidden action, hidden information, shirking, lack of commitment and trust has been a matter of interest for most of the organisations. However, in many cases the instruments to reduce these effects are still underdeveloped and organisations are looking for improvements. The use of robust design principles in an organisation will improve the effectiveness and efficiency of the organisation. Further research on these design principles in order to judge not only the availability of a category of mechanisms but also the effectiveness and efficiency of design principles is of considerable interest.

NOTES

1. Given the non-contractability of relationship-specific investments, incomplete contracts lead to hold-up problems. Changes in asset ownership can affect the severity of the hold-up problem (see Hart 1995, p. 87). Asymmetric information plays a very limited role in the analysis of hold-up problems.
2. See for shirking also Alchian and Demsetz (1972), Holmström (1982), McAfee and McMillan (1991) and Tirole (1993).

REFERENCES

Alchian, A.A. and H. Demsetz (1972), 'Production, Information Costs, and Economic Organisation', *American Economic Review*, **62**, pp. 777–95.

Cooter, R. and Th. Ulen (1996), *Law and Economics.* Second edition, Reading, MA: Addison-Wesley.

Cornes, R. and T. Sandler (1996), *The Theory of Externalities, Public Goods and Club Goods.* Second edition, Cambridge: Cambridge University Press.

CPB (Centraal Planbureau) (1997), *Challenging Neighbours: Rethinking German and Dutch Economic Institutions*, Berlin: Springer.

FitzRoy, F.R., Z.J. Acs and D.A. Gerlowski (1998), *Management and Economics of Organisation*, London: Prentice Hall Europe.

Furubotn, E.G. and R. Richter (1991), 'The New Institutional Economics: An Assessment', in Furubotn, E.G. and R. Richter (eds), *The New Institutional Economics: A Collection of Articles from the Journal of Institutional and Theoretical Economics*, Tübingen: J.C.B. Mohr (Paul Siebeck), pp. 1–32.

Furubotn, E.G. and R. Richter (1997), *Institutions and Economic Theory: The Contribution of the New Institutional Economics*, Ann Arbor: The University of Michigan Press.

Hart, O. (1995), *Firms, Contracts, and Financial Structure*, Oxford: Oxford University Press.

Hart, O. and J. Moore (1998), 'Co-operatives vs. Outside Ownership', National Bureau of Economics (NBER), NBER Working Paper No. W6421.

Holmström, B. (1982), 'Moral Hazard in Teams', *Bell Journal of Economics*, **13**, pp. 324–40.

Kasper, W. and M.E. Streit (1998), *Institutional Economics; Social Order and Public Policy. The Locke Institute*, Cheltenham UK and Northampton MA: Edward Elgar.

Kreps, D.M. (1990), *A Course in Microeconomic Theory*, New York: Harvester Wheatsheaf.

McAfee, R.P. and J. McMillan (1991), 'Optimal Contracts for Teams', *International Economic Review*, **32** (3), pp. 561–77.

Ménard, C. (1997), 'The Enforcement of Contractual Arrangements', Paper presented at the first Conference of the International Society for New Institutional Economics, Meeting, Saint-Louis, September 19–21, 1997, Centre ATOM University Paris.

Milgrom, P. and J. Roberts (1992), *Economics, Organization and Management*, Englewood Cliffs, New Jersey: Prentice Hall International.

Nooteboom, B. (1999), *Inter-firm Alliances: Analysis and Design*, London: Routledge.

Ostrom, E. (1990), *Governing the Commons; The Evolution of Institutions for Collective Action*, Cambridge: Cambridge University Press.

Slangen, L.H.G. (1997), 'How to Organise Nature Production by Farmers', *European Review of Agriculture Economics*, **24**, pp. 508–29.

Tirole, J. (1993), *The Theory of Industrial Organization*, Cambridge, MA: The MIT Press.

6. Environmental Co-operatives as Entrepreneurial Instruments for Farmers: Concepts and Experience

Gert van Dijk and Jifke Sol

1 INTRODUCTION: THE PROBLEM OBSERVED

Dutch agriculture was a leading sector in the eyes of the public for many years. Regarded as a love child and a national symbol of progressiveness, farming in The Netherlands expanded both in total value added and efficiency. The significance of the agricultural sector for the current account of the trade balance enhanced the feeling that this sector was the national economic hero. Various sectors in agriculture and horticulture earned the title of 'world market leader', as conceptualised by Porter (1997).

Indeed, the flower industry, in particular, and some other sectors such as the co-operative dairy industry are still at the frontiers of world market developments, although globalisation has set such a fast pace since the 1990s. However, as is well known now, the advantages have been partly overshadowed by the negative environmental effects that have become ever more apparent in the past few decades. The problems which arose were quite serious as the Dutch natural conditions are sensitive: high population density, high proportion of surface area covered by open water, and ground water at a level which is close to the surface of the soil. Most important, of course, is the intensive agricultural production system which characterises Dutch farming in general.

Problems of pollution were not combatted efficiently and effectively. Certainly, it took some time before the new reality was accepted. That is, however, more or less normal. Then there were the public interest groups, single issue movements which were so characteristic of the 1970s and 1980s. They managed to draw attention away from politicians and governments. Government policies were, however, not only late, they were also ineffective. The most important reason for the lack of impact was (and still is) that there was no way of introducing the 'polluter pays principle'. On the contrary, this still is) that there was no way of introducing the 'polluter pays principle'. On the contrary, this principle failed to take effect because the bill was presented exclusively to the farming industry. None of the costs of introducing new technology could be passed on to the final consumer.

Almost all attempts to introduce new production methods to new product market combinations for which consumers were meant to pay a premium failed completely. In short: the citizens asked the farmer for new production methods for products which they were not willing to pay for as consumers. This situation follows naturally from the fact that Dutch agriculture exports approximately two-thirds of its products. It also follows from the fact that the main market outlets are in consumer areas where low-cost standard products are most popular. So farmers were increasingly squeezed between price competition and new restrictions on production which implied investments without returns as far as one could see. (This is not to deny that there were also new production technologies which resulted both in lower pollution and lower cost per unit of production.)

By the end of the 1980s a situation was created in which farmers were opposed to the government (departments of agriculture and the environment), and environmental interests or pressure groups were in conflict with both of them.

2 HOW TO CHANGE BEHAVIOUR – THE PERSPECTIVE OF GOVERNMENT VS. THE PERSPECTIVE OF THE ENTREPRENEUR

Government policy ultimately has as its goal to change the behaviour of economic agents. The government can make use of three basic mechanisms: coercion, transaction and persuasion. Policy can be positioned in the public domain, the private domain and, lastly, government agencies can themselves act as participants. Combining these elements shows us a 3 x 3 matrix as in Table 6.1.

From the perspective of changing behaviour and appropriateness of instruments, three main categories can be distinguished:

- Method of measurement, for example of causal relationships between individual behaviour on pollution and the effect of the pollution itself.
- Structure of the sector such as the number of plants, number of farms, their influence in society, and so on.
- Variables which determine the resistance and the costs of the sector under consideration, that is the farmers, such as low price elasticity.

A situation of low price elasticity is usually taken as an argument for using direct regulation.

Table 6.1 Possibilities of changing economic behaviour concerning sustainability

	Role of government in the ...		
Behavioural mechanism	... public domain	... private domain	... as participant
Coercion	Direct regulation		
Transaction	Levies, subsidies for polluters	Contracts, liabilities, ownership	
Persuasion	Obligation to measure, to inform, subsidies to environmental organisations		Gentlemen's agreements, education, extension

Hatched area = tradable permits.

Source: WRR (1992).

In applying economic approaches to agricultural pollution problems, it turns out that most of these problems are reasonably measurable and there is knowledge of causality. The costs of technologies can be both low or high, and there are many sources of costs, that is, the behaviour of economic agents, that may have to change if costs are to decrease. The type of government instruments which are considered most effective under such conditions fall under the category 'transaction'. This conclusion was drawn by an extensive analysis done by the Dutch Wetenschappelijke Raad voor Regeringsonderzoek (WRR 1992), the Scientific Council for the Government (the approach used by this body is summarised in Table 6.2).

By comprehensively identifying the environmental problems of Dutch agriculture (with the exception of environmental pollution where farmers themselves experience the detrimental effects), the Council concluded that in all cases financial instruments are most adequate. In other words, the government should make use of transaction methods to influence behaviour. (Obviously, the Council took as its perspective that environmental problems are in essence behavioural problems. In other words, one should find incentives to effect behavioural change.)

Table 6.2 Situation type and policy instruments

Measurable/ identifiable	Sources of pollution policy subjects	Cost differences/ technological possibilities	Problem type	Primary type of policy instrument
Good	Few	Small	Simple	D
		Big	Distribution problem	FP
	Many	Small	Manageable	FP
		Big	Heterogeneous	FP
Low	Few	Not important	Not visible	D
	Many	Small	Diffuse	X
		Big	Complex	?

Notes:
D = Direct regulation by government
F = Financial instruments
P = Private domain solutions
X = Methods of persuasion
? = Undefined.

Source: WRR (1992).

Nevertheless, the government – even up to now – has not followed this route completely. Reluctantly, the government began to threaten, and to actually impose, levies. There was, however, no willingness to acknowledge the complete lack of acceptance by farm organisations. As a consequence, many years passed in which nothing happened save for the deterioration of the relationship between the ministry and the farming community.

3 THE BIRTH OF ENVIRONMENTAL CO-OPERATIVES

At the same time unity and solidarity among farmers began to crumble. In particular the problem of manure surpluses (phosphate in the soil, NH_3^+ in the air and NO_3 in the ground water) split farmers' interests. On a regional basis, the differences in problem pressure between the north and the south became visible. On a sectoral basis, the pig farmers were made scapegoats, although to a lesser extent, this happened to dairy farmers and poultry and egg producers as well. These groups felt that there was a need for countervailing power against too much government pressure. Hence, it can be said that basically it was the old co-operative concept that lay behind the establishment of environmental co-operatives.

Looking back to the early 1990s when this 'co-operative fever' began, it is interesting to note that it was mostly the dairy farmers who took the initiative. It is not difficult to explain why. The dairy industry is the sector which is most acquainted with co-operation. This is true for most countries in which farmers' co-operatives were established and it is certainly the case in The Netherlands. Other farm sectors were much more reluctant. The pig farmers, for instance, barely made use of the environmental co-operative. The best-known case is where a group of farmers bought a nature area and began to steward it. This was not due to their profound interest in natural areas as much as it was a way to maintain a buffer zone between themselves and other owners of natural areas, among them private foundations, interest groups such as the World Wide Fund For Nature and so on.

At that time there was a genuine interest in environmental co-operatives also because of the felt need for new approaches, new co-operation between farmers and the government, and new coalitions with the environmental groups which at that time were at the peak of their influence in society. The concept to which we turn in section 4 was, in fact, never put into practice. The reason was that at the same time there were other concepts of environmental co-operation which attracted attention. As a result, the concept 'environmental co-operative' became an umbrella-concept (or container concept) covering various and very diverse developments at the same time. Among others the following forms were established:

- introduction of mineral administration systems;
- local and farm-oriented research;
- optimising feeding systems;
- nature maintenance (meadow birds/nest protection);
- water maintenance;
- maintenance of tourist attractions;
- producing locally specific products.

In 1994 at least 30 groups calling themselves environmental co-operatives existed. There were 60 by October 1996 with a total of 4000 members. 'These groups are located throughout the country and differ greatly in focus and size. One thing they all have in common is a desire to apply locally-tailored solutions to national and regional environmental problems' (OECD 1998). What they also had in common in particular, was that they were too reliant on government stimulation through programmes and subsidies. Likewise they were poorly organised as concerns member commitment and member (self) control.

The first evaluations (van Broekhuizen and van der Ploeg 1997; IKC 1998) of environmental co-operatives concluded that they have been successful because

- breakthroughs have been realised in the communication between farmers and the government;
- co-operation between farmers' groups and regional clubs on environmental policy has improved;
- there is more integration of nature, landscape and environmental policy through a regional approach;
- a growing farmers' positive self-consciousness and self-image is created, that is, the shift from defeatism towards the positive initiative of farmers;
- the realisation of some environmental goals and the start of projects with new techniques aiming at, for example, measurement and reduction of NH_3^+ emissions;
- environmental co-operatives are able to define different projects in quantifiable terms and build in systems for monitoring, control, and keeping the process going.[1]

Studies revealed that more progress in environmentally friendly production methods had been realised with environmental co-operatives than without. At the same time it is strongly emphasised that more 'managerial room for manoeuvre' is very important. Without the right government support the whole project will slow down, 'lose its momentum and fail' (van Broekhuizen and van der Ploeg 1997).

'Self-management by environmental co-operatives of farmers is not yet well developed', concluded another study (Mijnders 1997). Research on self-management by five Dutch environmental co-operatives (Eastermar, de Peel, Overlegplatform Duinboeren, Achtkarspelen and Winterswijk) showed that the role of these groups is mostly limited to the development and the gathering of ideas. In addition, small-scale projects concerning nature maintenance take place. However, policy making and policy implementation do not belong to their field of activities. Reasons for this are the lack of time, knowledge, money and the legal position to exert self-control.

Another conclusion drawn was that environmental co-operatives were appropriate institutions by which farmers could engage in learning about how to accommodate individually and collectively the demands of society concerning environmental quality. By adjusting as individual farms to the demands of the public, farmers feel that they just keep their activities within the legal framework or always lag somewhat behind the rules set by the government. However, this is most unsatisfactory in the long run, as it creates a defensive style of entrepreneurial conduct.

Implicitly, the impression arose that it could not be the farmer who translated societal demands into new technologies and so 'keeps the licence to produce'. Indeed, farmers' unions felt that environmental groups never stop pressing for change. The concept of environmental co-operatives was also introduced to help farmers take the initiative and determine the political agenda. The expectation was that this would produce more opportunities to obtain investment subsidies from the government. This view was very much supported by regional governments and regional environmental groups.

The sort of learning capacity environmental co-operatives are supposed to provide may be similar to market learning, which is a concept taken from the theory of market orientation. It distinguishes between exploitative market learning and explorative market learning. Exploitation includes activities such as refinement and adjustment in which the farmers' world views remain unchanged and small incremental changes can be managed within the current routine repertoire. Exploitation relies on replicating institutionalised rules and practices. It is typically a function of well-exercised and well-learned sequences of actions. Exploitation can lead to new knowledge, but this is a refinement of current procedures and it operates within the boundaries of the dominant logic of organisation (Kyriakopoulos 2000). Exploitative learning was the rule at the farm level, and its logic has dominated the discussion between the farming community and the public.

Exploratory market learning refers to search, variation, risk-taking, experimenting, playing with new ideas, flexibility, discovery and innovation. Mental models and procedures are questioned and revised. Rules and world views are redefined. Exploration is not identical with innovation, but it is likely to embody innovation because innovation starts with exploration although not all exploration leads to innovation.

The environmental co-operatives no doubt have been set up in order to develop exploratory learning by farmers. Therefore various learning institutions were suggested: a national discussion forum, regional helpdesks, exemptions from general policy measures to try new methods. Except for the last point, most of these suggestions have led to requests to the government for financial help. Generally speaking, the farmer members were reluctant to invest in learning themselves. The regional and central governments have provided the environmental co-operatives with both financial help and advice.

If there were ever a chance to come to fundamentally new polluter pays relationships concerning the role of farmers in nature conservation and creating recreation opportunities in rural areas, it was in the 1990s. Yet both the new farmers' co-operatives and the government failed to make it a success. On the part of the government, it must be said that there was a grave lack of creativity in applying both transaction and persuasion type instruments. Farmers, in turn, were too much under the pressure of the big gap that existed between the demands of civil society and the lack of willingness to pay both as citizens and as consumers. The last element is, as was said in section 1, little wonder. Most consumers are found outside the country and in economic and cultural conditions that make up a low price market.

As a result, both types of market learning do not show any appreciable take-off. Exploitative market learning could have been a process relating environmental issues to marketing of farm products. It did not materialise because the markets were dominated by discounts and not by premiums. Exploratory learning could still have been a fruitful development by making the farm sectors more aware of the behaviour of various organisations in the public domain. It must be concluded, however, that although some good initiatives were made, this opportunity also did not work out. The main reason is that there was not enough engagement of the farming communities, probably because individual farmers could not transform the activities into opportunities to produce at their individual farm. In addition, there were not enough opportunities to distinguish between the quality differences of farmers. Thus, the question arises whether a better model would have been available.

4 THE ORIGINAL CONCEPT OF ENVIRONMENTAL CO-OPERATIVES (ECs)

4.1 General Concept

The original concept of ECs was an application of the typical co-operative institution facilitating self-control. As was analysed in 1997 by the National Council for Agricultural Research, the ECs should provide for the abolition of the opposition between the intervening government and the farmers. They should acknowledge the diversity between farmers and start with practice-oriented knowledge (Ettema, Frouws and van der Ploeg 1997, p. 7).

Firstly, conforming to the assessment that there is much diversity in farming regions and between farmers, the EC should accommodate for such diversity. Secondly, accepting the assessment of the Scientific Council of the Government concerning instruments for effective environmental policy, financial instruments should be used. Thirdly, the idea of co-operation has always proven to be most effective when there is strong pressure in the environment, be it from competitors or from society. (This leads to another hypothesis explaining why ECs may have failed: perhaps government did not exert enough pressure. Possibly this was because the farmers' unions were too strong in the 1990s, and the initiative would have had a much better chance at the beginning of the twenty-first century. In any case, ECs were conceptually based on strong societal demands with an effective government in which one or two ministries could have forced either self-control or accepting the higher cost of individual compliance to both adjustments and levies.)

In order to illustrate the original concepts of ECs, we take the cases of NH_3^+ and of phosphate in soil and surface water as examples. The sources of pollution can be identified at the farm level and there is a linkage to environmental quality at the regional level.

Technically, the EC was meant to act as a market creation institution. The economic logic is as follows: farmers who are able to reduce pollution faster than the average farmer are, in an economic sense, creating value because they move to desired goals at an above average speed. Therefore, they can be stimulated by subsidies. Of course, from an ecological point of view they may still be in the realm of unacceptable pollution. In practice, such differentiation exists. Farmers' interests in pollution-reducing behaviour and the reasons why they change technologies, and at what speed they do this, crucially depend on the characteristics of their individual farms and the life cycle of the farm family.

From where do the needed subsidies accrue? It was thought that there might be three different sources – one of course being the exchequer. But in this case payments should be regarded as investments in the farming sectors. The second source is 'ploughing back' general levies imposed on all polluting farms (in the ecological sense). The third source comes from dwellers in the region. Suggestions for the establishment of public authorities such as the current water boards came from the latter. In fact, the present water boards might have been the correct organisations.

If levies imposed were to be returned into the region in the form of subsidies for the progressive farmers, the general development of money flows would, schematically, have been as shown in Figure 6.1. Of course, farmers who are not in the position of ever reaching the necessary pace of pollution reduction here face ever increasing levies after a period of, say, six years, ultimately forcing them to make an adequate investment or to resign.

4.2 Institutional Concept: 'Corporate Governance'

From an institutional point of view, ECs are not different from ordinary, modern co-operatives. There is common interest based on solidarity. Solidarity does not mean that farmers co-operate because they are equal. They co-operate because they differ among themselves. Solidarity means to

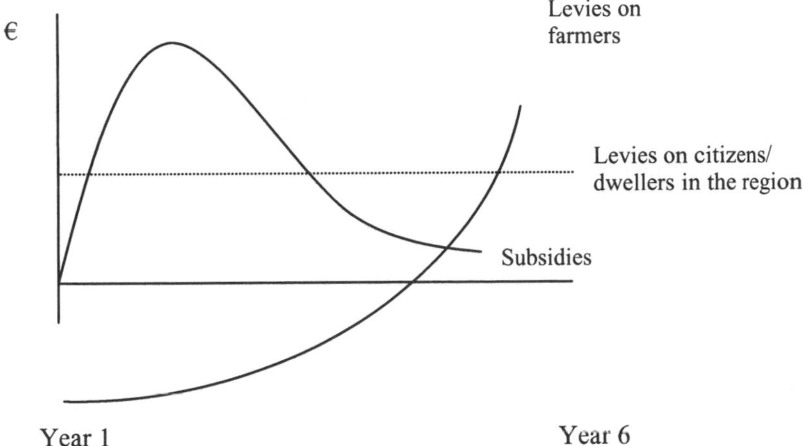

Figure 6.1 Levies and subsidies as basic instrumentation of environmental co-operatives

stay together despite differences. The farmers who improve faster than the average farmer have an interest because of subsidies accruing to them. Yet they take a position for the co-operative's region by which pressure is eased on the farmer who is not considering investments to the same effect.

As concerns democracy, the EC is an efficient institution since it allows farmers to exert self-control on the basis of democracy. Democracy in co-operatives never means that Mr Average Farmer or Mr Median Farmer determines the route, as is suggested by Hart and Moore (1998) (cited by Slangen and Polman 1999). As far as competition is concerned, it may be said that ECs make effective behaviour possible. In fact, the collective action of farmers to negotiate on averages for the country and for farms in certain regions and sectors is changed into a type of conduct by which individual farms can fully exploit their natural strengths as managers and entrepreneurs. All successful co-operatives have always applied this principle, for example by differentiating prices to members according to quality, and so on. So there is no fundamental difference with the EC concept.

As regards the corporate governance structure, the EC concept was meant to follow the general two-tier concept depicted in Figure 6.2. (In fact it is a three-tier system if the professional management also has statutory control.)

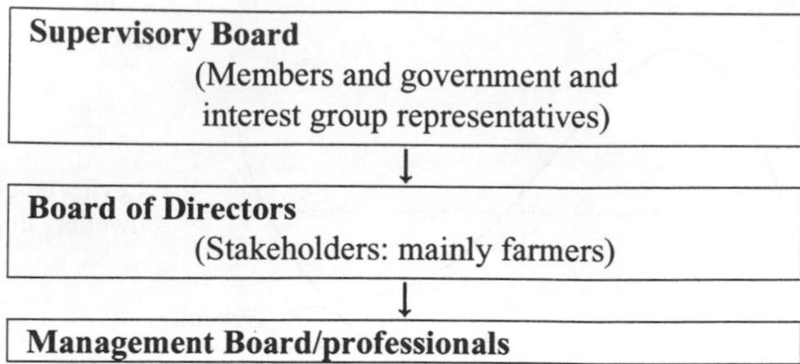

Figure 6.2 Basic governance structure of environmental co-operatives

In the Supervisory Board of market co-operatives there are normally also non-member supervisors. In the case of an EC it would be self-evident to have representatives of governments and possibly environmental interest groups on the Supervisory Board. This would seem the minimal position. The EC is based on differentiation between regions, between farms, and between their time paths. There is a trade-off between attractiveness of the EC to release the societal limitations and the effectiveness of reaching the results at a higher speed and lower cost. With so many variables at work the EC is caught between easing societal constraints and reaching desired results at a higher speed and lower cost.

4.3 Member Relationships

The previous section argued that the EC would have to adopt the normal user-control principle. It should be the members who discipline their organisation. The most important relationship is, of course, the transactional relationship between the members and the co-operative. There is a natural tendency to let property rights develop and to make them tradable. Pollution rights can be transferred between members through the co-operative acting as a sort of clearing house. Furthermore, such rights can be transferred between ECs when, for instance, manure surpluses from one region are to be transported to another region.

As regards residual claims, it should be kept in mind that co-operatives can be seen as 'a cost covering organisation' (in German: 'Kostendeckungs-betrieb'). ECs will result in losses and members can apply these as investment costs (for taxation purposes). But the principles of collective and individualised and tradable property rights are essentially the same as for marketing co-operatives which are yielding good milk prices, sugar beet prices and so on and financial performance on top of that (not to be confused with the concept of profit as defined for non-co-operatives or Investor Owned Firms).

5 CONCLUDING REMARKS

There has been a fair amount of theory building, discussion and participatory research on ECs. The original concept was, however, never put into practice. The reason why the EC has failed may be that co-operatives were 'children of emergency' when they came into existence as real social/economic innovations. Pressure was not strong enough. The willingness to co-operate along new lines between the public and the private domains was not strong enough. Institutional innovation requires much more effort, especially if it is intended to result in co-operation including transaction, ownership and control. In co-operation theory it may be said that theory is the flower of practice and not the root of it. Therefore, we have to wait and see whether we can add experience with ECs as institutional innovation to this important body of knowledge.

NOTE

1. Environmental goals are measurable, but sometimes the improvement of nature and landscape is very hard to measure. In that case, relative indicators will be more useful.

BIBLIOGRAPHY

Broekhuizen, R. van and J.D. van der Ploeg (1997), 'Anderhalf jaar milieucoöperatie, een voortgangsrapportage van het bestuurlijk experiment met milieucöperaties' (One and a Half Years' Environmental Co-operation. An Evaluation of the Progress in the Administrative Experiment with Environmental Co-operatives), Research Report, Department of Rural Sociology, Wageningen University, The Netherlands.

Bruin, R. de (1997), 'Dynamics and Sustainability. Views on Farming Styles, Governance and Policy', Dissertation, Circle for European Studies, Wageningen, The Netherlands.

Dijk, G. van (1993), 'Is it the Right Moment for Developing Environmental Co-operatives?', Working Paper, Nationale Coöperatieve Raad voor land- en tuinbouw NCR (National Council for Cooperatives), The Hague, The Netherlands.

Dijk, G. van (1997), 'Sustainable Agriculture and Environmental Co-operatives in the Netherlands', in *Livestock and the Environment – International Conference 1997*, Wageningen: International Agricultural Centre Wageningen, pp. 124–29.

Driessen, P.P.J., P. Glasbergen, P.P.P. Huigen and F. Hijmans van den Bergh (1995), *Vernieuwing van het landelijk gebied: een verkenning van strategieen voor een gebiedsgerichte aanpak* (*Renewal of the Rural Area: An Inventory of Strategies for a Regional Policy Approach*), The Hague: VUGA Publishers.

Ettema, M.T.A., J. Frouws and J.D. van der Ploeg (1997), 'Not through Government Regulation alone – Background Report of the NRLO Foresight Study Agrochemicals, Nutrients and Energy in Agricultural Systems in 2015', Nationale Raad voor Landbauwkundig Onderzoek NRLO (National Council for Agricultural Research), NRLO Report No. 97/8, The Hague, The Netherlands.

Hart, O. and J. Moore (1998), 'Cooperatives vs. Outside Ownership', National Bureau of Economics (NBER), NBER Working Paper No. W6421.

Haven, G.H.M. ten and H.J.W.M. Roefs (1993), 'Strong Together on the Environmental Market. Environmental Co-operative De Kop van Noord-Holland', Stichting PR Land- en Tuinbouw (Foundation for Public Relations of Agriculture and Horticulture), Brochure, The Hague, The Netherlands.

Hees, E., H. Renting and S. de Rooij (1994), *Towards Local Self Management. Co-operative Groups for Integration of Agriculture, Environment, Nature and Landscape*, Ministry of Agriculture, Nature and Fisheries; Wageningen, The Netherlands: Circle for European Studies.

Holmström, B. (1982), 'Moral Hazards in Teams', *Bell Journal of Economics*, 2 (13), pp. 324–340.

Horlings, I. (1996), 'Sustainable Farming through Policy. Innovative Groups in Dutch Agriculture', Dissertation, Circle for European Studies, Wageningen, The Netherlands.

IKC (Informatie- en KennisCentrum) (1998), 'Environmental Co-operatives. The Valuation of the Administrative Experiment with Self-management', Brochure, Ede: IKC, The Netherlands.

Kieft, H. and W. van Weperen (1999), 'Regional Co-operation between Farmers and Governments for Nature and Environment. Inventory of some European Experiences', ETC-Ecoculture, Publication, ETC Netherlands (Urban Agriculture Programme), Leusden, The Netherlands.

Kusiak, L. (ed.) (1994), *Tailor-made Steering. A Different Approach of Environmental Problems*, Ministry of Agriculture, Nature and Fisheries, The Hague: The Netherlands.

Kyriakopoulos, K. (2000), *The Market Orientation of Co-operative Organisations. Learning Strategies and Structures for Integrating Firm and Members*, Assen: van Gorcum.

Litjens, M.E.G., M. Rattink and W.S. van Wingerden (1995), 'Regional Initiatives for Nature and Environmental Co-operatives. Approach and Perspective', Scientific Report, Department of Knowledge Transfer, Wageningen University, The Netherlands.

Mijnders, I. (1997), *Self-management by Environmental Co-operatives still Restricted.* Wageningen University, The Netherlands.

OECD (1998), 'Voluntary Group Action in the Public Interest: Issues', in *Co-operative Approaches to Sustainable Agriculture*, Paris: OECD Publications.

Overveld, C., M. Vroom, L. Beijer, G. van Eck and C. v. d. Brand (1999), *Co-operative Groups. Future Perspectives for Co-operative Groups in Relation to Agricultural Policy in the Netherlands*, Ministry of Agriculture, Nature and Fisheries, Ede: Informatie- en KennisCentrum (IKC), The Netherlands.

Ploeg, J.D. van der (1999), *De virtuele boer* (*The Virtual Farmer*), Assen: van Gorcum.

Porter, M.E. (1997), *Perspectives on Strategy, Contributions of Michael E. Porter*, Boston: Kluwer.

Slangen, L.H.G. and N.B.P. Polman (1999), 'Environmental Co-operatives for Farmers: a New Institutional Arrangement', Scientific Report, Agricultural and Rural Policy Group, Wageningen University, The Netherlands.

Tatenhove, J. and H. Goverde (2000), 'Institutionalisation of Environmental Policy', in Driessen, P. and P. Glasbergen (eds), *Environmental Policy; an Introduction*, Amsterdam: Elsevier.

WRR Wetenschappelijke Raad voor Regeringsonderzoek (Netherlands Scientific Council for Government Policy) (1992), 'Environmental Policy: Strategy, Instruments and Enforcement', Report 41, The Hague, The Netherlands.

PART III

Governance Structures and Learning Processes for Changing Agricultural Practices

7. Collective Dimension and Learning Process: Coping with Change of Farming Practices to Preserve Water Quality

Mohamed Gafsi and Jacques Brossier

1 INTRODUCTION

This chapter analyses a local process of change in farming practices which focuses on preserving the quality of groundwater, threatened by a risk of diffuse nitrate pollution caused by farming. Public awareness of this type of agri-environmental problem (Deffontaines et al. 1994) has grown over the past few years (Loseby 1992, Barrué-Pastor et al. 1995), leading to a social demand plus considerable pressure for a change in farming practices, deemed to be largely responsible for the deterioration of the quality of the natural environment (Alphandéry and Bourliaud 1995, Whitby 1995). The changes are sought with a view to promoting a type of agriculture which is both sustainable and environmentally friendly. This aim is shared by many, but the key question remains: how can agri-environmental problems be tackled and adequate solutions be found whilst ensuring sustainability for agriculture?

In order to answer this fundamental question it is important to recall the main characteristics of agri-environmental problems which are both complex and localised. Complex because they possess a number of dimensions: bio-technical (new technical prescriptions), socio-economic (new conditions for exercising farming, farm sustainability, effects on production lines) and organisational (dynamic of local networks and role of institutions). The problems need to be examined in all of these dimensions, which bring certain interaction dynamics into play (negotiation, conflict, co-operation) between the actors faced with identifying and solving the problems. In addition, these problems are always localised within a certain land area. Agri-environmental issues reflect the spatial dimension of farming and its role in managing the natural resources on its territory. This means that the interaction dynamics mentioned above are localised, and thus management situations in farming involve new local actors and new forms of co-ordination.

The aim of this chapter is to demonstrate the importance of a co-operative approach when using a local interaction process for solving agri-environmental problems. A case study will show how the interactive strategies of the actors gradually took form, and learning processes were shaped, leading to the successful change in farming practices with a view to preserving the quality of groundwater.

2 CASE STUDY: FARMING PRACTICES AND GROUNDWATER QUALITY

Faced with an increase of nitrates in the mineral water it was marketing, the Water Company asked 40 farmers on the water body perimeter to change their farming practices (Box 7.1). The nitrates rate was practically non-existent in the 1950s. Beginning in 1970, a number of farmers affected by an increasingly demanding socio-economic context and quality constraints implemented certain changes in their activity. They turned over permanent grassland that was often replaced by maize, and increased crop yields and herd sizes, which were managed more intensively. Alarmed by the slight increase in the nitrates in the water body (research having proven the indisputable role of agriculture in this increase), the Water Company decided to take protective measures against agricultural pollution by limiting the maximum rate of nitrates in the water under the roots (groundwater) to 10 mg/litre, even though European regulations have fixed the nitrates limit at 50 mg/litre for drinking water and 15 mg/litre for mineral water suitable for infants (with certain countries requiring 10 mg/litre, the same limit set by the Water Company).

The problem of water quality represented, therefore, a major challenge for the Water Company,[1] as an increase in the nitrates rate would endanger its activity. In this situation, where there were conflicting interests between economic actor groups, the farmers were in a position to request considerable compensation in return for changing their practices. Current regulations (50 mg/litre for drinking water) do not oblige them to do so and the potential prejudice for the Water Company was great. The Water Company thus asked the French National Institute for Agricultural Research (INRA) to make an assessment of the problem and come up with proposals for negotiation between the Water Company and the farmers. A research programme was set up for this purpose by INRA, the objective of the researchers being to propose an operational farming production system which respected water quality and which was economically sustainable (see Figure 7.1, p. 136).

BOX 7.1: GENERAL PRESENTATION OF THE CASE

- A private Mineral Water Company, in order to avoid an increase in the level of nitrates, wanted to take preventive measures concerning the farming practices used in the perimeter.
- Cause of the increase in nitrates: human activity involving agriculture. Agriculture occupies practically the entire area and recent changes in farming systems (turning over of pastures, development of maize crops, increased fertiliser inputs) seem to be a major cause for the increase in nitrates.

In order to curb this rise, the Company asked the French National Institute for Agricultural Research (INRA) and the local Chamber of Agriculture to come up with some solutions.

Some agricultural facts:

- a relatively well delimited restricted area: 5000 hectares, of which 3500 are used as farmland (with wide soil diversity);
- people involved: 40 farmers, dairy and cereal companies, farmers' professional organisations; milk output: 60 000 hl; cereals: 8000 metric tonnes;

The Mineral Water Company is an important firm employing 1500 staff, is the leader in its market (1 million bottles per year), and the Company is the main employer in this rural area.

This case is unusual, compared to traditional environmental problems, due to:

- a major constraint arising from the targeted nitrate level (10–15 mg/l);
- a restricted area;
- the fact that the 'polluted' party is prepared to help the 'polluting' parties to curb nitrate leaching. Although the pollution does not exist as such, since the level is far below European standards, the private company could incur a prejudice to its economic activity if water quality deteriorates due to intensive cropping practices.

Finding a solution was thus a matter of transactions between private companies (farms and the Water Company), hence the interaction dynamics, negotiations and contractual procedures. We present briefly how these dynamics transformed over time.

If durable development is held to be socio-economic development for which the natural environment provides, on a permanent basis, the resources for changing and diverse activities, then the solutions sought by the Water Company fall within this category. Several conditions need to be met in order to achieve durable development and can be listed as follows. First, negotiation opportunities and procedures need to be re-assessed, created and adapted: (i) negotiations between the users of renewable natural resources (in this case, the farmers and the Company both using the water resource); (ii) negotiations between research teams from different disciplines (organisation of multidisciplinary research), (iii) negotiations between the different partners in this action research. The second condition, connected with the first, is to re-examine existing knowledge of the relationships between activities and resources (in this case between farming and the water resources). The researchers, since they contribute to the development of knowledge, become partners in the negotiations. It is important to emphasise this original role played by research.

3 PROCESS OF CHANGE IN FARMING PRACTICES

An overall study of the dynamics for solving the water quality problem shows three main phases of development (Gafsi 1999). First, after an exploration campaign launched in 1988 and involving various actor groups,[2] the Water Company proposed a number of drastic solutions to the farmers, particularly that of grassing-over the entire area of the water body perimeter, which was eventually facilitated by the purchase of land by the Water Company.[3] The farmers, considering these solutions non-adapted to their production systems, pronounced them unacceptable. After this refusal, the Water Company redefined its way of tackling the problem, that is, setting up research with the farmers in order to define new non-polluting and efficient practices.

Secondly, during the phase we call diagnostic assessment and experimentation, the search for solutions and experiments was undertaken through close collaboration between the farmers, the Water Company and INRA. Certain farmers were volunteers for participation in an 'action research' programme (beginning 1989 and ending 1991) with a view to defining new practices that respect water quality and also comply with the production systems in use. Using this large-scale test, specifications (elimination of maize, suppression of chemical fertilisers and plant health products, composting of animal waste) were worked out and proposed to farmers together with an estimation of the shortfall in revenue they would endure due to its implementation. The farmers ratified their participation in the action-research programme by signing 'experimentation contracts' with the Water Company, in which they committed to modifying their production systems and applying new practices.

As of 1993, a third stage consisting of negotiation, of contracting between the farmers and the Water Company, and of implementing change began. The Water Company proposed financial support through subsidies (1500 FF/ha of usable farmland for seven years) plus investments (1 million FF per farm) in return for applying the specifications. The Water Company, acting on advice from the research team, created a subsidiary company in 1992 in charge of negotiations with the farmers and providing back-up for implementing change on the farms having signed the contract. The subsidiary was to carry out on the farms all tasks connected with animal waste management: setting up a fertiliser programme, stable emptying, and manure composting and spreading. During this phase of the contract, farmer endorsement of the change process was gradual: from 5 per cent in February 1993, it reached 80 per cent in February 1996 and 92 per cent in 1998 (see Figure 7.1).

After this brief outline of the change process, we should like to emphasise the collective and gradual nature of this change. The solutions (new farming practices) were shaped and remodelled through interaction between actor groups. The example of composting serves to illustrate this recursive and gradual solution-finding dynamic. In 1988, the Water Company, along with the Chamber of Agriculture, asked the farmers to cover manure heaps in order to prevent nitrate leaking towards the water body caused by rain water. This protective measure was rejected by the farmers. But as of 1990, these same farmers agreed to carry out manure composting tests with INRA for three years. This resulted thereafter in animal waste composting becoming one of the new practices included in the specifications. This technique requires a cement platform for collecting the liquid in a liquid manure pit. This composting technique was readjusted over the following years.

4 INTERACTIVE STRATEGIES AND THE LEARNING PROCESS

Local interaction dynamics were crucial in solving the water quality problem. They enabled the strategies of the main actor groups to develop and converge, and also the learning process of these actors, including the researchers, to develop. Which strategies were adopted by the key actors in this management situation?

4.1 Development of Water Company Strategy: from Radical Solutions to Partnership for the Change

Faced with the urgency of finding a solution to its water quality problem, the Water Company adopted from the outset a four-tier strategy:

- Mobilisation of many actor groups for managing pollution risk, in order to qualify it as 'for the public good'.
- Proposal of ready-made and drastic technical solutions.
- Policy of land appropriation.
- Collective negotiation approach with the farmers via their professional representatives.

Not surprisingly, the Water Company soon found itself confronted with the negative reaction of the farmers and the complexity of the farming sector, co-user of the land area. A first shift in Water Company strategy was revealed by two new key points. First, the need to include the farmers in finding suitable solutions. Secondly, the need to recognise as legitimate the farmers' requirements concerning the viability of local farming activity, on a par with water quality protection as fundamental parameters of the final solution to the problem.

The second shift in the Water Company's strategy came about during negotiations for signing 18-year contracts and applying the specifications. The Water Company changed its strategy from a collective logic to an individual logic, because the collective logic, adopted up until then, was not problem-free, and often resulted in deadlock, mainly due to the positions adopted by the farming profession. This deadlock was also a determining factor in the rejection of the collective solutions proposed. Starting in 1992, the Water Company opted for individual negotiations and solutions, in order to get around these difficulties.

This second shift was concurrent with a new point in the Water Company's strategy in 1992. This consisted of steering the change and controlling the remaining potential sources of pollution through:

- the creation of a subsidiary and recruitment of a farming advisor as its director;
- the control of animal waste management via the tasks carried out by this subsidiary on the farms having signed the contract;
- co-steering of the change on the farms and technical back-up for farmers.

Lastly, beginning in 1994, realising the importance of the land factor in the farmers' decision to sign the contract, the Water Company introduced a new element into its strategy: play the card of farm enlargement in the negotiations with farmers. Owner of about 45 per cent of the farmland within the perimeter, the Water Company proposed that the farmers use the land free of charge, for a period equivalent to the length of the contract. The Company used this method to reorganise land-use in the area, by distributing the land in an advantageous way to those farmers having signed the contract. This strategy paid off. Many of the farmers, interested in acquiring land and in the new land organisation, signed the contract requiring them to apply the new specifications.

After having analysed the radical, albeit gradual, transformation of the Water Company's strategy and the emergence of new elements at different times during the problem-solving process, we shall now show the strategies adopted by the farmers.

4.2 Strategies of the Farmers: from Refusal to Partnership for the Change

The strategy of the farmers regarding the water quality problem was based on three main points:

- refusal to assume any responsibility for the deterioration in water quality. They did nevertheless admit how serious the problem was and accepted to solve it by negotiations between them and the Water Company;
- adoption of a collective approach involving all the farmers and professional representatives in order to define the terms of this negotiation;
- refusal of ready-made solutions proposed by the Water Company.

This farmer resistance soon shifted. The first shift concerned the refusal to co-operate in solving the problem. Certain farmers did co-operate with the Water Company and INRA in order to find suitable solutions. In addition, signing of 'experimental contracts' led, slowly but surely, to a commitment regarding the change in farming practices.

The second shift in farmer strategy appeared in 1992 during negotiations with the Water Company for the signing of 18-year contracts. An individual approach replaced the collective approach, due to the diversity of farmer reactions connected with their diverging interests. This tactic was put forward by the professional farming organisations, underlining the fact that farms are economic agents operating in a liberal economy and that collective solutions could no longer prevail.

In 1993, three main positions were adopted by farmers:

- 35 per cent considered that the water quality problem was an opportunity to create a new production model that was both economically and ecologically viable;
- 40 per cent showed prudence and adopted a wait-and-see attitude;
- 25 per cent refused to reason in terms of a water problem which did not concern them.

These positions were subsequently transformed by the negotiation dynamic, and the farmers gradually endorsed the process of change (Figure 7.1). The first two categories of farmer and part of the third category became supportive of the change. In 1996, only a minority of the farmers (about 20 per cent) continued to resist.

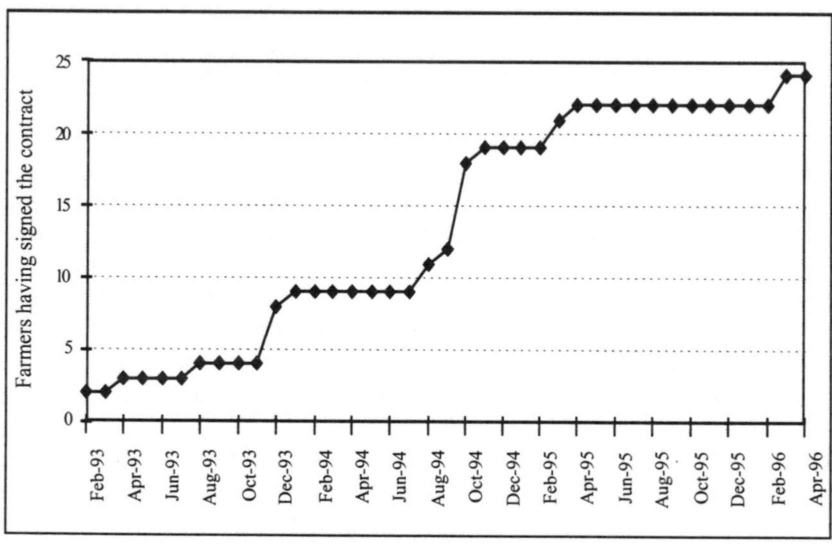

Figure 7.1 Evolution of cumulative number of farmers in the perimeter who signed the contract with the Water Company

4.3 Research Strategies: from Refusal of Expert Appraisal to Learning-Building

The research team was composed of a core of 16 people (of which six were postgraduate thesis students) coming from bio-technical and social science disciplines, plus 15 researchers from various institutions (CNRS, CEMAGREF, Universities), temporarily associated for ad-hoc operations. In order for such a group to function efficiently, the research programme was built up and organised gradually by various work teams and scientific commissions and by using a mediation technique between the research programme and the different participants. Once the final objectives had been discussed, and a scientific structure established, an interactive approach was adopted, for an agrarian system is collective in nature (see Figure 7.2, p. 140). It should be borne in mind that this type of on-going action research involves a number of uncertain elements relative to the number of actors involved, their diversity, their lack of experience in working as a group, insufficient knowledge of the phenomena involved, and so on. It is therefore most difficult to control the way it works and how to plan it. An ad-hoc method was therefore chosen.

In view of the complex nature of the problem, a study of social relationships was explicitly included in the initial project. The likelihood of the farmers adopting the proposals for technical changes depended on the way in which they could express their own viewpoints, using a co-operation procedure with other actor groups. An arrangement was proposed, the main purposes of which were to allow the farmers in the area to work together with the research team on the research programme and on the gradual elaboration of solutions, to create procedures and to find ways of concurring with these farmers. This point met with violent opposition on the part of the professional organisations for two reasons: not only did they consider this to be an unacceptable intrusion with respect to their status of 'sole representative body' of the farmers in negotiations with the Water Company, but also they felt that researchers should stay in laboratories.

As a result, there was a first shift in the ambitious strategy adopted by the research programme. While aware of the serious consequences attached to passing over the study of social relationships, the research team accepted this to continue working on the project because it seemed possible to get around this problem by engaging a mediator.

The mediator played a decisive role in several ways:

- by facilitating the contacts between the research team and the farmers,
- by working out the specifications,

- by creating and organising a network of three pilot farms on which the first concrete experiments were carried out to check the feasibility of the technical solutions proposed in the specifications,
- by participating in discussions leading to the necessary creation by the Water Company of a development structure (the subsidiary company Agrivair).

Unfortunately, the implementation of change and the recruitment of this mediator by the Water Company became obstacles to the integration of researchers in the development project. The Water Company tended to direct research capability towards immediate and concrete issues which turned the research function into an expert appraisal. This repeatedly caused tension between the research team and the Water Company.

Analysis of the behaviour of the main actor groups reveals two fundamental characteristics of their strategies that can be qualified as 'interactive strategies'. The first is the dynamic way in which these strategies were formed. The actor groups did not stick to their original strategies. On the contrary, their strategies were gradually and throughout the problem-solving process reformulated and readjusted. The interaction dynamic between the actor groups is responsible for the transformation in these strategies, which is why they can be qualified as interactive strategies. The second characteristic is the diversity of farmer reactions when confronted with a sole proposal from the Water Company, this being explained by the diversity of farmer projects. The strategy adopted is the product of the interaction that exists between project and action, between the means and the ends (Gafsi and Brossier 1996). This is also why they can be called interactive strategies. Lastly, it should be noted that the interaction dynamic between actor groups built up over a period of time, which was conducive to the change in positions adopted by the different actor groups. This change can also be put down to the learning processes undergone by the actor groups during the course of the interaction dynamic.

4.4 Learning Processes

Thanks to the interaction dynamic (co-operation, conflict, negotiation), the Water Company, the farmers and the research team developed several types of learning. According to Chia and Barbier (1999), organisational learning regarding the collective management of farming took place. We shall limit ourselves here to the analysis of negotiation learning. In actual fact, the transformations in actor group strategy were the result of this learning.

The Water Company learned to negotiate with the farmers. Two examples illustrate this point. First, the change in the negotiation procedure already mentioned above. Using a trial-and-error-correction technique, the Water Company drew conclusions of its four-year experience of collective negotiations with the professional representatives of farmers and, starting in 1992, opted for individual negotiations with each farmer. This approach allowed the Company to make progress in solving its problem. The second example is the use of land allocation as an incentive. As the negotiation dynamic progressed, the Water Company realised how important the land factor was in the farmers' strategy and was able to use this in its negotiations with the farmers.

As far as the farmers were concerned, the interaction dynamic created by the water quality problem allowed them to acquire some legal knowledge and new negotiation techniques. For example, certain farmers increased the proportion of maize crops in the cropping plan just before the negotiations with the Water Company, others signed a one-year experimental contract in order to obtain more from the Water Company, six farmers created a group for collective negotiations. Using these negotiation techniques, the farmers developed 'combination know-how' (Hatchuel 1994) concerning the organisation and co-ordination of different elements such as their resources, their objectives, the projects of other actor groups (the Water Company, other farmers, and so on).

The implementation of the management system of change, in which research played its part, albeit with difficulty, was made possible by the learning and back-up experienced by the actor groups. Back-up was provided by a subsidiary of the Water Company, Agrivair, which was created specifically as a result of collective learning by the research team and the Water Company. This company monitors transformations on farms, sets up contracts based on the specifications and provides technical and economic advice. Unfortunately, the elimination of the sociological study meant that a joint negotiation level including the researchers could not be created. Therefore, actor group learning was unquestionably limited by this restriction to the programme.

5 DISCUSSION

The case study presented above shows the importance of interaction dynamics and co-operation between actor groups in solving agri-environmental problems. These dynamics provided the context in which the actor groups developed interactive strategies and learning processes, which resulted in progressive change in farming practices. This novel approach is of interest to all those involved in the farming sector and political decision makers, and constitutes a marked departure from a linear conception of change to an interactive conception of change.

The interactive point of view sees change in farming practices as a continuous and recursive process (Le Moigne 1990) in which the project for change (solutions) is not given at the outset by 'experts' (exogenous project) but needs to be built up by the actor groups involved in the action dynamic (endogenous project). Change in this case is not just the simple implementation of a number of technical prescriptions delivered by some centralised institution, but a complex process based on a dynamic of interactions between actor groups locally concerned by the problem. This interactive point of view mobilises two complementary theories; first, the sociology of organised action (Crozier and Friedberg 1977) based on the power games and conflicts of interest existing between actor groups. In this duality between co-operation and conflict, the actor groups develop

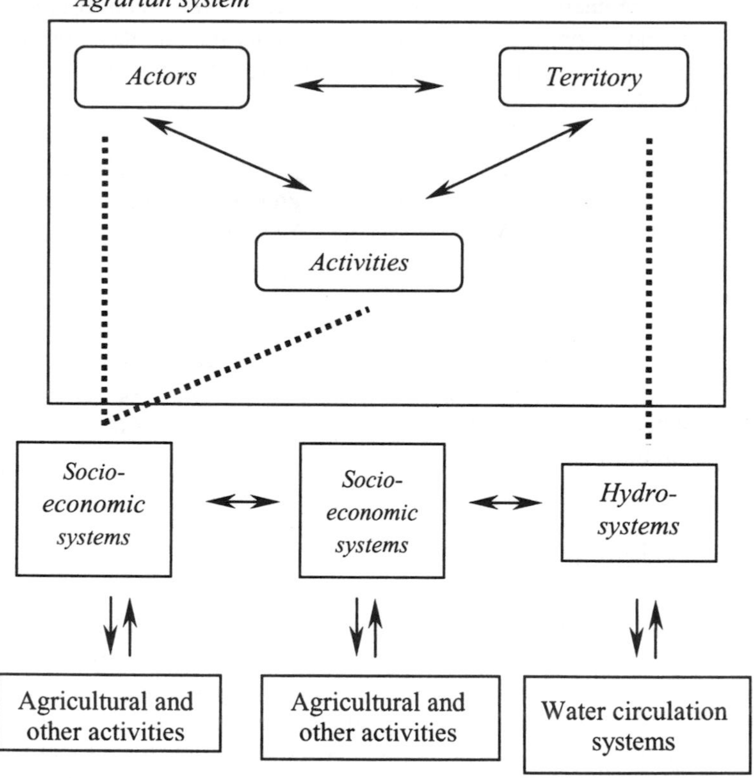

Figure 7.2 General structure of the programme

interactive strategies and thus the process of change can be built. The second theory is that of organisational learning (Bateson 1977, Argyris 1995). Thus, interaction means much more than power games and is necessarily accompanied by actor group learning. Confronted with the unpredictability of change together with bounded rationality (Simon 1982), individual actor groups can enter into a collective dynamic for producing and sharing know-how.

NOTES

1. Particularly because the mineral water market is highly competitive regarding quality and price. The Water Company is a major producer in the French mineral water market.
2. Farmers and their professional representatives, government bodies (local representatives of government, Ministries of Agriculture and Health and Social Services), researchers (French National Institute for Agricultural Research) and other actor groups involved in water (National Geological Institute, Water Board).
3. The Water Company proposed a very attractive price of FF 40 000 per hectare to farmers owning their land, while the market price was at that time FF 25 000 per hectare. Certain farmers made use of this opportunity of selling all or part of their land. This policy of land appropriation allowed the Water Company to become owner of about 45 per cent of the farmland by 1996.

REFERENCES

Alphandéry, P. and J. Bourliaud (1995), 'Chronique d'un mariage de raison: les Mesures Agri-environnementales dans la politique agricole', in Barrué-Pastor, M. et al. (eds), *Agriculture, protection de l'environnement et recomposition des systèmes ruraux: les enjeux de l'Article 19*, Paris: CNRS-PIREN, pp. 115–37.

Argyris, C. (1995), *Savoir pour agir*, Paris: InterEditions.

Barrué-Pastor, M., C. Deverre, J.-P. Billaud and P. Alphandéry (eds) (1995), *Agriculture, protection de l'environnement et recomposition des systèmes ruraux: les enjeux de l'Article 19*, Paris: CNRS-PIREN.

Bateson, G. (1977), *Vers une écologie de l'esprit*, Vol. 1, Paris: Seuil.

Chia, E. and M. Barbier (1999), 'Gestion de la qualité de l'eau: apprentissage collectif et rôle des prescripteurs', *Cahiers Agricultures*, **8**, pp. 109–17.

Crozier, M. and E. Friedberg (1977), *L'acteur et le système*, Paris: Seuil.

Deffontaines, J.P. and J. Brossier (eds) (1997), 'Agriculture et Qualité de l'eau: l'exemple de Vittel', *Dossier de l'environnement*, **14**.

Deffontaines, J.P., J. Brossier, M. Benoit, E. Chia, F. Gras and M. Roux (1994), 'Agricultural Practices and Water Quality. A Research Development Project', in Brossier J., L. Bonneval, de and E. Landais (eds), *Systems Studies in Agriculture and Rural Development*, INRA, pp. 31–62.

Gafsi, M. (1999), 'Farming Practices and Environment Quality: How to Manage the Changes on Farms', Communication to the IXth EAAE Congress, Warsaw.

Gafsi, M. and J. Brossier (1996), 'A New Perspective for Farms: Strategic Management and Conditions Required for Successful Adaptation', Communication to the VIIIth EAAE Congress, Edinburgh.

Hatchuel, A. (1994), 'Apprentissages collectifs et activités de conception', *Revue Francaise de Gestion*, **99**, pp. 109–20.

Le Moigne, J.L. (1990), *La modélisation des systèmes complexes*, Paris: Dunod.

Loseby, M. (ed.) (1992), 'The Environment and the Management of Agricultural Resources', Agrifutura Editrice Snc.-Roma. Proceedings of the 24th Seminar of EAAE.

Simon, H.A. (1982), *Models of Bounded Rationality*, Cambridge: MIT Press.

Whitby, M. (1995), 'Agri-environmental Policies in Britain', in Barrué-Pastor, M. et al. (eds), *Agriculture, protection de l'environnement et recomposition des systèmes ruraux: les enjeux de l'Article 19*, Paris: CNRS-PIREN, pp. 21–38.

8. Research Experience with Tools to Involve Farmers and Local Institutions in Developing More Environmentally Friendly Practices

Egon Noe and Niels Halberg

1 INTRODUCTION

As a response to the increasing public focus on the externalities of intensive farming and the resulting pressure to strengthen public regulation for farming practices, Danish farmers, within their own farming organisations, have begun to formulate their own goals and intentions for the development of environmentally friendly farming. Moreover, the number of organic farms is increasing all over Europe and the EU is presently trying to harmonise the organic rules. However, this coupling of a still more centralised formulation of organic rules and a broader group of farmers not involved in the original value debates in the organic movement might threaten to reduce the potential environmental benefits of conversion to organic farming. For these reasons, there seems to be a need for tools facilitating both conventional and organic farmers to reflect on their current practices and values in the light of society's demands for environmental goods and nature values.

With the overall aim to facilitate a learning process for farm families, the ethical accounting consists of group dialogues (to help the family clarify its own values and goals in the light of interests existing in society), a yearly accounting with indicators of resource use, environmental impact and animal welfare, and so on, and a MODS procedure ('multi-objective decisions support') for strategic planning on the farm including the new criteria on which the family might want to focus. On the basis of an evaluation of the 20 participating farmers' attitudes toward ethical accounting, a theoretical understanding of the important factors influencing the farmers' involvement in the reflection and farm development process was developed. This approach was subsequently used to structure a questionnaire concerning farmers' interests in decision aids, resource use and the environmental impact of farming. The questionnaire was mailed to about 1000 organic farmers. Results from this analysis will be presented and discussed in the light of the overall theme of possibilities for involving farmers in the development of farming practices in relation to local environmental goals. Finally, this topic will be discussed using preliminary results from a project using a social network theory to research 40 neighbouring farmers' possibilities of and motivation for developing environmentally friendly practices in a small region with sensitive groundwater resources.

With this background, the goal of this chapter is to present an empirical and theoretical reflection on how interactive decision tools can contribute to the involvement of farmers in developing more environmentally friendly farming practices.

2 DESCRIPTION OF THE DECISION AID: ETHICAL ACCOUNTING FOR A LIVESTOCK FARM AND STRATEGIC PLANNING USING ETHICAL ACCOUNTING (ETHICAL MODS)

The Danish Institute of Agricultural Sciences has developed an 'ethical accounting system' for livestock farms in a multidisciplinary project comprising agronomists, animal scientists, veterinarians, social scientists, professional philosophers and a group of farmers (Jensen and Sørensen 1998). The overall idea was that it would be beneficial for the farm family and for the farm as an enterprise to reflect on the farm's impact on relevant interests of different stakeholders (Pruzan and Thyssen 1990). From a systems point of view, this argument can be interpreted as the farm manager's need to reflect on his current management in the light of changes in the perception of farming on the part of the outside world (Kristensen and Halberg 1997). The stakeholders were broadly defined as present and future generations, the farm animals and the farm family (Jensen and Sørensen 1998). The ethical accounting consists of several components with the overall aim to facilitate a learning process for the farm family:

- A yearly account for each farm, including indicators of resource use, environmental impact, product quality and animal welfare in addition to the traditional technical-economic results.
- Group dialogues between farmers, with the aim of helping each family clarify their own values in light of the ethical conflicts in agriculture and letting the family formulate farm-specific personal goals to be included in the account.

The yearly account was used as a basis for a dialogue between researchers and the farm family regarding different possible interpretations of the results and the potential impact on other stakeholders' interests. For a description of the indicators, see Sandøe et al. (1997) and Halberg (1999). Most of the indicators were chosen in order to reflect the results of the farming practice. They should reflect changed management practice and thus be quantifiable and not just descriptions of the farmers' current practices (Halberg 1997).

3 STRATEGIC PLANNING USING THE ETHICAL ACCOUNT

One purpose of the group dialogues and the yearly accounts was that the families should clarify their own values and objectives in relation to the dimensions of animal welfare and environmental impact and so on. On this basis, they might want to include some of these aspects in their planning and management, especially in long-term (strategic) planning. However, because of the many new indicators of the results of their present farming practices, the families needed information about their alternatives to be able to decide whether they should change their practice and, in the affirmative, how. Moreover, the farmers could not be expected to have clear goals and preferences concerning these new dimensions of animal welfare and environmental impact.

Therefore, the farm families were invited to participate in an iterative multi-objective planning procedure based on ideas from multi-criteria decision making (MCDM) (see Romero and Rehman 1989; Bogetoft and Pruzan 1991). More specifically, an iterative procedure was set up allowing the participating families to clarify and change their goals and preferences when confronted with the predicted consequences of alternative plans (Bogetoft and Pruzan 1991). Thus, the learning process was assumed to be more important than a quick arrival at a specific plan:

> The choice of an alternative corresponds to the culmination of a learning process where values, objectives, criteria, alternatives and preferences continually interact and redefine each other and lead – explicitly or implicitly – to a compromise, which dissolves the intra-personal conflict. From this perspective, preferences are context dependent and therefore dependent on the set of alternatives being considered. (Bogetoft and Pruzan 1991, p. 49)

The procedure of this multi-objective decision support was as follows:

1. Each of the 14 interested families formulated ideas for a change in their current practice – in the form of goals they wanted to pursue or in the

form of alternative production plans following the distinctions between a so-called 'Prior Articulation of Preferences' method or a 'Prior Articulation of Alternatives' method (Bogetoft and Pruzan 1991).

2. The consequences of each alternative plan for the different dimensions were described by the researchers using predicted values for the indicators used in the ethical accounting. Some consequences, especially regarding animal welfare, could only be predicted in terms of the direction of change (that is, plan Y results in fewer cows with leg disorders compared to plan X).
3. The alternative plans and their predicted consequences were then discussed with the family, who were asked to give priorities to some of the plans or to give weight or to set goals for some of the indicators. With information about the family's preferences, the researchers reformulated alternative plans before returning to the family for a second and third time. In each round, some plans were given up and the direction in which to search for interesting solutions became clearer. The farm family decided when to stop the search. Thus, no mathematical modelling of the farmers' preferences was attempted and the search for optimal solutions used the farmers' indications of directions in which they wanted the plans to be changed and the relative importance of the different criteria. An example of how this procedure was carried out on a specific farm is presented in Halberg (1998).

The farmers' general evaluation of their experiences with ethical accounting was positive. After each visit for presentation of the ethical accounting all farmers were phoned and asked for their experiences with and opinion of the ethical accounting. On a scale from 1 to 9, with 9 as best, the outcome of the participation in the project on average was evaluated to be about 7 (Table 8.1). This evaluation of the project also reflects different perceptions of ethical accounting and the use of ethical accounting. Due to this quantitative evaluation by the farmers, there is hardly any difference between the various groups of farmers, but the conventional dairy farmers seem a bit more positive than the other farmers.

As already described, the indicators were selected from a scientific, ethical perspective, and the interviews reflect the farmers' different perceptions of these indicators. Some farmers find them very meaningful. Some of the organic farmers find that the indicators do not capture the idea of organic farming, and one finds them too theoretical. One of the pig producers finds the environmental indicators an expression of romanticism far removed from modern agriculture. The different attitudes towards the indicators reflect a different perception of the environment. This means that the indicators cannot

Table 8.1 The farmers' general evaluation of the ethical accounting on a scale from 1 to 9, with 9 as best

	N	Mean Score
Organic dairy farmers	9	6.9
Conventional dairy farmers	5	7.2
Pig farmers	5	6.8
All	19	6.9

Source: After Michelsen (1998, p. 118).

be selected to fit everyone, and, from a voluntary point of view, that the discussion of indicators is a very important part of the ethical accounting.

Many of the farmers stated that they feel more confident when the technical and economic situation of the farm serves as the point of departure for a discussion of what can be done with the other aspects of the accounting. Several farmers also found that the aggregation of otherwise scattered information into a coherent evaluation ('whole-farm-oriented') was a positive quality of the ethical accounting. It was a help to combine the different perspectives of the farm management.

Experiences from the presentation of the accounting to the farm families indicate different ways of using the ethical accounting. While some families reflected on the results and on how to improve in one or several aspects, a few farmers felt no need to change their management (but they were happy with the documentation, which they got via the accounting). Thus, not all farmers intend to use the ethical accounting to reconsider their ideals and goals in the light of the present results, for they find that they are already doing what they can. Some organic farmers, for instance, find that they are ahead compared with conventional farmers. Others have involved themselves in a search for solutions to cut down energy use or fodder import (Halberg 1998).

These experiences are supported by the qualitative interviews. Through the interviews, three different kinds of reaction to the ethical accounting can be identified: (1) Reflections, where farmers/farm families use the ethical accounting to reflect on their present farming practice. (2) As documentation – many of the farmers think they are doing quite well and see the accounting as a tool to document this for the surrounding society. (3) Rejection of the whole concept or parts of it. All three kinds of reaction were identified within all groups of farmers.

The group dialogue was met with very different reactions, too. During the interviews, many of the farmers/families referred to the group dialogue as a very interesting and inspiring part of the project. The confrontation of farmers with totally different values has been especially fruitful for the farmers' reflection on their own values. Other farmers said that they find that these group dialogues infringe on their privacy and that they do not want to discuss their values in such a context. Moreover, a few of the organic farmers claimed that they had already been through such value reflections and that the dialogues did not add anything new.

Of the 20 farmers co-operating in the project, 14 families decided to participate in the strategic planning process, the rest not finding themselves in a position to consider the long-term development of their farm. An average of 5–6 farm-specific plans was presented to each family, beginning with the family's choice of aspects to focus on. On all of the 11 dairy farms, changes of the stables were considered to improve animal welfare. Moreover, most families requested suggestions for reduction of energy use or other types of negative environmental impact, including the possibilities for a conversion to organic farming.

The farmers' responses were very different. It appears that for some farmers it is very difficult to formulate ideas to alternative plans or preferences, they are restricted to what they actually find realistic. Other farmers easily come up with several ideas for alternative plans. An explanation of these differences is the farmers' different ways of managing the farm. Some farmers do not think of alternatives to plans or preferences. These farmers have a clear perception of how their farm should be developed and managed. They do not seek alternatives, but strive to improve their specific way of farming. Other farmers are used to thinking in alternative solutions, they relate their goals and values less to the farming processes than to the outcome in terms of money, spare time, flexibility, and so on.

The interviews reflect that the attitude towards the ethical MODS tool and an involvement in a strategic planning process was more connected to the farmers' interest in actual relevance than to the concern with ethical aspects. This supports the hypothesis that the farmers' interest in such tools is much more linked to management strategies than to the farmers' environmental and ethical concerns.

The above evaluation shows that the farmers involved have a positive attitude to their participation in ethical accounting in general, but it also indicates very different ways of perceiving the concept and of applying it to the whole farm management process. This hypothesis is tested below in a survey among organic farmers using the 'farming styles' approach.

4 ETHICAL MODS AS A TOOL FOR THE ORGANIC FARMERS

Organic farming in Denmark, as in many other places in the 1980s, was formulated by farmers as values and objectives for organic farming. Some of these values and objectives were formulated as the rules we associate with organic farming today. The idea of a MODS tool based on ethical accounting could be relevant for organic farming when reflecting on the connection between objectives formulated for organic farming and the actual outcome. The organic farmers' motivation for using an ethical MODS tool is analysed in a survey of all organic farmers converted in the period 1995–97. A questionnaire was mailed to the 1004 registered organic farmers, of which 592 were returned completed.

To get a more in-depth analysis of the heterogeneity of interest in ethical MODS and to explore the above findings, the survey was analysed using a 'farming styles approach' which builds on a theoretical understanding of farm management as a socio-technical practice constructed through social processes (van der Ploeg 1995). In this chapter, styles of farming are defined as self-creating and self-organising communicative systems where the goals and significance of farming are created through communicative social processes. The theoretical and empirical foundations of the farming styles approach employed in this chapter are elaborated in the Ph.D. thesis by the author (Noe 1999). The farming styles approach has thus far only been applied to the group of dairy farmers in the Danish context. Therefore, the following farming styles analyses are only based on the sub-group of dairy farmers.

The classification builds on two pairs of opposing communicative systems. The first is a 'craft' versus a 'business' communication and the other is a 'turnover' versus an 'economic' communication. The pairs of communications are mutually dependent on each other to make each other meaningful and the individual farmers' orientations towards these communications are alternative to each other. The tension between these opposing communications is described in table 8.2.

Based on these communications, columns of value statement about farm management are formulated for the questionnaire. Factor analysis with an 'Oblimin'[1] rotation is used to extract the two fields of tensions and the factor scores are interpreted as the respondents' relative orientations toward these communications. The factor analysis simply reduces strongly correlated variables to factors, and the factor scores are the value of each observation regarding this new factor (Kim and Mueller 1994).

Table 8.2. Classification of opposing communicative systems

Craft →	**← Business**
'You have to be skilful as a farmer to make a living of it'	'You have to be flexible and market orientated to make a living of it'
Specialisation – Own skills and experience – Individual cow – Optimisation of production –	– Flexibility – Updated knowledge – Herd – Economic optimisation
Turnover →	**← Economic**
'You need to have a high turnover to develop the farm and make an income of it'	'Saved is earned'
Newest technology – Abrupt growth on borrowed capital – Rationalisation of size –	– Second hand – Gradual growth on own savings – Go simple

Based on these new variables of factor scores, four clusters of orientations were obtained by quick cluster analyses. This clustering procedure is a relatively rough categorising, but usable for analysing the connections between differences in management and attitudes towards MODS. The following descriptions of some of the key features of these farming styles are based on the Ph.D. thesis by the author (Noe 1999).

- The craftsman style is characterised by an orientation towards the values connected to a high yield per cow and personal skills where intuition and experience play a central role. The family and family labour play an important role and , finally, the style is characterised by a desire to be self-financing and less dependent on market fluctuations.
- The business style is characterised by a desire to be market orientated. Farmers orientated towards this style identify themselves more as business managers than as farmers. In the business communication the competent farmer can explore the financial possibilities of the market and quickly adapt production accordingly.
- The entrepreneur style is characterised by strong ideas and goals in farming and the development of the farm; choices are made with a long-term perspective. In this communication size, technology and, consequently, rationalisation of the farming processes are of great

importance. In contrast to the business style, farmers within this communication identify themselves very much as farmers.

– The intensive production style. This style is characterised by an orientation towards a large and intensive production and a clear vision of the enlargement of the production. Though skill orientated, this style is much more focused on technology than the craft style, and its orientation towards knowledge is linked to technology, for example complete feed mixer. This communication is mainly concerned with specialisation and rationalisation and is not particularly orientated toward market opportunities.

In the questionnaire the farmer was asked: To what extent do you think that a MODS tool would help improve farm management in general, and to what extent would you apply an ethical MODS tool in farm management in order to improve the environmental impact of your farming if such a tool were available?

If we look at the whole group of respondent organic farmers we find that approximately 25 per cent of the farmers have positive attitudes toward the possibility of applying a MODS tool, approximately 30 per cent are not sure, while the rest are not interested or do not believe in such a tool at all (Figure 8.1(a)). This picture does not change much for the attitudes towards an ethical MODS tool, although the percentage of farmers that 'might be interested' in such a tool has increased and the percentage of farmers that 'do not need such a tool' has decreased compared to the group of farmers that 'have enough tools'. The results suggest that approximately 25 per cent of the respondent organic farmers are likely to use an ethical MODS tool but only 10 per cent for certain, and that another 30 per cent of the farmers could possibly be motivated to apply such a tool. No such survey has yet been made among conventional farmers, but there is reason to believe that their attitude to MODS tools will not differ dramatically.

We will now take a closer look at the group of organic dairy farmers among the respondents. The survey provides an opportunity to analyse the relation between farm management and attitudes towards MODS from a farming styles perspective introduced above. Table 8.3 shows Parson's correlation between the attitudes towards MODS and ethical MODS and five variables constructed from the questionnaire. The first variable expresses the farmers' perception of the fulfilment of the organic goals on their own farm. The second variable expresses to what extent these goals are focused on their own farm. The third variable is an expression of the farmers' perception of their own general possibility of improving the farm management in relation to the organic goals. The last two variables are drawn from farming styles presented above.

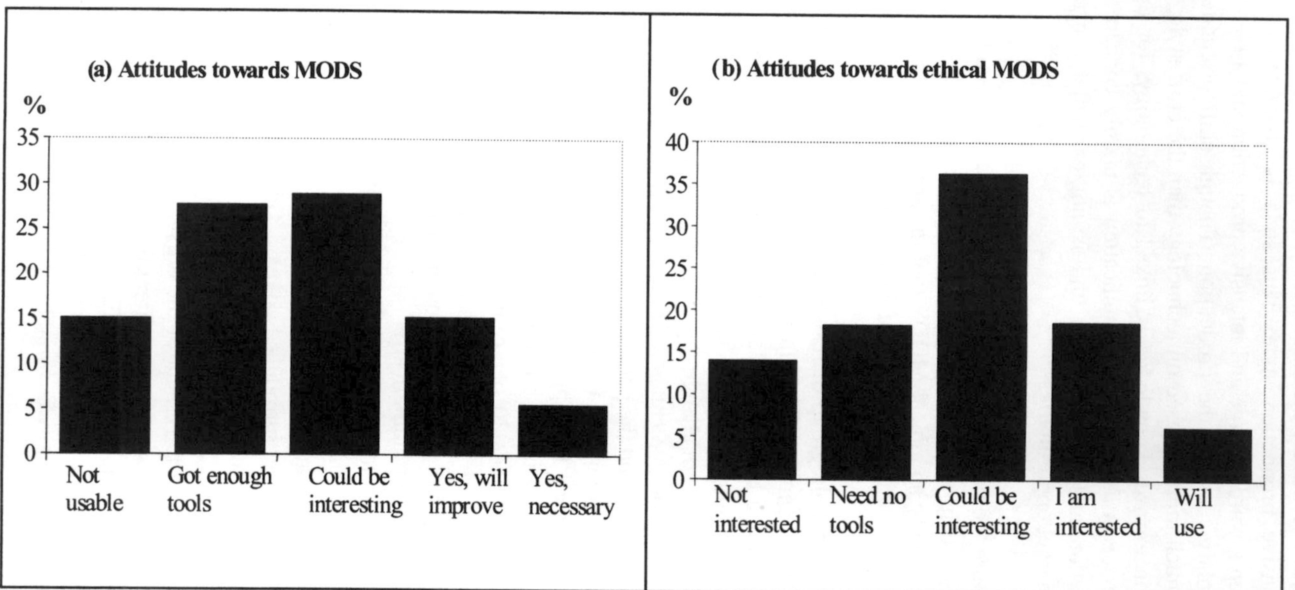

Figure 8.1 *Farmers' attitudes towards implementation of MODS tools (a) and the degree to which they expect to use a tool like ethical accounting if it were available (b) (N=512)*

Table 8.3 *Correlation coefficients between organic farmers' expected use of ethical MODS, conception of environmental problems and farm management*

Pearson correlation	Attitude towards MODS	Attitude towards ethical MODS tools	Perception of fulfilment of the organic goals	Organic goals in focus in management	Perception of possibilities to fulfil goals
Attitude towards MODS [(a)]	1.00				
Attitude towards ethical MODS tools [(a)]	0.57 **	1.00			
Perception of the fulfilment of the organic goals [(a)]	0.07	0.04	1.00		
Organic goals in focus in management [(a)]	−0.06	−0.08 *	0.66 **	1.00	
Perception of possibilities to fulfil goals [(a)]	−0.06	0.00	0.55 **	0.62 **	1.00
Economic versus turnover [(b)]	0.25 **	0.26 **	0.23 **	0.21 **	0.21 **
Craft versus business [(b)]	0.37 **	0.45 **	0.24 **	0.21 **	0.20 **

Notes:

** Correlation is significant at the 0.01 level (2-tailed).

* Correlation is significant at the 0.05 level (2-tailed).

(a) N = 537–597.

(b) N = 169–178.

Table 8.3 shows the extent to which the farmers find problematic areas within their farming and the extent to which they focus on these problems in their management. There is apparently no correlation between attitudes towards ethical MODS and the perception of the environmental situation of the farm. Furthermore, there is no correlation of the attitudes towards ethical MODS and the farmers' perception of their possibility of doing something about it in their management. This supports the findings of the qualitative evaluations of the MODS above that the attitudes towards ethical MODS are not correlated to environmental concerns but to the question of how such a concept fits into farm management.

This conclusion is supported by the very strong correlation between the attitude towards ethical MODS and the management dimension established from the farming styles approach. The highest correlation is found between the business-orientated farmers and ethical MODS. In the following, this will be analysed in the context of farming styles of the subgroup of dairy farmers within this group (Table 8.4).

Table 8.4 The attitudes of the dairy farmers orientated towards the different farming styles (in per cent)

Attitude towards ethical MODS tools	Strategy of farm management				
	Business	Craft	Entrepreneur	Production	Total
Not interested	3	12	3	9	7
Need no tool	18	36	5	5	17
Could be interested	37	38	31	58	41
I am interested	39	14	44	26	29
Will use	3		18	2	5
N of respondents	38	50	39	43	170

Compared to the whole group of respondents, the attitudes of this group of dairy farmers show the same patterns. Although a little more positive, still only about 25 per cent of the farmers have positive attitudes. The percentage of 'could be' is a little larger. If we look at the differences between the four styles, clear differences in attitudes can be explained by the differences in logic and values of the styles.

The craft style holds by far the most negative attitude towards an ethical MODS tool. Only 14 per cent of the farmers clustered into this style claimed an interest in an ethical MODS tool and none of the farmers in this group claimed that they would use such a tool for certain. This fits nicely with the description of this style as orientated towards one's own skills and experience. Their management is performed in the stable and not at the desk. The entrepreneur style, on the other hand, shows very positive attitudes towards MODS. This fits into the picture of this style as both orientated towards big enterprises, where management tools are needed, and towards external knowledge. The intensive production-orientated farmers show a mixed reaction to an ethical MODS tool. Almost 60 per cent hold a 'could be' attitude. This can be explained by the fact that, despite their large-size farms, these farmers are more focused on technology than on knowledge.

Table 8.4 shows clear differences between the different farming styles and their attitudes towards MODS tools. Craft and intensive production-orientated farmers will hardly make use of such a tool voluntarily, simply because it does not fit into their way of managing their farms.

5 FROM FARM LEVEL TO MICRO REGION/WATER CATCHMENT

Through their own farm organisations, Danish farmers have formulated goals and intentions of good farming practice – an introduction to integrated farming presented in a pamphlet called 'Good farming practice year 2000'. This introduction is primarily to be seen as a reaction to the environmental debate and as an effort to prevent more regulation. These goals are complementary to the organic movement's declarations of goals and include objectives to reduce pollution in agriculture, to minimise nutrient losses and to maintain biodiversity and landscape values. The hypothesis was that the ethical accounting could help farmers to pursue such goals within their economic and practical constraints.

There are, however, some obstacles to such a voluntary approach. First, as described above, only approximately 30 per cent of the farmers can be expected to employ such a tool. Another 30 per cent might be engaged, but this would probably require some kind of extension or pressure. Secondly, many aspects of a farm's environmental impact can only be evaluated in relation to locally defined goals for landscape and environment and in relation to the conditions on the neighbouring farms. Likewise, important environmental and landscape values can only be furthered if several farmers in a small region change production methods in the same direction. Therefore, the success of a voluntary approach might depend on co-operative strategies and farmers networking that might again require extensionists or external facilitators to support the process.

The evaluation of the possibilities for the development of a small region must, therefore, be based on the understanding of the farmer's motivation for participation in a co-ordinated implementation of some of the goals of good agricultural practice. This was also shown in an evaluation of the attempts to establish green corridors in two Danish counties (Just et al. 1996). Personal contact and public plans adjusted to local farmers' interests thus proved to be better than a simple introduction of general economic incentives to introduce environmentally friendly production methods (Wiborg 1997). Röling (1994) suggests the creation of local platforms for dialogue. Experience from different European projects suggests that the creation of a common understanding of problems and possible solutions among stakeholders in an area is a prerequisite for a fruitful development (Deffontaines et al. 1993; Hubert et al. 1993; van der Ploeg and Long 1994).

To research this potential for profiting from local resources when defining environmental problems of agriculture, and to find possible solutions, a project (the Fabjerg project) has been started in a small area with 40 neighbouring farms. Eight of these farmers have agreed to be pilot farmers. The area is situated in a region with important interests in drinking water and a traditional landscape undergoing changes. The work will use experience from the ethical accounting, including the group dialogues and the combination of natural and social science.

The main research topics are:

1. to develop farming systems that are economically viable and environmentally friendly in terms of locally defined goals,
2. to study the motivation of different types of farmers for including local goals for landscape and environment in their management,
3. to find ways to create a platform for dialogues between different stakeholders in the area, that is, intensive farmers, part-time farmers, local authorities, and so on,
4. to research the importance of farmers' networking for the implementation of environmentally sound agricultural systems.

In a first round of interviews the farmers in the area claimed to live up to the goals and intentions behind 'Good farming practice year 2000'. They reported that they have already done a lot to reduce the use of pesticides and the amount of fertiliser, and that they have applied new technology to improve the nitrogen utilisation of the organic manure. Generally speaking, the farmers interviewed stated that they see new problems in the present way of farming. Two of the farmers have recently converted to organic farming. The motivation for these farmers to convert was not any kind of critique of conventional farming, but rather they had converted primarily for economic reasons and in order to create a more positive image of agriculture. Obviously, the local farming discourse asserts that the present conventional farming is environmentally sound and that the problem is that the farmers have to convince the rest of society of the fact – a discourse shared by the local advisory centre and probably not far from the general agricultural discourse. This means that one of the major barriers for a voluntary change of farming practices toward a more environmentally sound approach is the farmers' perception of the ethical and environmental impact of their present farming practices. Therefore, any voluntary change must include a process of problem identification.

One of the main intentions behind the Fabjerg project is to involve local human resources and knowledge in such a process. The idea is to involve the farmers collectively in the discussion and improve environmentally friendly farming practices. To analyse the possibilities of such a collective local strategy, a network approach is employed (Wiskerke and Oerlemans 1998). A network analysis shows that farmers are not primarily forming technical-social networks within this narrow area but in a much larger regional area. Several factors play a role in the explanation of the weak local networking of both a social and a technical character. One of the factors apparently most important to stress here is the structural development, which here as elsewhere results in a tension between farmers in the competition for farmland. The network analysis therefore leads to the conclusion that the advisory centre is the only local social and technical platform that includes almost the whole group of farmers.

The Fabjerg project is centred around two kinds of tools: the already described MODS tool based on developed ethical accounting, and a GIS-based tool as a platform for identification and discussion of the problems of the area. Both tools need data from the farms in the area. The ethical MODS tool is employed in a process of interactions with the eight pilot farmers as a point of departure for discussion of the possibilities of improving the environmental impact of the farms. The results of these interactions with the individual farmers will be one of the inputs in the local discussion.

Another input will be a GIS-based tool to illustrate the geographical situation of different problems. As the central interest of the area is groundwater, the first figures presented to the actors involved in the project at a local meeting will be the nitrogen balance of the area, both at farm and field level. An example of such a visualisation of the problematic situation is presented in Figure 8.2, an ArcView map showing the estimated nitrogen surplus at field level.

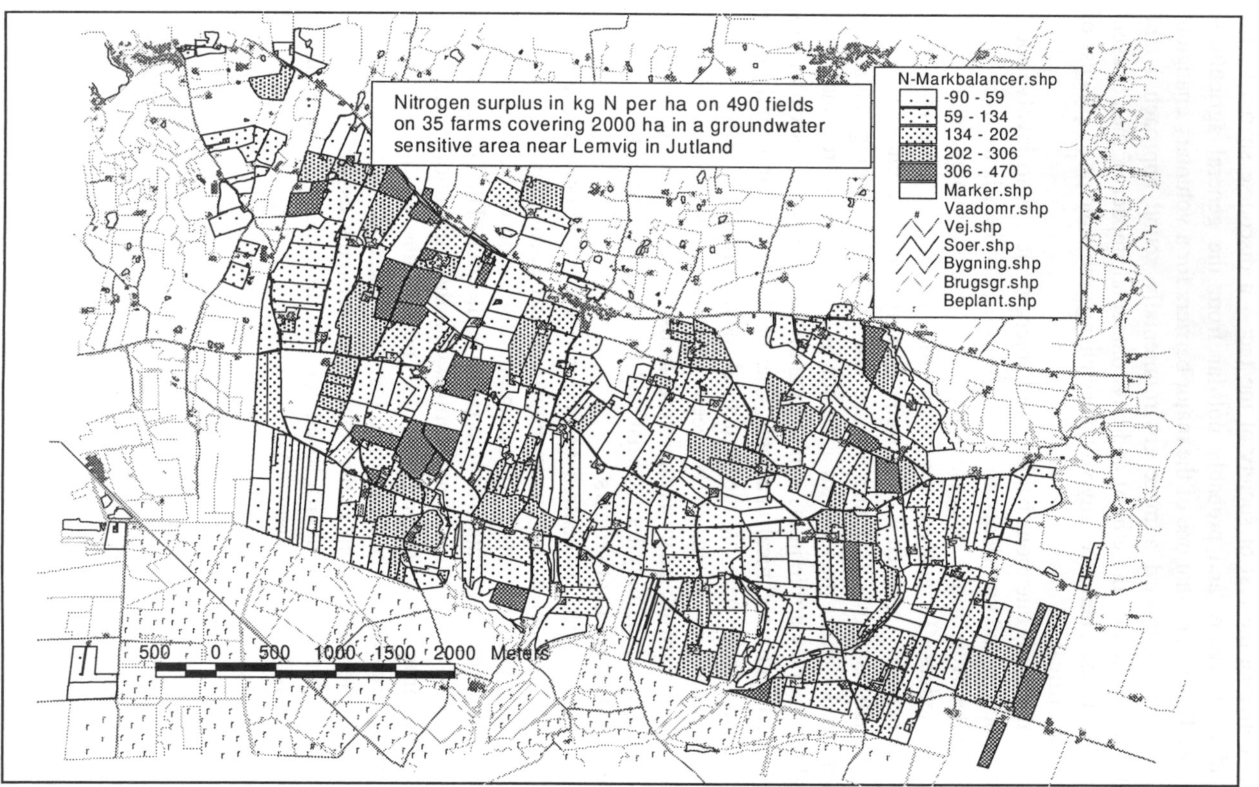

Figure 8.2 Presentation of the 1998 nitrogen surplus at field level for different crops

The idea is that these two processes represented by the two kinds of tools will support each other in a mutual process of discursive problem identification and contextual problem solving. Former experience and research show that MODS tools cannot stand alone, and that discursive problem identification plays an important role in such a developing process.

So far, there have been no local environmental revolutions, but through our contact with the farmers we recognise that the farmers are reflecting on the inputs. The success of such projects depends on the degree to which the relevant local actors are involved in the process. Furthermore, it is also important that the local advisors act as central actors in the local discourse and as facilitators of the process and that the other interested parties are involved. As researchers, we can stimulate such a process with knowledge and tools, but we cannot control the processes. In the role of facilitators, we have to be sensitive to the local social processes. Network analysis turns out to be a good point of departure for such reflections.

6 CONCLUSION

Indicators that quantify environmental and ethical aspects of farming have proved to be a good point of departure for a discussion with farmers on the environmental impacts of farming. Many farmers appreciate the whole-farm orientation of such a discussion that combines the environmental aspect with technical and economic aspects of farming.

Empirical studies suggest that only 25 per cent of organic farmers can be expected to voluntarily include an ethical tool that includes different environmental indicators. Attitudes towards such a tool are correlated with the way in which the farm is managed and not with the environmental concerns of the farmer. Studies of conventional farmers show that one of the major barriers for voluntary improvement of the environmental impact of farming is the farmer's perception of the environmental impact of the farm.

Researchers can possibly stimulate and facilitate local voluntary processes by means of knowledge and tools (top down) but they cannot control these processes. In the role of catalysts, we need to be sensitive to the local social situation and processes. A social-technical network analysis has proved to be a good tool for such sensitivity.

NOTE

1. Oblimin: 'a general criterion for obtaining an oblique rotation which tries to simplify the pattern matrix by way of reference axes' (Kim and Mueller 1994, p. 72). This method allows the extracted factors to be correlated but makes the interpretation of these easier.

REFERENCES

Bogetoft, P. and P. Pruzan (1991), *Planning With Multiple Criteria – Investigation, Communication and Choice*, Amsterdam: North-Holland.

Deffontaines, J.P., M. Benoit, J. Brossier, E. Chia, F. Gras and M. Roux (eds) (1993), *Agriculture et Qualité des Eaux. Diagnostic et propositions pour un périmetre de protection*, Versailles–Dijon–Mirecourt: INRA, URSAD.

Halberg, N. (1997), 'Farm Level Evaluation of Resource Use and Environmental Impact', in Isaart, J. and J.J. Llerena (eds), *Resource Use in Organic Farming*, Proceedings of the 3rd European Network for Scientific Research Co-ordination in Organic Farming, Workshop, Ancona.

Halberg, N. (1998), 'Researching Farmers' Possibilities and Motivation for Including Environmental Aspects in their Management', in Doppler, V. and A. Koutsouris (eds) (1999), *Rural and Farming Systems Analyses: Environmental Perspectives*, Proceedings of the 3rd European Symposium of the Association of Farming Systems, Hohenheim, Germany, March 25–27, 1998, pp. 103–13. http://www.agrsci.dk/jbs/bepro/Publications/body_afsre98_researching_farmers_po.htm

Halberg, N. (1999), 'Indicators of Resource Use and Environmental Impact for Use in a Decision Aid for Danish Livestock Farmers', *Agriculture, Ecosystems & Environment*, **76** (1), pp. 17–30.

Hubert, B., E. Rigolot, T. Turlan and N. Couix (1993), 'Forest Fire Prevention in the Mediterranean Region – New Approaches to Agriculture–Environment Relations', in Brossier, J., L. de Bonneval and E. Landais (eds), *Systems Studies in Agriculture and Rural Development*, Paris: INRA, pp. 63–86.

Jensen, K.K. and J.J. Sørensen (1998), 'The Idea of an Ethical Account for Livestock Farms', *Journal of Agricultural Environmental Ethics*, **2** (11), pp. 85–100.

Just, F., E. Noe and L.A. Rasmussen (1996), 'Korridorer i landskabet – En evaluering af Miljøministeriets Eksempelprojekt nr. 7', Working Paper, South Jutland University Center.

Kim, J. and C.W. Mueller (1994), 'Introduction to Factor Analysis: What It Is and How to Do It?', in M.S. Lewis-Beck (ed.), *Factor Analysis and Related Techniques*, London: Sage Publications, pp. 1–69.

Kristensen, E. Steen and N. Halberg (1997), 'A Systems Approach for Assessing Sustainability in Livestock Farms', in Sørensen, J. Tind et al. (eds), *More than Food Production*, Proceedings of the 4th International Livestock Farming Systems Symposium, Foulum, 1996.

Michelsen, J. (1998), 'Hvad syntes husdyrbrugerne om "Etisk regnskab for husdyrbryg"' (What Do Dairy Farmers Think about 'Ethical Accounting for Livestock Farms'), in Sørensen, J.T., P. Sandøe and N. Halberg (eds), *Etisk regnskab for husdyrbrug* (*Ethical Accounting for Livestock Farms*), København: DSR Forlag, pp. 113–31.

Noe, E. (1999), 'Værdier, rationalitet og landbrugsproduktion. Belyst ved en microsociologisk undersøgelse blandt danske økologiske og konventionelle kvægbrugere' (Values, Rationality and Farming – Examined in a Microsociological Study of Organic and Conventional Dairy Farmers), Ph.D. Thesis, Institut for Økonomi, Skov og Landskab. Den kgl. Veterinær- og Landbohøjskole.

Ploeg, J.D. van der (1995), 'The Tragedy of Spatial Planning', in Schoute, J.F.T. (ed.), *Scenario Studies for the Rural Environment*, Dordrecht: Kluwer Academic Publishers, pp. 75–90.

Ploeg, J.D. van der and A. Long (eds) (1994), *Born from Within – Practice and Perspectives of Endogenous Rural Development*, Assen: van Gorcum.

Pruzan, P. and O. Thyssen (1990), 'Conflict and Consensus: Ethics as a Shared Value Horizon for Strategic Planning', *Human Systems and Management*, **9**, pp. 135–51.

Röling, N. (1994), 'Platforms for Decision-Making about Ecosystems', in Fresco, L.O., L. Stroosnijder, J. Bourma and H. van Keulen (eds), *The Future of Land: Mobilising and Integrating Knowledge for Land Use Options*, Chichester: John Wiley & Sons Ltd, pp. 385–93.

Romero, C. and T. Rehman (1989), *Multiple Criteria Analysis for Agricultural Decisions*, Amsterdam: Elsevier.

Sandøe, P., L. Munksgaard, N.P. Bådsgård and K. Hjelholdt (1997), 'How to Manage the Management Factor – Assessing Animal Welfare at the Farm Level', in Sørensen, J. Tind et al. (eds), *More than Food Production*, Proceedings of the 4th International Livestock Farming Systems Symposium, Foulum, 1996.

Wiborg, I.A. (1997), *The Lack of Success of the Accompanying Measures in Denmark*, Proceedings from the 'Nordiske Jordbrugsforskeres Forening', Seminar on Alternative Use of Agricultural Land, Foulum, pp. 57–65.

Wiskerke, H. and N. Oerlemans (1998), 'Field Study Methodology', Working Paper of the EU Project: Making Agriculture Sustainable – Identification of Barriers and Driving Forces of the Unequal Dissemination of Sustainable Agriculture in Europe.

9. The Governance of Quality and Environmental Management Systems in Agriculture: Research Issues and New Challenges

Armelle Mazé, Marie-Béatrice Galan and Francois Papy[1]

1 INTRODUCTION

The extent of environmental pollution caused by the application of nitrates and pesticides or other agricultural activities keeps consumers' attention focused on the lack of transparency within production systems used by farmers. To cope with these agri-environmental problems, the implementation of quality and environmental management systems such as ISO 14000 and ISO 9000) at the farm level is regarded as a possible solution. Their adoption by farmers could improve process reliability regarding product quality, as well as environmental impact. However, implementation of the international standards of the International Standard Organisation (ISO) has been, until now, considered to be time consuming and difficult to carry out in small and medium-sized firms, like farms. How is it possible to develop co-operative strategies rather than regulatory rules through the implementation of quality and environmental management systems based on these international standards?

The adaptation of these general ISO standards to the specific dimensions of agricultural production has been emphasised in several European countries (Gottlieb 1997; Grolleau 1998; Castet 1999). However, these systems still remain at an experimental stage and involve only a few farmers. The aim of this study is to identify some of the organisational conditions to be met in order to facilitate their adoption and the overall reduction of quality control costs. One original aspect of the analytical approach developed in this study is the connection between recent advances in organisation theory and research on agricultural systems. A similar approach was adopted by Allen and Lueck (1999) through the incorporation of seasonal forces, crop cycle and task specialisation into a model of farm organisation. However, the diversity of farming systems is still introduced in their model as an exogenous variable.

The central proposition of this chapter is that the design of these governance mechanisms matters as much for the success of this management system at the farm level as does the complete implementation of normative rules. The nature of the interactions between the farm's organisation and its immediate economic environment (advisory services, agro-food firms, certifying bodies and neighbours) also matters. The point is, that with these quality and environmental management systems, problem solving relies primarily on the collective management of organisational change whereby farm activities are mostly individual. The major organisational innovation set up by these new management systems (in large firms) is mostly based on collective training and 'team groups' in order to prevent product and environmental defects, and hence to develop quality assurance. In the case of small firms, other methodologies are needed to promote similar organisational learning and process improvement.

In this chapter, we address some of the preliminary results of a research programme conducted with three Local Advisory Centres (Chambres d'agriculture) and their regional organisation in the French region Picardie. In this region, farming systems are primarily oriented toward crop production. However, specific dimensions of animal production (dairy farms, poultry production) are also emphasised, and an extension of the methodology is actually being exported to other regions. The chapter is organised as follows: first, we will investigate some issues surrounding the implementation of the international standards based on ISO 9000 and ISO 14000 in farms (section 2). Second, we will focus on some alternative strategies chosen in Europe for their adaptation to the agricultural context (section 3). Finally, we will identify some theoretical issues associated with the adoption of these quality and environmental standards on chain management and on information systems in agro-food sectors (section 4).

2 QUALITY AND ENVIRONMENTAL MANAGEMENT SYSTEMS IN AGRICULTURE

In agriculture, the adoption of quality and environmental management systems (QEMS) still remains at an experimental stage involving only a few farmers. However, in a context of increasing requirements for food safety and environmental protection, their implementation at the farm level covers important economic issues including traceability and the efficiency of farm organisation (section 2.1). This section intends to disentangle some of the main concepts that govern the use of these methodologies (section 2.2). As environmental concerns and food quality are increasingly linked in agriculture, the term 'quality management' means here both quality and environmental management systems.

2.1 Farm Certification between Quality Assurance and Environmental Management

Two different types of certification have been developed in agro-food sectors. Product certifications such as Protected Denomination of Origin (PDO), organic production or other official labelling systems are now well known by European consumers. These certifications are based on the definition of specification of a product's quality or production methods (Valceschini and Mazé 2000). More recently introduced quality and environmental management systems contrast with the former approach in that they focus primarily on the efficiency of the organisational design and process control implemented by the firms themselves. First used in large industrial firms as a way to improve their internal organisation, they are now viewed as reference standards[2] for a broad range of economic activities.

Several reasons justify their extension in agriculture. Customers and consumers or other landscape users now require farmers to give assurances as to the compatibility of their technical practices with specific environmental or quality requirements. This includes quality or environmental criteria that are not directly observable with the final product (that is, how animals are kept, for example). Thus, technical recommendations concerning 'good practices' in agriculture to cope with agri-environmental problems or traceability of information about farming systems are all converging toward a strengthening of these requirements.

Several sources of potential inefficiencies may appear regarding the multiplicity of requirements that farmers have to cope with:

- Systematic self-reporting of information by farmers and the collection of repetitive data with a limited technical interest for farmers increase the potential for measurement error or fraud, and risk a lack of motivation in the conservation of these information systems through time. Systematic recording of successive technical operations in the field is increasingly required by agro-food firms (on what they do, how, when, where, and so on).
- The absence of requirement harmonisation and the development of repetitive controls realised by different customers or certifying bodies

at the farm level increase the costs of controls without improving the reliability of the overall monitoring system.

For these reasons, systematic recording of information by farmers is not a sufficient condition to guarantee the reliability of farmers' practices. In fact, at this time most traceability systems in agriculture are designed for one particular production, instead of considering the farm as an overall entity with its own coherence.

However, recent research on farming systems leads to the conclusion that work organisation at the farm level is mostly realised through the aggregation of basic management units, for example through the bundling of several parcels or animals depending on the resource constraints of the farms (Ingrand et al. 1993; Papy et al. 1988).[3] These aggregation patterns are now limited by new requirements on product quality or environmental policy. Thus, the implementation of technical actions is supported by specific patterns of organisation which may influence the accuracy of information and traceability systems at the farm level. This is especially true in France, where farms are highly diversified and mostly multiproduct firms, including crop production as well as animal production, or other economic activities such as environmental services or direct-to-consumer sales.

Hence, the design of information systems at the farm level cannot disregard the specific rules of resource allocation chosen by farmers (Aubry et al. 1998). Focusing on the quality of farm organisation and its ability to give adequate assurances as to the application of these requirements is an alternative approach to increase the reliability of information systems. Hence, the use of quality and environmental management systems seems to be best suited to deal with the new societal requirements on traceability and environmental activities. However, new models of farmers' decisions are needed to implement quality assurance systems at the farm level, and thus improve the transparency of agricultural production processes.

2.2 An Integrated Management System Based on Continuous Process Improvement

In contrast to standard quality control systems in agriculture, these quality and environmental management systems, as defined by international standards, focus primarily on process requirements and, consequently, on the quality of the firm organisation, instead of on specific requirements for final product quality. In fact, the core of these integrated management systems is organised with an eye to continuous improvement in a rhythm defined by the firm 'according to its own economic constraints and depending on circumstances' (Schiefer 1997). The objectives are then mostly defined at an individual level.

The idea of a Continuous Process Improvement is a key point in international management standards (ISO 14000 and 9000).[4] This quality spiral, the so called 'Plan, Do, Control, Act (PDCA) cycle', is based on an individual and voluntary commitment on the part of the firms, allowing more flexibility than a regulatory approach. These integrated management systems are built on internal improvement efforts for the firms and attempts to fulfil the expectations of their customers for quality management and for environmental management, that is, the expectations of society regarding the effects of its process on the environment (De Haes and De Snoo 1997; Schiefer 1997).

As the process itself is controlled, these procedures must result in a reduced level of inspection concerning the final product. Thus, ex ante monitoring by the firm prevails over ex post inspection of the firm's output. These management systems based on ISO 9000 and ISO 14000 share the same organisational approach. They are able to promote practices which act as officially recognised standards and, at the same time, seek to be respectful of the environment and compatible with objectives of food safety and quality. However, some differences remain with respect to their specific objectives. Table 9.1 depicts some of the common features and differences between ISO 9000 and ISO 14000 standards.

Table 9.1 A comparison of ISO 9000 and ISO 14000

Area	ISO 9000 (1994)	ISO 14000
	Common features of the two ISO standards	
Organisation standards	Definition of an individual quality and/or environmental policy by the firm	
	Definition of organisational structure, responsibilities and resources requirements, that is, procedures needed to elaborate, implement, control and maintain the system	
	Divergent features of the two ISO standards	
Target definition and operator control	A static quality assurance approach	A dynamic PDCA cycle for continuous improvement
	Definition of the targets regarding individual customers' requirements Evaluation by a contract review	Definition by an environmental evaluation Control of environmental indicators

Quality and environmental management systems represent a methodological approach to arranging the planning, implementation and review of an organisation's attempt to manage quality or its impact on the environment. The main difference between these two management systems is related to the identification and the characterisation of the requirements that a firm's organisation has to deal with. In the case of the ISO 9000 standard, requirements are included in contractual arrangements with the customers, and can be easily identified through a specific procedure called a contract review. The aim of this procedure is to evaluate whether the organisation of the firm offers adequate guarantees to meet these contractual requirements.

In the case of the ISO 14000 standard, the procedure is different and is realised through an operational control of environmental indicators. Environmental evaluation is related to both intentional and non-intentional products of the firm. Requirements are mostly non-contractual in the sense that they could include collective environmental impact on third parties. These requirements are also mostly implicit, but there is an obligation for the firm to define indicators that allow for an evaluation of its environmental impact.

In both cases, the firms have to formalise their own organisation in order to prove their ability to cope with these requirements. The documentation and analysis of the production process are of central importance in supporting the design of information systems in farms. A reduction in co-ordination cost is then expected. However, economising on monitoring costs is related to their being accepted by customers and to their confidence in the certification process. The certification is a procedure by which a third party, in general a certifying body, gives a written assurance that a product, a service or a specific system quality is in keeping with specified requirements. It gives an assurance as to the commitment of the firm (that is, the farmer) to apply environmental or contractual specifications.

Despite these advantages, environmental and/or quality management systems have often been blamed for their high level of formalisation and administrative features that have to be fulfilled, especially in small firms. This creates excessive certification costs for the level of activity concerned. However, according to transaction cost theory, the central benefit that can be expected from these environmental and quality management systems is a reduction in excessive measurement cost induced by repetitive and useless controls implemented by separate customers.[5] Several options are available to firms to reduce these costs. They focus mainly on reducing the documentation requirements for processes, for example by adopting a joint quality manual in which general rules are defined, instead of a strictly individual approach as defined in the ISO standards (Schiefer 1997). Another point is to consider the design of alternative organisational patterns, that is, governance structures, needed to support the implementation of quality and environmental management systems in very small firms like farms.

3 FARM CERTIFICATION AND THE DESIGN OF GOVERNANCE MECHANISMS

The simplest strategy to guarantee the quality of farmers' practices regarding environmental or product quality would have been the direct application of these international standards (series ISO 9000 or 14000). However, in the case of very small firms, their adoption among farmers will remain marginal due to the specificity of a farm's organisation in agriculture. Two different options have been experimented with in Europe to adapt these international management systems to the European agricultural context (section 3.1). New methodologies are also needed to facilitate their appropriation by farmers and the creation of a collective learning process (section 3.2).

3.1 The Nature of Governance Mechanisms for Certification

The two alternative strategies developed in Europe to adapt these management systems share a common feature in the design of a specific governance structure, that is, the institutional matrix in which the integrity of a transaction is decided (Williamson 1996). They also include individual and bilateral relationships among agents as well as collective rules or organisations. The transaction analysed here is a support transaction as defined by Spiller and Zelner (1997), that is, a quality assurance service associated with the product transaction in order to facilitate the realisation of the exchange. Adoption of the management systems to quality improvements requires substantial training costs. The aim here is to economise on certification costs while preserving the reliability of the overall management system.

These governance structures are both based on a collective organisation model. They differ with regard to the institutional design of the intermediate organisation: co-operatives (or private firms) on the one hand, and extension services on the other. The first one is a vertical chain-oriented quality management system, mostly used in strongly coordinated production systems like the pork industry or specialised vegetable production (Helbig 1997; Castet 1999). Another option was developed by the Danish Kvamilla project (Gottlieb 1997), as well as by the French programme Quali'Terre.[6] The intermediate organisation here is an advisory service. This second approach is more in the spirit of ISO standards, taking the farm and its activity as a whole.

Agriculture's adaptation of these ISO standards for quality and environmental systems follows two different pathways in European countries according to their specific goals. In our opinion, these two systems are not competing, but are rather complementary. They share a common general architecture of certification in which the governance mechanisms are organised following a pyramidal certification system,[7] as opposed to a direct and individual certification of farms (Figure 9.1).

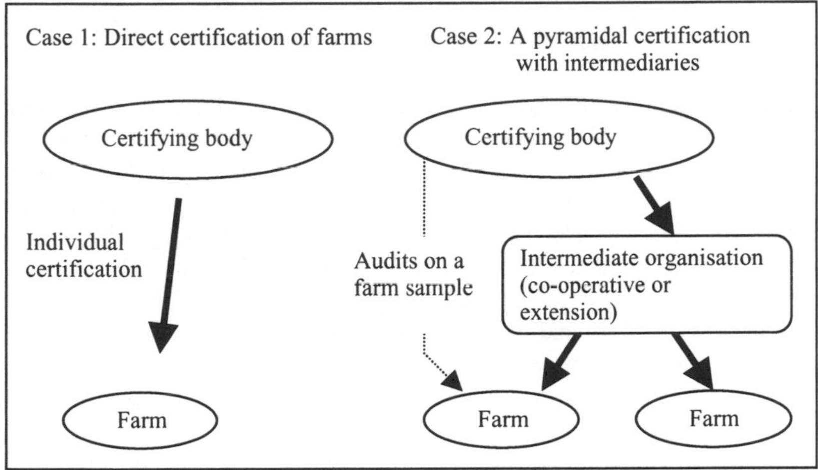

Figure 9.1 Alternative architectures of certification systems in agriculture

In this pyramidal certification system, the original feature is to combine the implementation of quality and environmental management systems in farms with technical support services given to the farmers by an intermediate organisation. The main expected advantage of this pyramidal organisation is to introduce farmers to a collective approach to quality assurance and to organisational improvement, thus reducing the limits of a self-evaluation by the farmer alone, as well as the costs of control and certification. The intermediate organisation is part of the overall management system, and is itself controlled by an independent certification organisation. These intermediate organisations may serve as a support to involve farmers' organisations in a dynamic process of continuous improvement through time. As a matter of fact, in large firms the major organisational innovation set up by these new management systems is mostly based on collective training and 'team groups' in order to prevent product and environmental defects, and hence to develop quality assurance. In the case of farms, these intermediate organisations may perform a similar training function.

Hence, the expected benefits of these management systems for farmers are related to: (i) an improvement in efficiency through a change in the internal organisation of the farm in order to cope with environmental problems and to reduce non-compliance, and (ii) a reduction of monitoring and inspection costs through mutual recognition of control systems by their customers or other inspection services. They also need to define new methodologies or rules in order to involve farmers in this quality spiral, as well as to facilitate collective and individual learning processes for farmers.

3.2 Farmers' Groups as a Support for a Collective Learning Process

Within this general organisation, more specific mechanisms have been implemented to facilitate their appropriation by farmers and to initiate a collective learning process through, for example, the creation of team groups where farmers can exchange experiences. The French programme Quali'Terre[8] has developed some original methodology. The initial motivation of professional organisations was threefold: (i) the adaptation of their regional production to new consumers and retail requirements concerning food safety and environmental concerns, (ii) the introduction of quality assurance systems to as many farmers as possible in their region, and (iii) the development of new methods for farm advisers to facilitate farmers' decision making.

The innovative part of this research programme in Picardie includes: (i) a combination of practice requirements and management systems requirements, but also (ii) new concepts concerning the relationship between adviser and farmer in a mutual learning process. Implementing a quality management system means that farmers have to explicitly define the rules of their technical decisions and their work organisation and formalise the way they will improve their practices regarding quality and environmental requirements. However, these rules of decision are mostly implicit for farmers themselves, making the identification of critical points in their organisation more difficult (Cerf and Hemidy 1999; Papy 2000). A consequence of this situation is that most farmers do not feel the need to take in external advice concerning their work organisation and farm management, even when strong improvement could be expected. These improvements are related here to quality and environmental issues, but they require as a precondition a change in the relationship between farmers and advisers. What is at stake is no longer the delivery of purely technical advice on crop management, for example, but the integration of an organisational diagnosis of the farm as a whole.

Instead of applying the general abstract rules of the ISO system, a progressive approach has been chosen in the Quali'Terre programme, including (i) the definition and application by farmers of general practice requirements according to the specific regional context in Picardie, and (ii) an individual approach to the farm organisation through a 'global diagnosis', including systems requirements, as well as technical and economic aspects. The aim of this two-step approach is to facilitate its implementation by farmers.

– In the first step, the farmers will apply good farming practices concerning food safety, environmental concerns, work safety and data recording for traceability (Figure 9.2). These good farming practices include additional requirements which go beyond the legal minimum standards to be fulfilled in agriculture. They are defined in a way that makes them operational regarding their implementation by farmers and their monitoring by auditors by using operational indicators. Farm audits are regularly made by trained advisers to control the compliance of the farm with the farming practices manual. The global quality of the farm is estimated through three different types of criteria:

(i) Monitoring systems and information support concerning technical practices, and production rules available on the farm, needed to support traceability systems.

(ii) The nature of agricultural practices, evaluated according to four objectives: food safety requirements, environmental specifications, technological quality of products, and farmer's health and security at work.

(iii) The outward image of the farm (cleanliness, outward appearance, integration in the landscape) provides indicators needed to be recognised as a quality agricultural enterprise.

– In a second step, groups of about 5–6 farmers (trained by 1 or 2 farm advisers) will use the PDCA cycle methodology[9] to develop the quality and environmental management systems in their own farms. Required competencies focus not only on the technical skills of farmers, but also on the overall organisation of the production process in farms. Co-operation between farmers and advisers is applied to formulate and to solve the farmers' problems and to develop the quality and environmental management systems. In contrast, organisation of the farming system, as well as labour allocation, stay exclusively under the individual farmer's responsibility. In this way, this organisation of the learning and innovation process based on groups of collaborating farmers may serve as a support for the formalisation of their own organisation patterns and decision-making processes. Figure 9.2 describes the overall organisation of the processing of quality and environmental management systems at the farm level in the Quali'Terre project.

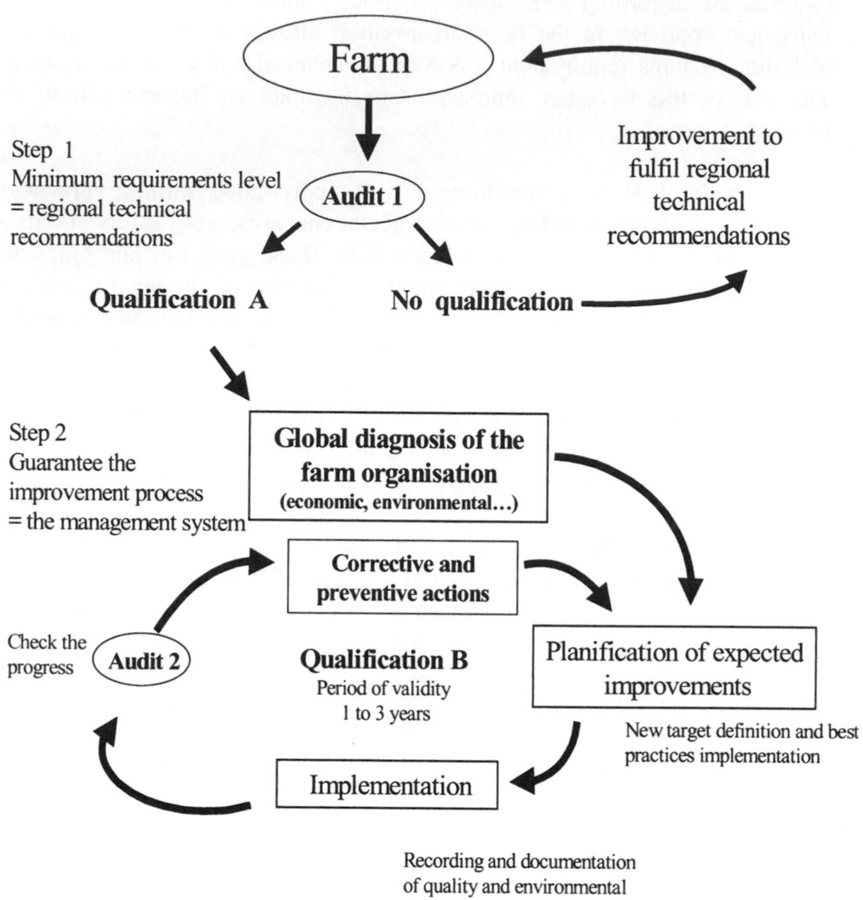

Source: Galan (1999).

Figure 9.2 The implementation of a quality and environmental management system in agriculture

The development of quality and environmental management systems at the farm level will increase the need for new competencies required to provide general advice on the efficiency of farm organisation. As a consequence, the role of advisory services will change. Presently, most advice given to farmers still focuses on specific technical recommendations such as fertilisation, pest management, and so on. For implementing the management systems, agricultural advisers need to acquire deeper knowledge of the rules of organisation used by farmers for their own activity and new methods to identify appropriate improvement targets. What is expected from agricultural advisers is not only highly specialised technical knowledge, but also much more integrative knowledge for defining and achieving, with the farmer, the definition of his own improvement targets. Hence, a change in the relationship between the farmers and their advisers is required. However, more studies are needed to identify and reveal the conditions under which farmers will be prepared to accept formal and informal rules of behaviour on such a voluntary basis.

4 CONTRACT DESIGN AND THE EFFICIENCY OF INFORMATION SYSTEMS

Co-operative strategies to cope with agri-environmental problems are an alternative to strictly mandatory regulations and can increase their effectiveness for a change in farmers practices. However, the question arises whether voluntary measures would not only lead to adequate consumer and environmental protection, but would also be adopted on a large scale by farmers. It is still not answered. Following transaction cost theory, their adoption depends on their capacity to reduce co-ordination costs. Accordingly, we will consider some issues concerning the identification of the quality and environmental management systems that are best suited to the individual constraints of farms (section 4.1), and the consequences of these systems for contract design between farmers and agro-food firms (section 4.2).

4.1 Information Systems: A Global Approach to Farm Organisation

Quality and environmental management systems broaden the scope to include the whole organisation of the farm, instead of one specific production process, as was usually done by the HACCP methodology (Caswell and Hooker 1996). The identification of HACCP in the production process focuses on situations in which hazards can be reliably monitored and controlled, and on a system of verification and documentation to ensure that controls are working effectively. Hence, this methodology is only a first stage in evaluating the overall efficiency of the farmers' organisation and their ability to deal with environmental or quality problems.

On a similar basis, the programme Quali'Terre in France applies this general HACCP methodology. Three quality indicators of farm organisation have been identified: work safety, environmental protection, and traceability.

For each of these quality indicators, various practices of the farmers were classified according to (i) their capacity to prevent risks, (ii) their ease of implementation on the farm, and (iii) the possibilities of third-party control. The good farming practices included in the regional requirements according to environmental or specific quality targets are summarised in Table 9.2.

Table 9.2 Process requirements for good farming practices at the farm level: a multicriteria evaluation

Types of devices	Detailed requirements
General requirements	Land history, adjacent land uses, information recording for technical decisions, worker formation, building and equipment security, waste management, landscape protection
Requirements for crop production	Pest and disease management, fertiliser input diagnosis, manure spreading control, water resources management and irrigation, soil erosion management
Requirements for animal production	Animal identification system for traceability, animal feeding recording, veterinary services, animal welfare, manure management

However, rules of resource allocation inside farms, as well as their organisational patterns, are highly diversified. Farm organisation can vary from a single production activity to very complex decision-making processes.[10] Agronomists and extension service advisers often still take the field as a primary unit for working out technical references and management advice. Recognising the existence of broader domains of management on the farm may help them to understand the needs felt by farmers when looking for decision support. Environmental requirements are not necessarily compatible with specific quality standards laid down by the agro-food industry (for example, barley production may require a high level of fertilisation, which may have harmful effects on water resources). The application of HACCP methodology will not help farmers solve such organisational dilemmas. Alternative decision-making models for farmers which take into account their specific organisational problems are needed for this purpose.

The advantages gained by the implementation of quality and environmental management systems at the farm level regarding these conflicting objectives are twofold. First, the conciliation between such conflicting objectives is realised according to the specific priorities of each farmer at an individual level. Farmers' practices reflect their particular aims and organisational constraints. Understanding the reasons for these practices is now regarded as a necessary step, especially for identifying farm organisation patterns. It is often noted that farmers do not (necessarily) follow the technical advice given by the extension service. This observation is one of the main motivations for farming systems research (Spedding 1975). Second, the farmer must commit himself to adjusting to his customers' requirements.[11] Thus the nature of the trade-off between these conflicting objectives has to be made visible to the customers. This obligation of transparency is based on the design of reliable information systems and on traceability inside the farms.

However, the collection of information about farmers' technical decisions is costly and time consuming with respect to the farmers' other production tasks. Simplification of information systems is a preliminary condition to facilitating the traceability of product specifications and production methods, and hence quality assurance. Recent advances in organisation theory have shown that several activities may compete for a manager's attention, and hence could cause someone to devote too much effort to one task while neglecting another aspect of the job (Holmström and Milgrom 1991). Alternative systems for managing incentives can be defined for the wide array of tasks for which a single farmer may be responsible. Hence, multi-task modelling includes task assignment and specialisation level.

In addition, modelling the diversity of a farm's organisation patterns requires the incorporation of seasonal forces, crop cycle, complementarities between tasks and random events (Allen and Lueck 1999). However, the diversity of farming systems is still mostly introduced as an exogenous variable. By means of a global approach to farm organisation, we are able to take into account these complementarities in task assignment and covariations in alternative incentive instruments (remuneration, monitoring, job design, and so on), as well as the realisation of savings in the collection of information and traceability systems. The design of adequate information systems inside the farm, as well as specific coordination mechanisms with the customers, represents a first way to reduce coordination costs. Another way is to change those coordination mechanisms that govern contractual arrangements between farmers and agro-food firms.

4.2 The Reduction of Co-ordination Costs and the Diversity of Contracts

Adoption of quality and environmental management systems may induce a change in coordination mechanisms between farmers and agro-food firms. Recent studies argue that information asymmetries concerning quality will lead to an increased vertical integration in food sectors (Hennessy 1996). However, no evidence of such a general trend has been reported, even if chain management systems in poultry or hog production, for example, seem to support such a hypothesis. A high diversity of contractual arrangements still remains in agriculture, including spot markets, production contracts and integration contracts. However, the obligation of transparency associated with these quality and environmental management systems may induce a real change in economic behaviour and bargaining positions.

Farmers often perceive these quality and environmental management systems as supplementary constraints, and almost as interference, when they are set up at the request of agro-food firms. But in the last instance, farmers keep the freedom to contract or not to contract depending on the existing commercial alternatives. As shown by transaction cost theory, several economic factors may influence the choice of contract, such as investment in specific assets, the level of uncertainty surrounding the transactions, their frequency or the intensity of specific measurement problems (Williamson 1996). The implementation of quality and environmental management systems at the farm level cannot ignore these economic factors.

In support of this point, the observation of the French programme 'Agri-Confiance®' managed by a co-operative, which is a 'vertical-chain oriented' quality management system, shows the predominance of agricultural production where there were already strongly co-ordinated contractual arrangements.[12] In the case of transactions with agricultural products organised through auction markets, or other relational contracts, such a 'vertical-chain oriented' quality management system seems to remain marginal (Table 9.3). As a consequence, farmers who sell their products through other marketing channels cannot join this type of management system, and they may prefer a global approach to their organisation through the implementation of the usual ISO standards, or similar standards such as in the Danish Kvamilla project or the French Quali'Terre programme. Their choice depends on the complexity of their own organisation (multiplicity of production, several employees, and so on), the specific nature of farming systems used, and the requirements of their specific customers. The implementation of quality and environmental management may follow different pathways.

However, recent advances in economic contract theories suggest that their adoption will result in the ability of firms to reduce co-ordination costs and to adjust their own organisation to this new context. Therefore, instead of a change in the contract form between farmers and their customers, one may expect an adaptation of the co-ordination mechanisms chosen by the firm to collect information, as well as to advise or monitor their suppliers. One major obstacle met by the Kvamilla project in the early 1990s was to establish a connection with agro-food firms and to obtain their recognition of the farmers' efforts for implementing these quality management systems (Gottlieb 1997).

Table 9.3 *The development of the Agri-Confiance® management system in France according to the type of production*

	Milk	Wine	Cereals (durum wheat, barley)	Chicken	Forestry	Maize seeds	Total
Co-op. involved	2	2	3	2	2	1	12
No. of producers	176-	339	1913	272	21	350	3071
Production	52 Mio l	1457 ha	27000 ha	-	-	-	

Source: Castet (1997).

Efficiency gains are primarily achieved by economising on transaction costs. Through mutual recognition of the management systems by firms, the aim is to reduce quality control and monitoring costs, as well as to reduce repetitive data collection in order to guarantee the traceability of information. Agro-food firms deliver a large part of the technical advice about herd or crop management directly to the farmers, regardless of extension services. The implementation of quality and environmental management systems creates a need for new forms of advice concerning organisational patterns in farms, and the design of adequate information systems.

This may be achieved by agro-food firms through a change in the organisation of their buying departments and the human resources devoted to providing technical advice to farmers. However, the delegation of some tasks in monitoring and advising farmers must be compatible with the objectives and the organisation of agro-food firms. This need for adaptation also applies to the organisation of extension services, and the definition of new forms of services to farmers, including quality controls at the farm level, organisational advice, and so on. In contrast to other countries, advisory services in France are provided through several competing channels. For the advisory services it is important to look for adequate concepts in general advice to farmers (economic, environmental), and to reorganise their activities around alternative functions such as monitoring and advice. These two functions (advising, auditing) must be separate in order to guarantee the credibility of the implementation of these quality and environmental management systems.

5 CONCLUSION

Voluntary management systems that focus on quality and the environment (based on ISO 9000 and 14000) are expected to gain importance in the future. They will, to a large extent, depend on the codification and on the increased transparency of the organisational rules and decision-making processes applied by farmers. Current research on farming systems and decision-making processes in farms may contribute to the codification process. In contrast to other concepts used for quality management (for example the HACCP method), the main innovation is the introduction of a comprehensive approach to the organisation of the farm, instead of considering each branch of production separately. Farms are usually multiproduct firms, inducing interactions between the production areas. The design of models of organisation that structure the farmer's own conception of his activities is required.

Most of the research on decision-making processes in farms includes the identification of the economic, psychological and environmental factors that influence farmers' decisions. It is usually based on case studies or quantitative models which lead to a ranking of these factors (Papy 2000). Further efforts are necessary to develop comprehensive models of decision making which can be instrumental in improving the organisational concepts farmers use, and hence their ability to achieve specific quality or environmental objectives. Agricultural production remains a highly unpredictable and variable multiproduct activity, and there is still a large number of small family farms. For these reasons, the connection between farming systems studies and modern theories of the firm may be useful in identifying the economic factors affecting the efficiency of the prevailing agricultural production systems.

Unfortunately, most agricultural economists have not subjected their insights regarding seasonal production phases, crop cycles, task specialisation and random events to interpretations provided by modern theories of the firm (Allen and Lueck 1999). Integrating these two traditions, that is, developing an economic model of farm organisation on which research on farming systems can be based, may help to deepen our knowledge of decision-making processes on farms and their capacity to guarantee the reliability of information that will, at the end of the chain, be presented to consumers.

The adoption of quality assurance or environmental management systems is also dependent upon the organisational design that supports them. In this chapter, we have identified three different organisational levels where a reduction of co-ordination costs may be expected through the implementation of these management systems, that is, the inside organisation of the farm, the inter-firm relationships, and the design of the certification process. More specifically, our analysis demonstrates that collective organisation of farmers may serve as a support mechanism for the implementation of these management systems. Hence, the implementation of the international ISO standard at the farm level cannot only be conceived of as a simple transfer of the normative rules applied in other industrial sectors, but requires the development of co-operative institutions.

NOTES

1. Thanks to J. Mousset and C. Aubry for their strong participation at the initial step of this programme. Part of this programme benefits from the financial support of the Conseil Régional de Picardie.
2. The economic literature introduces a distinction between three types of standards depending on their functions: (i) minimum quality standards, (ii) reference standards, (iii) compatibility standards (David and Greenstein 1990). ISO standards on management systems could also be included in compatibility standards, making the inspection of their organisation easier for customers or a certifying body.
3. This research demonstrates that farmers are often using some representative parcels or animals, instead of considering each one individually, as a reference in making technical decisions (fertilisation, and so on). Hence, the way the bundling of parcels and animals is realised influences the accuracy of this information. Another point is that information from monitoring and processing systems is highly diversified depending on customers' requirements, and on the farmer's own work organisation (field operation records, technical information synthesis, traceability worksheets required by agro-food firms, and so on).
4. Several concepts have been developed which support an improvement of process regarding customer orientation or environmental concern. A distinction is made between: (i) a comprehensive approach with the concept of Total Quality Management; (ii) a quality management based on anticipation; and (iii) the concepts of Quality (for example environmental) Management Systems based on quality assurance, like the ISO 9000 standard. It must be stated that these ISO standards will, in the future, include continuous process improvement.
5. The dissipation of rent through oversearching behaviour or excessive measurement has been analysed in other contexts by Barzel (1982) and Kenney and Klein (1983), among others. They focus on both the design of pre-contractual mechanisms used to screen and sort products according to their quality, and ex post enforcement mechanisms.
6. This programme Quali'Terre was developed at the beginning of 1997 at the initiative of the three Local Advisory Centres of the region of Picardie (Northern France). Extension at the national level is now beginning.
7. This approach may be interpreted as a collective certification. However, it is not. The certification involves the individual responsibility of the farmer. The original point is to combine advising farmers in the implementation of these management systems and monitoring systems included in a third-party certification. In fact, such a certification system is already used for product certification, like Protected Denomination (PDO), or the 'Label Rouge' system in France, where an intermediate collective organisation of producers is involved in the global certification organisation (Raynaud and Sauvée 1999).
8. This programme is still at an experimental phase. The first step focuses on the definition of general practice requirements following a Hazard Analysis and Critical Control Points (HACCP) methodology and according to specific regional problems. A second step has

started during Winter 1999–2000 with the realisation of audits (level I) and the introduction of the quality and environmental system (level II) to 30 farms. The objective is to involve about 3000 farms in step 1 in the region Picardie for 2005.

9. This methodology will be included in the modified ISO 9000 standard in 2000, converging towards the ISO 14000 standard. This PDCA cycle is organised through four steps in which the farmers have to (i) define and plan the actions that need to be realised (Plan), (ii) apply and record realised actions in order to give the proof of what has been done to a third party (Do), (iii) verify and control what was planned and check the progress (Check), and (iv) implement corrective action, as defined by needed improvements (Act). This second step is realised with the support of trained local advisers.
10. The farmer's decision-making process has to cope with several dimensions. On every farm, and every year, it occupies many fields that may vary widely in terms of soil type and preceding crop. It requires a large number of technical operations per field (7 to 11 for wheat management alone). On most arable farms, other crops sown in spring and harvested in the autumn (like sugar beet, potatoes, or maize) require work or natural resources (irrigation, fields without specific plant disease during the preceding crops) that are partly competing for labour or equipment (Aubry et al. 1998).
11. Investigations show that farms which have several employees and highly diversified production or which are involved in direct-to-consumer sales have more incentives to use these management systems in order to give increased assurance to their customers regarding the quality of their own organisation, resulting in a higher net value.
12. They mostly include specialised production such as barley production for breweries, durum wheat for pasta, and chicken and milk production, where the bilateral dependency between producers and dairy firms is strong.

REFERENCES

Allen, D. and D. Lueck (1999), 'The Nature of the Farm', *Journal of Law and Economics*, **61**, pp. 343–86.

Aubry, C., F. Papy and A. Capillon (1998), 'Designing Decision-Making Processes for Annual Crop Management', *Agricultural Systems*, **56** (1), pp. 45–65.

Barzel, Y. (1982), 'Measurement Cost and the Organization of Markets', *Journal of Law and Economics*, **25**, pp. 27–48.

Castet, R. (1999), 'Agriconfiance: le seul programme de mise sous Assurance-Qualité de l'amont agricole', in Lagrande, L. (ed.), *Signes Officiels de Qualité et Développement Agricole*, Paris: TECDOC, pp. 313–19.

Caswell, J.A. and N.H. Hooker (1996), 'HACCP as an International Trade Standard', *American Journal of Agricultural Economics*, **78** (3), pp. 775–79.

Cerf, M. and L. Hemidy (1999), 'Designing Support to Enhance Co-operation between Farmers and Advisers in Solving Farm Management Problems', *Journal of Agricultural Education and Extension*, **6** (3), pp.157–70.

David, P.A. and S. Greenstein (1990), 'The Economics of Compatibility of Standards: An Introduction to Recent Research', *Economics of Innovation and New Technology*, **1**, pp. 1–32.

Galan, M.B. (1999): 'La certification des exploitations agricoles en Picardie', Working Paper, Mimeo, Agro-Transfert, France.

Gottlieb, Ch. (1997), 'Quality and Environmental Management Systems on Sixty Danish Farms', in Schiefer, R. and R. Kühl (eds), *Quality Management and Process Improvement for Competitive Advantage in Agriculture and Food*, Proceedings, EAAE Seminar, University of Bonn, Germany.

Grolleau, G. (1998), 'La norme environnementale ISO 14001 est-elle applicable à l'exploitation agricole?', *Ingénieries EAT*, **14**, pp. 69–79.

Haes, U.H. de and G.R. de Snoo (1997), 'Environmental Management in the Agricultural Production-Consumption Chain', *International Journal of LCA*, **2** (1), pp. 33–38.

Helbig, R. (1997), 'Quality and Environmental Management Systems on Sixty Danish Farms', in *Quality Management and Process Improvement for Competitive Advantage in Agriculture and Food*, Proceedings of the 49th EAAE Seminar, Bonn: University of Bonn.

Hennessy, D. (1995), 'Microeconomics of Agricultural Grading: Impacts on the Marketing Channel', *American Journal of Agricultural Economics*, **77**, pp. 980–89.

Hennessy, D. (1996), 'Information Asymmetry as a Reason for Food Vertical Integration', *American Journal of Agricultural Economics*, **78**, pp. 1034–43.

Henson, S. and J. Caswell (1999), 'Food Safety Regulation: an Overview of Contemporary Issues', *Food Policy*, **24**, pp. 589–603.

Holmström, B. and P. Milgrom (1991), 'Multi-Task Principal–Agent Analysis: Incentives Contracts, Asset Ownership and Job Design', *Journal of Law, Economics and Organisation*, **7**, pp. 24–52.

Ingrand, S., B. Dedieu, C. Chassing and E. Josien (1993), 'Etudes des pratiques d'allottement dans les exploitations d'élevage', *Etudes et Recherches sur les Systèmes Agraires et le Developpement*, **27**, pp. 53–72.

Kenney, K. and B. Klein (1983), 'The Economics of Block-Booking', *Journal of Law and Economics*, **26**, pp. 497–540.

Papy, F. (2000), 'Farm Models and Decision Support. A Summary Review', in Colin, J.P., E. Crawford and C. Fillonneau (eds), *Research Methodology for Agricultural Systems Analysis*, Boulder: Lynne Rienner, USA.

Papy, F., J.M. Attonaty, C. Laporte and L.G. Soler (1988), 'Work Organisation Simulation as a Basis for Farm Management Advice', *Agricultural Systems*, **27**, pp. 295–314.

Raynaud, E. and L. Sauvée (1999), 'Common Labeling and Producer's Organisation: A Transaction Cost Economics Approach', Paper presented at EAAE Seminar 'The Socio-economics of Origin of Labelled Products in Agro-Food Supply Chain', October, 28–30, 1999, Le Mans, France.

Schiefer, G. (1997), 'Total Quality Management and Process Improvement: some Issues', in Schiefer, R. and R. Kühl (eds), *Quality Management and Process Improvement for Competitive Advantage in Agriculture and Food*, Bonn: University of Bonn, Germany.

Spedding, C. (1975), 'The Study of Agricultural Systems', in Dalton, G.E. (ed.), *Study of Agricultural Systems*, London: Applied Science Publishers, pp. 3–19.

Spiller, P. and B. Zelner (1997), 'Product Complementarities, Capabilities and Governance: a Dynamic Transaction Cost Perspective', *Industrial and Corporate Change*, **6** (3), pp. 561–94.

Valceschini, E. and A. Mazé (2000), 'La politique de la qualité agro-alimentaire dans le contexte international', *Economie Rurale*, **258** (juillet–aout), pp. 30–42.

Williamson, O. (1996), *The Mechanism of Governance*, New York: Oxford University Press.

PART IV

Implementation of Agri-environmental Policies as an Issue of Collective Action

10. How to Provide for Environmental Attributes in Rural Landscapes: Theoretical Analysis of Different Institutional Arrangements[1]

Christian Lippert

1 INTRODUCTION

The agri-environmental programmes first adopted under the framework of EU Regulation No. 2078/92 consist mainly in paying cost-covering premiums to farmers for certain precisely defined measures or farming practices (actions) which are supposed to promote environmental objectives. In contrast, in Germany the Council of Experts at the Federal Ministry of Environment repeatedly suggested granting payments based on the ecological results delivered (RSU 1994, p. 318; RSU 1996, p. 404). This contribution deals with the question of under what conditions such a result-related remuneration seems to be preferable and who (farmers, specialised organisations, co-operatives) might be the appropriate recipients.

After a short outline of some general institutional economics aspects (section 2), the relevance of these theoretical aspects to the provision for environmental attributes (that is, characteristics of goods or resources) is studied (section 3). Finally, some examples for useful remuneration modalities for different environmental attributes will be given in section 4.

2 AN INSTITUTIONAL ECONOMICS CONCEPT

In the following, an institutional economics approach (Barzel 1989; North 1990) which stresses the allocative effects of the costs of measuring and monitoring is applied to the problem of providing environmental goods in agricultural landscapes. According to the theory, various profitable attributes are connected to every asset (good or resource).[2] The 'production costs' of these attributes consist not only in (opportunity) costs of inputs but also in transaction costs for the definition, protection and enforcement of the corresponding property rights.

In general, the property rights related to a certain attribute are defined and assigned to a private owner (or to the state) only when the transaction costs for their enforcement do not exceed the profits which may be derived from the attribute. Because of elevated measurement and monitoring costs there are always some attributes of a certain asset the rights of which are not delineated, so that these attributes remain in the public domain (so-called 'free attributes') (Barzel 1989, pp. 1, 64; North 1990, p. 29). In the course of time new property rights are delineated (whereas others are released to the public domain) for the following reasons:

- The enforcement costs are now covered by a higher appreciation of a formerly 'free' attribute. (In the recent past this seems to have been the case for several environmental attributes, which explains the extension of nature reserves and national parks.)
- The enforcement costs have declined in a way that it becomes profitable to establish ownership over the attribute in question.

The economically efficient distribution of the property rights related to the (enforceable) attributes of an asset depends on who is most able to vary (to provide or to improve) the different attributes. The person most inclined to manipulate a certain attribute should – and in the case of existing markets will – finally become the residual claimant to the attributes' outcome. This person would increase his efforts as long as his additional opportunity costs did not exceed the corresponding increase in value of the attribute (North 1990, p. 30; Barzel 1989, pp. 36, 41).

Due to specialisation and scale effects this implies so called 'divided ownership' of the attributes of an asset, which means that different parties will hold property rights to different attributes of the same asset (North 1981, pp. 23, 26). In the past this has been particularly relevant to agricultural land (for example compulsory cultivation; water and irrigation management). The extension of 'divided ownership' is only restricted by increasing enforcement costs (North 1990, p. 33). It should be noted that, especially in the case of environmental attributes, (spatial) scale effects may occur.

Sometimes the value of an attribute will be significantly influenced by two or even more contracting parties, without the possibility of monitoring at low costs the efforts of each party (in other words to determine who is responsible for a change in outcome). When two or more inputs (to be more precise: attributes of inputs) are necessary to produce a good (attribute), an incentive problem between the different parties involved arises, similar to the question of optimal land and labour contracts in agriculture (Barzel 1989, p. 31).

Here the different inputs are land and labour attributes. When considerable monitoring costs (for the respective efforts) on the one hand, and opportunistic behaviour on the other hand, are very likely, this leads to a principal–agent relationship. Under these conditions and if the outcome is variable, different contractual arrangements are possible: wage contract, tenancy contract, 'sole ownership' (of all inputs) and sharecropping.[3] Each of these ideal-type arrangements shows typical advantages and disadvantages:

(1a) (Fixed) wage contract: The tiller gets a fixed wage for his labour. This may result in reduced labour efforts and opportunistic behaviour ('shirking') unless the principal (landlord) takes costly(!) monitoring measures. The landlord is the residual claimant to an increase in efforts.

(2a) (Fixed) tenancy contract: Here the tenant must monitor the efforts of the landlord, who is specialised in improving soil quality. The tenant is the residual claimant to an increase in efforts.

(b) Sole ownership by one party: In the presence of high monitoring costs for the enforcement of labour attributes as well as for soil-related attributes (and given a high variability of these attributes), sole ownership of all necessary inputs might be the best solution (that is, the landlord himself is the tiller). The disadvantage of this arrangement consists in the loss of potential gains from specialisation and/or scale effects.

(c) Sharecropping: This system – where the landlord and the tenant share the yield (as the result of their common efforts) – has the advantage of enabling the different parties to specialise and may therefore be the most efficient solution – at least if varying payments according to the quality of the inputs are not possible for the reason of high monitoring costs. The disadvantage of the sharecropping system compared to 'sole ownership' results from the distortions of marginal partial (land and labour) productivities. (Here the share rate works like a tax rate.) Thus both parties will undertake less effort (until their respective marginal productivities equal the opportunity costs of their inputs) than in the sole ownership case.

Thus, which of the contractual arrangements outlined above should be preferred depends on the variability of the respective inputs and on the corresponding enforcement costs (that is, the costs at which the attributes of the diverse inputs can be monitored).

3 THE RELEVANCE OF THE CONCEPT FOR THE IMPROVEMENT OF ENVIRONMENTAL ATTRIBUTES

In the following the multitude of environmental and landscape-related attributes of agricultural areas are of particular interest. The capability of land to satisfy an environmental function (see de Groot 1992, p. 13) (for example to serve as a habitat for certain endangered animal or plant species) will be called an environmental attribute.

One conclusion from the theory expounded above is that the different agricultural and environmental attributes of an area (or CCAs, see note 2) must not necessarily be controlled by the same person. This is all the more so as – due to gains from specialisation and spatial scale effects – in many cases the different agricultural and environmental attributes' values are expected to be optimised by distinct persons or organisations, which leads to 'divided ownership'. This means that the property rights to agricultural attributes of farmland will be held by farmers whereas the environmental attributes may finally be in the hands of a person or organisation that operates on a larger (area) scale than the farmers ('nature agent').

In this connection, particularly interesting environmental attributes of an area are groundwater quality, accessibility, landscape amenity, but also attributes like biodiversity or suitability as a habitat for particular species. The following sections deal with (i) remuneration modalities concerning the payment for the provision for such attributes, and (ii) the question of who might best provide for them (farmer, 'nature agent', or both together).

3.1 Remuneration Modalities

The transaction costs (here: costs of enforcing the property rights) occurring in providing and transferring environmental attributes are closely related to the specific remuneration modality chosen in paying for an environmental attribute. In the following, three kinds of transaction costs are distinguished:[4]

- costs of excluding (exclusion costs), that is, costs incurred when an attribute is traded within markets (which is necessarily result related and works only if the costs of excluding third parties from consumption are not prohibitive[5]).
- costs of measuring (measurement costs), that is, costs incurred when result-related payments are granted by the state (in this case costs of measuring the attribute in question – the output – must be sufficiently low).

- costs of monitoring, that is, costs incurred when certain – environment improving – actions are remunerated (in this case monitoring of inputs becomes necessary).

(1) Provided that the sum of 'production costs' (including opportunity costs) and costs of excluding other users ('consumers') is significantly below the (expected) value of an environmental attribute, private ownership seems to be the best solution. That means remuneration will sooner or later occur within markets (automatically according to the results of the providers' 'efforts').
(2) On the other hand, when the sum of production costs and costs of excluding other consumers is significantly higher than the (expected) value of the attribute, there will be no measures to provide for it at all or its provision will be promoted by a territorial authority, if at least its production costs are less than the corresponding value. In the latter case there are two possibilities:

(2.I) Costs of excluding are prohibitive but costs of measuring the output are low. Then a result-related remuneration by the state of the person or organisation improving the environment will be preferable.

(2.II) Costs of excluding as well as costs of measuring are prohibitive. In such a situation – and given a close relationship between certain cultivation measures (farming practices) and the expected (environmental) outcome – fixed payments for well defined actions should be given to the farmers. As long as the expected value of the relevant environmental attributes exceeds the sum of production and corresponding monitoring costs, contracts should be concluded with farmers, specifying the necessary actions. That means that then (and only then) a solution similar to the present payments made under EEC Regulation No. 2078/92 would be useful.

Thus, payments varying according to the results of environmental improvement are useful when the value of the attributes concerned can be measured at justifiable costs. As long as this is not possible, the production of environmental attributes which are of high value to society should be induced by granting cost-covering payments for suitable farming practices or services.[6]

In other words, whether an 'action-related' remuneration (entailing monitoring costs) or a result-related one (entailing measurement costs) of agri-environmental improvement should be chosen must be decided by considering the respective amount of the different kinds of transaction costs under the possible institutional arrangements. An important condition for the – often demanded – 'result-related payment solution' is the relatively low costs of measuring the 'results'.

The following considerations start from a point of view where a result-related remuneration seems to be useful.

3.2 Provision for Environmental Attributes by Whom?

When payments based on the results of environmental improvement seem to be useful (because of a high value of the attributes as well as moderate measuring costs) *and* when specialisation and scale effects can be expected, introduction of a so-called 'nature agent' should be considered, who has to be the 'residual claimant' to the outcome of his efforts. The main idea (see Lippert et al. 1999, p. 110) is represented in Figure 10.1: the nature agent purchases from the different owners (O_j) the property rights to 'inputs' (z_i) which he needs in order to improve the environment. Other inputs (to be more precise: attributes which are inputs for the production of environmental attributes) whose property rights have not yet been delineated may be taken from the 'public domain' (for example z_4 in Figure 10.1). By combining these inputs he produces 'his' environmental attribute(s) and puts it (them) at the disposal of the consumers. He is paid by the latter either directly (if costs of excluding are low, that is, the Coase solution) or indirectly via the appropriate territorial authority (if excluding third parties from consumption is impossible, that is, the Pigou solution).

The notion of inputs here covers a wide range of possible productive factors. They can be different labour qualities (more or less skilled, with or without engines), ecological know-how or different attributes of agricultural land like nutrient contents in soil or the kind of land utilisation (for example intensities, arable or grassland farming, the kind and time of tillage or time of mowing). The nature agent pays a compensation to the respective owner for the ceding of the property rights to these inputs for environmental improvement. The amount of this compensation depends on the opportunity costs of the acquired inputs.[7]

The functioning of this organisation is similar to that of the 'Conservation, Recreation and Amenity Trusts (CARTs)' described by Hodge (1988, p. 371; 1991, p. 191): a CART

> can fully determine the form of land use, either by directly managing the land itself or through a tenancy which includes clauses defining the appropriate requirements. It can then select the appropriate management which will generally involve some trade-off between agricultural income and countryside benefits. Because the CART represents the residual claimant and to the extent that it values all benefits, it faces the full opportunity costs of its actions. (Hodge 1988, p. 371)

In particular, some attributes related to a wider area (for example biodiversity, see below) may be influenced in equal shares by different parties, each contributing to environmental improvement (similar to the example of the variation of agricultural output given above).

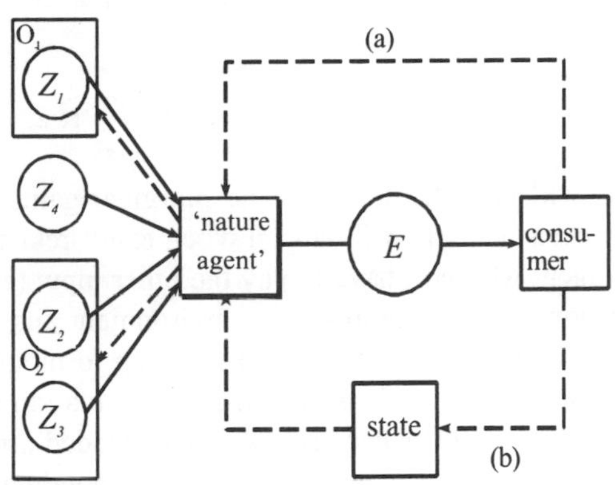

Notes:

E = Value of the provided environmental attribute

Z_i = Amount of input i used for the production of the environmental attribute

O_i = Owner of the inputs Z_i

Bold arrows: transfer of property rights; broken line arrows: payments.

(a) Coase solution.

(b) Pigou solution.

Source: Lippert (1999, p. 423).

Figure 10.1 Provision for an environmental attribute by a nature agent (example)

The following simplified profit function f for an environmental attribute serves to illustrate the two possible remuneration solutions arising in this context (see Lippert 1999):

$$\text{(E1)} \qquad f = E\,(z_1; z_2) - w_1\, z_1 - w_2\, z_2 \;\; \text{max!}$$

$$\text{with } \partial E/\partial z_i > 0; \quad \partial^2 E/(\partial z_i)^2 < 0; \quad i = 1; 2.$$

As in Figure 10.1, E stands for the environmental attribute's (assumed) value, which has to be optimised. E is a function of two different inputs z_1 and z_2; the wage rates w_i are the corresponding opportunity costs per unit of input *i*. The partial marginal productivities $\partial E/\partial z_i$ are supposed to be positive and decrease with the amount of input units (z_i) used.

The first remuneration solution, which we call the 'sole ownership case', corresponds to the cases (a) and (b) in section 2. It is characterised by the equations

$$\text{(E2)} \qquad \partial E/\partial z_i = w_i; \quad i = 1; 2.$$

Both inputs will be extended until the marginal gains $\partial E/\partial z_i$ will equal the opportunity costs w_i. This will happen when result-related payments are given to a nature agent who will have to pay the other input (z_2) necessary – besides his own efforts (z_1) – to improve the environment and when the other input (for example a certain kind of labour) is cheap to monitor (corresponding to the cases (a) in section 2). This is similar to a situation where the problem of monitoring does not occur because all inputs needed are owned by one party (therefore called the sole ownership case, corresponding to case (b) in section 2).

However, considering some environmental attributes, sole ownership by one person or cheap monitoring have to be excluded. So the conditions for birds brooding on grassland are equally influenced at the farm level (by the time of mowing and the care taken by the farmer) as well as on a wider spatial scale (for example when improving habitat patch connectivity). Both activities are difficult to monitor.

Such a situation – when prohibitively high monitoring costs for both inputs (z_1 and z_2) have to be faced and solution (b) does not seem possible – leads to the second solution, which is to pay shares (here αE and $(1 - \alpha) E$) of the realised attributes' value (E) to the parties involved. This corresponds to the 'sharecropping case' in the classification of land and labour contracts (case (c) in section 2) and means that a nature agent operating on a large area scale and the farmers would both be given result-related pay. But compared to the sole ownership case and given decreasing marginal productivities $\partial E/\partial z_i$ there will be a loss in efficiency which results from the distortions of the marginal productivities by α and $1 - \alpha$ respectively:

$$\text{(E3)} \qquad \partial E/\partial z_1 = w_1/\alpha \quad \wedge \quad \partial E/\partial z_2 = w_2/(1 - \alpha)$$

with $0 < \alpha < 1$; α = share of the attribute's value paid to agent 1; $1 - \alpha$ = share paid to agent 2 (i = 1; 2 here refers to two inputs owned by different agents).

The problem occurring here is a prisoner's dilemma: each party knows that the other party will extend his efforts (that is, increase his input z_i) until the equations (E3) hold, so that a Nash equilibrium will be reached. But from a further increase of input z_1 the other party could take unfair advantage by not increasing his input z_2 or vice versa.

A way out of this dilemma could be sole ownership by an organisation. In this sense sole ownership would imply that every member of a nature agent organisation is motivated to such a degree that monitoring becomes unnecessary. (Given mutual trust everybody will extend his efforts until his marginal gains ($\partial E/\partial z_i$) will equal his opportunity costs w_i.) Result-related payments are granted to the organisation that distributes them to its members according, at the least, to the amount of their opportunity costs.

Thus if it is rather expensive to monitor all agents (nature agent, farmers) involved in the production of the attributes in question, these attributes may best be provided by a co-operative nature agent as long as his members are sufficiently committed to environmental improvement and as long as there is mutual trust (that is, sole ownership of the corresponding inputs). The second best solution would be to share the yield from improving the attributes among the different agents.

4 EXAMPLES FOR DIFFERENT REMUNERATION MODALITIES

When choosing how environmental attributes will be provided it should first be examined whether an exclusion of consumers is possible at sufficiently low costs. In such cases the environmental attribute in question is suggested to be brought about by market co-ordination (for example the attributes of golf courses).

Second, given the impossibility (or inefficiency) of excluding 'consumers' and taking into account the respective monitoring and measurement costs related to the provision for a certain environmental attribute, it should be thoroughly examined which form of remuneration is most appropriate (fixed payments to the farmers for certain practices or services versus variable payments based on the attribute delivered to the farmers and/or a nature agent).

Then the question arises who – apart from the agriculture-related attributes which are obviously best managed (varied) by the farmers – should provide for, or improve, the environmental attributes of agricultural landscapes: (i) a specialised organisation (nature agent), (ii) farmers, or (iii) a co-operative consisting of farmers and environmental experts? In other words and in the case of payments based on the attribute delivered: who should be the residual claimant to the different attributes' values? The first arrangement leads to divided ownership, the latter two induce different forms of sole ownership of agricultural and environmental attributes.

Table 10.1 shows some selected attributes (examples, without aiming at completeness!) and tries to outline their relevant provision-related characteristics such as measurability (second column) and costs of excluding from consumption (third column). Here the attributes of a golf course (quality of the green, site, and so on) are an obvious example for high attribute values which justify elevated exclusion costs (fences, guardians, and so on). This is not the case as far as the attribute 'landscape amenity' is concerned because, in general, people would not pay enough entrance fees to cover the corresponding enforcement costs.

The fourth column gives some remarks related to possible gains from scale and specialisation effects. Optimal specialisation concerning traditional farming activities (including specialised extension services) is suggested to be brought about by market mechanisms. Particularly interesting are spatial scale effects when optimal area sizes related to distinct attributes differ.

Finally, we try to specify the remuneration modality which seems to be most suitable (fifth column): remuneration within markets (1), result-related remuneration (2.I) or fixed payments for precisely defined actions by a local authority (2.II). Further, considering the 'measurable' farmland attributes mentioned in the table which have the character of a public good, the question of who might be the most appropriate residual claimant to its improvement and should consequently be the recipient of result-related payments (institutional arrangements (a), (b, c), see footnote of the table) may be asked. Here the modalities which seem to be preferable 'at first sight' are given. Sometimes the preference of the modality indicated is obvious. In other cases further investigation should be undertaken. It should be stressed that the contents of Table 10.1 are not the final results of thorough case studies but first (intuitive) reflections, which may be discussed and modified later, serving to illustrate the institutional economics concept applied here. Furthermore, it should be noted that some environmental attributes may be linked closely, which we have neglected in order to keep analysis simple. Moreover, the following remarks should be added with respect to the farmland attributes contained in Table 10.1:

- Cropping capacity and soil structure: for the improvement of these attributes the farmer is paid either indirectly (by higher agricultural yields) or directly within the land market.
- Landscape amenity: as long as it is plainly agreed upon that landscape amenity is improved, for example when planting single trees or hedges, this attribute mostly depends on the efforts (know-how, care) of *one* agent. Then this agent should preferably be paid for it based on

Table 10.1 Characteristics of selected land attributes and corresponding payment modalities

Attribute	Measurability	Possibility of excluding from consumption	Scale and specialisation effects	Payment to ...; preferable remuneration modality [*]
Cropping capacity	Is given at relatively low costs (soil analysis)	At low costs (under the institutional conditions in Europe)	Often exhausted (depending on farm size and farmers' know-how)	Farmers; (1)
Soil structure	(?)	At low costs (see cropping capacity)	See cropping capacity	Farmers; (1)
Golf course attributes	Attempts (guides describing the qualities of the courses)	At significant costs (fences etc.) but justified by the value	In practice probably exhausted	The golf club; (1)
Landscape amenity	Possible at low costs	Only at prohibitive costs not to be covered by entrance fees	Considerable	Nature agent; (2.I), (a)
Biodiversity	Attempts (Shannon index etc.)	Only at prohibitive costs	Inevitable, not to provide for at farm size level	Co-operative or nature agent *and* farmers; (2.I), (b, c) or (2.II)
Suitability as habitat for a certain species	Possible (e.g. counting individuals of a species)	Only at prohibitive costs	Inevitable, not to provide for at farm size level	Nature agent, co-operative or nature agent *and* farmers; (2.I), (a) or (b, c)

Table 10.1 (continued)

Groundwater quality	Depending on farm size and on the watershed area	(?)	Considerable	Farmers; (2.II) (?)
Pollination by insects	Impossible	Only at prohibitive costs	Considerable	Beekeepers; (2.II)

Notes:

(*) Here the respective remuneration modality which seems to be preferable at first sight is indicated by a symbol corresponding to those used in section 3. Sometimes the preference of the indicated modality is evident. In other cases further investigation should be undertaken. The meaning of the symbols is as follows:

(1) remuneration within markets;

(2.I) result-related remuneration by a local authority;

(2.II) fixed payments for precisely defined actions (contracts between providers and a local authority specifying the necessary actions have to be concluded);

(a) environmental attribute influenced by different parties, nevertheless the value of its improvement should be paid to one specialised agent;

(b, c) environmental attribute considerably influenced by different parties; the value of its improvement should be paid to a co-operative (sole ownership of all inputs needed) or, in the case that this solution seems impossible, should be paid to a specialised agent *and* to farmers at proportionate shares.

the principle of 'attribute delivered'. It is true that besides the planning nature agent the attribute is influenced by many other persons (needed for planting, and so on) but these are supposed to be monitored at relatively low costs. When the state grants a fixed premium for every new hectare of hedges in an area, a nature agent might be brought about by markets.

- Biodiversity: this attribute is certainly influenced by various parties. With regard to the complex ecological relationships the fixed payment solution (2.II) here seems to be less appropriate because of high monitoring costs and because of the insecurity concerning the actions actually needed in an area. But to apply the other solution (2.I) biodiversity (and its value) has to be measured. Thus, in recent years many attempts have been made to assess this environmental attribute.[8] Furthermore, result-related payments to (small size) farmers turn out to be inefficient because normally one farmer has only a little influence upon this attribute (see Lippert 1999, p. 424).
- Suitability as habitat for a certain species: an improvement of this attribute consists, for example, in protecting and/or connecting the habitats of endangered birds or beavers. This attribute is easier to measure than biodiversity (for example by counting individuals of a species) but it is normally also influenced by different parties. In this context, one large area scale objective is to improve the habitat patch connectivity, while at farm size level appropriate farming practices have to be applied. Which institutional arrangement is most suitable has to be decided upon from case to case and depends on the species considered. In Bavaria the concept of 'beaver management' has been successfully introduced (Schwab 1999). One important function of the 'beaver manager' (a single person acting in a defined region) consists in developing and implementing solutions for conflicts between farming and beaver protection at minimum social costs.
- Groundwater quality: in general this is influenced by many different parties. The measurement costs of the attribute delivered by one party depend on the structure of farm size as well as on the natural conditions (see note 6). At present in Germany, local authorities often pay for certain farming practices, supposed to improve groundwater quality. It should be added that remuneration can take place only when property rights related to groundwater attributes have been assigned to the farmers.
- Pollination by insects: it is quite obvious that a premium per flower pollinated would entail extraordinary transaction costs. If pollinators become scarce (for example to an extent that fruit-growing farms may

be harmed) it would be better to pay for beehives to be put up in the area in question.

Obviously, which payment modality should be chosen depends on the relative weight of the advantages and disadvantages of the options compared. Fixed payments for defined actions entail monitoring costs (or the possibility of shirking) as well as the risk that the relationship between the actions and the expected results will be insufficient. Payments according to the result, on the other hand, may imply the introduction of a nature agent, otherwise there would be a significant loss of specialisation gains. Potential gains from specialisation and scale effects have to be compared to the transaction costs involved in the development of such an organisation (see Lippert and Rittershofer 1997, p. 205).[9]

A co-operative solution is advantageous if, on the one hand, important spatial scale effects have to be expected and if, on the other hand, the farmers involved possess a large endogenous potential of environmental knowledge (for example concerning the behaviour of certain animals whose habitats have to be protected or improved). The alternative would be the 'sharecropping solution', probably entailing higher transaction costs for the state (finding the adequate shares, and so on) and leading to less efforts for the reason mentioned in section 3.2 (social dilemma). In contrast, co-operation, mutual trust and commitment within a co-operative may strongly improve the results. Thus, developing a corporate identity may lead to an organisation achieving environmental improvement as a sole owner of all necessary inputs. This may help to overcome the prisoner's dilemma outlined above, which occurs whenever an environmental attribute is influenced by several parties whose contributions are difficult to monitor *and* when a result-related remuneration seems to be preferable.

5 SUMMARY

Starting from a specific institutional economics concept which does not consider goods but the different attributes of goods as well as the property rights related to them, the notion of 'divided ownership' of an agricultural area is introduced. This means that the different – agricultural and environmental – attributes of an area (for example cropping capacity, soil structure, groundwater quality, accessibility, landscape amenity, but also attributes like biodiversity or suitability as habitat for particular species) need not necessarily be controlled by the same person. This is all the more as – due to specialisation and spatial scale effects – in many cases the different agricultural and environmental attributes' values are expected to be optimised by distinct persons or organisations.

Apart from the agriculture-related attributes which are obviously best managed (varied) by the farmers, the question therefore arises by whom the environmental attributes of agricultural landscapes should be provided (or improved): (i) by a specialised organisation (nature agent), (ii) by farmers, or (iii) by a co-operative including farmers and environmental experts. If payments are based on the attribute delivered, the residual claimant to the different attributes' values has to be selected. The first arrangement leads to divided ownership of agricultural and environmental attributes, the latter two entail sole ownership of environment improving inputs. Finally, considering some selected environmental attributes as well as the corresponding transaction costs and different payment modalities, the advantages and disadvantages of the above-mentioned institutional arrangements are discussed.

NOTES

1. The author is indebted to Heinz Ahrens for valuable comments.
2. A plot of land as an example for a resource has – besides attributes like accessibility or diverse soil qualities (for example soil structure) and the corresponding agricultural productivities – the attributes groundwater quality, suitability as habitat for certain species, biodiversity and landscape scenery, attributes which can be subsumed under the notion 'countryside and community attributes (CCAs)' (Bromley 1991, p. 189).
3. An exhaustive analysis – including risk aspects – of the underlying ('classic') principal–agent relationship in agriculture is made by Otsuka et al. (1992, p. 1965). It is supposed that the principal has two possibilities to induce the agent to make an effort: (a) by monitoring or (b) by giving incentives. In the following we assume risk neutrality of the parties involved, so that each party is supposed to accept a varying (completely result dependent) remuneration, without insisting on a fixed (risk independent) wage component.
4. Within the context of this contribution the focus is on certain kinds of transaction costs. It should be noted that some kinds of transaction costs (for example information costs incurred at the state level when designing agri-environmental programmes) are neglected in the following. Falconer and Whitby (1999, p. 14) give a large typology of transaction costs entailed by current agri-environmental programmes in Europe: costs for acquiring information, costs incurred when contracting, enforcement costs and so on. The different sub-categories of these costs are more or less relevant at the private or at the state level. The same authors show the considerable magnitude of administrative costs (for information, monitoring, and administration) resulting from programmes under EEC Regulation No. 2078/92.
5. Prohibitive costs of excluding others from consumption are a characteristic of public goods.
6. For example, in case the reduction of nitrate contents in groundwater is of high value to society, but the measurement of the contents at the farm level is rather costly (for example for the reason of many small farms, working within the same watershed area), it would be

better – provided that the property rights to this groundwater attribute are given to the farmers – to pay for certain actions (for example for the reduction of fertilising or for the cultivation of catch crops). Then there would not be any measurement costs at all, but costs of monitoring, which have to be taken into consideration when talking about how to organise the provision of low nitrate contents in water (for 'optimal' monitoring costs see Hanf 1993, p. 139 and Brandes et al. 1997, p. 371).

7. Whether a nature agent is useful or not also depends on the transaction costs involved in his implementation. Transaction costs may be reduced by distributing the property rights to the attributes of an area in such a way as to minimise the number of transactions necessary to reach the optimal allocation of property rights. (This implies a different initial distribution of property rights in ecologically and agriculturally different areas.)
8. See, for example, the 'indices of species diversity' (Shannon Index and so on) enumerated by de Groot (1992, p. 293) or the sophisticated 'yardstick for biodiversity on farms' developed by Wossink et al. (1996).
9. If a nature agent is brought about by market mechanisms (see remarks under landscape amenity) and subsists for a long time, this indicates that transaction costs are outweighed by scale and/or specialisation effects.

REFERENCES

Barzel, Y. (1989), *Economic Analysis of Property Rights*, Cambridge: Cambridge University Press.

Brandes, W., G. Recke and T. Berger (1997), *Produktions- und Umweltökonomik*, vol. 1, Stuttgart: Ulmer.

Bromley, D. (1991), *Environment and Economy. Property Rights and Public Policy*, Cambridge MA: Blackwell.

de Groot, R. (1992), *Functions of Nature. Evaluation of Nature in Environmental Planning, Management and Decision Making*, Groningen: Walters-Noordhoff.

Falconer, K. and M. Whitby (1999), 'Transactions and Administrative Costs in Countryside Stewardship Policies: An Investigation for Eight European Member States', Research Report, University of Newcastle, Department of Agricultural Economics and Food Marketing, Newcastle upon Tyne.

Hanf, C.-H. (1993), 'Ökonomische Überlegungen zur Ausgestaltung von Verordnungen und Verträgen mit Produktionsauflagen zum Umwelt- und Naturschutz', *Agrarwirtschaft*, **42** (3), pp. 138–47.

Hodge, I.D. (1988), 'Property Institutions and Environmental Improvement', *Southern Journal of Agricultural Economics*, **20**, pp. 369–75.

Hodge, I.D. (1991), 'The Provision of Public Goods in the Countryside: How Should it be Arranged?', in Hanley, N. (ed.), *Farming and the Countryside: An Economic Analysis of External Costs and Benefits*, Oxford: CAB International, pp. 179–96.

Lippert, C. (1999), 'Institutionenökonomische Überlegungen zur optimalen Bereitstellung und Entlohnung von Umweltattributen in Agrarlandschaften', *Agrarwirtschaft*, **48** (11), pp. 417–30.

Lippert, C. and M. Rittershofer (1997), 'The Role of the Common Agricultural Policy in Inhibiting Afforestation: The Example of Saxony', in Adger, W., D. Pettenella and M. Whitby (eds), *Climate-Change Mitigation and European Land-Use Policies*, Wallingford: CAB International, pp. 199–213.

Lippert, C., H. Ahrens and M. Rittershofer (1999), 'The Significance of Institutions for the Design and Formation of Agro-environmental Policy', in Frohberg, K. and P. Weingarten (eds), *The Significance of Politics and Institutions for the Design and Formation of Agricultural Policies*, Kiel: Vauk, pp. 105–22.

North, D. (1981), *Structure and Change in Economic History*, New York/London: Norton.

North, D. (1990), *Institutions, Institutional Change and Economic Performance*, Cambridge: Cambridge University Press.

Otsuka, K., H. Chuma and Y. Hayami (1992), 'Land and Labor Contracts in Agrarian Economies: Theories and Facts', *Journal of Economic Literature*, **30,** pp. 1965–2018.

RSU (Rat von Sachverständigen für Umweltfragen) (1994), *Umweltgutachten 1994. Für eine dauerhaft-umweltgerechte Entwicklung*, Stuttgart: Metzler-Poeschel.

RSU (Rat von Sachverständigen für Umweltfragen) (1996), 'Umweltgutachten 1996. Zur Umsetzung einer dauerhaft-umweltgerechten Entwicklung', in *Deutscher Bundestag – 13. Wahlperiode*, Drucksache 13/4108, Bonn.

Schwab, G. (1999), 'Modellhaftes Bibermanagement in der Region 10 mit Kelheim', Zwischenbericht 1998, Biberkoordinationsstelle 'Haus im Moos', Karlshuld und Wildbiologische Gesellschaft München e.V., Ettal.

Wossink, G., J. Buys, C. Jurgens, G. de Snoo and J. Renkema (1996), 'What, How and Where: Nature Conservation and Restoration in Sustainable Agriculture', Paper presented at the VII European Congress of Agricultural Economists, Edinburgh, 3–7 September 1996.

11. Auction Mechanisms for Soil and Habitat Protection Programmes

Klaus Müller and Hans-Peter Weikard*

1 INTRODUCTION

Land use has an important impact on the environment. Externalities from agricultural production must be accounted for in the economic analysis of land use. Here we focus on the provision of public goods from agriculture. Public goods are underprovided in a market economy with rational maximising agents. Hence, efficiency of land use can be enhanced when demand for public goods is organised by government regulations or some other form of collective organisation. We consider the use of auction mechanisms to co-ordinate the supply of public goods from agriculture for a given public demand.

Farmers who participate in programmes for environmental protection and accept particular rules of land use accordingly receive a fixed rate compensation payment under EU regulations.[1] In this chapter we argue that auctions are more efficient allocation mechanisms than fixed rate payments. Using auctions, a given environmental standard can be met with a smaller budget, or given a fixed budget the environmental standard can be improved. This has been pointed out by Latacz-Lohmann and van der Hamsvoort (1998), who discuss the benefits of 'green auctions'. We want to contribute to this discussion in two different respects. First, we explicitly focus on multi-unit auctions, pioneered by Vickrey (1962) and further developed by Harris and Raviv (1981), Maskin and Riley (1989) and others. Also, we take into account the government's budget constraint and its consequences for bidders' expectations. This has not been done in earlier auction models. Secondly, we discuss some specific design problems for two possible applications of auctions: programmes for erosion reduction and habitat protection.

In the next section we present the multi-unit versions of the two basic auction mechanisms, the lowest rejected bid pricing and the individual bid pricing auctions. This serves as a framework for analysis. In section 3 we compare auctions with fixed rate compensation schemes which are used by most existing environmental protection programmes. We find auction mechanisms to be more efficient. In section 4 we discuss how auctions can be adapted to the particular informational and structural features of an erosion reduction programme. In section 5 we consider the use of auctions in habitat protection programmes.

2 AUCTION MECHANISMS FOR THE PROVISION OF PUBLIC GOODS FROM AGRICULTURE

We consider an agency in charge of a nature conservation programme. The programme defines rules for land use. Farmers who participate in the programme agree to accept these rules. Let's assume each farmer can contribute to the programme with one unit of land. Her or his costs to participate are c_i. Costs are private knowledge. However, it is common knowledge of the agency and all farmers that everyone's c_i is drawn independently from a common distribution with probability density function f. Let n be the number of farmers in the region where the programme is to be implemented. Thus, the size of the potential area covered by the programme is n. We examine two cases: (i) The agency limits the programme to the area necessary to meet some environmental standard.[2] (ii) The agency faces a budget constraint and seeks to maximise the area covered by the programme subject to this constraint.

(i) Let $k < n$ be the size of the area necessary to be covered by the programme in order to meet a given environmental standard. Farmers who want to participate in the programme are asked to submit a bid, which states their minimum compensation claim. A bid b_i is successful if it is among the k lowest bids. Denote the lowest bid $b_{(1)}$, the second lowest $b_{(2)}$, and so on. Thus, $b_{(1)} \leq ... \leq b_{(k)} \leq b_{(k+1)} \leq ... \leq b_{(n)}$ and $\{b_{(1)}, ..., b_{(k)}\}$ is the set of successful bids. We consider two selling procedures: lowest rejected bid pricing and individual bid pricing.[3] The former assigns to each successful bidder i a payment equivalent to the bid of the lowest unsuccessful bidder $b_{(k+1)}$. The latter assigns to each successful bidder a payment equal to her own bid b_i. Under both procedures winners have to cover their cost c_i.

The lowest rejected bid pricing is the multi-unit analogue of a second price auction.[4] In this type of auction it is a (weakly) dominant strategy to bid according to one's own cost. A bid higher than c_i decreases the probability of winning (participation in the programme), but does not change the payment in case of winning. Hence, it cannot be optimal. Lowering the bid to $b_i < c_i$ can change the outcome only when for $c_i > c_{(k)}$ the bid b_i becomes a winning bid, that is $b_i < c_{(k)}$ (assuming others bid according to their cost). Since $c_i \geq c_{(k+1)}$ a loss may result. Hence, deviating from bidding according to one's true cost does not pay. Hence, it is a Nash equilibrium strategy to bid

$$b_i = c_i. \tag{11.1}$$

With individual bid pricing a higher bid lowers the probability of the bid being successful, but increases the payoff in case of winning. Assuming risk neutral farmers, *i*'s decision problem is to choose a bid such that her or his expected payoff is maximised. Formally *i*'s decision problem is

$$\max_{b_i}\left[(b_i - c_i)\cdot Prob(b_i \le b_{(k+1)})\right]. \tag{11.2}$$

Since farmers differ only in their costs and are assumed to be identical otherwise, each uses the same bidding strategy β in this auction game:

$$\beta(c_i) = b_i \tag{11.3}$$

which is strictly increasing in *c*. Thus, in any symmetric equilibrium:

$$c_i \le c_j \Leftrightarrow b_i \le b_j \tag{11.4}$$

By assumption all c_i are drawn independently from the same distribution *f*. The probability of *i*'s bid being a winning bid is the probability of c_i being no larger than the *k*th smallest cost $c_{(k)}$, that is $\text{Prob}(c_i \le c_{(k)})$.[5] Therefore, *i*'s expected payoff from her equilibrium bid is given by

$$(\beta(c_i) - c_i)\cdot Prob(c_i \le c_{(k)}). \tag{11.5}$$

Vickrey (1962) has shown that the lowest rejected bid pricing and the individual bid pricing both lead to the same total expense of the agency. This result is known as the revenue equivalence theorem.[6] We can use this result to calculate the expected expense from the equilibrium bids under the lowest rejected bid pricing scheme according to equation (11.1). The payment $c_{(k+1)}$ (= lowest rejected bid) is paid to the *k* successful bidders. The expected payment is $\int c f_{(k+1)}(c)dc$, where $f_{(k+1)}(c)$ is the probability density for a given value *c* to be in *k* + 1st position.[7] Then the expected budget requirement for a conservation programme of size *k* is given by

$$\hat{B} = k\int c f_{(k+1)}(c)dc. \tag{11.6}$$

We compare this result to the budget of a fixed price scheme in the next section.

(ii) In the remainder of this section we focus on the case of a fixed budget of the conservation programme. The budget B is assumed to be common knowledge to all bidders and the agency. Given this budget the agency seeks to maximise the number of participants. The agency's problem is to select an appropriate auction mechanism. In the model discussed by Latacz-Lohmann and van der Hamsvoort (1998), the agency invites bids (compensation claims) from farmers. Farmer i's bid is successful if it is lower than a maximum acceptable bid $\overline{b}$ which is announced ex post by the agency. In the model of Latacz-Lohmann and van der Hamsvoort, farmers' expectations about the maximum acceptable bid are exogenous. However, given common knowledge of the budget, expectations can be endogenised. We provide a brief sketch of such auctions with endogenous expectations.

In a lowest rejected bid pricing auction the agency chooses the number of accepted bids k to be the largest number such that

$$kb_{(k+1)} \leq B[< (k+1)b_{(k+2)}]. \tag{11.7}$$

The choice of k and, therefore, the probability of b_i being a winning bid crucially depends on others' bids. Under the assumption of common knowledge of B and f, the auction mechanism is a symmetric non-cooperative n-player game.[8] Recall that with lowest rejected bid pricing it is optimal to bid according to one's true cost. Thus, the k bidders with lowest costs are the winners.

In the individual bid pricing auction the agency chooses a maximum acceptable bid $\overline{b}$ such that

$$\sum_{b_i \leq \overline{b}} b_i \leq B. \tag{11.8}$$

The strategic situation is more difficult to analyse, since there is no simple dominant strategy (see equation (11.2)). However, by the revenue equivalence theorem we can conclude that the same number of bids is accepted as with lowest rejected bid pricing.

3 AUCTIONS VERSUS FIXED RATE PAYMENTS

An agency which designs an environmental programme must address the problem of incomplete information. It is useful to distinguish two levels of decision making. First, an appropriate environmental standard must be defined. Second, given an environmental standard the agency faces the choice of a mechanism, that is, a set of rules designed to meet the standard. Here we deal with the second problem. In the following we will assume that the desired standard, for example the size of a protected area, is given exogenously. We compare an auction mechanism and fixed rate payments used to compensate participants of environmental programmes. We show that auctions perform generally better than fixed rate payments.

An auction mechanism uses the dispersed knowledge of bidders' costs to determine the compensation for participation in the environmental programme. In contrast, fixed rates are based, at best, on guesses about the actual costs of the potential participants. Let us assume, as in section 2, that an agency wants to establish a protected area of size k to meet a given environmental standard. With fixed rate payments it is unlikely that by announcing compensation $\bar{b}$ exactly k participants will be attracted by this offer. Assuming individual farmers' costs are private knowledge and only the distribution of costs is known, the agency can only guess the right compensation level. The best guess is a compensation level $\bar{b}$ which maximises the probability that precisely k farmers' costs are lower than $\bar{b}$. These k farmers would then be willing to participate in the programme. Formally the best guess is:

$$\arg\max_{\bar{b}}\left[Prob(c_{(k)} \leq \bar{b} < c_{(k+1)})\right] \tag{11.9}$$

In the following we compare the two auction mechanisms introduced in section 2, *individual bid pricing* and *lowest rejected bid pricing*, with *fixed rate payments*. Costs, if ordered from lowest to highest, are represented by an increasing function $C(x)$; see Figure 11.1. As we have noted, this function is not known precisely. In a world of perfect information the fixed rate compensation could be set at b^* where exactly k farmers are willing to participate. Under cost uncertainty the agency is at risk of setting $\bar{b}$ either too low or too high.

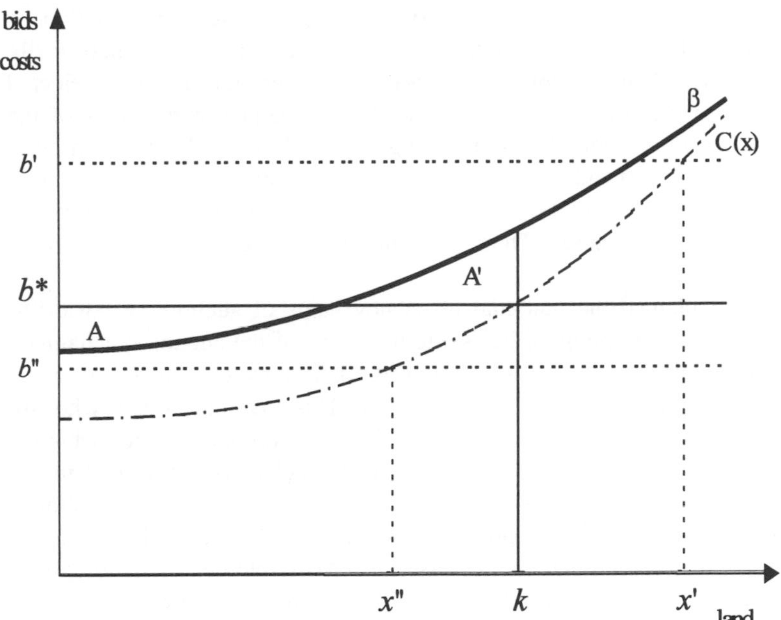

Figure 11.1 Auctions versus fixed rate payments

Assume that the compensation is set according to b'. In this case $x' > k$ farmers would like to participate in the programme. Since the desired number of participants is given by k, we have an excess supply $x'-k$. If a first-come-first-served allocation scheme is chosen, it is easy to see that not necessarily the farmers with the lowest cost will participate. Farmers with high costs $c_i > c_{(k)}$ (but $c_i < b'$) will have an equal chance to participate compared with low cost farmers $c_i \leq c_{(k)}$. Then the environmental protection measures are not undertaken at the lowest possible cost. Thus, in this case we find an inefficiency. Furthermore, farmers receive an additional rent which may also distort the land market.

If the compensation is set too low at level b'', the number of participants is $x'' < k$. Then there is too little supply of land to meet the environmental standard. Again, we find an inefficiency provided the right standard k is chosen.

Using an auction mechanism the agency selects the k lowest bids. The auction mechanism is efficient, because the selected bidders are those with lowest costs. This holds for lowest rejected bid pricing and individual bid pricing auctions. With many bidders (which comes close to the continuous case displayed in Figure 11.1) the lowest rejected bid is only marginally higher than $b_{(k)}$. Thus the total compensation payment under lowest rejected bid pricing is given by $k\,b^{*}$. The optimal bids are equal to the costs of the bidders $C(x)$. In an individual bid pricing auction bids are higher than costs (see equations (11.2) and (11.3)). Farmers' compensation is according to their bids β (see Figure 11.1). Under the given assumptions the revenue equivalence theorem holds. Thus, in Figure 11.1 the areas A and A' are of equal size.[9]

Having explained the potential efficiency gains of auctions, we want to close this section by pointing out some problems of the auction mechanism. First, efficiency is not always guaranteed. Inefficiencies may occur when farmers are uncertain about their own cost. This favours bidders who are overly optimistic about their own costs. Bidders end up in a situation which is known as the winner's curse.[10] However, this problem is not special to the auction mechanism. With a fixed rate compensation scheme a similar problem can also occur.[11] Second, auctions can be inefficient under collusion. In lowest rejected bid auctions bidders can form stable coalitions to exploit the agency. In the coalition bidders reveal their true costs to each other and determine the prospective winners. The following bidding scheme is optimal for the coalition: k farmers with the lowest cost bid according to their true cost while all others submit the highest eligible bid. The winners earn a maximum rent and give a small side-payment to the losers. There is no incentive to deviate from this agreement. If a high cost farmer reduces the bid to get into a winning position she or he would incur losses because the farmer in position k according to cost would now deliver the lowest rejected bid which does not cover the costs of the high cost farmers. The possibility of collusion is limited by the transaction costs necessary to arrange a bidder cartel and reach agreement about the side-payment. In reality it is often observed that bidder cartels break down when one participant is not satisfied with her or his payment. In general, the transaction costs of the co-ordination rise with the number of bidders.

4 AN AUCTION MECHANISM FOR EROSION REDUCTION

The simple auction mechanisms presented in section 2 can be refined in various ways to take into account specific features of the environmental good that is to be provided. This section seeks to capture one particular feature of the erosion problem, its site-specificity. Two types of site-specific environmental problems are distinguished. First, the environmental problem may be less severe on some lands than on others. Second, due to differences in type of land or location, a protection measure which is effective on one site may not be effective on another. In this section we shall briefly discuss a framework to deal with both problems focusing on erosion protection.

(i) When erosion is less severe on some sites and more severe on others, priority should be given to the latter. Ceteris paribus the funds of an erosion protection programme should be directed towards lands with a higher risk of erosion. We will assume that the agency attaches a value v_i to the participation of farmer *i*. v_i captures the risk of erosion on *i*'s lands. A higher v_i means a higher erosion risk and a greater importance of protection measures. For an efficient use of the programme's funds compensation should be allocated taking into account the participation values v_i as well as participation costs c_i. Under the constraint that the agency limits the programme to *k* units of land (as discussed in section 2) it is one possibility to select the *k* most valuable lands. However, such a mechanism can be exploited if v_i is observable and, therefore, commonly known. Then, those farmers with the *k* most valuable lands will know that their bids are going to be accepted. Thus, they can claim a higher compensation than in a competitive situation. Under such a scheme the erosion protection programme can be very expensive.

A superior way to select participants is to invite bids from farmers and select the *k* bids with the highest difference $v_i - b_i$. Under lowest rejected bid pricing it is a (weakly) dominant strategy to bid according to one's true cost. No bidding strategy which over- or understates the costs can improve upon a 'truthful' bid (see section 2). Notice that the farmers selected by this rule may not be those who bid lowest, since some of them offer land which is not at much risk of erosion. Also, some highly erodable land may not be enrolled in the programme if implementing the protection measures is too costly.

(ii) In an area with different types of soil the choice of a particular erosion protection measure will not be adequate everywhere. Also, it is informationally too demanding to select the specific protection measures for each piece of land. Under such conditions a sealed bid mechanism may be an efficient way to use the decentralised information about specific soil conditions. Here our suggestion is to invite bids in the form of management plans for erosion reduction together with a claim for monetary compensation. Let ϕ_i be *i*'s management plan. Then a bid is a pair (ϕ_i, b_i). To select the best bids the agency must rank these pairs. This requires, first, a valuation of the management plans ϕ_i. The agency must assess what each plan ϕ_i contributes to erosion reduction as compared to the management plans submitted by other bidders. If no quantifiable information is available, the selection of bids can be based on an (ordinal) ranking of the management plans. In a second step such ranking must be combined with information about costs as revealed by the bids. At this stage the ranking of management plans is transformed into a monetary evaluation. A value w_i is assigned to each management plan ϕ_i. Finally, bidders with the highest $w_i - b_i$ are selected to participate in the programme.

5 AN AUCTION MECHANISM FOR HABITAT PROTECTION

Certain agricultural lands are habitats of endangered species. In order to protect these species particular modes of land use are required. This can increase production costs and decrease the yield from land use. As in the model of section 2, each farmer incurs costs c_i when participating in the habitat protection programme. Suppose the programme is restricted to a particular region known to be the habitat of a species to be protected. The protected area should be sufficiently large, but it is also of importance that the lands covered by the programme are not isolated from each other. Ecological effectiveness requires that the lands in the programme are connected. Thus, from the agency's point of view, the ecological value of i's participation in the programme depends on whether or not i's neighbours also participate. Here we consider a mechanism to select the winning bids such that ecological value for money is maximised. We also consider the rational bidding behaviour under the proposed selection rule.

We assume the ecological value of participation depends on the total size of connected lands. Furthermore, we assume that all farmers in the region considered are willing to participate if their costs are covered. Thus, each farmer is assumed to deliver a bid $b_i > 0$ as a compensation claim. The total size of the region is n. The size of the protected region is $k < n$. The agency chooses a connected area of size k such that the total compensation payment is minimised. Without concern for the location the number of possible groups of size k to be selected from n bidders is

$$\frac{n!}{(n-k)!k!} = \binom{n}{k}. \tag{11.10}$$

How many of those are connected depends crucially on the shape of the region considered. In the simple case where the habitat of a protected species is at the bank of a river, all lands are located on a line. In this case there are $n-k+1$ groups of bidders whose bids have to be considered. Let us assume an individual bid pricing where i is compensated according to her own bid if she is in the group of winners. In this case, unlike in the model of section 2, the bidding process can be inefficient. The reason is that an externality exists in the bidding behaviour. A high bid of farmer i decreases not only i's but also i's neighbours' probability of winning.

A possible solution to this externality problem is the formation of co-operatives who submit a bid for the group. If the auction is restricted to groups who are invited to submit bids for connected areas of size k, the agency can use an efficient auction mechanism as described in section 2. However, if k is large it will be difficult to organise a co-operation. Also, competition is restricted and the formation of co-operations might lead to collusion in the bidding process.

6 CONCLUDING REMARKS

The use of auction mechanisms for nature protection programmes and the provision of public goods from agriculture can lead to efficiency gains when compared to the commonly used fixed rate payments. The efficiency gains are a sufficient reason to propagate the use of auctions. However, for practical purposes a number of problems must be addressed. In this chapter we have discussed some of the problems that may arise in the context of erosion reduction and habitat protection. We do not claim to offer a solution to all the problems; however; our discussion shows the potential and the flexibility of auction mechanisms to be adapted to various special situations. A number of possible extensions of the simple auction model used in this chapter are implicit in our discussion. First, farmers may submit bids for a variable supply of the environmental services. Secondly, extending the model further, the assumptions of a common distribution of costs and private information may be dropped. A third extension might consider bidders' risk aversion.

NOTES

* We would like to thank participants of the 64th EAAE Seminar and our collaborators in the GRANO-Project (Research Project) for stimulating discussions. Financial support from the Federal Ministry of Education, Science, Research and Technology, Grant No. 0339694A is gratefully acknowledged.

1. See EU regulation 2078/92.
2. The US Conservation Reserve Programme sets enrolment targets for the size of the protected area. However, these targets are not only set according to environmental goals. Additional objectives of the programme are agricultural surplus reduction and income support for farmers; see Shoemaker (1989).
3. See Vickrey (1962). For an introduction to the analysis of auctions see Milgrom and Weber (1982) or McAfee and McMillan (1987).
4. Second price auctions are also called Vickrey auctions in the literature.

5. We implicitly use a tie-breaking rule to the effect that all bids equal to the k-lowest are accepted.
6. The revenue equivalence theorem was first formulated for auctions where a seller sets up an auction for a single good. It holds if bidders are risk neutral and if costs are drawn independently from a common distribution; see Vickrey (1961), Myerson (1981), Harris and Raviv (1981), Maskin and Riley (1989).
7. In other words, $f_{(k+1)}(c)$ is the probability density function of the $k + 1$st order statistic of cost. See Pitman (1993, p. 325) for an introduction to order statistics.
8. Latacz-Lohmann and van der Hamsvoort (1998) essentially consider a game between one bidder and the agency. Their model does not fully grasp the strategic situation. In our model the agency is not considered to be a player. The behaviour of the agency is strictly determined by the rules of the game. In other words, the agency does not make a strategic choice, but just selects k bidders according to a given rule. The rules of the game are also common knowledge.
9. Note, however, that the revenue equivalence theorem does not hold if bidders are risk averse, if costs are correlated and drawn from differing distributions; see Maskin and Riley (1989).
10. See, for example, McAfee and McMillan (1987).
11. Ministry of Agriculture, Nature Conservation and Environment of Thuringia (1999, pp. 140–42) reports that the compensation of losses from conservation measures was not sufficient for all participants when a fixed rate payment scheme was used.

REFERENCES

EU Regulation 2078/92.

Harris, M. and A. Raviv (1981), 'A Theory of Monopoly Pricing Schemes with Demand Uncertainty', *American Economic Review*, **71**, pp. 347–65.

Latacz-Lohmann, U. and C.P. van der Hamsvoort (1998), 'Auctions as a Means of Creating a Market for Public Goods from Agriculture', *Journal of Agricultural Economics*, **49**, pp. 334–45.

Maskin, E. and J. Riley (1989), 'Optimal Multi-unit Auctions', in Hahn, F. (ed.), *The Economics of Missing Markets, Information, and Games*, Oxford: Clarendon Press, pp. 312–35.

McAfee, R.P. and J. McMillan (1987), 'Auctions and Bidding', *Journal of Economic Literature*, **25**, pp. 699–738.

Milgrom, P.R. and R.J. Weber (1982), 'A Theory of Auctions and Competitive Bidding', *Econometrica*, **50**, pp. 1089–122.

Ministry of Agriculture, Nature Conservation and Environment of Thuringia (1999), *Erhaltung der Kulturlandschaft, Umweltgerechte Landwirtschaft, Naturschutz und Landschaftspflege – Evaluierung des KULAP Thüringen*.

Myerson, R. (1981), 'Optimal Auction Design', *Mathematics of Operations Research*, **6**, pp. 58–73.

Pitman, J. (1993), *Probability*, New York: Springer.

Shoemaker, R. (1989), 'Agricultural Land Values and Rents under the Conservation Reserve Program', *Land Economics*, **65**, pp. 131–37.

Vickrey, W. (1961), 'Counterspeculation, Auctions and Competitive Sealed Tenders', *Journal of Finance*, **16**, pp. 8–37.

Vickrey, W. (1962), 'Auctions and Bidding Games', in *Recent Advances in Game Theory* (Conference Proceedings, Princeton University Press), Reprinted in Vickrey, W. (1994), *Public Economics*, Cambridge: Cambridge University Press, pp. 85–98.

12. Institutional and Political Economy Modelling of Nature Evaluation and Provision by Rural Communities

Ernst-August Nuppenau

1 INTRODUCTION

Nature evaluation and provision is confronted with the serious problem of the public good character of nature, being mostly non-rival and non-exclusive. It is currently heavily debated whether standard consumer choice theory can be applied to the evaluation and provision of nature, or whether citizens' evaluation should prevail (Blamey 1995). Those who criticise monetary evaluation on the basis of individualistic evaluation techniques and the usual property rights solution, prefer participatory, community-oriented and co-operative action approaches. These approaches implicitly comprise institutions that are no longer individualistic and voluntary; rather they expose nature evaluation to multilateral negotiation, political bargaining and political economy options. The envisaged institutions go beyond property rights distribution. Political co-ordination, as compared to market co-ordination, is seen as a better opportunity to develop public preferences (Bartsch et al. 1993). Apparently, that raises the question of whose interests are pursued (Pashigian 1985), and one has to reconsider mandatory and statutory regulations by authorities that apply to all individuals in communities. Regulations can either be efficiency enhancing, or they are rent-seeking activities, and it is not clear where the border has to be drawn (Rausser 1992). The agricultural sector has an especially strong history of rent seeking (Swinnen and van der Zee 1993; Bullock 1994), and it would be naive to think that politically motivated actions equally improve the welfare of all participants.

However, whether communally agreed upon or democratically legitimised, decisions on environmental regulations, that are based on certain institutions like majority rules in democracy or based on moral consensus in traditional societies, impose norm-constraining behaviour. Hence, it would be even more naive to think that participatory approaches are free of interest conflicts, smoothly abstract from political power, and simply reflect public preferences.

As has been shown by the political economy and game theory literature, co-operative action is mostly biased by pressure groups and managers are partial. This is not a very big problem if free riding is avoided and the tragedy of the commons problem is solved. It only becomes a problem if preferences of those who have limited power are strongly overruled. In contrast, as Hodge (1988 and 1991) and Hanley et al. (1997) have remarked, a pure property rights solution may also not be the best choice due to transaction and control costs; or not even politically feasible, either.

In the political sphere, political procedures, such as participatory approaches, to solve conflicts between agriculture and the environment are becoming increasingly popular. In contrast to previous research, pure property rights solutions are increasingly discarded as being narrow and inappropriate in solving conflicts in nature conservation on the basis of market transactions. Many studies suggest that this is due to high transaction costs on environmental goods markets. The political process is considered a substitute for market transactions of environmental goods because political decisions require consultation of the public, offer legitimisation, and policy makers want to avoid pure property rights regimes as the basic institution.

Also, due to public pressure, detailed planning of nature provision in communities has become increasingly attractive to governments. Governments seek to promote nature and landscape provision by farmers based on landscape planning and user regulation (Peltzman 1976). However, planners frequently do not know what communities want, and contingent valuation results are regarded as insufficient for detailed planning. There is scope for a longer lasting co-ordination process between vested interests in the environment and planning. It is hoped that different interest groups will gain insights into the needs of preserving nature if they participate in planning. Proponents of socially oriented preference gaining processes are also confident that all groups can express their preferences, though power of groups plays a major role in preference formation. Contingent to these problems, the chapter shows that an application of a political economy model helps in understanding the formation of social preferences and institutions.

A political economy model of social bargaining is applied to the provision of an ecological main structure by farmers and other rural residents. First, a spatial framework for investigating collective decision making in a community of farmers and residents is provided. Second, it will be shown how a tragedy of the commons problem prevails in the individual calculations of farmers for contributions to the main structure. Third, we will see how residents that have the alternative of accepting income reducing contributions for financing land set aside by farmers, will respond to fees or compromise on land provision to the main structure. Fourth, we outline a theory of a social optimum of field margin provision and its finance, presuming ill-defined property rights. In doing so, a public good manager will be entitled to charge individual contributions to beneficiaries and guarantee compensation payments to providers of nature. That approach adopts the predatory versus productive government framework of Rausser and Zusman (1992). It distinguishes between the process of public preferences formation and the process of social power involvement. The concept of bargaining is presented, and, finally, this chapter discusses potentials for application. The chapter also provides a theoretical procedure for solving the problem of establishing rules for collective action and coercion in a political framework. In that politically based solution, farmers', residents' and a manager's interests are explicitly considered and modelled.

2 FRAMING INTEREST FUNCTIONS AND PROVISION OF LAND FOR ENVIRONMENTAL SERVICES

As a basis for studying the interest function of residents and farmers in an ecological main structure, we must develop a treatable description of a settlement structure. Figure 12.1 presents a stylised version of a settlement structure where farm land is surrounded by residential areas. This stylised mixture of farm and residential land use provides a minimum for structuring arguments on nature provision by field margin provision. In order to establish an interest function that depicts private interest and allows political economy modelling, we have to formalise the argument for nature provision. Moreover, we presume that the community has some right to interfere in private land rights. In Figure 12.1, we see illustrated how ill-defined land rights enable political disputes: the political dispute on land use is confined to field margins that have to be devoted to an ecological main structure by farmers and residents. Land in field margins is subject to ecologically prescribed land use; for instance, hedgerows, ditches and other landscape elements. Residents and farmers negotiate on the size of margins.

Having set the basis for a structured description of settlement patterns such as land devoted to conventional use and land devoted to nature preservation, we can study the analytical framework for a biological networking. Such descriptions of community participation in ecological main structures and ecological networking focus on the spatial allocation of land by farms and residents for ecologically upgraded land use patterns (Wossink et al. 1998).

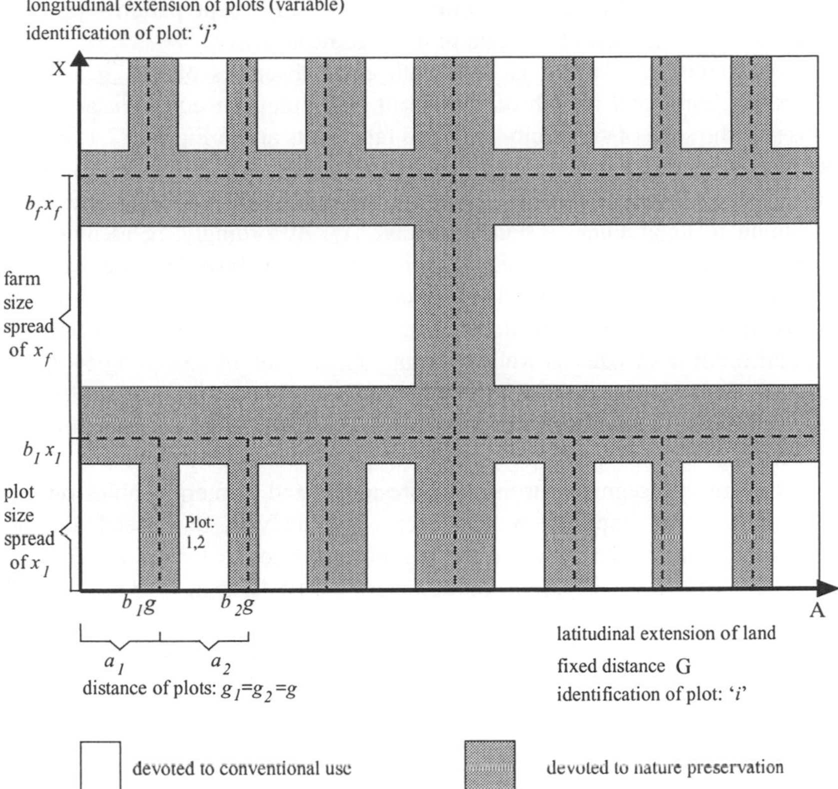

Figure 12.1 Settlement structure and nature preservation in mixed land use of farmers and residents

Source: Own design.

The framing enables a reformulation of Rausser's and Zusman's (1992) initially time-oriented model of market failure in the provision of public goods by communities. This reformulation uses a spatial dimension instead of a time dimension. The introduction of Figure 12.1 is motivated by three aspects. First, it shows the basic idea of a plot-oriented type of settlement pattern that compromises on agriculture, residential use and nature preservation. On the basis of a rectangular and easily quantifiable structure, such as given land use patterns, we will be capable of formulating interest functions. Second, pre-structuring enables the most simple specification of field margins devoted to ecological main structures, and, third, ecological and economic effects can be investigated. Finally, settlement patterns provide access to a mathematical treatment of the arguments.

In particular, the latitudinal axis with equal distances of $g_1,\ldots,g_i,\ldots$ to g_n shows the horizontal stretch of a resident community at equal distances of plots (for the sake of simplicity only two farm plots are in Figure 12.1, but, in general, a farm area contains a number of *m*-fields). The plot size differs on the longitudinal axis, allowing residents to have different sizes of homesteads according to longitudinal distances $x_1,\ldots x_j,\ldots x_m$. Accordingly, residential and farm size can vary on the x-axis, extending the sketch above to more than one combination of residential and farm land. In total, such framing of residential and farm plots enables us to depict land allocation of residents and farmers with different farm sizes as well as the implementation of an ecological main structure, subject to individual field margins. In Figure 12.1, the ecological main structure (shaded area) is formed by individual plots of residents and farmers.

Extending the segments to multiple residents and farmers enables one to cover a range of impacts on land users. For analysis, the stretch on the horizontal axis is fixed at *G* and the variation of sizes of land is covered by the stretch of the x-axis. The framing determines individual land sizes *l* and the recognition of the community as a whole. For instance, confining, firstly, the analysis to farms and neglecting residents, by definition of size l_{ij} we get:

$$l^*_{ij} = g_i \times x'_j \tag{12.1}$$

Next, the area contributed by a farmer to an ecological main structure f_{ij} is identified as plot *i* and homestead *j*, and it can be depicted as a percentage of the size of the plot using Taylor expansion for a rectangular field $g_i . x_j$. Multiplying the area by a percentage b^*_j gives

$$f_{ij} = g_i\, b^*_j \times x'_j + x'_j\, g_i \times b_j - g_i\, b^*_j \times x'_j\, b^*_j \cong 2\, x'_j\, g_i \times b^*_j \tag{12.2}$$

for example, with $0 \leq b_j \leq 0.2$ the approximation is fine, since still $g_i\, b^*_j \times x'_j$ $b^*_j \cong 0$, that is close to zero.

Accordingly, the remaining area that is not subject to ecological margins is defined as:

$$l_{ij} = (1 - b_j)\, l^*_j = (1 - b_j)\, 2\, x'_j\, g_i \tag{12.3}$$

Note, in the two formulas, the part of the latitudinal axis, that is, the distance of the field g_i on the horizontal axis, is fixed, and, since the stretch of g_i has been assumed to be equal to all fields, the length becomes proportional to the absolute length G. If the absolute length is G, it prevails that $g_i = G/n$; then the remaining area for farming and residential activity is subject to G:

$$l_{ij} = (1 - b_j)\, l^*_{ij} = (1 - b_j)\, 2\, x'_j\, G/n \qquad (12.3')$$

The same argument applies to the size of any other farm plot and also residential plots. In the given example of Figure 12.1, four residents share the length of one farm field and two fields may compose a farm, but that is arbitrary. More importantly, the area (size) of a farm is measurable by a proportional part of the length G multiplied with the distance on the vertical axis. Alternatively, farms with more than two fields can proportionally increase their area (size) by the number of segments to $2n \times G$ (presuming equal length of fields or segments). The same applies to the number of plots of residents by whom farmers are surrounded. In principle, all sizes of farms and homesteads can be expressed by a proportional factor z to the fixed distance G. If the provision to the main structure, as a percentage, is deducted, the remaining area for 'non-nature' use becomes dependent on margin b_j and distance G:

$$l_{ij} = (1 - b_i)\, l^*_{ij} = (1 - b_j)\, z\, x'_j\, G \qquad (12.3'')$$

The advantage of this explicit modelling of farm and residential areas can be seen in an equivalent expression of a communal constraint on land use B, imposed by an ecological main structure in terms of a horizontal stretch of farms (see Rausser and Zusman 1992). For instance, if 40ha have to be proportionally accrued for the main structure from 2000 residents, each having approximately 600 square meters, and 10 farmers, having approximately 100ha, each resident has to provide 50 square meters and each farm has to provide 3ha: more generally, if we consider only farm area, we can formally derive the link between area B^f

$$B^f \leq \sum_i \sum_j z_j\, g_i\, x_j\, b^f_j \text{ ; and since } G = \sum_i g_i \text{ by this assumption:}$$

$$B^f \leq \sum_j G\, z_j\, x_j\, b^f_j \Leftrightarrow G \leq \frac{B^f}{\sum_j z_j\, x_j\, b^f_j} \qquad (12.4)$$

of the main structure and individual contributions b^f_j (now b^f_i for farmers) using G. Or having farms and residents (b^r_i for residents):

$$B = B^f + B^r \leq \sum_j G z_j^f x_j^f b_j^f + \sum_i G z_i^r x_i^r b_i^r \Leftrightarrow$$

$$G \leq \frac{B}{\sum_j z_j^f x_j^f b_j^f + \sum_i z_i^r x_i^r b_i^r} \tag{12.4'}$$

The presentation of B helps to specify any individual use of land in terms of a constraint:

$$l_{ij} = (1 - b_j)\, l^*_{ij} = (1 - b_j)\, z_j x_j G/m$$
$$l_{ij} = (1 - b_j)\, z_j x_j \frac{B}{\sum_j z_j^f x_j^f b_j^f + \sum_i z_i^r x_i^r b_i^r} \tag{12.5}$$

Having specified the land use, we can proceed to model farm behaviour (section 4). Correspondingly, the size of area devoted to ecological activities on plot i of a farm j (no. of plots m) is:

$$b^*_j = b_j\, l^*_{ij} = b_j z_j x_j G/m$$
$$b^*_j = b_j z_j x_j \left\{ \frac{B}{m\left[\sum_j z_j^f x_j^f b_j^f + \sum_i z_i^r x_i^r b_i^r\right]} \right\} \tag{12.5'}$$

Note, regulations on margins imply interdependencies between individual and collective decisions.

3 FRAMING BIOLOGY, SPECIES OCCURRENCE AND LAND ALLOCATION IN A MAIN STRUCTURE

The above argument allows a closer look at management aspects in terms of ecological needs in conjunction with spatial land use. At places where individuals in a community of residents explicitly contribute and benefit from an ecological main structure, one can perceive land use for ecological purposes as a network of land. Voluntarily reallocating land is nature preservation. The crucial thing is the recognition of dependency between species prevalence and habitat appearance on individual plots in that net. Let us assume that a matrix Ω exists that 'converts' a vector of habitats on field margin b into a vector of species s. Then, sites and size of the main structure have an impact on species appearance. The two aspects reflect advantages accrued from increased eco-nets in terms of mobility and diversity:

$$s = \Omega_1 b + \varpi B \tag{12.6}$$

In equation (12.6), the matrix Ω and the vector ϖ can be thought of as a probability function, depicted as a Markov process. That process models the relationship between land for ecological needs on field margins, expressed as habitats, and ecosystem functioning. The model tells us, as a bilateral measure, with which probability we may get a sequence of species s_i living in habitats b_j. Since species need support by multiple habitats b, a linear combination Ω guarantees a composition of habitats that supports s, whereas $s' = [s_1,s_2,\ldots,s_i,\ldots,s_n]$ is a vector of species appearance (trees, birds, and so on). In terms of interest of residents as members of the community, s is a public good, being non-rival and non-exclusive in consumption. Note: a broad range of nature elements such as oak trees, owls, and so on should be included. Moreover, the habitats on specific field margins that generate, support or coincide with species composition, for instance, in terms of gardening, can be identified and be described by the sizes: $b = [b_1,b_2, \ldots,b_i,\ldots,b_m]$. It is up to the ecologist to classify and constitute these habitats and convey information on habitat requirements to a manager of the eco-net, defined as 'environment'. The description relies on biological information and non-human activities are involved. Presumably, the manager is fully informed as to the complexity of species' needs, appearance and ecological activity; individuals may only see the size of B, the relevant public good.

4 FARMERS AND VOLUNTARY FIELD MARGIN PROVISION FOR AN ECOLOGICAL MAIN STRUCTURE

In this section we deal with farm behaviour. We show why a possible theoretically voluntary provision of field margins by farmers will not be established. Deliberations should be explicitly based on farm behaviour and correspond to the micro-economic theory of farms. We will see that an ordinary profit maximising farmer has limited incentives to provide field margins (tragedy of the commons: Rausser and Zusman 1992). Note that we have no payments introduced yet. The institutional change that can be investigated in a first round is a voluntary provision versus statutory regulation by a manager of the common. For the sake of simplicity, farmers are the only providers of the main structure in this section and residents enjoy the main structure required at a predetermined volume B. Increases in the size of the main structure itself are acknowledged by the farmer. There is sufficient knowledge in the farm community that an increased ecological main structure reduces costs due to improved ecological conditions in the countryside. The question is, do they appreciate this by behaviour?

Allocation of field margins towards ecological main structures has to be seen in conjunction with the overall use of agricultural land. The applied micro-theory approach of a farm is similar to the one of Nuppenau and Slangen (1998). It distinguishes between conventional operation on the remaining field and conditional farming on field margins, given restrictions in farm practices (as a special case, field margins are, with no tillage, used for ecological reasons, only). Frequently mentioned restrictions are 'no spraying of chemicals, lower fertiliser rates' and so on (Wossink et al. 1998). Positive ecological effects (cost reduction due to higher biological activity) from the main structure are regarded as public goods B. Harvests from field margins remain private. The adjusted total profit P is calculated using both crop yields on field i and the margin. Thus, profits are essentially determined by land allocation between the rest of the field and the margin. Theoretically, the objective function of a representative farmer in field margin provision corresponds to a constrained optimisation approach (Chambers 1988).

$$P_{i,A} = \sum_{i} \left\{ \underset{(+)}{p_j} l_{ij}^f - C[\underset{(+)}{l_{ij}^f}, \underset{(-)}{b_j^f}, \underset{(-)}{B}, \underset{(+)}{r_j}] \right\} \tag{12.7}$$

where: increase: ⇑ and decrease ⇓:

p_j = gross margins per hectare (profit ⇑)

l_{ij} = size of the field i on farm j, area cropped (profit ⇑)

$C(.)$ = cost function on quantity of q_{ij} at field l_{ij} with the yield $h = q_{ij}/l_{ij}$, (cost ⇑ = > profit ⇓)

b_j = field margins, *individual* cost reducing effect by biological activity (cost ⇓ = > profit ⇑)

B = size of the *community's* ecological main structure and effect from main structure (cost ⇓ = >profit ⇑)

r_j = input costs, farm specific (cost ⇑ = >profit ⇓)

For the sake of simplicity, equation (12.7), the objective or interest function of farmers, only recognises the size of the main structure, to be obtained collectively as argument, in the cost function (no s). If a regulator can influence field margin provision, as a percentage, profits are adjusted:

$$P_{i,G} = \sum_i \left\{ p_j x_j^f g_i^f (1 - b_j^f) - C[x_j^f g_i (1 - b_j^f), b_j^f, B, r_j] \right\} \quad (12.8)$$

with constant $x_j = x_j^f$

Assuming linear homogeneity in land with respect to the cost function and equal distance of fields on the horizontal axis, $\Sigma g = G$, the sum of profits from all fields i can be rewritten as:

$$\Pi_{i,G} = G\left\{ p_j x_j^f (1 - b_j^f) - C[x_j^f (1 - b_j^f), b_j^f, B, r_j] \right\} \quad (12.9)$$

Introducing the ecological constraint B, depicted as the recalculated G from farm length in equation (12.4), profits on an individual farm can be expressed as dependent on individual allocation b_j of field margins *and* communal achievement (requirement) of field margin B.

$$P_{j,A} = \frac{B\left\{ p_j x_j^f (1 - b_j^f) - C[x_j^f (1 - b_j^f), b_j^f, B, r] \right\}}{\sum_j x_j^f b_j^f + \sum_i x_i^r b_i^r} \quad (12.10)$$

In words: the community of farmers 'decide' on B, but only because a pressure on all of them requires the allocation of field margins. The question is: will individual optimisation behaviour go for the b_j s, appreciating the positive effects on B? Nothing has been said about voluntary provision of field margins for the ecological main structure and benefits to individual farmers. As a public good, the ecological main structure B, that is the empirically measurable equivalent of nature provision by the community of all farmers, is only of potential interest, since it may not appear due to common property problems. To see the argument, we look at the optimisation of (12.10) by setting the first derivatives (12.11) equal to 0:

$$\frac{\partial P_{j,A}}{\partial b_j^f} = \frac{-B\left\{p_j^f x_j^f + C'[x_j^f(1-b_j^f), b_j^f, B, r]\right\}}{m\left\{\sum_j x_j^f b_j^f + \sum_i x_j^r b_i^r\right\}} +$$

$$\frac{B\left\{p_j x_j^f(1-b_j^f) - C[(x_j^f(1-b_j^f), b_j^f, B, r]\right\}}{-m\left\{\sum_j x_j^f(1-b_j^f) + \sum_i x_i^r(1-b_i^r)\right\}^2} = 0 \Leftrightarrow \tag{12.11}$$

$$\frac{\partial P_{j,A}}{\partial b_j^f} = \left\{p_j x_j^f - C'[x_j^f(1-b_j^f), b_j^f, B, r]\right\} - \frac{P_{j,A}}{B} = 0 \tag{12.12}$$

Equation (12.12) consists of two parts. The first part {...} shows that the determination of field margin size is dependent on *private* marginal costs. The second part can be interpreted as the share of farm *j*'s profit in the provision of the public ecological main structure. We assume that this share is small for a large number of farms. Selfish and narrowly rational farmers will not provide the envisaged main structure (as Rausser and Zusman (1992), already argued in the time frame). Instead, farmers focus on the first part {...}. If no political pressure exists, that is, no institution comes up with statutory regulations, the impact of the main structure is marginal or zero, if $\lim B \rightarrow 0$; a dominant strategy is defection, the tragedy of the commons argument!

However, the size x_j and intensity of farming normally matter. The situation is verified in Figure 12.2. Farmers will contribute differently, but at very low levels, to the main structure. The willingness to contribute, in the case of the tragedy of the commons (equation 12.12), is independent of the level of B and a divergence between social and private (tragedy) marginal willingness to contribute occurs.

While farmers will not voluntarily contribute to the main structure (tragedy of the commons as Nash equilibrium), there is scope for institutional change, either statutory regulations or financial transfers or both together. As suggested in Figure 12.2 (sketched line and indicated as social), a shift in the marginal willingness to contribute to the main structure may occur and it is welfare improving. If farmers were sure that others would also contribute, they would voluntarily increase the size of land strips for nature preservation. The questions are: how can we establish a social objective function by political bargaining processes and how can we include residents?

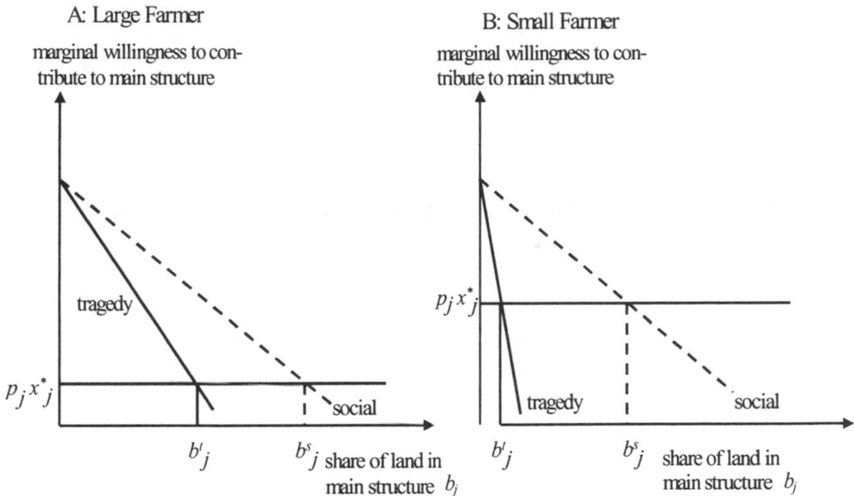

Figure 12.2 Farmers' individual willingness to contribute

Source: Own design.

5 RESIDENTS AS VOLUNTARY CONTRIBUTORS OF LAND AND FINANCE TO THE MAIN STRUCTURE

We will now investigate how individual objective or interest functions of residents can be modelled in the case of a more authentic allocation, making individual farmers *and* residents interested and presuming, as a collective, all together they become interested in the ecological main structure. This more authentic case may include statutory regulations on land allocation and financial contributions of residents. The first step is to specify welfare functions including nature s. The welfare function is modelled on the basis of a constrained indirect utility function and we ask: how can we achieve a comparable description of 'nature' provision on the basis of land allocation versus money provision for obtaining the main structure from farmers? For accruing the main structure from farmers we may need money. Essentially, given this background of allocation, the utility function of a consumer is given as:

$$V_i = V_i\,[p, y - a_i^r \frac{G}{n} x_i^r\,(1 - b_i^r),\ \frac{G}{n} x_i^r (1 - b_i^r),\ s,\ B] \tag{12.13}$$
$$\qquad (-) \qquad\qquad (+) \qquad\qquad (+) \qquad (+)\,(+)$$

where:

p = price vector of indirect utility function of marketable goods
y = income
a_j = land tax
x_i^r = size of homestead of resident r in longitudinal distance
G/n = size of homestead in lateral distance
s = species combination
B = size of the main structure in terms of land and absolute size

In explanation: a homestead owner (resident) is constrained by income, land and public good preference. In principle, public good preferences are separated in species appearance s, that is, the quality aspect, though species are recognised in terms of quantities, and the size of the main structure B, that is, the quantity aspect. The size of the homestead is the product $G \times x_i$.

Again, the introduction of such a welfare function allows a re-specification of residents' ecological and economic preferences in terms of collective land allocation and finance. That includes three fundamentally important welfare aspects: Resident preferences for species, the size of the structure, and a concrete payment scheme. The species aspect needs further explanation: We adopt the above framing of a vector of species s that is supported by a composition of land parcels: $s = \Omega \cdot [b^1, \ldots, b^i, \ldots, b^m, b_1, \ldots, b_j, \ldots, b_n]' + \varpi \cdot B$. Ω is the transition matrix that describes the transition from the present residents' plots b^i to s; it includes needs for the size of B to get species s. Apparently, the argument is imposed by the introduction of the previous specification of the species composition as a welfare function recognising collective action.

$$V_i^r = V_i^r \left[p, y - a_i^r \frac{B}{n\left[\sum_j x_j^f b_j^f + \sum_i x_j^r b_j^r\right]} x_i^r (1 - b_i^r),\ \frac{B}{n\left[\sum_j x_j^f b_j^f + \sum_i x_j^r b_j^r\right]} x_i^r (1 - b_i^r),\right.$$

$$\left. \Omega \cdot [b_1^f, \ldots, b_m^f, b_1^r, \ldots, b_n^r]' + \varpi \cdot B, B \right] \tag{12.14}$$

This formulation makes the individual objective function dependent on allocation decisions of all individuals in the community, say all b_is, b_js, and finance a^i. The collective decision on providing nature s can be expressed as a vector b. Moreover, the formulation still fits in the given frame for the political economy analysis. In the equation the arguments for the welfare of residents are, first, the 'traditional' price vector and income which are exogenous, and, secondly, the fee to be paid for the appearance of nature a^i, the individual land b^i to be made as physical contribution, the collective action as vector b, and B as size of the main structure in the community. These variables are endogenous to individuals and politically decisive. Thus, individual welfare is contingent on collective decision making.

6 POLITICAL BARGAINING SOLUTION AND INSTITUTIONS

6.1 Principles

In contrast to a situation in which a benevolent manager of the club is the manager of nature, this chapter uses a political economy bargaining model drawing on a game structure. The manager collects financial contributions for the public good provision from citizens as club members and 'organises' provision of the public good being a non-impartial manager. The manager has to negotiate contributions a^i in a power struggle, modelled as a political economy bargaining process, and can redistribute benefits (Harsanyi 1963). He also is interested in his own benefit. The envisaged political economy bargaining process appeals to a structure of bilateral negotiations on individual contributions. Negotiations are between the manager of the environmental good and residents of farmers (or group wise). The manager is entitled to raise money and uses the money for payment to farmers. The beneficiaries, who enjoy amenities from the environment, have to pay or provide land, but, due to political power, can gradually take free rider positions. Nevertheless, as a manager with statutory power, the manager guarantees finance and nature provision on the community level. These features imply a multiple bargaining model (Harsanyi 1963). A multiple bargaining model, as in real politics, enables one to depict the heterogeneity of interests in public goods provision, asymmetry in power, and enforcement. In comparison with the benevolent dictator model, it is the more realistic model that includes social power and individual preferences.

As a participatory approach, political economy bargaining models can also recognise a diversity of residents' interests in the provision of public goods and can serve as an analytical tool to merge individual interests to public interest. Due to the bargaining involved, specifics on nature and prevailing interests in nature preservation are revealed to the manager. However, because the manager as a mediator has to consider the interests and the political power of individuals and groups, his final decision will not only be subject to overall welfare but also to his political support function. The support function increases his economic and social position. A model on bargaining in participatory or public domain decision making adopts that framework and uses above specified welfare functions. In doing so welfare functions are converted into interest functions. The formulation of interest functions in a modern game theoretical fashion has the advantage of recognising the bargaining positions of each participant. In particular, strategic behavioural functions of individuals are recognised. Therefore, response functions to conflicts in interest are modelled. Further, note that only one *s* prevails.

6.2 Interest Functions, Institutional Amendments and Payment Scheme

In section 5 it was discussed how the decision making of residents concerning financial contributions and land allocation to the main structure can reveal preferences for nature as a public good. The sum of financial contributions serves as a manager of the public good to create incentives for farmers who contribute land to the main structure. Thus, provision of land from the farm side no longer relies solely on statutory regulations. Practically, for the sake of integration of payments as variable in negotiations and institutions, we can use equation (12.8), objective function of farmers, to implement compensation payments on land devoted to the main structure. In the revenue part, we have to recognise additional revenues from payments on land devoted to the main structure as field margins. Payments always have a price component, that is as a^f_j, the negotiated compensation for land, and a quantity component, b^f_j, the area.

$$P_{i,G} = \sum_i \left\{ p_j x^f_j g^f_i (1 - b^f_j) + a^f_j b^f_j - C\left[x^f_j g_i (1 - b^f_j), b^f_j, B, r_j \right] \right\}$$

$$\text{with constant } x_j = x^f_j \qquad (12.15)$$

The payment may not totally compensate farmers or might overcompensate some farmers. The effect crucially depends on the change of the cost function as dependent on the size of the main structure. Hence, negotiation in communities can alter both payments and costs.

6.3 Complete Bargaining Equilibrium

The model of the bargaining centres around Harsanyi's (1963) multiple agent model (equation 12.16) using interest functions I_j^f (farm profits), I_i^r (citizens' utility) and I^m (manager's utility), as well as $I_j^{f,0}$, $I_i^{r,0}$ and $I^{m,0}$ as reference for not co-operating.

$$L = [\prod_j \prod_i (I_j^f - I_j^{f,0})](I_i^r - I_i^{r,0})(I^m - I^{m,0}) \tag{12.16}$$

Moreover, an interior solution, to be derived, is similar to the one prescribed by Rausser and Zusman (1992), resulting in a weighted objective function (logarithmic presentation of (12.16)). In that function, individual weights correspond to the power of pressure groups. As Zusman (1976) has shown, the bargaining solutions are not the same as policy preference function approaches. Instead, the author (Zusman) shows that the weights reflect the analytic properties of both aspects, the 'production function' aspect and the 'resources devotion' aspect, in bargaining. The weight can be computed from the production function. However, it gives:

$$W = \sum_j (1+w_j^f) \left\{ \frac{B[p_j x_j^*(1-b_j) + a_j^f b_j^f - C(x_j^*(1-b_j), b_j, r)]}{m\left[\sum_j x_j^f b_j^f + \sum_i x_j^r b_j^r\right]} \right\} +$$

$$\sum_i (1+w_i^r) V_i^r \{p, y - a_i^r [x_i^r(1-b_i^r)] \left\{ \frac{B}{n\left[\sum_j x_j^f b_j^f + \sum_i x_j^r b_j^r\right]} \right\},$$

$$\left\{ \frac{B}{n\left[\sum_j x_j^f b_j^f + \sum_i x_j^r b_j^r\right]} [x_i^r(1-b_i^r)] \right\}, \Omega\, [b_1^f, \ldots, b_m^f, b_1^r, \ldots, b_n^r]' + \varpi B, B\}$$

(12.16')

The weights $w_1, \ldots, w_j \ldots, w_m$ on the farm side and weights $w_1, \ldots, w_i, \ldots, w_n$ on the residents side correspond to the ratio of achievements in the bargaining process (optimal interest function in the bargaining process). They can also be expressed as the first derivative of the strength or power in bargaining, that is, acquired from the threat strategy not to co-operate minus the reference interest. Formally, weights can be derived as ratios on deviation from initial wealth subject to a situation of not attending. For example, the ratio for farm j is:

$$\ldots; w_j = \frac{(I_m^{opt.} - I^{m,0})}{(I_j^{opt.} - I_j^{f,0})} = \frac{\partial s(c_j, \delta_j)}{\partial c_j}; \ldots; w_i = \frac{(I_m^{opt.} - I^{m,0})}{(I_i^{opt.} - I_i^{r,0})} = \frac{\partial s(c_i, \delta_i)}{\partial c_i} \tag{12.17}$$

Calculating derivatives of the public welfare function W provide a bargaining solution:

$$\frac{\partial W}{\partial b_j^f} = B(1+w_j)\left\{ \frac{\left\{ p_j x_j^* + a_j^f - \frac{\partial C[.]}{\partial b_j} \right\}}{m\left[\sum_j x_j^f b_j^f + \sum_i x_j^r b_j^r \right]} + \frac{\left\{ p_j^f x_j^f (1 - b_j^f) + a_j^f b_j^f - C[.] \right\}}{-m\left[\sum_j x_j^f b_j^f + \sum_i x_j^r b_j^r \right]^2} \right\} +$$

$$(1+w_i^r)\frac{\partial V_i^r[.]}{\partial l_i^r}\frac{\partial l_i^r}{\partial b_j} + \frac{\partial V_i^r[.]}{\partial s}\frac{\partial s}{\partial b_j} = 0 \tag{12.18a}$$

$$\frac{\partial W}{\partial a_j^f} = B(1+w_j^r)\left\{ \frac{b_j^f}{m\left[\sum_j x_j^f b_j^f + \sum_i x_j^r b_j^r \right]} \right\} = 0 \tag{12.18b}$$

$$\frac{\partial W}{\partial b_i^r} = (1+w_j)\frac{\partial P_j^f(.)}{\partial l_j}\frac{\partial l_j}{\partial b_i^r} + (1+w_i^r)$$

$$\left\{\frac{\partial V_i^r[.]}{\partial y}a_i^r x_i^r + \frac{\partial V_i^r[.]}{\partial l_i^r}x_i^r \frac{B}{-n\left[\sum_j x_j^f b_j^f + \sum_i x_j^r b_j^r\right]}\right\} + \left\{\frac{\partial V_i^r[.]}{\partial y}a_i^r x_i^r\right.$$

$$\left.(1-b_i^r) + \frac{\partial V_i^r[.]}{\partial l_i^r}x_i^r(1-b_i^r)\frac{B}{n\left[\sum_j x_j^f b_j^f + \sum_i x_j^r b_j^r\right]^2}\right\} + \frac{\partial V_i^r[.]}{\partial s}\frac{\partial s}{\partial b_i^r} = 0$$

(12.18c)

...

$$\frac{\partial W}{\partial a_i^r} = (1+w_i^r)\left\{\frac{-x_i^r(1-b_i^r)}{n\left[\sum_j x_j^f b_j^f + \sum_i x_j^r b_j^r\right]}\right\} = 0 \quad (12.18d)$$

...

$$\frac{\partial W}{\partial B} = (1+w_j^f)\left\{\frac{\{p_j^f x_j^f(1-b_j^f) + a_j^f b_j^f - C[.]\}}{-m\left[\sum_j x_j^f b_j^f + \sum_i x_j^r b_j^r\right]}\right\} + (1+w_i^r)\frac{\partial V_i^r[.]}{\partial B} = 0$$

(12.18e)

As we can see, this solution to the complete bargaining process is a complicated mathematical expression. However, as has been shown (Zusman 1976), it is possible to rccognise the various necessary elements for co-operative provision, that is of nature. For simplification, one can imagine that a partial solution already reveals crucial aspects. For instance, as we will see, a restricted analysis that primarily deals with farmers easily provides an analytical solution.

6.4 Simplified Bargaining Equilibrium with Lobbying Farmers and a Resident Group

To solve the above system explicitly, assumptions on the cost (farmers) and indirect utility functions (residents) are needed. Linear supply and factor demand functions correspond to quadratic cost and utility functions. For instance, assuming a linear quadratic cost function (Nuppenau and Slangen 1998) for the provision of field margins to the main structure as

$$C\,[x_j^*(1-b_j),b_j,B,r]=\gamma_{0j}b_j+0.5\,\gamma_{1j}b_j^2+\gamma_{2j}b_jr_j+\gamma_{3j}B+\gamma_{4j}B^2+\gamma_{5j}Bb_j \tag{12.19}$$

and a simple quadratic utility function that only refers to the size of the main structure for residents, we can comparatively easily model a situation that reflects the problem of collective provision of an ecological main structure from the farm side. However, from an institutional point of view we have excluded payments. To solve that simplified system, let us also assume that we have only one lobby group for residents and that payments are not involved. If the 'demand' for the nature of that group of residents is a linear function, depending on B only, surplus or welfare is quadratic and interest can be modelled quite straightforwardly as:

$$V_r=\omega_0 B-\ 0.5\omega_1 B^2+\omega_2 Bp \tag{12.20}$$

This would give us, after individual market optimisation, that is as a reference system, an equilibrium condition of $\omega_0-\omega_1 B = a^r$, if a market would prevail. But depicting the interest function in situations of collective bargaining, surplus *and* payments remain with the lobby group.

Inserting the condition for total provision to the main structure (in the equation (12.18e)) and using the explicitly specified quadratic approximation of individual optimality conditions for farms and residents, we receive, as result of bargaining:

$$(1+w_j)\left\{p_jx_j^*-\gamma_{0j}+\gamma_{1j}b_j-\gamma_{2j}r_j\right\}-(1+w_E)\left\{\ \omega_0-\omega_1\ \left\{\sum_j Ax_j^*b_j\right\}\right\}=0 \tag{12.21}$$

For all b_j, that is field margins of the farmer, we get a new system of m equations that can be solved for $b^f=[b^f_1, ..., b^f_j, ..., b^f_m]$ analytically by inverting the right-hand matrix of the system:

$$\begin{bmatrix} (1+w_j)\gamma_{11}+(1+w_E)\omega_1 Gx_1^* & \cdots & (1+w_E)\omega_{11} Gx_1^* \\ (1+w_E)\omega_1 Gx_1^* & & (1+w_j)\gamma_{1m}+(1+w_E)\omega_1 Ax_m^* \end{bmatrix} \times$$

$$\begin{bmatrix} b^f_1 \\ \cdots \\ b^f_m \end{bmatrix} = \begin{bmatrix} (1+w_1)[p_1 x_1^* - \gamma_{01} - \gamma_{21} r_1] + (1+w^r)[\omega_0 + \omega_2 p] \\ \cdots \\ (1+w_j)[p_m x_m^* - \gamma_{0m} - \gamma_{2m} r_m] + (1+w^r)[\omega_0 + \omega_2 p] \end{bmatrix} \tag{12.22}$$

To summarise, the left-hand side can be expressed as a matrix Γ^*_1, multiplied by a vector of bargained field margins b^b(farmers and residents) and the right-hand side can be expressed as a vector taking care of exogenous factors such as input prices r and consumer prices p for residents. It shifts the solution. In the case of a specified indirect cost and utility functions, we receive

$$\Gamma^*_1\, b^b = (1 + w^f)[p - \gamma_0 - \gamma_2 \mathrm{r}] + (1 + w^r)\omega_0$$

$$\Leftrightarrow b^b = \Gamma^{*\,-1}_1\, (1 + w^f)[p - \gamma_0 - \gamma_2 r] + (1 + w^r)\omega_0 \tag{12.23}$$

The vector $b^b=[b^b_1,...,b^b_j,...,b^b_m]$ becomes calculable from the system of equations in (12.22). It depicts a bargaining solution, and vice versa the bargain solution reflects the political power structure. As we can see, if power is equally distributed, a reference vector b^s can be calculated showing the situation of a benevolent dictator. At least in theory, comparing three situations, the impacts of power on allocation of field margins and preferences can be distinguished. It could be assumed that large farmers have more bargaining power than smaller farmers. Figure 12.3 depicts such a situation, where small farmers (right side) are pushed into an oversupply of field margins while large-scale farmers (left side) may even enjoy a better position (undersupply; their bargaining of the supply function shifts to the left and in linear models the intercept may also change due to political power). The 'social' objective function is theoretically achieved if weights for different pressure groups are equal; a special case! It is therefore an empirical question to show how bargaining shifts the regulation of the manager.

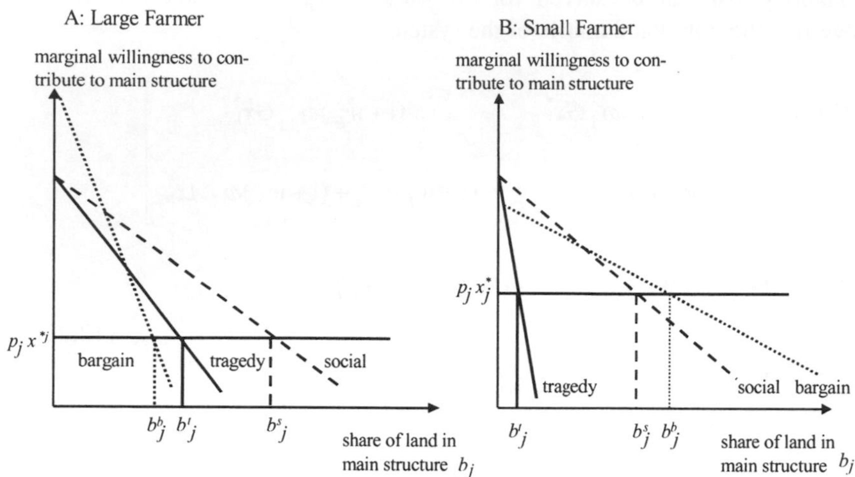

Figure 12.3 Bargaining solution and modified willingness to contribute after bargaining

Source: Own design.

With regard to empirical application, the individual cost functions on the farm side can be derived from behavioural estimations (see Nuppenau and Slangen 1998 for hints), and the welfare function of the residents is approachable from contingent valuation. Since the size of the main structure is normally referable from design of contingent valuation of particular studies, and the price or willingness to pay, per se, is part of the investigation, estimations of coefficients of the demand function for nature can be obtained from cross-section analysis.

7 SUMMARY AND OUTLOOK

The chapter started with the premise that the political process is considered as a substitute for market transactions of environmental goods, primarily because political decisions require consultation with the public and participatory approaches contain a bargaining element. That bargaining element was further developed. In doing so, we outlined a spatial framework for investigating collective decision making in a community of farmers and residents. Then we showed how a tragedy of the commons problem may prevail in the individual calculations of farmers for contributions to an ecological main structure. Extending the exercise, we contemplated how a mechanism could be designed that forces residents to reveal their preferences for nature. We thought that residents having the alternative of accepting income reducing contributions for financing land set aside by farmers or setting aside some of their own land will reveal preferences. Revelation of preferences will be done by responses of the land contribution alternative or accepting fees on land not devoted to the main structure.

Then, we sketched how a social optimum of field margin provision and finance of the main structures can be reached by multilateral bargaining. In pursuing that idea, a public good manager was entitled to charge individual contributions to beneficiaries and guarantee compensation payments to providers of nature. That approach adopted the predatory versus productive government framework. The concept of bargaining and, in particular, the specification of interest functions in bargaining were presented. Finally, for simplification, we showed that the general framework can be used to solve simpler partial problems.

In this chapter we also looked at potentials for empirical application. However, the chapter primarily provided a theoretical procedure to solve the problem of establishing rules for collective action and coercion in a political framework. In that solution, farmers', residents' and a manager's interests are reconsidered.

REFERENCES

Bartsch, E., M. Rauscher and I. Thomas (1993), 'Environmental Legislation and the Impact of Lobbying Activities', Working Paper No. 562, The Kiel Institute of World Economics.

Blamey, R., M. Common and J. Quiggin (1995), 'Respondents to Contingent Valuation Surveys: Consumers or Citizens?', *Australian Journal of Agricultural Economics*, **39** (3) (December), pp. 263–88.

Bullock, D.S. (1994), 'In Search of Rational Government: What Political Preference Function Studies Measure and Assume', *American Journal of Agricultural Economics*, **74** (3), pp. 347–61.

Chambers, R.G. (1988), *Applied Production Analysis: A Dual Approach*, Cambridge: Cambridge University Press.

Hanley, N., J. Shogren and B. White (1997), *Environmental Economics in Theory and Practice*, London: Macmillan.

Harsanyi, J.C. (1963), 'A Simplified Bargaining Model for the N-person Co-operative Game', *International Economic Review*, **4** (2), pp. 194–220.

Hodge, I.D. (1988), 'Property Institutions and Environmental Improvements', *Journal of Agricultural Economics*, **39** (3), pp. 369–75.

Hodge, I.D. (1991), 'The Provision of Public Goods in the Countryside: How Should it be Arranged?', in Hanley, N. (ed.), *Farming and Countryside. An Economic Analysis of External Costs and Benefits*, Wallingford: CABI, pp. 179–96.

Nuppenau, E.-A. and L.H.G. Slangen (1998), 'Nature Provision by Farmers and the Principal Agent Framework. How to Achieve Environmental Improvements in Agriculture through Improved Payment Schemes', *Forum*, **24**, Kiel.

Pashigian, B.P. (1985), 'Environmental Regulation: Whose Self-Interests are Being Protected?', *Economic Inquiry*, **23** (4), pp. 551–84.

Peltzman, S. (1976), 'Toward a More General Theory of Regulation', *Journal of Law and Economics*, **23** (2), pp. 211–40.

Rausser, G.C. (1992), 'Predatory versus Productive Governments. The Case of US Agricultural Policy', *Journal of Economic Perspectives*, **6** (3) pp. 133–57.

Rausser, G.C. and P. Zusman (1992), 'Public Policy and Constitutional Prescription', *American Journal of Agricultural Economics*, **74** (2), pp. 247–57.

Swinnen, J. and F. van der Zee (1993), 'The Political Economy of Agricultural Policies. A Survey', *European Review of Agricultural Economics*, **20** (3), pp. 261–90.

Wossink, A., C. Jurgens and J. van Wenun (1998), 'Optimal Allocation of Wildlife Conservation Areas within Agricultural Land', in Dabbert, S. et al. (eds), *The Economics of Landscape and Wildlife Conservation*, Wallingford: CABI, pp. 205–16.

Zusman, P. (1976), 'The Incorporation and Measurement of Social Power in Economic Models', *International Economic Review*, **17** (2), pp. 447–62.

PART V

The Role of Co-operative Arrangements in Implementing Environmental Policies

13. Developing Co-operative Approaches to Agri-environmental Policy: a Transactions Cost Perspective on Farmer Participation in Voluntary Schemes[1]

Katherine Falconer

1 INTRODUCTION

There is a perceived under-supply of agri-environmental goods in the EU, with continuing discussion of how provision could be increased. Agri-environmental policy across the EU is dominated by schemes implemented under Regulation 2078/92 which motivate individual farmers to commit voluntarily to produce countryside goods in return for compensatory payments. However, problems have been increasingly evident. For example, there is no back-up mechanism to persuade reluctant farmers to enter into management agreements and, in any case, participants may discontinue their participation at the end of the agreement or at an opt-out point several years after its start. Furthermore, the production of some important countryside goods such as landscape by individuals is 'non-separable': the co-operation of a number of producers is necessary. A fundamental problem is the absence of incentives for landholders to provide conservation goods collectively. Consequently, conservation management is fragmented, with a risk of lacking real ecological, landscape or amenity value.

An important policy need is the mobilisation of conservation scheme participation by groups of landowners to achieve a greater output of jointly produced countryside goods and services. Considerable academic and policy-making attention at present is focused on the development of a new model for rural support measures to maximise the environmental and economic benefits of policy reforms. Institutional development for sustainable rural development should aim at the encouragement of local, area-specific initiatives; bottom-up (participatory); multi-sectoral; innovation-orientated; and within national networks (von Meyer 1999). Centralised decision making may fail to produce adequate solutions if it is not linked to decentralised institutional arrangements. Therefore, consideration should be given to how appropriate strategies can be implemented and how participation can be motivated.

A basic assumption of the analysis presented here is that policy makers will wish to continue along 'soft-regulatory' lines, that is, maintaining the voluntary approach to land management improvement to achieve social goals. However, the aim is to foster stewardship, rather than to achieve the merely temporary provision of agri-environmental goods in return for payment. Furthermore, changes will not be made overnight. Thus, it is important to assess the scope for improvements to be made within the current institutional system. Transactions-cost economics is used here as a framework to guide thinking about the development of collective strategies to improve the provision and protection of natural resources and countryside goods. This chapter considers the transactional advantages and disadvantages of co-operative approaches to the procurement of agri-environmental goods from the private sector. Section 2 considers some problems of collective management in the context of current, voluntary policy. Section 3 outlines transactions-cost economics and its implications for agri-environmental policy. Section 4 assesses a new model for agri-environmental policy based on collective scheme entry, with further discussion in section 5.

2 FLAWS IN THE CURRENT VOLUNTARY APPROACH

2.1 Ecological Gaps and Fragmentation

Current agri-environmental schemes incorporate an individual basis to scheme entry, which is associated with significant transactions costs for both farmers and government agencies (see Falconer and Whitby 1999) and the risk of a fragmented response by landowners. There has been a preoccupation on the part of agricultural ministries with scheme recruitment rather than with environmental gain (Morris and Potter 1995) and, furthermore, participation has not been considered strategically by policy makers, in terms of its geographical patterns and relevance to ecological systems. These aspects result in low policy effectiveness and value for money.

There are strong ecological rationales for an underlying spatial strategy in agri-environmental policy, in order to reduce habitat fragmentation and to maintain ecological networks (Hobbs 1990; Adams et al. 1994; Kirby 1995). The physical isolation of conserved sites can have significant implications for habitat diversity, extinction rates and population genetics; micro-habitats need linking together through conservation management in the wider countryside. Furthermore, sites which are not of particularly high conservation value in themselves may nonetheless have conservation value by virtue of their location with respect to other sites (Adams et al. 1994). However, there is only limited scope for individual agri-environmental management agreements to deliver comprehensive conservation management reliably. Management agreements are generally negotiated with minimal reference to factors outside the farm boundary; the participation of one landholder is unconnected to the participation of his neighbour. Agreements are, at most, at farm level rather than having any inter-farm element to their design and, under some schemes, entry may be merely at the plot level. Survey work by Adams et al. (1994) suggested that farmers and conservation advisors in East Anglia in general do not think about conservation problems and solutions at a strategic level.

Farm conservation-management could be improved by being guided more by the needs of ecological systems and landscape attractiveness principles (O'Riordan 1994; Forman and Godron 1986; Selman 1993). MacFarlane (1998) called for a re-scaling of agri-environmental policy to a landscape or regional level, arguing for whole-farm or business targeting and for inter-farm co-operation. Schemes might be based on a broader system of environmental contracts to secure particular forms of conservation management in the wider countryside; such a structural approach could promote co-ordination between holdings. However, the achievement of this vision would require some degree of institutional reform (see Hodge et al. 1994); this chapter aims to assess the potential for such change. The next section assesses some current aspects of agri-environmental resource allocation where collaborative management is needed.

2.2 Common Land and Agri-environmental Schemes in the United Kingdom

The key, and the challenge, to the maintenance of the value of common land lies in collective management. A practical problem facing any person or body who wishes to change the management of a common is that some interference with the rights of commoners is usually required, so their agreement is needed. The greater the number of commoners, the greater the problems of achieving full co-operation (Howarth and Rodgers 1992). Frequently, commoners are represented by a voluntary management association (Countryside Commission 1986). An association might have powers relating to the implementation of approved co-operative management schemes, turning out of animals on to the common and gathering them in, the appointment and remuneration of officials and agents, and revenue raising by means of levies on members to cover administrative costs (Countryside Commission 1985).

An association cannot bind its members unless it is expressly authorised by each and every one to do so, and has no legal status as the representative of individual commons rights-holders (Countryside Commission 1986; Rodgers and Bishop 1999). The Commons Act 1899 allows a local authority to propose a commons management scheme, but nature conservation per se is not an objective for which the power may be exercised.[2] Furthermore, any such scheme is still subject to veto from the owner of the soil, or from one third of the commoners by value (ibid.). Given these constraints, it is unsurprising that common ownership poses challenges to the entry of the land into agri-environmental schemes.

The Environmentally Sensitive Area (ESA) scheme is the largest agri-environmental scheme in the UK. There are 43 designated areas at the sub-regional level; landowners within these may enter voluntarily into management agreements with the government in return for compensatory payments. For each ESA, there is a menu of conservation options and fixed-rate payments. The participation of all registered commoners is required for a satisfactory management agreement for common land within ESAs. However, universal agreement on entering common land into the scheme is rare, especially where agri-environmental management restrictions must apply to the whole farm. The lack of legal status of commons management associations means that management agreements under which stocking levels will be regulated in accordance with the overall management strategy for the site as a whole must be concluded with individual farmers (Rodgers and Bishop 1999).

Rodgers and Bishop (1999) found that in some areas, although the Ministry of Agriculture, Fisheries and Food (MAFF) had included common land in the ESA land designated as eligible for entry into the scheme, it was unwilling to negotiate with each individual farmer. Where a Commons Association is authorised to act on behalf of commoners, government agencies no longer have to approach each individual separately. If a management agreement to regulate the use of a common could be concluded with the Commons Association on behalf of individual commoners, policing issues could then be left in the hands of the Association. Guidelines (DETR 1998) now set out the circumstances in which MAFF will conclude joint management agreements with commoners through an association, with a view to self-regulation. Internal negotiation determines the division of payments and stocking reductions.

A problematic aspect in relation to agri-environmental scheme entry for common land is that if full participation is impossible, a risk assessment of the likelihood of non-participating farmers exercising their rights must be carried out. If the stocking on the commons exceeds the agreed figure, MAFF will hold the Commons Association responsible, and make reductions to all members' stocking limits, unless the culprit can be identified (Rodgers and Bishop 1999). This produces a substantial disincentive to participation, since it places the burden of risk firmly on those commoners who willingly participate in the conservation scheme (ibid.).[3] On 'hefted' commons, livestock are 'acclimatised' on a particular hill, and it is unnecessary to fence the holding and shepherding is made easier; hence it is fairly easy to target individual producers for management agreements and to reject spurious claims (Rodgers and Bishop, 1999). Open commons pose a less tractable problem, as it is easier for individual producers to vary their stocking levels which, given opportunistic behaviour, may undermine any conservation strategy for the site. In fact, at present, some large, geographically isolated commons are currently excluded from designated ESA scheme areas because it is impossible to prevent encroachment. Low observability of individuals' grazing is a fundamental problem: information asymmetry, often coupled with opportunism, is endemic.

Thus, to summarise, collective land ownership and its institutional requirements have contributed to a failure to achieve widespread participation in agri-environmental schemes for coherent agri-environmental management to be achieved. For example, the geographical pattern of ESA enrolment for the Lake District shows notable gaps in coverage; many of these gaps coincide with areas of common land, which is often of high conservation, landscape and access significance (MacFarlane 1998). Since landholder co-operation is needed to achieve agri-environmental objectives in areas of common land, it is necessary to identify and to overcome the constraints. However, while the complexity of common land management might pose barriers to agri-environmental management, it may in fact also offer opportunities for improved management at a more appropriate spatial level, lifting the focus up from individual farms. Some progress is now being made in some areas through the formation of commons management associations. The next section outlines the transactions-cost economics perspective on policy.

3 TRANSACTIONS-COST ECONOMICS AND AGRI-ENVIRONMENTAL POLICY

3.1 Transactions Attributes and Organisation

Standard, neoclassical economic theory considers a set of institutions that govern and regulate the process of exchange, and then proceeds to show that, given these institutions and other variables related to the economic system, one final allocation is superior to all others. However, transactions between economic agents are not costless and independent of their institutional context, and many phenomena can only be explained by explicitly stating the nature of such costs. Transactions-costs (TCs) are related to the institutional environment; choosing one institutional system may involve higher or lower TCs than another institutional system (Dahlman 1980).

'Transactions-costs economics' (TCE) can provide a fresh perspective on the organisation of agri-environmental provision. If TCs are non-zero, organisational choice will have a resource allocation impact. Different approaches will not be equally efficient in achieving policy objectives (Williamson 1985), so one final allocation may be superior if fewer resources are expended in moving to that rather than to any other final allocation. Institutional developments such as policy formation can contribute to the reduction of the TCs of allocating resources to different uses to achieve particular goals. The high TCs of resource allocation directed by private, atomised markets to provide agri-environmental goods and services has resulted in market failure and externalities. Policy mechanisms have developed across the EU to provide alternative ways to move towards the optimal provision of such goods, primarily through the establishment of quasi-markets, using a state agency as a nexus for landowner/society transactions to provide agri-environmental goods. However, any chosen policy mechanism will need to cope with the unavoidable transactional attributes of agri-environmental goods, particularly low observability coupled with opportunism of suppliers.

It is necessary to identify the defining attributes of transactions in order to identify the best mode of organisation for any given resource use or exchange. A transactional perspective is highly appropriate, given the procurement basis of much EU agri-environmental policy. This approach necessitates substantial transacting between economic agents. Policy design could be improved by relating policy features to the existence of TCs between stages of resource allocation, the factors linked to TCs and participants' resultant strategies.

A hurdle for analysis is the absence of a clear definition of TCs. A cost typology might be developed in general terms based on the phases of exchange (see Coase 1960). There is a spectrum of organisational costs to consider. At root are information deficiencies. The reason for the existence of TCs in many scenarios is the degree of heterogeneity of the characteristics of the commodity to be exchanged, and the difficulties of specifying precisely every potential contingency. For example, in the agricultural sphere, no two plots of land are identical; consequently, extensive and costly measurement is needed to determine the properties of each unit, for example in terms of agricultural productivity and conservation potential. To assess whether there are alternative organisational forms to quasi-markets that might be more effective, in transactional terms, it is necessary to establish when and why differential TCs arise between feasible alternative modes of organisation, along the spectrum from discrete market exchange to centralised hierarchical organisation. The factors leading to TC differences are examined next.

3.2 Transactions Attributes and Governance Structures

The characteristics of transactions have significant consequences for the structure of formal organisations. Williamson (1985) focused on several attributes: asset specificity; the observability of the asset at the level of the individual; the jointness of production (separability) of the asset; asymmetric information; and opportunistic behaviour.

Asset specificity refers to durable investments that are undertaken in support of particular transactions. Crucially, the value of the investment is usually much lower in its best alternative use, which means that the specific identity of the parties is very important and continuity of relationships is valued. Asset specificity distinguishes between the relative appropriateness of the competitive and governance contracting models; competition works well where asset specificity is negligible. Unified ownership (vertical integration) is more likely where investment is specific. Strategic hazards must be traded against the benefits of specific investments.

The degree of observability of the contributions of individual transacting parties is another important parameter, and is an aspect of the information asymmetry problem. For example, while individual farmers' tree-planting activities can be clearly attributed to each one, the provision of other agri-environmental goods and services, such as reductions in the level of pesticide contamination of water-courses is less easily linked to individuals. Where agents' objectives are imperfectly aligned, opportunism must be taken into account if the transaction is to achieve its planned outcome, and compliance monitoring and enforcement may be necessary. However, the influence of opportunism on economic organisation is conditional on the degree of asset specificity and the agent's capacity to respond to disturbances.

The production of various goods and services may also have various degrees of linkage between them. For goods of low separability, that is, high jointness of production, such as landscape, the inputs of different individuals are complements rather than substitutes. For example, water contamination levels will be the outcome of the agro-chemical usage of all landowners within that catchment, acting on an individual basis. In principle, individual emissions could be measured and controlled. Moreover, the abatement actions of one landowner might be traded-off against a failure to abate by another individual. The problem for policy makers is one of low observability, given the often prohibitively high costs of measuring individual contributions to an overall observed level. In contrast, consider the production of landscape, for which the actions of different landowners cannot be traded-off against each other. If one landowner refuses to maintain landscape features on his land, extra landscape management activity by another landowner will not compensate.

The presence, and degree, of the transactional characteristics outlined above have a major influence on the efficiency of alternative transacting modes (governance structures). Williamson (1985) developed four typologies or 'modalities' of labour market contracting according to cross-combinations of low/high specificity and the absence of the presence of output. The modalities are summarised in Table 13.1.

Table 13.1 Summary of Williamson's four organisational modalities

	Low asset specificity	High asset specificity
Separability	*Spot market*: short-term contracts and highly individualised incentives (e.g. piece-work) – easy monitoring as high observability	*Obligational market*: specificity means that contracts of longer duration are likely. High separability implies that implementation should be easy.
Non-separability	*Primitive team*: problems in identifying individual contributions to overall performance. Contracts are more complex than the spot market, with more costly monitoring required. Longer duration (given the costs of re-negotiation) but could be relatively short term still as low specificity	*Relational team*: complex organisation. Co-operation and shared values are needed to reduce opportunism. Contracts are likely to be relatively long term, to capitalise on the costs of building team-capabilities, with a greater role of organisational incentives over monetary incentives.

3.3 Agri-environmental Transactions Attributes

The focus of this research is on mechanisms to increase the provision of agri-environmental goods, particularly through the encouragement of private landowners to provide higher levels of public goods and hence to increase social welfare. TCE focuses on system-wide efficiency; economic actors are assumed to economise on both production and TCs. The economic problem of the provision of agri-environmental goods and services can be re-cast as a problem of how to organise the production of agri-environmental assets where some form of exchange is needed, rather than just a problem of measuring the costs of changing management practices more towards conservation-orientated goals. Agri-environmental goods comprise a very heterogeneous assortment, encompassing amenity landscapes, biodiversity, habitats, water quality and so on. Transactional problems such as asymmetric information (low observability of the output of the transaction), opportunism, locational asset specificity and non-separability (that is, the degree of jointness of production) will affect the relative TCs of different policy approaches and thus the appropriateness of different governance structures. For example, we might expect different structures for the provision of the various goods shown in the matrix in Table 13.2.

Table 13.2 A two-dimensional typology of agri-environmental assets

	Low separability	High separability
Low asset specificity	Water contamination from nitrates and pesticides	Hedges, stone walls, traditional farm buildings
High asset specificity	Habitats (moorland and wetland conservation or re-creation)	Micro-habitat protection (for example, ponds)

A major problem of agri-environmental contract design lies in the difficulty of observing changes in production practices and compliance with the terms of an agreement. The contractor (the state agri-environmental agency) must incur costs in obtaining the necessary information, or, given the likelihood of opportunism, must risk breaches of the agreement. TCE suggests that internal governance can reduce opportunism if it is related to the specificity of assets involved; otherwise, contracts should prevail. In terms of agri-environmental provision, this might imply public ownership and management of land, or control over land by another body (such as a Commons Management Association), perhaps in return for compensation payments made to landowners. The long-term nature of development of some goods (especially bio-diversity) also, in effect, amounting to asset specificity, implies that on-going relationships are needed with land managers. A particular characteristic of agri-environmental goods is asymmetric asset specificity.[4]

Given the non-separability of environmental goods such as landscape, issues relate to how co-ordination between landholders can be achieved, as the activities on one parcel of land will affect the productivity of management activities on another (for example, in terms of landscape effects and wildlife movement) because of its proximity. Landscape value-added from conservation management by one landowner may only be possible to the extent that neighbouring landowners similarly maintain grazing practices, engage in hedge and wall maintenance and so on. So, for example, there could be benefits for agri-environmental provision of the increased integration of supply. The rest of the chapter focuses on the organisation of the supply of non-separable agri-environmental goods, given the problems of current schemes outlined in section 2. Transactions-cost analysis implies that the relational team-work mode might be most appropriate, although few forms have developed so far in the agri-environmental sphere. Therefore, the next section discusses the potential role for environmental co-operatives to form to achieve policy objectives.

4 A NEW MODEL FOR AGRI-ENVIRONMENTAL SCHEMES

Policy has developed to procure goods from the private sector, but there are flaws and inadequacies in the current framework, suggesting that improvements should be made to improve environmental effectiveness and value for money. The proposed future direction of the Common Agricultural Policy towards greater subsidiarity could perhaps include more devolution of conservation procurement mechanisms to the local level, with the development of new approaches to agri-environmental organisation (and especially a more integrated spatial strategy to ecological management) while building on the policy of management agreements between individual farmers and the state.

4.1 Co-operative Approaches to Agri-environmental Management

The collective dimension to procurement contracts deserves particular consideration. Having started from Coasian free market negotiations between individual farmers and individual members of society, agri-environmental policy has developed based on voluntary management agreements between individual farmers and the government, representing the interests of members of society. 'Collectivisation' in the agri-environmental sphere could now develop beyond state–farmer contracting (collectivised demand) towards state–farmer association contracting (collectivised supply, perhaps through co-operatives). In terms of Williamson's typology, co-operatives are a mixture of market and hierarchical transactions, or a third institutional dimension, the network (Bager 1996).

Hence, one approach to policy development might be a focus on co-operative conservation management by private landholders, as part of a new policy direction building on the existing policy framework. Some elements of the present system likely to be maintained for the time being include procurement of agri-environmental goods from the private sector by the state; compensation payments to private landholders who participate in agri-environmental schemes; and varying degrees of differentiation of these payments (scheme targeting). However, there is scope to make significant incremental improvements within the present system of property rights assignments. Policy development should include the creation of mechanisms and incentives for collaborative action. A re-orientation of agri-environmental policies is now needed – away from the present focus on individual farms and holdings towards broader geographical coverage and management of land across ownership boundaries.

MacFarlane (1998) suggested that spatially adjacent farms should co-operate through multi-farm management agreements. Bilateral state–landowner transactions would be replaced by trilateral (or greater) transactions at the horizontal level. Slangen (1994) suggested that 'environmental co-operatives' could permit considerable cost savings (for example, in terms of government administration) in relation to the achievement of agri-environmental policy goals, and could be an appropriate way of providing agri-environmental goods produced jointly by different landowners. New or better-promoted collaborative entry options could also assist the functioning of current schemes: for example, small landholders are effectively disadvantaged under the English Countryside Stewardship Scheme for which payments are made on a discretionary basis, although their plans may well be of high conservation value. Combined, collective applications would assist them to participate and improve their conservation management. Some transactional and institutional aspects of collaborative agri-environmental management agreements are considered in more detail below.

4.2 Co-operative Formation and Willingness to Co-operate

'Market failure', for example relating to the sub-optimal provision of public goods in the countryside, is a necessary but insufficient pre-condition for co-operative formation. Farmers must see a need to counteract market failure, but they must also possess the ability to act collectively, taking into consideration the possible divergence of their individual interests. Farmers may form co-operatives for positive reasons; there may be non-economic motives, such as co-operative membership being 'the right thing to do', based on shared values. Farmers may thus be acting on the basis of legitimacy, rather than efficiency, with ideological reasons for membership. Where there is a tradition of co-operation, reviving the co-operative form ethic (see Dahlman 1980) may be easier than where there is not (see Brown 1997).

The processes of co-operative formation and the role of attitudes and changes in these, and the incentives that might need to be created for partnership approaches, should be considered. Several stages of development can be identified: a recognition of a need for co-operative management; the establishment of a management association (and determination of constitutional aspects such as the scope of membership, decision-making procedures and sanctions); internal negotiation over strategies (including agri-environmental scheme participation); external activities to influence the economic conditions within which the collective is to operate (for example, through lobbying); and the provision of information and advice. Support from external bodies may be needed, for example in terms of conservation management extension.

There will be problems for collective management schemes to address, for example relating to potential unwillingness to work with neighbours or problems determining liability in the event of non-compliance with prescriptions. Behavioural aspects may be of high importance if schemes are to be based more on co-operative actions: for example, trust of neighbouring landowners is needed if successful co-operative agreements are to be made. MacFarlane (1998) investigated the scope for farms to facilitate landscape-scale management through management agreements that explicitly specify the ecological and aesthetic linkages between holdings. MacFarlane found that 72 per cent of a survey sample were already involved in co-operative arrangements with one or more of their neighbours, for example for equipment sharing and livestock gathering. A relatively small number of farmers were in favour of a co-operative option for ESA entry, but the proportion in favour who also enjoyed good relations with their neighbours was significantly higher (83 per cent) than for those who were against the proposal (55 per cent).

4.3 Transactions Costs

The advantages and disadvantages of co-operative approaches to agri-environmental provision need careful consideration. A problem is that inter-farm co-operation, especially for conservation, is a radical idea for farmers. A workable approach must not be more administratively cumbersome than the current system. Environmental co-operatives must still perform the same transacting activities as individual scheme participants and more, given the need for internal co-ordination prior to interaction with the government agency charged with implementing any particular scheme.

An important issue is whether collective approaches to the provision of conservation through public procurement can play an economising role in organisational terms, and if so, to what extent. The competencies and responsibilities that are transferred from conventional policy administrative units to environmental co-operatives will influence transactions costs. Collective management bodies could have transactional advantages through substituting some external transactions (such as compliance monitoring and enforcement by the state) by internal activities, although the relative costs in each sector need consideration.

There may be scope for economies of scale, for example in relation to providing advice, the initial conservation audit, the formulation of a conservation management plan and compliance monitoring. Co-operative agri-environmental schemes may have lower aggregate transactions costs as, for example, there will only be one set of negotiations with the government agency implementing the management agreement scheme. Environmental co-operatives may be able to perform some tasks at a lower cost, for example monitoring the management activities of participants because they may have transactional advantages in terms of lower information asymmetry and perhaps lower opportunism given social sanctions. Members of an environmental management association will be contained within a small geographical area, and will probably be friends or family, strengthening the potential for social sanctions. However, such ties may also have negative effects on the achievement of conservation goals by the organisation, for example if members turn a blind eye on breaches of any management agreement. Penalties might be applied on a pro-rata basis across the whole co-operative, rather than just levied on the individual defaulter, to strengthen incentives for enforcement. Ideally, that mix of policies which minimises total costs, that is, both scheme compliance and organisation costs, should be selected, so it is important to consider problems of market failure if provision is to be through collectives (locational oligopolies). Collusion against the implementing agency is a risk; external policing of the associations will be needed.

Co-operatives may constitute a more efficient mechanism than other arrangements for the procurement of agri-environmental goods, avoiding the inflexibility and administration costs associated with full integration of provision into the public sector (for example, by land ownership and management) while potentially providing transactional cost advantages compared to the pure market solution. However, at the same time, other transactional factors may reduce the advantage of the co-operative form. The transactions-cost burden may simply be shifted from public sector agencies to the co-operative (through the need to conduct non-trivial internal negotiations). This is inevitably an issue for empirical investigation.

4.4 Incentives for Participation

The co-operative agreement needs to be attractive for participants, if it is to be sustainable. Members must be able to benefit as well as there being an overall increase in welfare more broadly. Co-operatives might fulfil a number of tasks likely to be beneficial to members, such as information collection and exchange, which could reduce information asymmetry to facilitate the efficient functioning of economic mechanisms in addition to having a suasive role. Co-operatives might also stimulate research, extension and education, since a collective can take advantage of greater economies of scale than can an individual producer. A co-operative could also provide a consultative body for members, and an intermediary body for interactions with government or other groups within society, with scope for the better protection of members' interests. There is also the possibility of pre-empting stricter legislation, and perhaps political benefits of improved public relations for the sector following wider recognition of its activities and achievements (Wallace-Jones 1998).

There may be a problem of reluctance to participate in co-operative management efforts given the extra burden that would be entailed in terms of independent verification procedures and self-reporting or monitoring for external credibility of the voluntary approach. Additional premiums for collaboration would probably be required, in addition to existing compensation payments for conservation management (available on an individual basis), to stimulate adequate participation. Extra payment might be made per additional participant in a joint management agreement, or on a per-hectare basis if the area of land entered into a particular scheme is above a specified size.[5] These premiums would compensate for the costs of the additional negotiating activity required between landholders in order to enter a scheme as a group. Extra premiums may also be needed given the risks of opportunistic behaviour by some members of the co-operative.

4.5 Human Capital and Social Aspects of Environmental Management Co-operation

Voluntary co-operation among farmers could contribute to the achievement of a number of longer-term objectives. For example, co-operatives could facilitate the process of consensus building for protecting natural resources by making use of the networks and communication channels constructed as a result of improving the acceptability of agri-environmental schemes. Interaction in a semi-formalised way should assist the mobilisation of farmers' endogenous potential of knowledge and motivation. From an institutional perspective, the initiative would signal an increased emphasis on decentralised regional approaches to policy. Positive aspects of agri-environmental co-operatives relate, for example, to being rooted in the local community, having a strong sense of historical continuity, and local pride in caring for a valued community asset (Countryside Commission 1985). However, these advantages must be balanced against negative aspects such as the fact that an emphasis on local issues may mean that insufficient attention might be paid to regional recreational pressures and national concerns of landscape and nature conservation (ibid.).

Co-operatives may have a number of advantages in terms of the social aspects of decision making. For example, voluntariness and consultation can increase the legitimacy and support for a policy. Linked to the encouragement of longer-term conservation management, individuals may be more reluctant to drop out of schemes if they are part of a collaborative strategy given social sanctions. However, being tied in to a collective scheme will inevitably reduce flexibility, since a deeper commitment has been made by an individual than if he were simply to enter a conservation scheme by himself; higher compensation may be required for this aspect, too. The specificity of human capital within government agency staff related to the management of the site for conservation (and perhaps also agricultural) objectives must also be considered. Breaking off a transaction may lose a significant part of its value, especially where it is embedded socially. The behavioural assumptions commonly applied in modelling transactions must be carefully assessed, particularly that of opportunism (Granovetter 1985). Personal relations between co-operative members may discourage malfeasance, quite apart from any incentives generated by the formal, institutional arrangements, and can strengthen contracts and improve performance. Reputation effects may deter breaches of agreements; peer pressure on farmers to be environmentally sound may be useful in countering opportunism. However, some management practices are more observable than others.

Attitudes, and variation in these across different parties, are central.[6] Co-operative agri-environmental schemes would be expected to be more successful given more farmers with positive attitudes towards conservation, which might have a reinforcing effect on the conservation decisions of farmers in that area due to peer pressure and moral suasion.[7] Farmers are highly diverse in terms of their degree of business ownership and control, personal characteristics, knowledge and skills, and outlook as managers. If management agreements are to be entered on an area basis, the dispersion and interaction of different types of farmer will be crucial to the participation outcome. Better awareness of a scheme and its objectives might improve participation (Morris and Potter 1995). If passive participants make up the bulk of farmers enrolled or enrolling in schemes, there will still be a very strong need for pro-active promotion by the agency.

5 DISCUSSION

Transactions-cost economics has been examined as a theoretical perspective to conceptualise new forms of participation and co-operation to improve the protection of natural resources and to guide agri-environmental policy developments. Different institutional arrangements will be of varying appropriateness for any given transacting scenario. This chapter has focused on the relative appropriateness of the collective organisational mode for providing non-separable agri-environmental goods most effectively. Particular interest lies in the benefits that greater partnership might bring, particularly within the private sector, to achieve public policy goals. Collectivisation through the development of agri-environmental co-operatives can have a number of benefits, for example in terms of transactional economising to facilitate the provision of non-separable goods such as landscape and wildlife habitat networks, as well as in terms of the social benefits of interaction.

Given at least some joint production of, for example, stonewalls and landscape, co-ordinated action by all landowners in the area may be needed, ideally, although so far little has been achieved in this area of policy making. It would be possible to develop broader landscape management schemes, instead of just focusing on individual contracts with farmers. However, the opportunities and risks for such mechanisms to work successfully, and their viability over time, need careful assessment. First of all, the focus should be placed on promoting participation; a critical mass is required for any collective management association (for example, for the fixed set-up costs to be worthwhile). Hence, examination of the factors likely to influence participation by individual farmers is important. There are significant hurdles to overcome, particularly given the novelty of the approach. A supporting framework will undoubtedly be needed: for example, in addition to additional inter-farmer negotiations, extra project officer involvement would be essential. There will be a number of basic requirements for successful environmental co-operatives:

1. positive environmental attitudes (support for policy goals);

2. existing collaborative networks with good communication channels and positive attitudes;
3. incentives for co-operative formation to cover the additional costs of collaboration and perhaps to cover the costs of increased risk;
4. standard form constitutions and collective management agreements to guide internal organisation and reduce set-up transactional costs;
5. promotion of collective approaches and their support by government project officers;
6. possibly, designation of high-priority areas for collective management.

Collective management agreements, for example for schemes similar to the UK ESA scheme, will in all likelihood entail greater administrative costs than individual management agreements.[8] However, it is essential to weigh the benefits of collective approaches to environmental goods provision against the extra administrative costs of co-ordination. Of central interest here are the likely outcomes, for example in terms of more coherent ecological and landscape management plans and higher social capital in localities, and the effectiveness (in environmental or other terms such as social capital building) of co-operative management. Organisational costs will affect the value-for-money of any expenditure to achieve agri-environmental objectives. Additional scheme costs should be considered in relation to the output brought forth under the policy that would not otherwise have occurred (in terms of conservation maintenance or enhancement, and also the development and maintenance of social capital). The additional costs of any proposed area-based management agreements should be linked to an assessment of the ecological and/or landscape connectivity of different land parcels, and the worth of co-operation.

Another issue is the long-run stability of co-operatives, and whether collective approaches to schemes can promote sustainable conservation management. This will depend on their promotion, members' experiences and the degree of capacity building over time. The evolutionary dynamics of the agri-environmental policy sphere cannot be over-emphasised; many schemes are largely exploratory still, and non-routinised. 'Learning by doing' is usually necessary given the limited scope for controlled experimentation, so responsiveness in organisations is essential for capacity building. Collective management through co-operative work could engender a stewardship ethic. In the future, if environmental co-operatives are successful as institutions and organisations of collective action, what processes of decision making and what policies of resource protection might be adopted by them in the long run? Could there be an increase in decentralised environmental management? It might be possible for environmental co-operatives themselves, by increasing participation and the responsibilities of their members, to develop opportunities for farmers to design environmental management measures to correct existing systems and take their own initiatives for new measures. Political legitimacy and acceptability are also important though (for example, in terms of who co-ordinates the process). Sustainability suggests that there should be greater decentralisation and more bottom-up rather than top-down institutional development, in the interests of social capital formation.[9]

6 CONCLUSION

Current policy is based on particular presumptions about property rights assignments, namely that farmers are to be compensated for the agricultural income foregone as a consequence of increasing the supply of agri-environmental goods. Management agreements are needed on a whole-farm and a neighbouring-farm basis, with guidance from ecological, landscape and catchment criteria. There is a value to contiguous conservation management: the non-separability of many agri-environmental goods has been much underrated in policy making to date. Co-ordination is needed if individuals' conservation actions are to have real value.[10]

Policy objectives should relate to the creation of landscapes and ecological networks on both area and regional scales, rather than just on the scale of individual sites. For agri-environmental policies to achieve their objectives, they need high uptake and integrated patterns of participation over large areas. This chapter has considered agri-environmental scheme administration and the potential to use existing frameworks to achieve improvements through the encouragement of collective (collaborative) management. Co-operative and individual management agreements need not be mutually exclusive. A suggested improvement to the existing framework is an additional entry option for agri-environmental schemes based on the joint entry into schemes by neighbouring landowners. This will probably involve incentives to encourage the development of collective, local-area management agreements. However, the benefits of co-operative approaches must be considered in the light of their costs, particularly as non-trivial organisational resources are likely to be needed if policy value-for-money is to be increased above that of the current system; organisational efficiency and cost-effectiveness are an area for further investigation.

NOTES

1. Grateful acknowledgement is made to Martin Whitby for comments on an earlier draft.

2. There are possibilities for controlling stocking levels through other legislation too, for example under the Commons Act 1908, and Local Acts, for example the Dartmoor Commons Act 1985 (see Howarth and Rodgers 1992).
3. Rodgers and Bishop (1999) found that of their survey sample, some scheme negotiators wanted at least 60 per cent of registered commoners to participate in the ESA scheme before a final management agreement was concluded, while others wanted a 70–80 per cent participation rate.
4. The supplier may have a relatively low commitment to transaction, given easy reversibility of conservation investments, while the 'buyer' is much more highly committed.
5. Some landholders might not have the potential to work with others, for example if they own large areas of land or whole catchments, hence a design solution could include a premium for entering large, contiguous areas.
6. An agri-environmental scheme participation spectrum can be identified, ranging from active adopters to resistant non-adopters (Morris and Potter 1995).
7. However, while enthusiast adopters may persuade laggards to enter, the direction of persuasion may work the other way too.
8. Falconer and Whitby (1999) found some evidence that in the English ESAs, extra administrative costs arose from the need to co-ordinate farmers' participation in relation to common land entry for ESAs.
9. An important issue is whether political decision makers (regional, national and EU) will in fact delegate responsibilities to environmental co-operatives, or whether they will consider them to be undesirable competition.
10. Although collaborative conservation management may be of varying importance in different areas, depending on the extent of fragmentation of land ownership in any given area.

REFERENCES

Adams, W.M., I. Hodge and N.A.D. Bourn (1994), 'Nature Conservation and the Management of the Wider Countryside in Eastern England', *Journal of Rural Studies*, **2** (10), pp. 147–57.

Bager, T. (1996), *Organisation in Sectors*, Denmark: South Jutland University Press.

Brown, A. (1997), 'The Re-making of Community: Crofting, Forestry and the Construction of the Crofter-Forester', Working Paper 27, Centre for Rural Economy, University of Newcastle.

Coase, R. (1960), 'The Problem of Social Cost', *Journal of Law and Economics*, **3**, pp. 1–44.

Countryside Commission (1985), *Management Schemes for Commons*, CCP 197, Cheltenham: Countryside Commission.

Countryside Commission (1986), *Common Land: The Report of the Common Land Forum*, CCP 215, Cheltenham: Countryside Commission.

Dahlman, C. (1980), *The Open Field System*, Cambridge: Cambridge University Press.

DETR (1998), *Appendix 4 to the Good Practice Guide on Managing the Use of Common Land*, London: HMSO.

Falconer, K.E. and M.C. Whitby (1999), 'Transactions and Administrative Costs of Countryside Stewardship Policies: an Investigation for Eight European Member States', Final report to the STEWPOL project (FAIR CT95/0709).

Forman, R.T. and M. Godron (1986), *Landscape Ecology*, Chichester: Wiley.

Granovetter, M. (1985), 'Economic Action and Social Structure: the Problem of Embeddedness', *American Journal of Sociology*, **91** (3), pp. 481–510.

Hobbs, R.J. (1990), 'Nature Conservation: the Role of Corridors', *Ambio*, **19**, pp. 94–95.

Hodge, I., W.M. Adams and N.A.D. Bourn (1994), 'Conservation Policy in the Wider Countryside: Agency Competition and Innovation', *Journal of Environmental Management and Planning*, **37**, pp. 199–213.

Howarth, W. and C.P. Rodgers (eds) (1992), *Agriculture, Conservation and Land Use: Law and Policy Issues for Rural Areas*, Cardiff: University of Wales Press.

Kirby, K. (1995), *Rebuilding the English Countryside: Habitat Fragmentation and Wildlife Corridors as Issues in Practical Conservation*, Peterborough: English Nature.

MacFarlane, F. (1998), 'Implementing Agri-environmental Policy: a Landscape Ecology Perspective', *Journal of Environmental Planning and Management*, **41** (5), pp. 575–96.

Meyer, H. v. (1999), 'Sustainable Development in Rural Europe: is Agenda 2000 a Step Forward?', Paper presented at the Agricultural Economics Society Conference, March 27–29, 1999, Belfast.

Morris, C. and C. Potter (1995), 'Recruiting the New Conservationists: Farmers' Adoption of Agri-Environmental Schemes in the UK', *Journal of Rural Studies*, **11**, pp. 51–63.

O'Riordan, T. (1994), 'Creating Whole Landscapes', *Countryside*, September/October, p. 7.

Rodgers, C. and J. Bishop (1999), *Management Agreements for Promoting Nature Conservation*, London: Royal Institute of Chartered Surveyors.

Selman, P. (1993), 'Landscape Ecology and Countryside Planning: Vision, Theory and Practice', *Journal of Rural Studies*, **9** (1), pp. 1–21.

Slangen, L.H.G. (1994), 'The Economic Aspects of Environmental Co-operatives for Farmers', *International Journal of Social Economics*, **21** (9), pp. 42–59.

Wallace-Jones, J. (1998), 'The Use of Voluntary Approaches as Environmental Policy Instruments', *FEEM* (*Fondazione Eni Enrico Mattei, Italy*) *Newsletter*, **3**, pp. 15–17.

Williamson, O.E. (1985), *The Economic Institutions of Capitalism*, New York: The Free Press.

14. The Role of Co-operative Agreements in Agriculture to Achieve EU Water Policy Targets

Floor Brouwer, Ingo Heinz and Thomas Zabel

1 INTRODUCTION

The application of the polluter pays principle has been an important factor for the achievement of environmental policy targets to control pollution from agricultural sources. According to this principle, 'the polluter should bear the expenses of carrying out . . . measures . . . to ensure that the environment is in an acceptable state'. The prevention of pollution at source is important in the attempt to achieve sustainable development. A more rational use of agro-chemicals, for example, could already provide a major contribution to the prevention of pollution. The directions towards sustainable agriculture are identified by the European Commission in its Communication (CEC 1999). Sustainability entails preserving the overall balance and value of the natural stocks and the inclusion of reflections on socio-economic costs and benefits of consumption and conservation in the short, medium and long run.

Environmental policy rests on four main types of instruments: regulatory instruments, market-based instruments (including economic and fiscal instruments, and voluntary agreements), horizontal supporting instruments (research, information, education, and so on) and financial support mechanisms (European Commission 1992). Until very recently, regulatory instruments through command-and-control measures have been the main policy instrument to control pollution from agriculture. In its Fifth Environmental Action Programme 'Towards sustainability', the Commission recommended to broaden the type of policy instruments, also incorporating economic instruments and voluntary approaches. The Programme states that 'in order to bring about substantial changes in current trends and practices and to involve all sectors of society, in a spirit of shared responsibility, a broader mix of instruments needs to be developed and applied'. This Action Programme reflects the calls for shared responsibility, as highlighted in the Brundtland Commission Report in 1987 (WCED 1987) and the 'partnership approach' which was endorsed during the Earth Summit in 1992 (UNCED 1992). A Communication of the European Commission concludes that environmental agreements 'can offer cost-effective solutions when implementing environmental objectives and can bring about effective measures in advance of and in supplement to legislation' (CEC 1996).

Traditionally, voluntary and farmer-led groups have been vital to the innovation into the agricultural sector. Study groups, for example, are seen as a type of self-regulation to cope with specific issues of concern. In the Netherlands, for example, study groups are an important instrument in fulfilling environmental goals (Just and Heinz 2000). Economic efficiency and effectiveness of achieving policy targets increasingly become important. In addition to the programmes that are based on measures taken by farmers, there is an increasing societal interest to involve the private domain in reducing pollution from agriculture. There exist some examples of voluntary arrangements made between farmers and water supply companies to reduce pollution and adapt more sustainable farming practices.

The objective of this chapter is to review the current and potential role of co-operative agreements between farmers and water supply companies and/or nature conservation organisations as an instrument to meet water policy objectives in a cost-effective manner. It is argued that these types of arrangements in the private domain would be a suitable instrument at regional level. It would at least complement and may even strengthen the current trend to further integrate environmental concerns in the Common Agricultural Policy (for example cross compliance and agri-environmental measures). Following a summary of the context of this type of instrument, some examples are provided of arrangements made within the European Union. The examples are drawn on the basis of their targets and type of support provided. Targets of these agreements may include groundwater and surface water quality, availability of water and conservation of ecosystems and conservation of aquatic ecosystems. The provision of aid to farmers might be based on direct payments from water supply companies, nature conservation bodies, subsidies or water intake charges.

2 THE PUBLIC AND PRIVATE DOMAIN IN ACHIEVING POLICY TARGETS

This section identifies co-operative agreements as arrangements in the private domain, either between farmers and water supply companies, or between farmers and nature conservation bodies. This type of instrument is typically based on bottom-up approaches with a high level of self-regulation through interaction among local and regional actors (for example water supply companies and farmers) (Figure 14.1). In contrast to such measures, agreements based on Regulation 2078/92 (or other agricultural support programmes) typically are in the public domain, possibly with private participation. We will identify some main features of the various types of policy instruments, allowing for comparison of co-operative agreements with other types of instruments to achieve more sustainable production methods in agriculture.

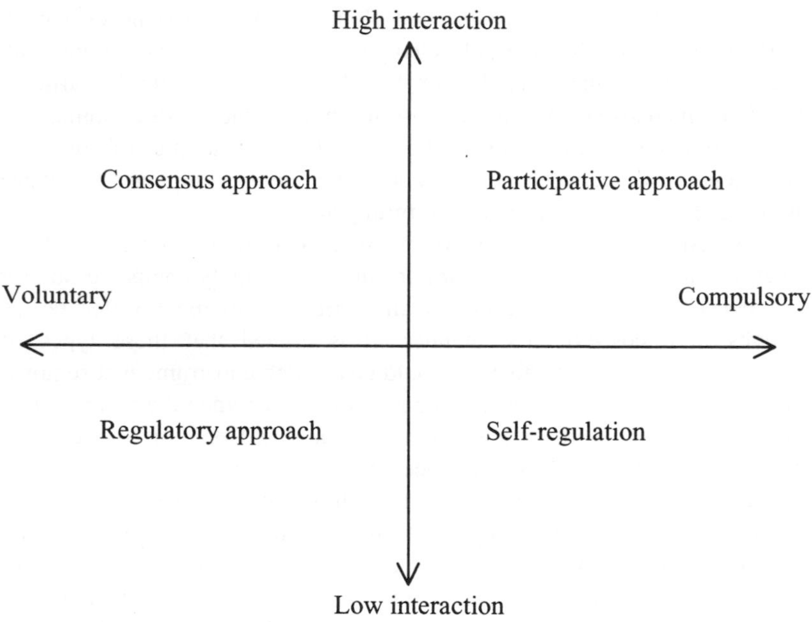

Source: Adapted from Liefferink 1997.

Figure 14.1 Alternative means to achieve environmental policy objectives

The traditional approach of achieving environmental targets in agriculture is regulatory, and a wide range of compulsory measures currently exists to control pollution. These measures are characterised by a low degree of interaction among public and private groups, and compliance is compulsory.

Command-and-control measures are commonly characterised by a high degree of policy intervention and limited interaction with the private groups. Measures taken are normally not compensated. The Nitrates Directive, for example, prohibits compensation being paid to farmers for observing the required standards with Nitrate Vulnerable Zones. However, Member States can and do offer limited aid to assist farmers in nutrient budget preparation and also in making capital investments to adjust their fertiliser usage practice so as to ease compliance with the Directive.

The interest has gradually increased over time to improve the interaction between public and private groups. This is reflected, among other indicators through the development of covenants. This approach is largely reached through regulation by consensus and negotiations. Covenants constitute a key policy instrument in the Netherlands to bring the national economy towards sustainability. An agreement was signed between the national government, the agricultural business sector and the pesticides industry to meet the targets of the Multi-Year Crop Protection Plan. As a result, the achievement of the objectives became a joint responsibility of these three partners. The agreement essentially includes measures which are agreed upon among the partners involved. Additional instruments might be introduced if the objectives are not met with the existing instruments. The provision of compensatory payments in the context of the agreements is rather uncommon, since it mainly provides a tool to achieve policy targets through interaction between public and private groups.

In contrast to the regulatory approach, the participative approach has also been developed over the past decade to reduce pollution through voluntary measures. It included a high level of interaction between the public and private sector. Many initiatives have been taken over the past couple of years to enhance environmentally friendly production methods in the European Union. They are increasingly based on voluntary approaches with the involvement of local groups and regional-specific measures. The 1992 reform of the Common Agricultural Policy recognised the need to contribute to an environmentally sustainable form of agricultural production and food quality and formalising the dual role of farmers as food producers and guardians of the countryside. This is reflected primarily by the aid scheme under Regulation 2078/92, which is aimed at encouraging farmers to introduce or continue with agricultural production methods compatible with the requirements of the protection of the environment and the maintenance of the countryside. Regulation 2078/92 currently is an important type of voluntary instrument in the context of the Common Agricultural Policy. At present, the Commission has approved more than 125 programmes and well over 2000 different measures. The programmes allow for aid to farmers who undertake certain measures, and are based solely on voluntary agreements made between farmers and government. The Regulation allows for compensatory payments to farmers taking action on the implementation and maintenance of agricultural production methods compatible with the requirements of the preservation of the environment and the maintenance of the countryside.

The provision of compensatory payments under Regulation 2078/92 depends on the effort made by the farmer, the loss of net income and the costs incurred as a result of compliance with the additional requirements. The premium may be increased by a margin not exceeding 20 per cent to encourage participation in the scheme. In this programme, effort must go beyond the requirements laid down in a Code of Good Agricultural Practice.

Finally, co-operative agreements are a type of self-regulation which is based on voluntary participation. The agreements are established mainly through efforts between water supply companies and the agricultural sector. Although we are well aware that many water supply companies are presently in the public domain, there is a vested interest in meeting quality requirements for the supply of water to consumers.

Some examples of co-operative agreements are presented in the next section, putting the instrument in the context of national policy requirements. The overview is aimed at exploring critical success factors for improving the economic and ecological efficiency of the European Union Water Policy through the provision of such agreements.

3 SOME EXAMPLES OF CO-OPERATIVE AGREEMENTS

Co-operative agreements have been used in Germany, in particular, and also to a lesser extent in Austria, the Netherlands and the United Kingdom, to achieve compliance with environmental and drinking water constraints. In such cases, the cost savings in drinking water treatment may well exceed the costs to agriculture arising from changing the farming methods. On the other hand, the use of co-operative agreements is presently rare in many Member States. Some examples of co-operative agreements are presented in this section.

3.1 Voluntary Agreements between Farmers and Water Companies in Germany

At present, approximately 400 co-operative agreements between farmers and drinking water companies exist in Germany. Compared to other Member States, the number of agreements is by far the highest in Germany. Decisive reasons for this are the very large number of often very small water companies (approximately 6600) and the relatively high proportion of drinking water abstracted from groundwater including artificial groundwater recharge (72 per cent). However, these two influences vary between the different regions in Germany. For instance, in Bavaria, which has about 2800 water companies and abstracts 94 per cent of its drinking water from groundwater, there are 143 co-operative agreements. In the other 'Bundesländer' where the proportion of groundwater is also above average, as in Lower Saxony and in Hesse, the use of these agreements is also widespread. An exception is North Rhine-Westfalia, where many co-operative agreements exist, but the proportion of drinking water derived from surface waters is relatively high (about 60 per cent) and the number of water companies is less than 100. Consequently, there must be further reasons for creating co-operative agreements between farmers and water companies in Germany.

Obtaining high quality drinking water seems to be a main incentive for the water companies to enter into negotiations with farmers. Most German water suppliers are reluctant to treat drinking water by using chemicals or other means. They prefer to protect the raw water sources by preventative measures wherever possible. This attitude is influenced strongly by the Germans' demand for pure 'natural' drinking water quality and the health concerns related to treated water. Furthermore, the requirement to comply with the maximum allowable concentrations (MACs) of 50 mg/l for nitrate and 0.1μg/l for individual pesticides, laid down in the EU Drinking Water Directives of 1980 and 1989, together with rising water pollution caused by agriculture, required actions by the water companies with potentially very high costs. Whereas in some EU member countries the water companies reacted by installing expensive water treatment facilities, for instance in the UK and in France, in Germany the companies strove to achieve a reduction in water pollution.

The problems experienced by the regulatory authorities to control compliance with legal regulations by farmers was an additional complication factor, mainly due to the diffuse character of the agricultural pollutants. Only in a few cases can the pollution be traced back to certain farmers, because the influencing factors, such as the type of soil, gradient of the slope, different rainfalls and complex groundwater flows, make this extremely difficult. Agricultural water pollution could not be prevented sufficiently even in those regions where statutory water protection zones with rigorous obligations for the farmers exist. Consequently, the water suppliers themselves have been forced to act. In most cases, the regulatory authorities are assisting in the establishment and operation of these voluntary co-operative agreements with farmers by partly funding the costs of changing agricultural practices.

A typical example can be found in the water catchment area 'Stevertalsperre' (River Stever Reservoir) located on the northern outskirts of the Ruhr area, from which drinking water for 1.8 million people is produced (Kooperation Land- und Wasserwirtschaft im Einzugsgebiet der Stevertalsperre 1998). Participants in this co-operative agreement are three water suppliers, including Gelsenwasser AG, one of the largest water companies in Germany (which supplies 210 million m³/year, one-third of which is to private households). About 3000 farms are located in this water catchment area of 90 000 ha. The co-operation between farmers and water suppliers was established in 1990 because the MAC for pesticides in the raw water was exceeded significantly, especially in the inflows to the Stevertalsperre. Nevertheless, Gelsenwasser AG had to treat the water in the meantime by activated carbon. In addition, the nitrate concentrations increased from year to year. Since the conflict between the water suppliers and farmers could not be solved by regulations, the government of North Rhine-Westfalia, together with the water companies, developed a joint arrangement.

3.1.1 Requirements for participation

In order to limit the water pollution and the increasing treatment costs, Gelsenwasser AG and the other water suppliers entered into negotiations with the farmers. An important incentive was a governmental announcement containing several measures, such as a ban on the use of atrazine and simazine in water catchment areas and the establishment of special programmes to promote the application of more environmentally friendly farming practices. A systematic advice programme for the farmers was developed, including demonstration projects and special rules for a better use of agro-chemicals and for extensifying farming.

There was a general understanding that the farmers should not suffer income losses. Therefore, the water companies and the government were ready to finance the advice programme. The underlying assumption was that the farmers' additional expenditures and yield losses would be more or less outweighed by their cost savings resulting from improved farming. Already at this early stage of the co-operative agreement, the government created the so-called 'Uferrandstreifenprogramm' (bankside protection strip programme) by which farmers are compensated for not using fertilisers and pesticides inside a zone of 3–5 metres along the banks of the rivers and streams flowing into the Stevertalsperre. The water companies provide additional funding for this programme. Presently, a total area of about 250 000 m² is regulated under this programme.

In order to motivate the farmers to enter into the co-operative agreement, they did not have to pay for the advice provided by agricultural authorities if they participated in the co-operative agreement. The farmers were contractually obliged neither to fill nor to clean their pesticide spraying machines on a hard surface (for example concrete) or near water courses. These measures were taken to reduce the risk of leaching of pesticides. Additional requirements were to avoid run-off during the application of pesticides by using suitable atomiser nozzles and by considering the weather conditions, to take into account the nitrate balance of the soils in applying fertilisers, to measure the nitrate content of manure, to abide by the rules of good agricultural practice as laid down in the new Düngeverordnung (fertiliser regulations) and in the Federal Plant Protection Law, and to participate in advice programmes.

3.1.2 Compensatory payments

If a farmer enters into the co-operative agreement, he will receive free advice on how to improve his production methods, and he will be allowed to participate in governmental funding programmes (for instance the 'Uferrandstreifenprogramm' or other special funds). As a result of the co-operative agreements, the legally binding controls, especially the obligations in statutory water protection zones, have become increasingly less significant. In the water catchment area of the Stevertalsperre there are some voluntary obligations agreed to by the farmers which take precedence over those usually required by the regulatory authorities in catchment areas. The regulatory authorities are accepting this, because they are convinced that advising farmers is more effective than regulating them.

Although farmers can claim compensation payments for compulsory obligations in water protection zones (according to §19 of the German Federal Water Act – Wasserhaushaltsgesetz), this policy instrument has contributed but little to the protection of waters. The main reasons are the compulsory character of this instrument and the insufficient level of compensating payments. In contrast, the voluntary agreements aim to help farmers to improve their practices on the basis of a dialogue with the water suppliers, who prefer to pay the farmers for changing their behaviour instead of paying compulsory compensations. The expenditure of the Gelsenwasser AG for the precautionary measures, such as the advisory service, water monitoring, research projects and compensation payments, amounts to 510 000 EURO/year on average (or 0.008 EURO per m^3 drinking water supplied to households).

3.1.3 Outcomes

Since the creation of the co-operative agreement 'Stevertalsperre' in 1990, a reduction in water pollution by nitrate and pesticides has been observed. In particular, the concentration of atrazine has decreased considerably although this is mainly a result of its ban. But without the co-operative agreement this significant improvement would not have taken place. On the other hand, the concentrations of nitrate and of individual pesticides, such as terbutylazine, bentazone and isoproturon, are still high and must be reduced by further efforts. As a consequence of the high water pollution the activated carbon treatment is still necessary. The treatment costs amount to about 1.5–2.0 million EURO/year (or on average 0.027 EURO per m^3 drinking water supplied to households). A comparison of the expenditures for precautionary measures with the treatment costs shows a high cost–benefit ratio (about 3.5) for the voluntary co-operative approach which would result if the raw water quality could be improved sufficiently to avoid the need for the activated carbon treatment (Heinz 1998). This is based on the assumption that, as already mentioned, the farmers do not suffer income losses and that the co-operative agreement will continue successfully over the coming years.

3.2 Voluntary Agreements between Farmers and Water Companies in the Netherlands

The Netherlands currently has 22 water supply companies, which in total extract about 1280 million m^3/year. About two-thirds of the extraction originates from groundwater. The organisations are public companies in which public authorities participate (provincial boards and municipality boards). In total there are around 10 agreements between water supply companies and farmers. They are in different stages of development. Some of them were already formed in the early 1990s, whereas others were only implemented very recently. Most programmes exist in the eastern and southern part of the country. The agreements typically allow farmers to join schemes with a wide diversity of options.

Nitrate levels in groundwater and the occurrence of pesticides are main issues in groundwater protection areas in the Netherlands. Most serious pressures on the environment are faced in the eastern and southern part of the country. That area is composed of sandy soils with a high share of intensive livestock production systems and arable production (for example growing potatoes with high levels of pesticide use). Concern about the pollution of groundwater resources from nitrates did induce debate to purify the water. Around 1990, the nitrate concentration in the upper groundwater (10 to 25 metres below the surface) exceeded the drinking water standard (50 mg per litre) in about 70 per cent of the agricultural land in sandy soils. The total expenses of drinking water companies for the removal of nitrates are assessed to be some NLG 17 million per year. In addition, the costs to remove pesticides from water resources amount to slightly more than NLG 20 million. Several drinking water supply companies have taken measures aimed at reducing pollution from pesticides and nitrates. Together with farmers, they take measures in groundwater protection areas at the farm and regional level, which go beyond national limits. Compensatory payments are provided for farmers joining such schemes. In addition, desiccation is also an issue of increasing concern in some parts of the country.

3.2.1 Requirements for participation

Several agreements have been developed among drinking water supply companies and individual farmers. Programmes are focusing on groundwater protection areas. Mineral accounting at farm level is a central part of the legislation to control standards in the context of the Nitrates Directive. National rules require farmers who need to prepare a mineral declaration system to apply their manure in an environmentally sound manner. Several programmes have focused on the provision of compensatory payments for programmes to reduce nitrogen surpluses. In addition, the environmental yardstick approach is applied as well as a basis for payments.

An agreement of the Water Supply Company in the province of Overijssel 'Gezonde Landbouw, Goed Drinkwater' (Health Agriculture, Good Drinking Water) provides incentives to farmers in their groundwater protection areas to reduce leaching of nitrates and pesticide use. Farmers may choose between six different options to stimulate environmentally friendly production methods:

- mineral balance (fixed payment);
- nitrogen reduction plan (fixed payment);
- integrated herbicide control in maize production (payment by result);
- integrated herbicide control in potatoes and cereals (payment by result);
- reduce the application of nitrogen from livestock manure on grassland (payment by result);
- reduce nitrogen surplus (payment by result).

Total costs for drinking water companies amounted to NLG 330 000 in 1998. Sixty per cent is used as direct income transfers through payments to farmers; the remaining part is mainly to facilitate the programme, provide information and support study groups. The provision of payments by result in the context of the programme to control herbicides in potatoes contributed to a substantial reduction in the environmental yardstick, as it reduced from around 1100 points per ha in 1996 to less than 300 in 1998. According to the method of environmental yardstick, the norm is 100 points per ha.

An agreement to provide incentives to farmers in the groundwater protection areas of Groningen and Drenthe was recently signed, and only started mid-1999. Requirements for joining this co-operative agreement focus on a reduction in pesticide use and use of organic fertilisers in groundwater protection areas. Essentially, the programme is developed such that farmers are compensated for the income foregone due to the tighter rules in groundwater protection areas. Some pesticides are not allowed to be used in the groundwater protection areas. Also, farmers are given incentives to reduce the use of livestock manure.

3.2.2 Compensatory payments

Several agreements provide compensatory payments to farmers for income foregone due to the measures taken. The project for agriculture in the groundwater protection areas of the provinces Drenthe and Groningen ('Uitvoeringsregeling voor landbouw in de grondwaterbeschermingsgebieden van Drenthe en Groningen 1999') include payments in the field of pesticides and manure.

Payments regarding the use of pesticides:

– potatoes: fixed payments of NLG 188 per ha are provided to meet the requirements of groundwater protection areas. Additional payments are provided in the case that extra measures are taken;
– seed potatoes: no cost differences of measures to meet the legal requirements of groundwater protection areas. Payments are only provided in the case that additional constraints are put to the use of pesticides;
– maize: the legal requirements of groundwater protection areas can be met without income loss, and no payments are provided for meeting the requirements of groundwater protection areas. Payments are only provided in the case that additional measures are taken.

Fixed payments are also provided for meeting the constraints on the use of organic manure. Payments depend on crop type and animal type. Payments also differ across provinces, since different rules apply to groundwater protection areas in the province of Groningen and of Drenthe. Whereas the supply of phosphate from livestock manure in groundwater protection areas should not exceed 75 kg per hectare, the province of Groningen puts an additional constraint limiting the application of phosphate to a maximum of 70 kg per hectare.

In addition, fixed payments are provided to dispose of excess manure outside groundwater protection areas. They cover the costs of transport, and amount to NLG 6 per m^3.

3.3 Voluntary Agreement between Farmers and a Water Supplier in the United Kingdom

The first such agreement has been made in the UK between Wessex Water and a number of farmers (ENDS 1998).

3.3.1 The main issues of concern

Nitrate levels in groundwater have increased steadily as a result of intensive farming in most of Wessex Water's groundwater resources. These comprise about 35 per cent of the Company's raw water resources for abstraction to drinking water. It is expected that a number of the sources will in the near future (5–10 years) exceed the drinking water standard of 50 mg nitrates per litre, if present farming practices continue.

3.3.2 Requirements for participation

To avoid the need for the construction and operation of nitrate removal facilities at water treatment plants, Wessex Water has offered financial assistance to those farmers who convert to organic farming in its catchment area. This subsidy is offered initially for two years to assess its effectiveness in reducing nitrate leaching by converting to organic farming. Research by the Elm Farm Research Centre, which will be involved in the administration of the scheme, has shown that careful management of the nutrient supply can lead to a significant reduction in nitrate leaching.

Independently of the above scheme there is some movement to organic farming in the UK encouraged by the higher prices paid for organic crops and the Organic Aid Scheme operated by the Ministry of Agriculture, Fisheries and Food (MAFF). The conversion process is strictly controlled in accordance with EC Regulation 2092/91, such that it is illegal to sell food as organic until the end of the five-year conversion period. At the end of 1998, a total of 138 242 hectares had been entered in the organic farming scheme across the UK constituting 0.6 per cent of the total UK land area (MAFF 1998a).

3.3.3 Compensatory payments

The Organic Aid Scheme offers farmers a one-off payment of currently £250/ha over five years for converting to organic farming. However, a recent review of the scheme noted the low rate of uptake of the scheme despite the potential profitability of organic farming (MAFF 1998b). This has been attributed to the low aid provided for the conversion and insufficient advice and information to encourage farmers to convert.

In order to make it attractive for farmers to convert to organic farming, Wessex Water offers to pay an additional £40/ha per year to those farmers who convert to organic farming in its catchment area. Wessex Water plans to partly finance the compensation payment to the farmers by landfill tax credits obtained by its partly owned waste company. The landfill tax regime was introduced in 1996 to reflect the environmental damage being caused by landfills in the UK and to encourage reductions in the production of waste. The charges were set at £2/ton for inert waste and £7/ton for other waste, which is to be increased to £15/ton by 2005. Under the UK landfill tax regime a waste company can donate up to 20 per cent of its landfill tax liabilities to approved environmental projects although 10 per cent of the funds the waste company contributes to the project must come from its own resources.

3.3.4 Outcome

The Wessex Water scheme has only recently been initiated and it is therefore difficult to assess its effectiveness. However, an assessment of the level of uptake and early successes of the agreement will be attempted as part of the EU funded research project on co-operative agreements in agriculture currently being undertaken by the three research teams of the Institut für Umweltforschung (INFU), University of Dortmund, Agricultural Economics Research Institute (LEI-DLO), The Hague, and Water Research Centre (WRc plc, UK).

3.3.5 Why are co-operative agreements not widely used in the United Kingdom?

The UK has traditionally applied the command-and-control approach with strict enforcement. Economic instruments have so far played only a minor role in environmental management. This is partly a result of the long-term tradition of river basin management, with the same organisation discharging into a river also being responsible for the abstraction of drinking water from the same river. Thus there was no need to collect charges for abstractions or discharges from one part of the organisation only to return it to another part of the same organisation as subsidy. The level of charges for abstractions and discharges in the UK has been restricted to cover only the costs of the regulatory authorities. Any additional charges would be seen as taxes, which would have to be passed on to the Treasury unless the current laws are changed.

The current system of economic regulation of the water companies favours the provision of infrastructure to treat water to comply with quality requirements, as there is a guarantee that the infrastructure will allow the companies to meet their quality standards. In addition, water companies favour this approach as they can derive financial benefits for additional infrastructure projects by, for instance, building the infrastructure cheaper than allowed for by the regulator and by future potential savings in operating costs.

Under the voluntary agreement scheme there is a degree of uncertainty as to whether the agreement made is adequate to solve the problem (for example whether sufficient farmers can be persuaded to participate or whether the agreement can be adequately enforced). This uncertainty may be too great for the rigid UK regulatory regime for either the water company or the regulator. This may be an additional reason why this approach has not yet been more widely accepted.

There may also be physical reasons why voluntary co-operative agreements are not widely used in the UK. In many aquifers, especially in some of the more intensively farmed areas, the time of travel of the water in the aquifers is very slow, requiring more than 20 years before effects can be detected. In addition, in some areas the aquifers are very large which would require large numbers of farmers to participate to achieve effective reductions.

Finally, there is little experience of voluntary agreements in the UK, perhaps partly because there is insufficient advice and information available as to the benefits of such agreements and how they can best be negotiated and enforced. In addition, UK regulators may not accept long delays in meeting standards, which may well be the case for many aquifers, and the water companies would therefore still have to introduce, in many cases, intermediate solutions. The current EU research project should provide a deeper insight into why voluntary co-operative agreements have not been more widely used in the UK and possible changes required to make their use more widespread.

4 CO-OPERATIVE AGREEMENTS ARE RARE IN SOME MEMBER STATES

Co-operative agreements remain unusual in certain Member States. We will explore this in the context of Finland and France in more detail.

4.1 The Significance of Co-operative Agreements in Finland

Finland is a large country with a total area of around 340 000 km^2, with almost 190 000 lakes of at least 500 m^2. In 1996, about 87 per cent of the population were connected to the public water distribution network. The remaining part of the population mainly takes their water from private wells. The share of public water service coverage is rather low compared to other European countries. This is mainly due to the long distances in sparsely populated areas and the abundance of water available. The use of groundwater and artificial groundwater for public water supply has increased over the past few decades. The share of groundwater was only 30 per cent during the beginning of the 1970s, which, however, gradually increased to slightly above 56 per cent in 1996. The number of drinking water supply companies has almost doubled over the past decades from about 600 (in 1970) to a current level of around 1100. In 1970, only slightly more than half of the population (57 per cent) got their water from such companies; the remaining part of the population had their own wells. This figure went up to 87 per cent in 1996. About 1000 of these companies serve between 50 and 500 inhabitants; only some 10–20 companies serve more than 50 000 inhabitants. Local municipalities normally own the companies.

4.1.1 A voluntary initiative in Finland

The Lake Pyhäjärvi Protection Fund is one of the few examples of voluntary controlling of water pollution. The objective of this programme is to develop new methods for water protection and land use planning. The drainage basin area of Lake Pyhäjärvi (inclusive of surface area) is some 615 km^2, which is small compared to the surface area. Total water volume of the lake is 840 million m^3, and only 20–25 per cent of the water is replaced each year. Therefore, more than 60 per cent of the phosphorus coming into the lake stays there. The water retention time is 3–5 years. The eutrophication process has rapidly increased during the past couple of years. During the 1970s, water quality was classified as excellent. During the 1990s, however, it was only classified as good. The main sources of the phosphorus load are farming within the catchment area and the large number of summer cottages on the lakeshores. The coastal zone of this lake has about 2500 households without sewage treatment (including summer cottages).

The greatest threat to the lake is the nutrient load, which exceeds its tolerance level. Lake Pyhäjärvi has no point source of pollution. Point source pollution sewage treatment is outside the drainage area. A large part of the drainage area is forests but the area has a relatively large share of agricultural land. Most of the fields are along rivers, and most of the nutrient load, therefore, originates from agriculture. Phosphorus content in the lake had increased in the past. This affected the drinking water supply companies, which provide their water to the municipality of Eura.

The Lake Pyhäjärvi Protection Fund is seeking to stop the eutrophication process in the lake. In order to achieve that, the external phosphorus load must be reduced by some 40 per cent. This is to be achieved during the period 1995–99. Examples of activities:

- Fishermen provide small fish to the fur farmers, who pay about 45 mark per kilo of fish. Reducing the small fish stock increases the plankton in the lake, and they contribute to reducing the algae levels. The role of the Protection Fund is to facilitate and organise this type of arrangement.
- Farmers may have problems with disposing of livestock manure, and part of the manure, indeed, needs to be transported. This is partly solved by composting, which again can be used in organic farming.
- Growing potatoes requires irrigation water during the spring period, and experiments have been initiated to establish irrigation reservoirs. This is also aimed at reducing nutrient loads into the water.

Farmers do not have a formal agreement in the context of the Lake Pyhäjärvi Protection Fund, neither do drinking water supply companies. The municipalities are owners of the drinking water supply companies. Farmers, however, do join the various projects.

4.1.2 Compensatory payments

The drainage basin has about 400 farmers, and some 22 per cent of the land is cultivated for agriculture. The northern part of the region is focused on crop production (sugar beet, wheat, barley and oats), with emphasis on livestock in the remaining part of the region (cattle, pigs and poultry). Farmers presently understand and accept the objectives of the project, join the various initiatives and participate in village plans. There is no direct transfer of incomes involved. However, some support was given to a few farmers who left cultivation, and accepted a sort of buffer zone (width of about 40 metres along the river). Investigations are being undertaken to assess the reduction of nutrient leakage when the area is not cultivated any more.

Farmers in the drainage basin have taken part in water protection projects. Mitigation actions taken well before the agri-environmental programmes under Regulation 2078/92 were implemented. Agricultural loads are reduced through a wide range of on-farm and off-farm actions, including conservation tillage to reduce erosion, and filter strips of vegetation to prevent nutrient loads from surface runoff.

The Lake Pyhäjärvi Protection Fund has contributed to this by additional actions which are not covered by the agri-environmental measures:

- filtering ditches to collect nutrients;
- ditch waters, which lead to sandfilters;
- treatment of washing waters of a building used for poultry production (in a small sewage treatment plant).

More than 95 per cent of the farmers in this region have joined the General Agricultural Environment Protection Scheme (GAEPS), which is part of the agri-environmental measures. A potential reduction of the phosphorus load of 30 per cent was estimated following participation of GAEPS. Therefore, more efforts would be required to achieve the 40 per cent reduction target of the Lake Pyhäjärvi Protection Fund. Therefore, in addition to the GAEPS, the supplementary protection scheme (SPS) is applied as well, providing support for:

- organic agriculture;
- wider riparian zones on river or lake banks;
- treatment of runoff waters (sedimentation basins or wetlands, special drains);
- efficient use of manure;
- special areas within the landscape.

Presently, farmers understand far better the need to take action, and also accept the objectives of the programme. They are involved in projects and in the village plans as well.

4.2 The Significance of Co-operative Agreements in France

According to the results of preliminary investigations, co-operative agreements in France are not practised in the same way as in Germany. The reasons are probably the different political structure, which is more centralised, and the small number of very large water companies supplying drinking water to households in numerous municipalities under concession contracts. Furthermore, the regulation of farmers and water suppliers seems to be less stringent, that is, the authorities are made more responsible than the water companies for guaranteeing a sufficient quality of drinking water. Furthermore, there are legally authorised derogations in certain cases where the MAC cannot be complied with by the water suppliers. Consequently, the water suppliers are not under the same pressure as the German water companies to enter into co-operative agreements with farmers for the reasons explained above.

On the other hand, there are co-operative agreements in France between farmers and regulatory authorities in which water suppliers participate. They assist in the development of agricultural advisory programmes and contribute to special funds for changing farming practices. An example is the Ferti-Mieux project, which is led by the National Association for the Improvement of Agriculture (ANDA). The goal is to help farmers to better manage the use of nitrogen. The money spent in the Ferti-Mieux project is used for council actions, research and payments for the planting of temporary crops to limit the losses of nitrate to ground and surface waters. This project covers at present about 1.8 million ha of agricultural land (or 6.1 per cent of the total agricultural area) and about 29 000 farmers (or 3.9 per cent of the total number of farmers) are incorporated. In addition, there is the Phytomieux project for improving the usage of pesticides.

As far as it is known there are no direct contractual agreements between farmers and water companies in France, although some interesting cases exist between farmers and the mineral water industry (Gafsi 1999).

5 CONCLUDING REMARKS

This chapter has as its source the study 'Co-operative agreements in agriculture as an instrument to improve the economic and ecological efficiency of the European Union water policy'. It is based on a first inventory of agreements which currently exist. The project aims to analyse the political feasibility of co-operative agreements as an instrument to meet environmental standards as economically efficient and ecologically effective as possible. It also aims to assess the significance of this type of instrument as regards a more efficient water policy and in reforming the Common Agricultural Policy.

- Command-and-control measures are the main instrument to reduce pollution of agriculture. Long delays in the implementation of the Nitrates Directive already indicate the difficulty of achieving water quality targets through the regulatory approach. Voluntary schemes have become increasingly important, and the implementation of cost-effective measures is an important criterion for their evaluation. Co-operative agreements should be given priority over other policy instruments to control pollution (including command-and-control).
- The participative approach has gained importance with the implementation of Regulation 2078/92. It allows for compensating farmers for any income loss if efforts are made which exceed policy constraints. This programme currently applies to 20 per cent of farmland. Many of the programmes which aim to limit input use show substantial reductions in the use of fertilisers and improvements in application techniques. The agri-environmental programmes do not necessarily take into account the nitrogen pollution problems faced by drinking water supply companies.
- A number of conditions are important to the incentives given to co-operative agreements between water supply companies and the

agricultural sector. In order to be effective, national legislation, and the way it is implemented, needs to be consistent with the role of self-regulation by the main actors. The adoption of site-specific rules at the regional level may improve the effectiveness of self-regulation.

– Analyses of the costs and benefits of self-regulation *vis-à-vis* other approaches thus far remain scarce. Farmers need to be offered the proper incentives to reduce pollution. Co-operative agreements, which take into account the site-specific nature of environmental concerns, may be cost-effective in the case that payments coincide with the loss of net income and the costs incurred as a result of compliance with the additional requirements. In addition to compensatory payments, other support programmes (including advice) are important instruments in adopting more environmentally friendly farm management practices.

REFERENCES

CEC (1992), *Towards Sustainability: a European Community Programme for Policy and Action in Relation to the Environment and Sustainable Development*, Commission of the European Communities, Brussels, COM(1992) 23.

CEC (1996), *Communication from the Commission to the Council and the European Parliament on Environmental Agreements*, Commission of the European Communities, Brussels, COM(1996) 51 final.

CEC (1999), *Directions towards Sustainable Agriculture. Communication from the Commission to the Council, the European Parliament, the Economic and Social Committee and the Committee of the Regions*, Commission of the European Communities, Brussels, COM(1999) 22 final.

ENDS (1998), ENDS Report 279, April.

Gafsi, M. (1999), 'Farming Practices and the Environmental Quality: How to Manage the Changes on Farms', Paper prepared for the EAAE IXth Congress, Warsaw, 24–28 August 1999.

Heinz, I. (1998), 'Costs and Benefits of Pesticide Reduction in Agriculture: Best Solutions', in Wossink, G.A.A., G.C. van Kooten and G.H. Peters (eds), *Economics of Agro-chemicals*, Aldershot, UK: Ashgate.

Just, F. and I. Heinz (2000), 'Do "Soft" Regulations Matter?', in Brouwer, F. and P. Lowe (eds), *CAP Regimes and the European Countryside: Prospects for Integration between Agricultural, Regional and Environmental Policies*, Wallingford: CAB International, pp. 241–55.

Kooperation Land- und Wasserwirtschaft im Einzugsgebiet der Stevertalsperre (Hrsg.) (1998), *Ein Bericht über die Ergebnisse der Beratung 1998*, Coesfeld.

Liefferink, D. (1997), 'Joint Environmental Policy Making', Summer Symposium, The Innovation of Environmental Policy, Bologna.

MAFF (1998a), *Agriculture in the United Kingdom*, Ministry of Agriculture, Fisheries and Food, London, UK: HMSO.

MAFF (1998b), *Review of the Organic Aid Scheme*, Ministry of Agriculture, Fisheries and Food, Internet homepage http://www.maff.gov.uk.

OECD (1998), *Voluntary Approaches for Environmental Protection in the European Union*, Paris: Organisation for Economic Co-operation and Development, ENV/EPOC/GEEI(98)29 Final.

UNCED (1992), *Earth Summit 1992: the United Nations Conference on Environment and Development*, London: Regency.

World Commission on Environment and Development (WCED) (1987), *Our Common Future*, Oxford: Oxford University Press.

15. Transboundary Co-operation in Terms of Environmental Protection

Mieczysław Adamowicz and Arkadiusz Gralak

1 INTRODUCTION

Changes in the border adjacent areas are one of the important elements of the transformation processes occurring across Central Europe. The development of these areas is particularly important in the context of efforts made by these countries (including Poland) to access the European Union. Different forms of transboundary co-operation have been animating growing interest for several years. The most favourable conditions for transboundary co-operation may be found in western Poland. Relations between the neighbouring regions of Poland and Germany have taken the most developed institutional and organisational forms, particularly in light of establishing a chain of Euroregions. Through regions situated along the Odra and Nysa Rivers, Poland adjoins both the united German State and the integrated market and territory of the European Union.

Simultaneously, regions situated on both sides of the Odra and Nysa Rivers face many difficult and complex problems which need to be solved as soon as possible. These problems become more daunting in the border adjacent areas because of a considerable distance from the national administration and economic centres. In spatial and environmental terms the border adjacent areas of the three countries are the source of a number of problems. Many reasons can be given to explain the poor state of the environment on the Polish territory adjacent to the Czech and German borderline. The main reason, however, is the pillage economy of the locally available natural resources (such as lignite) and construction of heat generating plants which discharge noxious substances into the atmosphere. Therefore, the development and implementation of a special ecological scheme in the areas where the integrity of the natural environment is threatened appears to be a particularly important domain of transboundary co-operation.

Unquestionably, the Euroregion 'Neisse-Nisa-Nysa' is the precursor of such co-operation.

The above justifies a review of the transboundary co-operation record in environmental protection. This chapter provides an analysis of major achievements resulting from a number of initiatives and undertakings meant to stop environmental degradation and to ensure the gradual improvement of environmental quality in the ecologically jeopardised areas using the example of the Polish division of the 'Nysa' Euroregion. An important aspect of this analysis is the identification of the possibility of using the acquired knowledge in other regions with environmental hazards. An interesting cognitive purpose of the chapter is the experience of a Euroregion related to the search for funds necessary to invest in environmental protection in the border adjacent areas.

2 EUROREGION AS THE SUPREME ORGANISATIONAL FORM OF TRANSBOUNDARY CO-OPERATION

The idea of transboundary co-operation consists in the mitigation of the adverse impact of the existing borderline, elimination of the consequences of peripheral location of these areas, developing contacts with the neighbouring nations and taking advantage of historical, cultural, economic and social similarities and natural geographic proximity. The European Outline Convention on Transfrontier Co-operation between Territorial Communities or Authorities of 1980 (known also as the Madrid Convention) defines this co-operation as 'any joint action intended to normalise and to develop further neighbourhood contact between the Communities and territorial authorities of two or more States, and conclusion of agreements and approval of opinions necessary to put such intentions into force'. Transboundary relations between these countries may be of a different nature and at different levels: informal, spontaneous or organised (Malendowski and Ratajczak 1998).

An agreement on the transboundary co-operation between the border adjacent regions is determined as a Euroregion. From the institutional and legal point of view, a Euroregion constitutes a formal co-operation structure reaching beyond the border of one State and based on the agreement concluded between the regional or local authorities or with the participation of business and social partners. Euroregions are established in the form of agreements or arrangements concluded generally between the unions (associations) of the territorial units of at least two foreign partners. A Euroregion is an institutionalised transboundary working community of towns and communes; however, it does not compose an autonomous and State structure with its own jurisdiction, administration or control (Malendowski and Ratajczak 1998). Legal acts which control the transboundary co-operation rules explicitly stress the primary character of the jurisdiction of the given State in relation to the provisions set out in the transboundary agreements. The agreements neither exclude nor limit the autonomy of a State with respect to this part of its territory which has become a component of a Euroregion. Neither is there any assignment of the local authorities' qualifications to the common Euroregional structures or bodies (Toczyński et al. 1997).

From the operational point of view a Euroregion should be considered a geographically determined territory including the border adjacent areas of two or more States, where local communities co-operate in different fields of activity. There are many possibilities to co-ordinate actions of local authorities of specific countries, to launch joint undertakings, to solve conflicts and to ensure that they do not arise without engaging the central administration bodies of a given State. The integration of the border adjacent territories within the Euroregional structures consists in undertaking joint actions which serve the purpose of both sides.

3 ESTABLISHMENT OF THE NYSA EUROREGION

Neisse-Nisa-Nysa Euroregion is the first to include a Polish border adjacent area. The idea of establishing the first transboundary co-operation region in Central–Eastern Europe, and at the same time the first on the eastern EU border, obviously sprang from the democratic transformation processes of the late 1980s and early 1990s in this part of Europe as well as in German unification. The initiative of Euroregion establishment was launched in 1991 by the local interest groups in the communes of Bogatynia, Liberec and Zittau. From the very beginning, the Euroregion idea was initiated by the local administration (Panorama Euroregionów 1997).

Nysa Euroregion was formally established in December 1991. It includes three border adjacent areas located in the centre of Europe and joining the Polish, German and Czech borders. The specific geo-political location of this Euroregion is connected with the fact that it is situated between two EU Member States and two applicant countries. Therefore, this is one of those territories where relations between the West and the East will assume a new European level.

From the legal and formal point of view, the Nysa Euroregion is a voluntary community of interests for counties and basic administration units (communities) for the territory of 'Three Lands Region', that is, the border adjacent areas of the Czech Republic, German Federal Republic and Republic of Poland. The Euroregion members are three commune associations:

- in the Polish territory – Nysa Euroregion Association of Polish Communities which includes 39 communities of Lower Silesia Voivodship and four communities of Lubuskie Voivodship;
- in the Czech territory – Nysa Euroregion – Regional Municipal Association of Towns and Communities of the Southern Czech Republic which includes five county units: Liberec, Jablonec nad Nisou, Czeska Lipa, Semily and Dieczin.
- in the German territory – Municipal Association of Nysa Euroregion – German Section which includes five counties of Saxony: Löbau-Zittau, Niederschlesischer Oberlausitzkreis, Bautzen, Hoyerswerda and Kamenz and the provincial capital Görlitz.

The Euroregion has been established in order to ensure the development of the areas through mutual co-operation beyond the State borderlines. The aims of Euroregional activities include the following:

- maintenance and improvement of the natural environmental conditions;
- co-operation with regard to spatial development;
- boosting the economy and providing equal standards of living;
- construction of infrastructure facilities and their adaptation to the needs over the borders;
- co-operation in emergency situations, such as fire fighting, floods, and so on;
- co-operation related to the development of personal communication means and tourism in the border adjacent areas;
- cultural exchange and care of the common cultural heritage.

According to the declarations of all parties concerned the close co-operation of the border adjacent areas within the Upper Łużyce, Lower Silesia and the Northern Czech Republic should contribute to the gradual elimination of economic, social, ecological and cultural problems and to the establishment of viable structures serving the future needs of the Three Lands Region. These three territories have many common problems and interests resulting from similar system transformation processes, a long history and various misunderstandings and prejudices built up along the centuries (Förster 1995). Awareness of the need to solve common economic, ecological, infrastructural and social problems led to the development of transboundary co-operation between the local administration units of Poland, the Czech Republic and Germany.

4 NYSA EUROREGION – ECOLOGICAL DISASTER AREA

The Nysa Euroregion incorporates the so-called 'Black Triangle', which is considered one of the most contaminated European areas. Across the Black Triangle there is a strip of lignite deposit running from Polish Lower Silesia through Southern Saxony in Germany and the Northern Czech territory. This strip incorporates a huge international 'power centre' which is formed by a group of over a dozen power generating plants which are fuelled with lignite. They constitute the biggest source of sulphur compounds emission. The emissions from the Black Triangle are estimated by experts to provide 30 per cent of all the sulphur compound emissions in the whole of Europe. The largest clouds of noxious gases and dust are emitted by the western and northern Czech power plants, German power plants (Hagenwerder, Boxberg) and Polish plants (Turów). The ecological emergency area includes territories inhabited by about a million people.

The industrial pollution has led to the total degradation of the natural environment in the region. The Nysa Łużycka River, which is a symbol of the Euroregion, does not comply with any water quality standard along its border section. Pollution of the atmosphere, which leads to that of water and soil causes huge areas of forests to die. Weakened forest with reduced density suffers additional mass damages from winds and snow falls. In the Western Sudety Mountains this process has already developed into an ecological disaster. High concentrations of air and soil pollutants have devastated over 10 thousand ha of forest in Saxony, over 15 thousand ha in the Polish Sudety Mountains and about 10 thousand ha of forest in the Czech Republic and Morawy. On the Polish territory the most extensive ecological damage is suffered by the Izerskie and Karkonosze Mountains. As a result of the dying spruce population, these areas almost totally lack live forests above the level of 800 m above sea-level. The dying of large forest areas starts at the mountain ridges and moves down to the higher and lower subalpine forest (Szymański 1994). Forestless slopes exhibit progressive escape and infestation of weeds in habitats. The research carried out with respect to the ecological impact of pollution has shown that the forests in the Karkonosze and Izerskie Mountains are dying because of the acidification of soil which produces large amounts of toxic aluminium and impedes root development.

As compared with other European mountains (such as the Black Forest, the Bavarian Forest, the Austrian Alps) also suffering forest devastation, in the Sudety Region the specific problem consists in absorbing huge amounts of sulphur dioxide emitted in the Black Triangle and brought over to Poland by western winds. Tests carried out on atmospheric pollution have proven that only 26 per cent of pollutants in the Sudety Mountains are emitted by the sources located in the Polish territory while the remaining portion originates from Germany and the Czech Republic. This is definite evidence that the transboundary migration of pollutants in the Black Triangle area is particularly annoying for Poland as the 'import' of pollutants prevails over their 'export' because of the wind pattern effect.

Particularly severe consequences of environmental pollution are suffered, though indirectly, by agriculture. This is manifested by a lower production (reduced crops), the necessity to set aside jeopardised areas, incurring the costs of land reclamation and restoration of environmental productivity and hence a decrease in agricultural productivity with respect to the agricultural production space. Lower quality of food products which contain substances from air and soil, harmful to human health, is another effect of environmental contamination.

5 TRANSBOUNDARY CO-OPERATION AREAS

When addressing questions concerning specific actions undertaken since the establishment of the Euroregion and their consequences for environmental protection, we should take into consideration uneven development tendencies in the particular parts of the region. Though the particular areas of the Three Lands Triangle have been facing similar problems (such as single-function economic structure, prevalence of large industrial establishments and complexes, low level of productivity and innovations, the detrimental effect on the environment), the starting point in terms of the capacity for restructuring and elimination of threats in each of them was different. As in the case of all border adjacent regions of new States the German portion of the Euroregion was also included in the restructuring policy of the Federal Government and obtained support of the EU Structural Funds, whereas the Polish and Czech border adjacent areas facing similar structural depression did not obtain any such support (Förster 1995). Furthermore, despite the desperate ecological situation of the whole region, difficult economic and social problems had priority in the mind of the central administrations and local authorities.

During the first stage of Euroregion development attempts were made to include the border adjacent areas in the development plans of the particular countries. This particularly concerned the German portion of the Euroregion which constitutes the EU border adjacent area, the co-operation development in the border adjacent areas being determined by the opportunities of obtaining assistance funds from different sources. Establishment of joint development and restructuring concepts was the condition for obtaining EU financial support for the development of the areas situated beyond the

German territory. This requirement had been met through the co-operation of the Polish, Czech and German local administration units leading to a number of joint initiatives and many projects of transboundary scope. It was agreed that the final target of the trilateral co-operation will be the agreement and establishment of a common regional development strategy including the interests of all partners.

Trilateral action with regard to environmental protection was recognised as the highest priority. The projects established emphasise a lasting inhibition of the deterioration of nature, gradual improvement of the environmental quality of the ecologically deteriorated areas in the future, and prevention of the expansion of deterioration to the ecologically sound areas. The Euroregion area is very important in terms of the protection of natural features. Apart from the areas deteriorated by excessive mining and concentrated environmentally noxious industries, the Euroregion also comprises areas of the highest natural and landscape values for tourism, recreation and mineral baths of both local and international interest. The Karkonosze National Park area offers particular natural values.

In this context the joint actions of local authorities with regard to the establishment of special ecological remedial schemes for the environmentally jeopardised areas and joint protection of the areas particularly attractive in terms of natural value are of great importance since they determine the area's attractiveness for tourists. Poland is very particular about the protection of natural values in this region, because they are regarded as priorities for tourism development – primarily for the development of farm and ecological tourism.

The massive destruction of the natural environment within the Three Lands Triangle could be first and foremost prevented by counteracting and eliminating ecological threats. The most spectacular example is the transboundary Phare funded Black Triangle Scheme. Between June 1991 and the end of 1998 Phare funds allocated to this programme amounted to EUR 12.4 million. The Black Triangle Scheme copes with the restructuring of mining and power generating industries noxious to the Euroregion environment. The restructuring and modernisation projects of the power generating plant in the northern Czech lignite basin (mainly around Liberec) are particularly important for the protection of the natural environment against total devastation as they counteract the pollution exports into the Sudety Mountains area. The modernisation investments which have been carried out in the Turów power generating plant for several years now are also of crucial importance.

The implementation of the Black Triangle Scheme has allowed considerable reduction of air pollution. The most recent air quality tests have shown that the pollutant emission has declined by 50 per cent as compared with 1998.

The joint monitoring system operating since mid-1996 is a great achievement of the transboundary co-operation between Poland, Germany and the Czech Republic. The system comprises 43 automatic gauging stations (10 in Poland, 12 in Germany and 21 in the Czech Republic) fitted with satellite signal receivers. The exchange of data between the countries is supported by the Meteosat satellite and by the numerical data transmission network and the Internet. The State borders are obviously not an obstacle for ecological damage; therefore, the actions undertaken within the Euroregion aim at the elaboration of joint observation, and warning and disaster intervention systems via the collection and exchange of data.

The inauguration of the monitoring system finally settled the dispute between the three countries concerning the transboundary displacement of pollutants. The measurements of air pollutant concentrations proved that the wind pattern in this region causes the majority of the emitted pollutants (almost 75 per cent of sulphur dioxide, nitrogen oxides, carbon dioxide and dust) to be blown into the Polish territory.

Euroregional co-operation in the field of environment protection relates to the specific undertakings and joint investments which involve a strict co-ordination of local communities. Over the period 1994–98, the Phare Programme Management Committee approved the financing of 46 large investment projects from the Phare Transboundary Co-operation Programme fund amounting to EUR 37.32 million; of these, 22 projects related to environmental protection to the amount of EUR 12.8 million. Financial support from the CBC Phare budget was mainly intended for investments concerning the establishment and modernisation of municipal infrastructure such as waste water disposal systems, waste storage and treatment and heating network development.

Within the frames of large project implementation in the Polish Nysa Euroregion territory four municipal waste water treatment plants (in Sieniawka, Lubawka, Kamienna Góra and Msciwojów) and one waste water pumping station (in Zgorzelec) were constructed. In Bogatynia and Olszyna two waste water treatment plants were extended and improved; furthermore, the existing domestic waste water trunk sewers were extended and a local sludge treatment plant near Bogatynia waste water treatment plant was built, whereas in Boleslawiec community, domestic waste water piping has been laid. The above mentioned investments consumed EUR 3.72 million from the Phare fund.

The municipal infrastructure investments co-financed by the CBC Phare budget also included municipal waste disposal. Within implemented projects six waste dumping sites were provided for (in Leknica, Wegliniec,

Boleslawiec, Luban, Lwówek Śl. and Ścięgna-Kostrzyca) and three waste utilisation plants (in Zgorzelec, Bogatynia and Luban). Over the period 1994–98 the Phare programme fund contribution for these purposes amounted to EUR 5.35 million. As for the improved thermal energy supply, a power generating plant was constructed in Zgorzelec and the Bogatynia heat distribution network was extended and improved. The EU allocation for these investments was EUR 3.7 million. Besides financing the investments to improve the municipal infrastructure, a couple of large projects were implemented within the framework of transboundary co-operation with regard to wasteland afforestation. Allocation of funds from different sources, including Phare Programme allocation of EUR 118 000, allowed the planting of forest over an area of 620 ha, including abandoned farmland.

In the face of the spruce population dying out in the Izerskie and Karkonosze Mountains, it is necessary to develop and to carry out a forest management and reconstruction programme. Reinstatement of the degraded mountain areas is necessary to protect mountain soils against erosion and to restore water retention normally provided by the forests. Work carried out within transboundary co-operation with regard to this problem is in its early conceptual stage. It shows that the reinstatement of the ecological disaster areas should begin in the highest part of the mountains, that is, at the upper subalpine forest level which provides protection against snow and wind for the forests located at the lower level because the high mountain forests control the destructive impact of winds, capture thick layers of snow and prevent snow avalanches, check the spring water flows, and prevent superficial soil erosion and floods in the lower course of rivers (Szymański 1994). Only the reinstatement and reconstruction of these protective forest zones will allow for a safe development of the lower level areas. However, the most severe problems originate from the costs of the planned investments. Therefore, the support provided by EU assistance funds will be necessary in this respect.

Spatial development is a meaningful element of co-operation within the Euroregion. The Polish, Czech and German local authorities are very active in this respect. On both sides of the border many studies have been carried out with respect to the future spatial development of these areas. So far two documents have been produced: 'Case Study of Spatial Development for the Area along the Polish–German Border Line' (1994) and 'Co-ordination Study for the development of Polish–Czech Border Adjacent Areas' (1993). These are preliminary documents which precede the establishment of a uniform concept of border adjacent area spatial development which would include supraregional spatial relationships of the three regions with respect to infrastructure, water courses, cultural landscapes, biocenoses, ecologically valuable areas, transboundary town associations, and so on. The agreed upon joint strategy of spatial development will be based on the sustainable development idea which ensures harmony between spatial development nature and structure and the features and values of the natural environment. In order to guarantee the sustainability and protection of the natural environment the rural area economy should be mainly based on the ecological and landscape conditions.

6 TRANSBOUNDARY CO-OPERATION FINANCING

The most promising opportunities which would facilitate development of the border adjacent areas include the availability of financing from many sources. Support provided by international, inter-governmental institutions and organisations as well as by the national commissions and boards dealing with the relevant problems may stimulate the development of transboundary co-operation at the regional and local levels. Since 1994 Poland has had access to EU financial support intended for regional development purposes, including environmental protection.

The Phare programme plays a particular role in the financing of the transboundary co-operation undertakings. It is the main source of grants provided by the European Union for Central and Eastern European countries. For the countries which have signed the European Agreements, the Phare programme is a financial instrument which enables the European Union to support the implementation of pre-accession strategy to prepare these countries for EU accession.

Phare programme priorities include areas such as infrastructure investments, particularly environmental protection and contamination control, power supply, transport and telecommunications infrastructure development. The programme also provides funds for know-how transfer, feasibility studies, research and analyses. A part of the financing is constituted by grants, but another part of it is allocated on a repayment basis and in the form of guarantees. The programme is carried out by the Directorate General I of the European Commission. The specific feature of the Phare programme is that its priorities and fund allocation lines are laid down in close co-operation with the beneficiary countries.

When allocating funds from the assistance programme budgets, the rule of co-financing is complied with, which means that the EU funds cannot constitute the only source of project financing. As a result, the parties concerned and participating in the project are more dedicated to the project implementation and financing. Also the subsidiarity rule is respected when allocating funds so that EU assistance is granted only when the necessary investments exceed the budget means of the local and regional authorities.

Among the EU programmes which provide support for transboundary co-operation at the regional and local levels the most important are the Cross-border Co-operation Phare Programme (CBC Phare), Phare Credo, Ecos-Ouverture, Phare Small Baltic Facility and Fiesta. Only the first and the second programme require the intervention of the Governments, which determine the final form of the projects approved for financing. The remaining programmes have a horizontal character, that is, it is communities and regions which apply for European Commission financing. In both cases, however, the successful application depends upon the connections between the local authorities and between local and regional authorities.

At the beginning of Phare programme operation 80 per cent of its funds were allocated to projects which had been bilaterally agreed upon between a given country and the EU. Since 1994, at the suggestion of the European Parliament, a Phare CBC has been launched within the Phare programme to support transboundary co-operation between countries receiving Phare assistance and EU Member States. At present Phare CBC is the leading programme in supporting transboundary co-operation between community and regional authorities within the Euroregion.

Under the programme, financing is granted for undertakings carried out by a number of partner countries with regard to the protection of the natural environment and transport infrastructure restructuring. From the total amount of EUR 1.015 billion allocated for Poland from the Phare fund for the period 1995–99, 26.1 per cent was intended for the implementation of the CBC programme. In Poland, the Phare CBC programme has been divided into two budgets:

1. Phare – Transboundary Co-operation Poland–Germany (about EUR 50 million/year)
2. Phare – Transboundary Co-operation Poland–Baltic Region (about EUR 4 to 6 million/year).

In 1995, the Phare programme for Transboundary Co-operation Poland–Czech Republic–Germany (trilateral co-operation) was launched.

The Poland–Germany Transboundary Co-operation Programme is intended for Euroregional operation on both sides of the Polish-German border, namely: Nysa Euroregion, Sprewa-Nysa-Bóbr Euroregion, Pro Europa Viadrina Euroregion and Pomerania Euroregion. It is the equivalent of the European initiative INERREG II – a programme carried out in Germany. Both programmes are complementary in solving common problems existing in this area.

Now the support for transboundary co-operation is focused on financing (in the form of grants) the 'hard projects', that is, those related to infrastructural investments. Phare CBC programme priorities include the following: transportation (55 per cent of the budget), environmental protection (25 per cent of the budget) and municipal infrastructure, economic development, research and analysis aid, and programme technical servicing. Within the framework of the programme a Small Project Fund (Euroregional Fund) has been established. This Fund provides financial support for all the 'soft' undertakings of non-investment character which promote direct contact between people living on both sides of the border line. Most often these are cultural events, seminars, conferences, workshops, publications, tourist agencies, and so on.

The Phare CBC programme financially supports such undertakings which may be beneficial to the regions on both sides of the border line (that is, to their inhabitants, local administrations, institutions, and so on). A respective application may be submitted by any institution, that is, central body, community, social organisation association, Euroregion, and so on. The most important requirement which should be met by the suggested project is a very detailed justification of its transboundary co-operation related relevance. Furthermore, the project undertakings must positively affect the natural environment. Therefore, the descriptions of infrastructure related undertakings should comprise relevant reports. They must include the calculated investment pay-back period or the internal rate of return. The possible risk should also be determined. Phare financing should not exceed 75 per cent of the project costs. The remaining costs must be covered by Poland. The intended undertakings must not be of a commercial nature.

Selection of projects submitted for financing from the CBC Fund is carried out by the Phare Programme Management Committee working with the European Commission. After an opinion is delivered by the Voivodship Parliament or Voivodship Board and a recommendation is given by the Transboundary Co-operation Department of the Council of Ministers, the projects are presented at a meeting of the members of European Commission and the Polish–German Transboundary Co-operation Programme Steering Committee. The projects are assessed by EU Consultants and the final decision on their financing is made by the Phare Management Committee.

The environmental protection related problems have been recognised as one of the priorities of the Agenda 2000 pre-accession strategy approved at the Berlin Summit in March 1999. It was agreed that within the framework of all assistance programmes for the ten countries of Central and Eastern Europe, the financial means amounting to EUR 21.8 billion (subject to valorisation by the inflation rate) will be allocated from the next tranche of Structural Funds for the years 2000–2006. As of the year 2000 two new pre-accession funds will be launched: ISPA (Instrument for Structural Policies for Pre-accession) and SAPARD (Support for Pre-accession Measures for

Agriculture and Rural Development). Taking into account the distribution of the financial means under these programmes, we may assume that Poland may expect an ISPA support of about EUR 400 million and a SAPARD support ranging between EUR 125 and 190 million.

ISPA operations based on its EUR 1.04 billion/year budget will be modelled after the Cohesion Fund. This instrument will cope with two elements only – environmental protection and transport network development. It is intended to support the financing of large investment projects (above EUR 5 million) related to water management, water source protection (waste water plant construction) and road network and telecommunications development, whereas SAPARD, with its EUR 520 million/year, will support activities related to agriculture modernisation and rural area development. The following priority support areas have been selected:

- development of the framing technologies which are environment and landscape friendly;
- revival and development of rural areas and protection of their cultural heritage;
- water resource management in the agricultural sector;
- farmland afforestation and tree planting.

The ISPA and SAPARD programmes will be complementary. This means that their implementation will require co-financing of at least 25 per cent of costs from the Polish public budget. Therefore, there is a necessity to aggregate funds from different sources – mainly from the State budget and local administration budgets (at the voivodship, county and community levels). However, it is worth noting that 25 per cent of financing is already a very serious challenge for Poland to face. Possible introduction of higher levels in the future could call into question Poland's ability to absorb Structural Funds.

For the countries which will become EU members by the end of 2006 the SAPARD and ISPA assistance funds will be withdrawn and Structural Funds will be introduced instead. Thus, Poland will be able to obtain support reaching 4 per cent of GNP. As of 2000, besides the SAPARD and ISPA, the main instrument of EU support will still be the Phare 2000 programme. The candidate countries will be able to have access to support of EUR 1.5 billion/year provided within this programme for areas which are not included in the SAPARD or ISPA scope, that is, mainly for the development of infrastructure and adjustment to EU legislation.

7 CONCLUSIONS

(1) The development of comprehensive, multifarious transboundary co-operation is one of the key elements of European integration. The idea of this co-operation consists in mitigating the adverse impact of the border line, overcoming the inferiority resulting from the peripheral location of the border adjacent territories, and multidirectional and sustainable social and economic development. Transboundary co-operation is able to produce many positive effects: people on both sides will be brought closer together and there will be a chance to benefit from the partner's experience in different domains of public services and to have better access to different external assistance funds. At present, the Euroregions, which operate on the grounds of agreements concluded between the territorial unit associations in the border adjacent areas of two or more countries, are the most sophisticated form of transboundary co-operation.

(2) Development of co-operation within the Euroregions leads towards full European integration. Models established during these co-operation processes will play an important role in the integration process of Poland with the EU. Therefore, Euroregions situated in the Polish territory along its western border are perceived as integration laboratories which help acquire experience before European integration reaches higher levels. In this way Poland may demonstrate its ability to co-operate internationally at the basic level of organisational structures.

(3) During the 1990s 12 Euroregions were established along the Polish borders with the most advanced transboundary co-operation along the western border line. This co-operation is a forerunner and may serve as an example for transboundary co-operation initiatives in other border adjacent areas. So far the co-operation related experience accumulated in the Nysa Euroregion – the first to be established in the Polish territory – is the most important in this type of initiative.

(4) Joint environmental protection actions have been recognised to be the highest priority in the trilateral transboundary co-operation between the Polish, German and Czech local authorities. Transboundary co-operation in this domain brings about the following advantages: establishment of a uniform system of monitoring stations, development of common environmental remedy programmes and determination of the protected areas. Phare funds have helped the development and implementation of the Black Triangle Scheme which is intended to ensure restructuring and technical modernisation of the environment deteriorating mining and power generating industries. In order to achieve gradual improvement of environmental quality within the Euroregion territory, a number of joint investments have been carried out in the area. These investments have consisted of the improvement

of the municipal infrastructure facilities related to water management, waste storage and disposal, and heating system extension.

(5) Apart from the construction of roads and sewage treatment plants, several years of experience in dealing with the funds which ensure financial support for the Nysa Euroregion operations have allowed the establishment of qualified staff who may work with their German and Czech counterparts on the preparation and supervision of projects and settling accounts concerning assistance funds. Successful financing of Euroregional co-operation requires so-called financial aggregation, that is, combining financial means from different public and private sources. Therefore, communities need experts capable of obtaining grants and additional financing from the EU and of raising internal resources at the regional and local level.

(6) Co-operation of the border territories faces various obstacles. The major one is a strong differentiation of social, economic and physical development in these areas. Furthermore, differences between the territories on both sides of the Polish–German border quickly become more pronounced as the Germans invest huge amounts of money from the Federal budget and the budgets of particular states and from the European Fund for Regional Development, whereas the Polish border adjacent territories lack such support. They are not able to overcome the problems of differentiated development without active assistance from the Government and financial support from the Pre-accession Funds.

BIBLIOGRAPHY

European Outline Convention on Transfrontier Co-operation between the Territorial Communities or Authorities (Madrid Convention), 1980.

Förster, H. (1995), 'Possibilities of Transboundary Co-operation in Nysa Euroregion', in: *Polska i Niemcy. Geografia sąsiedztwa w nowej Europie* (*Poland and Germany. Geography and Neighbourhood in New Europe*), Kraków: UNIVERSITAS.

ISPA (Instrument for Structural Policies for Pre-accession) (2000), *Materiały Komitetu Integracji Europejskiej*, Warsaw.

Jakubiec, J. (1994), 'Nysa Euroregion (Genesis, Structure, Function)', in: Arawczuk, F. and Z. Przbyła (eds), *Nysa Euroregion. Three Years of Experiences: The Development of Polish Eastern and Western Areas Adjoining the Border*, Warsaw: Institute of Geography and Spatial Planning PAS.

Malendowski, W. and M. Ratajczak (1998), *Euroregiony. Pierwszy krok do integracji europejskiej* (*Euroregions. First Step towards European Integration*), Wrocław: Atla2.

Mierosławska, A. (1999), 'Euroregiony na granicach Polski' (Euroregions at the Polish Frontier), *Studia i Monografie*, **91**, Warsaw: Institute of Agricultural Economics and Food Economy.

Panorama Euroregionów (1997 and 1998), *Panorama of Euroregions I i II*, Jelenia Góra: Statistical Office.

Regional Office Jelenia Góra (1994), 'Case Study of Spatial Development for the Area along the Polish–German Border Line', Brochure, Jelenia Góra: Regional Office.

Regional Office Katowice (1993), 'Co-ordination Study for the Development of Polish–Czech Border Adjacent Areas', Brochure, Katowice: Regional Office.

SAPARD (Support for Pre-accession Measures for Agriculture and Rural Development) (2000), *Report of the Committee of European Integration*, Warsaw.

Szymański, S. (1994), 'Problemy zagospodarowania i przebudowy lasów sudeckich' (Problems of Development and Reconstruction of Sudety Forests), *Prace Instytutu Badawczego Leśnictwa (IBL)*, Seria B, Nr 21, Warsaw.

Toczyński, W., W. Sartorus and J. Zaucha (eds) (1997), *International Co-operation of Regions*, Warsaw: Przedświt.

PART VI

Knowledge Systems, Stakeholders' Interests and Conflict Resolution in Protected Areas

16. Co-operative Conflict Resolution in a Nature Conservation Area in Brandenburg, Germany: a Case Study

Andrea Knierim

1 INTRODUCTION

There is a common understanding that conflicts should be solved in a co-operative way. Constructive behaviour, principled bargaining and procedural justice are the keywords which characterise the idea of successful conflict resolution with respect to the interests of all actors involved (Deutsch 1976, p. 35; Fisher and Ury 1987, p. 10; Thibaut and Walker 1975). Empirical research in all domains of human interaction suggests that these concepts might also work at a micro-level (for example in partner or family conflicts) as well as in cases of inter-group or international conflicts. Nevertheless, these concepts and methods have to be adapted to the specific situation and adjusted according to the needs and the capacities of the people involved.

This chapter focuses on the conflictive land use situation in a nature conservation area in the state of Brandenburg, Germany, and on efforts undertaken by different stakeholders to handle conflicts in a co-operative way. This process was initiated and supported by an action-oriented research project analysed by the author. The results presented here concentrate on the content of the process examined and on the question as to when and how co-operation was achieved. The analysis of the results is based on theoretical concepts of social psychology which will be presented shortly. The aim of the research project itself was to initiate a process of dealing with land use conflicts in a co-operative way and to demonstrate the usefulness of the method for similar situations in Brandenburg and elsewhere. The project was designed to adapt and apply appropriate methods of considering the specific, and sometimes contradictory, demands of all interest groups in a way to realise a common process of decision making.

2 CO-OPERATIVE CONFLICT RESOLUTION IN THEORY

Conflict analysis and resolution is a complex subject with multiple factors to be considered on both the societal (political, legal, economic and cultural conditions) and on the individual level (personal perceptions, experiences and values and norms). Predominant scientific fields which deal with conflicts and conflict resolutions include sociology, economics, political science and social psychology. Each field has its own definitions and areas of focus.

In political science and sociology, key elements of research are social actors as collective entities with 'power of agency' (Long 1992, p. 23). In the analysis of conflicts, these entities have various roles, interests, and formal and informal functions in the public realm (Jänicke 1994, p. 10). In these contexts, conflicts are usually analysed on a macro level. Economics, especially game theory, concentrates rather on conflict issues such as the distribution of goods and resources, and the benefits and costs of decisions made in conflict situations. From this perspective, a conflict is understood as a decision dilemma: two actors can choose between co-operation (which maximises the joint benefit) and defection (which probably maximises the individual benefit). This decision-making process has to be undertaken in a state of uncertainty with regard to the behaviour of the co-actors – this can lead to disastrous results for both (Weimann 1991, p. 203; Hofstadter 1998, p. 60). The modelling and economic analysis of these decision-making situations provides indications as to the importance of an issue and the possible strategies of the actors; however, this approach still operates with assumptions such as *no* or *limited* communication between the actors, predetermined fixed interests and the rational behaviour of the individuals (Kesting 1998, p. 1053). For the research question outlined here, such an economic approach to conflict and conflict resolution is of limited practical validity.

New institutional economics tries to link the macro with the micro perspective through the definition and analysis of economic and political institutions, such as transactions, property rights and governance structures. Co-operative structures among actors like farmers or between farmers and other actors with the goal of solving land use problems and conflicts can constitute one important governance institution, in addition to markets, hierarchies and other contractual relations (see Hagedorn, Chapter 1, this volume). In Germany, as in many other European countries, co-operative conflict resolution is not yet institutionalised in the field of agri-environmental conflicts (Hoffman-Riem 1990, p. 41; Fietkau and Weidner 1998, p. 199). A series of theoretical and empirical questions remain as to under which conditions these institutions are competitive and hence preferable. Some practical evidence on how to proceed on the organisational level can be found in countries like The Netherlands (Wagemans and Boerma 1998; Woerkum and Aarts 1998), Australia (Curtis et al. 1995), the United States (Lawrence et al. 1997) and in developing countries (AGILNP 1995).

Theoretical concepts which focus on the interaction process among the involved actors on the personal level can be found in social psychology. From this point of view, the conflict issue is of a wider dimension than in the economic case: it may be a question of distribution or (a lack) of institutions, but is also one of a difference in personal perceptions, values and norms, or information deficits, as well as simple misunderstandings among people (Deutsch 1976, p. 18). The essential point that creates a conflict situation is that activities or communicative acts of one party are perceived as offensive, aggressive or harmful by the other side (Grunwald 1981, p. 70; Glasl 1994, p. 14). From this point of view, conflicts occur as a result of human actions and reactions – so the crucial step in reaching a solution is changing the mutual human perceptions and the resulting behaviour and action.

Research on the behaviour of people in interpersonal and inter-group conflicts revealed two typical strategies in conflictive situations: co-operation or competition (Deutsch 1976, p. 30). While co-operative strategies can be characterised by personal openness, the willingness to exchange information, the search for common interests and response to external demands in the form of mutual support; competitive behaviour typically consists of communication with a hidden agenda, mistrust and a hostile attitude towards others, as well as a clear tendency to maximise one's own advantages. Competitive behaviour usually leads to an escalation of a conflict in the direction of struggle and mutual destructiveness (Glasl 1994, p. 215). More recent research states that competition is one important aspect of conflicts, but that in conflict situations and processes competitive as well as co-operative attitudes among actors are possible and frequent (Grunwald 1981, pp. 62 and 95).

For constructive conflict resolution, co-operative behaviour on the individual level is one of the preconditions. Other important elements for co-operative processes and results are

- common objective(s) (Deutsch 1976, p. 31),
- the focus on interests, not on positions (Fisher and Ury 1987, p. 41) and
- procedural justice (Thibaut and Walker 1975, p. 2).

Procedural justice is a subjective concept, which can also be understood as fairness and is evaluated by the distribution of controlling or influencing power among the actors in a decision-making process. An important means of appreciating the power distribution is transparency of interaction. This transparency can be achieved either through already established and recognised standards and structures or through procedures and criteria that have been jointly developed (Thibaut and Walker 1975, p. 7).

Obviously these preconditions have to be realised if a co-operative conflict resolution is to be achieved. This can be done with the help of a third party who demonstrates co-operative behaviour and who has the power to adequately guide the other actors in this process.[1] Another possibility is that one of the actors introduces these conditions.[2]

Frequently, land use conflicts involve more than two actors (individual persons or groups). This means, when focusing on the interpersonal interaction and communication among all actors, working with groups and hence the dimension of group dynamics has to be taken into account. Adequate procedures and rules for joint work in a non-hierarchical group have to be adopted or developed. This is a process involving several phases (Langmaak and Braune-Krickau 1987, p. 78), which can be supported by a third party (a moderator). The successful working of a group can be characterised by a goal-oriented and constructive attitude of the group members on the objective level and a fair and open way of dealing with one another on the personal level.

Summarising the discussed concepts, the following criteria can be used to analyse and evaluate a co-operative conflict resolution process:

1. common objective(s);
2. information exchange;
3. joint efforts, supportive activities;
4. respect and understanding of mutual interests;
5. joint decision making, transparency of structures and procedures; and
6. satisfaction with the results.

These criteria will guide the evaluation of the results obtained in one case study in a nature conservation area in Brandenburg (see section 4).

3 THE INITIAL SITUATION IN THE NATURE CONSERVATION AREA IN BRANDENBURG

In March 1990, the last government of the German Democratic Republic (GDR) implemented a 'national park programme' in which several nature conservation areas of considerable size (> 100 km^2) were identified (Reichhoff and Böhnert 1991, p. 200). Today there are about 13 such areas in the federal state of Brandenburg alone, which cover in total about 30 per cent of the state's surface (MUNR 1999, p. 14). These conservation areas can be divided into three categories: national parks, biosphere reserves and nature parks. The last one is the most frequent form; it has at the same time the lowest degree of protection. Its aim is to conciliate tourist and economic interests with the environmental goals (MUNR 1994, p. 22). In accordance with the federal legislation, public agencies were established in subsequent years in each of these conservation areas with the task of realising the necessary legal conditions (protection decree) and to manage and co-ordinate the specific conservation measures.

During the implementation phase (that is realisation of the protection decree) the environmental agencies found themselves frequently confronted with serious resistance by some of the local communities and inhabitants. Stakeholders and different interest groups such as farmers, local and regional community representatives, entrepreneurs, sportsmen and others were opposed to the planned restrictions on their conventional use of land. By way of written objections, public demonstrations and the use of the media, the actors tried to get their opinions across (Siebert and Knierim 1999).

These conflicting situations were more or less frequent in the different conservation areas with a varying degree of escalation. As a result, a research co-operation was constituted among the responsible administration unit on the federal state level (Landesanstalt für Großschutzgebiete Brandenburg, LAGS), the environmental agency of one conservation area (the Park Administration) and the Chair of Agricultural Extension and Communication at Humboldt University. A preliminary analysis of the conflict situation in the nature park revealed the main actors and their respective interests, shown in Table 16.1.

The conflict situation at the end of 1996 can be described as follows:

- The overall subject is the decree of the landscape protection area[3] and the respective regulations for different kinds of land use.
- Other important subjects are the plans or rumours concerning the plans of the Park Administration to
  - move a dyke and to re-naturalise the river bank and
  - re-naturalise a meliorated small river.
- Finally, there were a lot of misunderstandings and a lack of understanding for one another which led to an unfriendly, semi-aggressive atmosphere between the environmentalists and the other land users in the nature park (Knierim 1997, p. 11).

In spite of the somewhat tense atmosphere and the specific conflicts, many people expressed their willingness to contribute to the maintenance of the landscape and the precious nature goods of the region in personal interviews (Knierim 1997, p. 23).

Table 16.1 Main actors and their interests

Main actors	Their interests (as expressed in interviews and publications)
– The Park Administration (locally based), – Board of Environment (district level)	to achieve an acceptable degree of protection for the whole area and a differentiated protection according to the specific nature resources and their protection needs
– The farmers – Board of Agriculture (district level)	to reduce land use regulations as much as possible to minimise regulation of grassland use to minimise the damage through birds and other protected animals or to obtain adequate compensation
– The communal representatives (mayors, administrative directors[a] etc.)	to minimise communal planning and construction regulations in the area of building and infrastructure
– Other land users like foresters, hunters, fishermen and tourists	to maintain protection of the environmental resources but also to get free access to the resources they intend to use (river banks, woods etc.)

Note: [a]Administrative Direktor: Amtsdirektor.

4 THE PROCESS OF CO-OPERATIVE CONFLICT RESOLUTION

The co-operative conflict resolution process in sensu stricto started after six months of preparations. At first, a group of land users (mainly farmers) declared their interest in conflict management and co-operation with the Park Administration. As the overall subject to be dealt with they chose the extensive use of grasslands.

Under this heading several problems and conflicts were slated to be dealt with in relation to the local agricultural situation, that is the important number of grassland dominated livestock farms:

- the consequences of the European Union Agrarian Reform ('Agenda 2000');
- the uncertainty of the state (Brandenburg) programme to support extensification of grasslands, with which
- the (regionally offered) programme of land care on a contract basis is linked;
- different planning horizons between official environmentalists and farmers;
- the competition for land resources;
- the dissatisfaction with the implementation of land care on a contract basis; and
- the uncertain legal and natural consequences of extensive grassland use.

These issues were mainly presented by the land users. The only point added from the side of the Park Administration was the dissatisfaction with the implementation of land care.

During the same meeting the group formulated a series of goals for the common process as follows:

- The actors of the nature conservation area represent their interests jointly to externals such as the ministries of agriculture or environment.
- The agricultural land users and the Park Administration look at each other as partners/treat each other as partners.
- The land care on a contract basis is efficiently arranged for everyone.
- All farms in the nature conservation area are maintained.
- All information on the subject 'extensification of grasslands', especially on supporting governmental programmes, will be exchanged.
- Additionally, the farmers claimed that in order to build up confidence the Park Administration had to put its plans on the table and to pass on information at its disposal.

Based on these objectives and with a focus on the above-mentioned problems and conflicts, a group of 8 to 12 different stakeholders met during a period of one and a half years in 14 meetings. The contents of the different meetings are presented in Table 16.2 in a very abbreviated form.

Table 16.2 The meetings during the co-operative conflict resolution process

Meeting no.	Date	Subject and contents	No. of partici-pants
1	Feb. 98	*Problem definition and goal setting* The different actors agreed on a subject to work on, and identified common objectives (on a rather general level). A topic for the next meeting was defined and contributing activities formulated.	11
2	March 98	*Analysis of the situation* Some of the actors presented data on the extensive use of grasslands in the park supported by the federal state and the regionally offered environmental programmes. This appraisal of the regional land use patterns gave an idea of the concerns of land users concerning federal, national and EU agrarian policies. Because of its relevance, the group decided to talk about the Agenda 2000.	8
3	April 98	*Agenda 2000* The Director of the Board of Agriculture (district level) gave information on the expected reform of the Common Agricultural Policy. The group tried to evaluate the consequences for the regional land users and decided to appraise the Agricultural Minister of Brandenburg concerning the specific regional situation.	15
4	May 98	*Letter of invitation* A letter had been drafted by three members of the group inviting the Agricultural Minister of Brandenburg to the meeting on November 9, 1998. The letter contained proposals on how to improve the situation for extensive agricultural land use in the nature conservation area. These proposals were discussed in detail.	10
5	June 98	*Competition for land resources* The presentation of the – now completed – land acquisition by the Park Administration with the funding from an EU project resulted in an emotionally intense debate over the competitive situation, the relatively weak position of farmers in this case and the general lack of information about the goals and plans of the Park Administration concerning that land.	10

Table 16.2 (continued)

6	Sept. 98	*Preparation for the visit of the Minister of Agriculture* The group agreed on a goal for the visit and a list of subjects to be covered. Preparations for the visit *vis-à-vis* the content and on the organisational level were initiated.	12
7	Sept. 98	*Preparation for the visit (continuation)* On the content level, the group went into detail as to which common proposals for supporting measures could be made through the Agricultural Ministry of Brandenburg. On the organisational level, the different actors disagreed over the characteristic sites to visit during an excursion.	10
8	Oct. 98	*Preparation for the visit (continuation)* The suggestions for the measures of the Ministry were completed. The route of the excursion was determined after clarifying the different interests of the actors with respect to the sightseeing tour.	11
9	Nov. 98	*Visit of the Minister of Agriculture* The visit permitted an open exchange between the ministerial guests from and the members of the group and allowed them to get acquainted with the regional specifics.	
10	Dec. 98	*Evaluation of the visit; monitoring and evaluation* The evaluation of the visit showed quite a satisfaction with the event, but also a very realistic perception of the effects on the Minister. The Park Administration presented its monitoring and evaluation results of the land care measures on a contract basis. Thirdly, it was proposed to cover another subject of conflict: the ploughing up of grasslands.	9
11	Feb. 99	*Ploughing up of grasslands* The group analysed the conflict situation which was due to different agreements (one in the form of the final decree, the other in the form of a protocol) in a former working group on the landscape protection decree. A solution had to be found that neither violated the now existing law (the decree), nor hurt the concessions made in informal papers. Proposals for solutions were developed.	9

Table 16.2 continued

12	March 99	*Ploughing up of grasslands (continuation)* A paper from the district administration was presented and discussed, in which a solution was proposed according to the legal requirements. The different aspects of the conflict were separated as to a local and a federal level and it was decided to invite representatives of the involved Ministries of Agriculture and Environment to take up the problem on the federal level.	10
13	April 99	*Ploughing up of grasslands (continuation)* The meeting with the Ministries' representatives was planned and prepared, tasks were distributed.	9
14	May 99	*Ploughing up of grasslands (continuation)* The meeting with the Ministries' representatives was fruitful as they were well prepared and the discussion produced several proposals as to how to proceed.	12
15	June 99	*Evaluation and scenery of the region* The last meeting was evaluated. The Park Administration presented its criteria to determine the preservation degree necessary for different grasslands in the region (scenery). The farmers showed their actual and potential grassland use in a map.	9

5 ANALYSIS OF THE RESULTS

The analysis of the results follows the above-mentioned criteria to evaluate a co-operative process:

5.1 Common objective(s).
5.2 Information exchange.
5.3 Joint efforts, supportive activities.
5.4 Respect and understanding of mutual interests.
5.5 Joint decision making, transparency of structures and procedures.
5.6 Satisfaction with the results.

5.1 Common Objective(s)

In the beginning of the co-operative process, common objectives were formulated, of which the first ones can be classified as very general. They are not linked to a concrete conflict, but express the kind of relationship people wished to create (partnership, unity *vis-à-vis* external actors). The third objective – efficient execution of land care on a contract basis – is concrete and linked to an identified conflict. Like the conflict, this objective had been proposed by the environmentalists. The fourth objective – maintenance of all farms in the area – can only be understood as indicative or as a political claim, for it is not within the scope of the actors involved to maintain or to support maintenance of every single farm. The last two objectives are rather suggestions of activities and wishes expressed by the agricultural actors and directed at the environmentalists.

These objectives did not lead the co-operative process explicitly – participants hardly ever referred to them. On the incentive of the author, the first objective – being/becoming partners – had been discussed with the aim to qualify 'partner' in order to be able to judge the degree of achievement. This happened in the third meeting, and because the group members were not very interested in this kind of discussion it was not extended. Nevertheless, the objectives 1, 2, 5 and 6 were indirectly but continually present and seemed to be guiding the whole co-operative process.

5.2 Exchange of Information

Exchange of information was an issue of surprising importance. Rather than starting the process with a conflictive subject of local relevance the group decided to talk about some burning questions induced by the federal state and the Common Agricultural Policy of the European Union (meetings 2 and 3). In both cases, the exchange of information, mainly given by the Director of the Agricultural Board to the working group, especially to the farmers, aroused great interest. In several other meetings the group started the session with an exchange of information. This happened either when someone felt his information might be relevant to the other participants, or when questions were raised as to how to understand certain events or activities in the environmental sphere (mainly by the agricultural land users, meetings 5, 10 and 12). Through these activities the group members contributed to objectives 5 and 6.

In final evaluation sheets and remarks this exchange of information was highly appreciated because of the directness and the topicality of the news, as well as the possibility to clarify misunderstandings and open questions. Sometimes an information exchange was accompanied by an attempt to evaluate the news obtained and to forecast consequences.

5.3 Joint Efforts, Supportive Activities

The overall subject to be dealt with was mainly of agricultural interest. Interestingly enough, the process did not start with a conflict but rather with 'external subjects': the agricultural policies at the state and at the European Union level. The first activity in this context was the analysis of the situation in the region with the aim of evaluating the state of concern of the farms. This was supported by several members of the working group by a supply of data (meetings 2 and 3). A second activity in this sense was the idea to invite the Agricultural Minister to the meeting on November 9, 1998. This was the result of an analysis which had shown that the specific regional situation with grassland dominance and livestock farms is insufficiently considered in the federal and the European agricultural policy, and that even the federal state Minister seemed to underestimate the problems of the area. The letter of invitation was formulated by some members of the working group and included proposals for future agricultural guidelines with respect to agricultural and environmental objectives. The formulation of the letter can be seen as an expression of 'joint efforts'. The process of agreeing on the different proposals constitutes a series of supporting activities. Especially in the case of one item, which corresponded to the environmentalists' interest but was judged by some agricultural land users as uncertain if not slightly risky to them, it was not an easy decision for the farmers to support it (meetings 4, 6, 7 and 8). The supportive activities become even more evident when looking at the concrete preparations for the visit: several members of the working group contributed through small presentations and on the organisational level (meeting 8). The meeting with the Agricultural Minister must be seen as one result contributing to achieving objective 2.

A real conflict was tackled when the subject 'ploughing up of grassland' was dealt with (meeting 10). Early on the group started to identify directions of solution (meeting 11) and formed sub-groups to work on propositions (meeting 12). When someone reported that a regional politician had proposed to intervene at ministerial level, the group quickly came to the conclusion that they should first solve the conflict at their own level.

5.4 Respect and Understanding of Mutual Interests

In personal interviews before the co-operative process, different actors talked about their interests and – sometimes – also about the assumed interests of the other actors. At the beginning of the co-operative process, the actors did not talk explicitly about their general interests. It can be assumed that these were sufficiently covered by the common objectives. However, when it came to conflicting questions during the process of co-operation, the group tried to clarify the different interests by listing them. This happened explicitly at least three times (meetings 8, 11 and 12), informally more often. Nobody had problems with the interests of the other actors, at least no one contested them in public.

5.5 Joint Decision Making, Transparency of Structures and Procedures

As a rule, decision making happened in consensus and discussions continued until the item was clarified. If necessary, proposals for decisions were collected and debated. Without major problems or endless argumentation, the group came to common agreements. In addition to the co-operative attitude that was shown by nearly every member of the group, these successful decisions may be due to the fact that, up to the fourteenth meeting, no conflicts of direct material relevance to any member had to be resolved by the group.

Transparency of structures and procedures was an issue that the author tried to pursue. It was done through presentation of her own concepts (co-operative conflict resolution, problem-solving cycle, evaluation of achievement of objectives, and so on) and by asking, from time to time, whether the 'chosen' structure and procedures of the group were still adequate. Transparency of structures and procedures is of continuing importance for the group members, as shown by the fact that the group wishes to maintain an external moderation function (meetings 12, 14 and 15). Activities to raise funds for the financing have already been started.

5.6 Satisfaction with the Results

From the researcher's point of view there are as yet no concrete results regarding conflict solutions. The group is still working on a major conflict on two levels (local and federal state), proposals have been formulated and realisation has just begun. Nevertheless, the participants are satisfied with the joint work – as expressed in an anonymous questionnaire and in interviews – and they have decided to continue their co-operative process.

6 CONCLUSIONS

It is obvious that no classical 'conflict resolution process' took place. What happened was rather a slow formation process of a long-term working group which is able and motivated to deal with topical questions and conflicts. What was reached in this case is the practice of co-operative behaviour in an informal semi-public group of different stakeholders which are all more or less concerned with the agricultural land use in the area. What kind of co-operative behaviour and activities could be observed?

- The environmentalists accepted the overall subject with the sub-points proposed by the agricultural land users. Their own conflict issue 'efficient land care on a contract basis' was not treated during the fifteen meetings.
- The agricultural land users supported proposals made to the Agricultural Minister which corresponded explicitly to the interests of the environmentalists and were unimportant, or possibly or slightly risky, to them (meeting 9).
- In general, agreed upon activities were executed, small inputs prepared and extra meetings in sub-groups took place. Beside the time spent in the meetings (normally 3 h), people were ready to contribute extra time and their knowledge (meetings 2, 3, 5, 10 and 12).
- Information that seemed interesting for the other actors was given voluntarily.
- External support was only demanded after common agreement and not to support one side only.

This process shows that, for the people involved, the co-operative atmosphere in the region and the establishment of a common structure were more important than the specific conflict resolution. Open information exchange seems to be an important instrument in achieving trust and co-operation. After a period of nearly one year (nine meetings) in which the exchange of information and the discussion of external problems predominated, the group started to resolve a pressing conflict. This happened in a very constructive and goal-oriented manner. This latter process is an indication of the newly achieved ability of the group members to deal directly with conflictive situations without producing major misunderstandings or emotional complications.

NOTES

1. The role and the inherent ambivalence of such an advisory work is discussed in detail by Glasl (1994, p. 304, p. 360).
2. For example land use planning in third world development projects is nowadays based on participation of and co-operation with the different stakeholders, even in conflict situations. Participation and co-operation as key ideas will be introduced by the project representatives (AGILNP 1995, p. 92).
3. Decree of landscape protection area: Landschaftsschutzgebietsverordnung.

REFERENCES

AGILNP (Arbeitsgruppe Integrierte Landnutzungsplanung) (1995), *Landnutzungsplanung Strategien, Instrumente, Methoden*, Eschborn: GTZ Deutsche Gesellschaft für Technische Zusammenarbeit.

Curtis, A., J. Birckhead and T. de Lacy (1995), 'Community Participation in Landcare Policy in Australia: The Victorian Experience with Regional Landcare Plans', *Society and Natural Resources*, **8**, pp. 415–30.

Deutsch, M. (1976), *Konfliktregelung. Konstruktive und destruktive Prozesse*, München, Basel: E. Reinhardt.

Fietkau, H.-J. and H. Weidner (1998), *Umweltverhandeln: Konzepte, Praxis und Analysen alternativer Konfliktregelungsverfahren*, Berlin: edition sigma.

Fisher, R. and W. Ury (1987), *Getting to Yes. Negotiating Agreement without Giving In*, London: Arrow Books.

Glasl, F. (1994), *Konfliktmanagement. Ein Handbuch zur Diagnose und Behandlung von Konflikten für Organisationen und ihre Berater*, Bern, Stuttgart: Paul Haupt.

Grunwald, W. (1981), 'Konflikt–Konkurrenz–Kooperation: Eine theoretisch-empirische Konzeptanalyse', in Grunwald, W. and H.-G. Lilge (eds), *Kooperation und Konkurrenz in Organisationen*, Bern, Stuttgart: Paul Haupt, pp. 50–95.

Hoffmann-Riem, W. (1990), 'Verhandlungslösungen und Mittlereinsatz im Bereich der Verwaltung. Eine vergleichende Einführung', in Hoffman-Riem, W. and E. Schmidt-Aßmann (eds), *Konfliktbewältigung durch Verhandlungen*, Baden-Baden: Nomos, pp. 13–42.

Hofstadter, D.R. (1998), 'Tit for Tat. Kann sich in einer Welt voller Egoisten kooperatives Verhalten entwickeln? Kooperation und Konkurrenz', *Spektrum der Wissenschaften*, Special Issue, **1**/98, pp. 60–66.

Jänicke, M. (1994), 'Akteure der Umweltpolitik', in Junkernheinrich, M. v., P. Klemmer and G.R. Wagner (eds), *Handbuch zur Umweltökonomie*, Berlin: Analytica, pp. 10–15.

Kesting, S. (1998), 'A Potential for Understanding and the Interference of Power: Discourse as an Economic Mechanism of Co-ordination', *Journal of Economic Issues*, **XXXII** (4), December, pp. 1053–78.

Knierim, A. (1997), 'Analyse der Konfliktsituation im Naturpark. 'E.' Erster Zwischenbericht', Unpublished Manuscript, Chair of Agricultural Extension and Communication, Humboldt University of Berlin.

Langmaack, B. and M. Braune-Krickau (1987), *Wie die Gruppe laufen lernt*, München: Psychologie Verlags Union.

Lawrence, R.L., S.E. Daniels and G.H. Stankey (1997), 'Procedural Justice and Public Involvement in Natural Resource Decision Making', *Society and Natural Resources*, **10**, pp. 577–89.

Long, N. (1992), 'From Paradigm Lost to Paradigm Regained?', in Long, N. and A. Long (eds), *The Battlefields of Knowledge*, London, New York: Routledge, pp. 16–43.

MUNR (Ministerium für Umwelt, Naturschutz und Raumordnung Brandenburg) (1994), 'Brandenburger Naturschutzgebiete', *Brandenburger Umwelt Journal*, August, pp. 21–23.

MUNR (Ministerium für Umwelt, Naturschutz und Raumordnung Brandenburg) (1999), 'Die Großschutzgebiete in Brandenburg', *Brandenburger Umwelt Journal*, August, p. 14.

Reichhoff, L. and W. Böhnert (1991), 'Das Nationalparkprogramm der ehemaligen DDR', *Zeitschrift für Naturschutz, Landschaftspflege und Umweltschutz*, **66** (4), pp. 195–203.

Siebert, R. and A. Knierim (1999), 'Divergierende Nutzungsinteressen in Schutzgebieten – Konflikte und Lösungsansätze in Brandenburg', *Zeitschrift für Kulturtechnik und Landentwicklung*, **40** (4), pp. 181–86.

Thibaut, J. and L. Walker (1975), *Procedural Justice. A Psychological Analysis*, Hillsdale, New Jersey: Erlbaum.

Wagemans, M. and J. Boerma (1998), 'The Implementation of Nature Policy in the Netherlands: Platforms Designed to Fail', in Röling, N.G. and M.A.E. Wagemakers (eds), *Facilitating Sustainable Agriculture*, Cambridge: Cambridge University Press, pp. 250–71.

Weimann, J. (1991), *Umweltökonomik. Eine theorieorientierte Einführung, 2. verbesserte Auflage*, Berlin, Heidelberg, New York, Tokyo: Springer.

Woerkum, C. van and N. Aarts (1998), 'Communication between Farmers and Government over Nature: A New Approach to Policy Development', in Röling, N.G. and M.A.E. Wagemakers (eds), *Facilitating Sustainable Agriculture*, Cambridge: Cambridge University Press, pp. 272–80.

17. Ecotourism, Stakeholders and Regional Sustainable Development

Michael Getzner[1]

1 INTRODUCTION

The establishment of the 'Gesäuse National Park' has been discussed on a regional level for a long time. A number of concepts focusing on the regional development of the poor and peripheral region of Upper Styria (Austria) stress the need for sustainable regional development. One major asset of the region of the Gesäuse National Park is a unique landscape with high mountains, deep gorges and wild rivers and creeks. The Gesäuse National Park is situated in the districts of Liezen and Leoben (see Figure 17.1 for a map showing the location within Austria). These regional development concepts report a number of problems in the region: particularly high unemployment rates, low productivity, high dependence on economic activities outside the region (high import rates) and on the primary sector (agriculture and forestry). Furthermore, many young and skilled professionals leave the region in order to find adequate jobs elsewhere in Austria. As regions today face international, often global, competition regarding foundations of new firms as well as visits by tourists, the region of the Gesäuse National Park has failed in promoting its assets to international businesses and particularly to the tourist industry. Nowadays, tourists are mobile, and lower airfares may also decrease European demand for tourist services in regional European tourist destinations.

One major step towards ecologically and economically sustainable development in the region can be seen in a recently finalised feasibility study of the establishment of a Gesäuse National Park which includes ecological, social, political and economic issues.[2] There are two main objectives for founding a national park. First, the landscape as well as wildlife are worth protecting according to the rules and regulations of the IUCN (International Union for the Conservation of Nature). The Gesäuse National Park will comply with category II of the IUCN rules (thus the national park would become internationally acknowledged as such).[3] Second, a number of past strategies and options for regional development were not successful. The establishment of a national park can therefore be considered as an opportunity and new challenge for sustainable economic development in the region. As one important part of the feasibility study, an ex ante regional economic impact analysis was carried out.

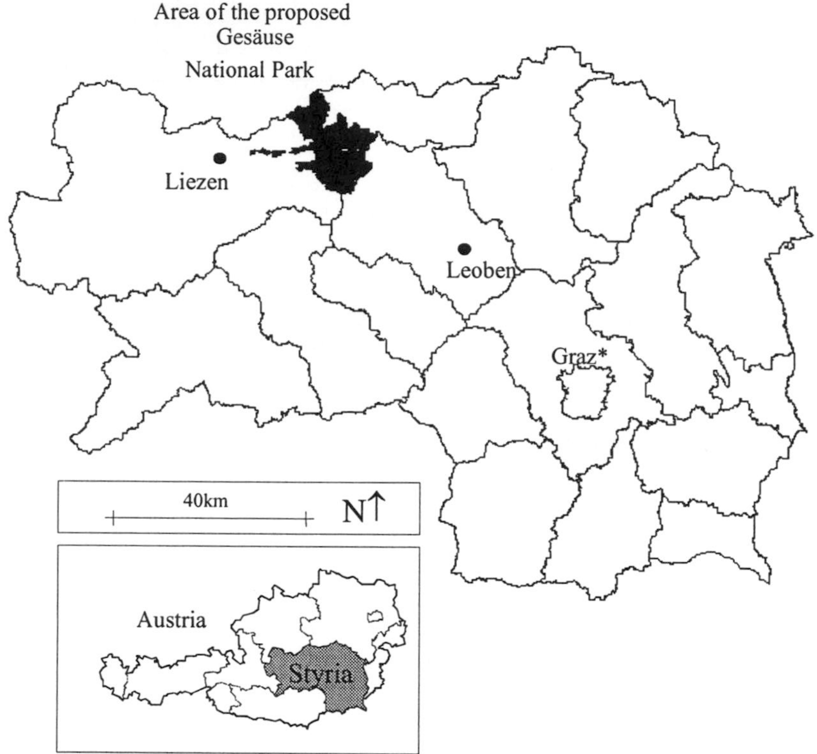

* capital of Styria

Figure 17.1 Overview of the location of the Gesäuse National Park in Upper Styria (Austria)

A major part of the development and establishment process for the Gesäuse National Park is the involvement of all stakeholders in the region. These are not only the local and regional population (residents), but also the tourist industries, the primary sectors (agriculture, forestry, hunting, fishing) and the mining industry, as well as regional opinion leaders and decision makers. The main objective of this discursive process is not only to assure the acceptance of a national park or to mediate opposition but also to collect regional, often tacit, knowledge which is not codified or cannot be quantitatively expressed in terms of inputs for economic modelling. Furthermore, environmental decisions are not only based on individuals' utility maximisation but on a number of institutional and social circumstances[4] which can only be elicited by the involvement of stakeholders.

The Gesäuse National Park would be the seventh national park in Austria. Three of them are internationally acknowledged as category II national parks according to IUCN guidelines (Neusiedler See, Donau-Auen, Kalkalpen). The others meet most of the criteria for category II but face some local and regional problems (for example continuing agricultural production). They are protected landscapes according to the IUCN's category V. However, the goals of Austrian national parks can be split in two major points. First, the ecosystems as well as the landscape should be protected. Second, regional development and ecological education should be improved (Tiefenbach et al. 1998). Public involvement with every national park project was intensively encouraged, especially through open debates, public information and by institutionalising a 'national park forum' (see, for example, Nationalparkplanung Donau-Auen (1994) for the 'Donau-Auen National Park').

The chapter is structured as follows: Section 2 provides a short discussion of regional sustainable development and of ecotourism. Section 3.1 gives an overview of the model used to calculate and project the economic impact of the establishment of the Gesäuse National Park, while section 3.2 describes in short the main economic problems of the region and the main future trends of regional development, and provides an empirical discussion of the potential economic impact in different sectors. The calculation of the economic impact as well as the realisation of the national park itself presupposes a network of stakeholders. Thus, section 4 describes the stakeholder network and the institutional framework on which the results of this chapter as well as the acceptance and (possible) realisation of the national park rests. Section 5 summarises the results and discusses the main findings of the chapter.

2 REGIONAL SUSTAINABLE DEVELOPMENT AND ECOTOURISM

From an abstract point of view, sustainable development is often defined in terms of the Solow–Hartwick rule stating that 'development based on the depletion of natural capital may be sustainable, as long as a) there exist substitutes for such capital, and b) investment on those substitutes at least compensates for the loss of natural capital' (Perrings 1995, p. 122). The debate in economics about sustainable development focuses to a great extent on substitutability, which leads to a number of valuation problems (Getzner 1999a). The 'quality' of ecological and economic systems is determined by the system's resilience, that is, the ability of the system to absorb and deal with shocks without losing stability. Perrings (1995, p. 133) shows that co-dependent ecological and economic systems can have multiple equilibria. Whenever one subsystem dominates the other, resilience and stability are in danger. Regional economic development within the framework of ecologically sustainable development can be considered as contributing to the resilience of the whole system. The region becomes more independent and resilient to shocks from the outside.[5] Theoretically speaking, a regional system consisting of a balance between the ecological and the economic spheres can be a regionally sustainable one.

In practice, regional sustainable development is usually addressed in regional development or structure plans. A thorough analysis of regional structure plans in England and Wales finds that the main issues of regional sustainable development in these plans are manifold, ranging from ignoring the broader concept of sustainable development to very specific definitions of regional criteria of sustainable development (Counsell 1998). A major problem arises with a proper definition of regional (or local) sustainable development. Building on definitions, for example by WCED (1987), regional structure plans try to operationalise sustainable development within eight sub-categories (Counsell 1998, p. 181): natural resources; land use and transportation; energy; pollution; waste management; wildlife and countryside; economic and social well-being; and built environment. While 'working within the carrying capacities of natural systems' and 'maintaining levels of critical natural capital', the adoption of a 'holistic approach across policy areas' and the 'precautionary principle' are equally important for sustainable development (Counsell 1998, p. 180). Among the fields of policy areas, economic and social well-being implies sustaining local communities, improving awareness and involvement, supporting local economic activity, mitigation measures for industrial development, and environmentally sensitive tourism and recreation (Counsell 1998, p. 182).

To secure ecologically sound development and economic benefits by means of ecotourism, a number of crucial factors have been determined (see for example Blangy and Nielsen 1994; Inskeep 1995; MacIntyre 1998). Ecotourism and recreation experiences themselves depend directly on the physical environment as well as on the social and cultural framework (Cable and Udd 1990). Ecotourism thus presupposes ecologically sound development. Ecotourism 'generally refers to travel to relatively undisturbed or uncontaminated natural areas with the specific objective of studying, admiring and enjoying the scenery and its wild plants and animals as well as any manifestation found in these areas' (Baud-Bovy and Lawson 1998, p. 11). Recreation experiences in the Gesäuse National Park clearly fall into that definition of ecotourism.

A number of studies show that (eco) tourism can contribute to regional sustainable development both in the ecological and economic sense (Sinclair 1998; Theophile 1995). Ecotourism can be considered 'as a means to sustain use of natural resources and provide income and economic security for a region' (Wagner 1997, p. 592). Outdoor recreation and development of recreation sites and natural scenic attractions may provide a viable development alternative for rural areas (Bergstrom et al. 1990). When ecological constraints are considered, ecotourism can crucially contribute to regional sustainable development because 'recreation-based jobs can typically be maintained for a long period of time' (Douglas and Harpman 1995, p. 246). A number of publications deal with ecotourism in Austrian national parks (for example Ullmann and Klauß 1993; Zimmermann 1993; Jülg 1993; Fontanari 1993). These authors generally stress the opportunities of ecotourism for the tourist and agricultural sectors, but they also consider the possibly negative impacts of tourism on regional ecosystems (too many ecotourists can be harmful as well).

3 THE REGIONAL ECONOMIC IMPACT OF THE GESÄUSE NATIONAL PARK

3.1 Overview of the Regional Multiplier Model[6]

The regional effects on employment and production (direct and indirect as well as secondary effects) are calculated by means of a regional multiplier model. The basis for the empirical analysis is the Austrian input–output table for the base year of 1983 which was adapted for the year 1994 (according to the methodology presented in Farny et al. 1988; ÖSTAT 1994; Eichler 1998; Getzner and Schneider 1999). The model itself has been used in a number of studies regarding the economic impact of infrastructure projects in Austria that have an environmental impact (for example Adensam 1995; Kosz 1996). Without going into detail, the results are average multipliers for production (value added) and employment for 177 economic activities of the Austrian economy, producing the respective number of goods and services. The general problems with this approach for our problem setting are especially (1) that effects at the regional level can only be computed with auxiliary hypotheses regarding the regional location of enterprises that satisfy additional demand when founding a national park; (2) that without more concrete data marginal effects are treated as if they compare to average effects; and (3) that no regional input–output table or other detailed regional economic data in consistent form are available. However, the use of average multipliers is nevertheless an appropriate and standard model for estimations of the regional economic benefits of a particular project. The use of input–output tables for (eco) tourism is especially emphasised in the US (see, for example, Frechtling 1994; Douglas and Harpman 1995).

Figure 17.2 shows the methodological framework for estimating the regional economic impact. The first step towards calculating the regional economic impact of the Gesäuse National Park is an analysis of current regional activities, including regional development concepts. The problem here is that many regional concepts do not include quantitative goals for regional development. Thus, building on these concepts to describe the status quo and future development only indicates possible future development paths (a number of assumptions have to be made). A very important method in projecting the status quo into the future are workshops and stakeholder interviews that create more or less realistic pictures and prognoses for future regional development (stakeholders' involvement in the planning process is discussed in section 4). Environmental impact assessment as well as legal and political frameworks provided further information (some in physical terms) for drafting future development paths (see section 3.2.2).

On the basis of these results and assumptions, expenditures, losses and changed regional economic activities can now be projected to mirror possible future development when a national park is founded. On the one hand, these expenditures concern mainly one-off and annual costs of the national park itself (infrastructure, personnel). On the other hand, additional visitors to the region demand tourist goods and services bringing additional money to the region. Tourism is considered as an export industry where tourists contribute to a local or regional economy through their trip-related expenditures (English and Bergstrom 1994). Transactions in agriculture, forestry, fishery as well as other economic activities (especially mining) are also discussed below.

All (changed) regional transactions that are caused by the establishment of the national park lead to a demand for goods and services which have to be allocated to the 177 economic activities of the input–output table. On the basis of existing studies as well as on a number of assumptions, all transactions were allocated in that way. Combined with multipliers for employment and production, the regional economic impact of the national park is calculated.[7] Again, we have to make assumptions on transactions made directly within the region as well as on the location of enterprises able to satisfy the additional demand and thus benefit from these transactions. The regional economic impact depends crucially on community level multipliers,

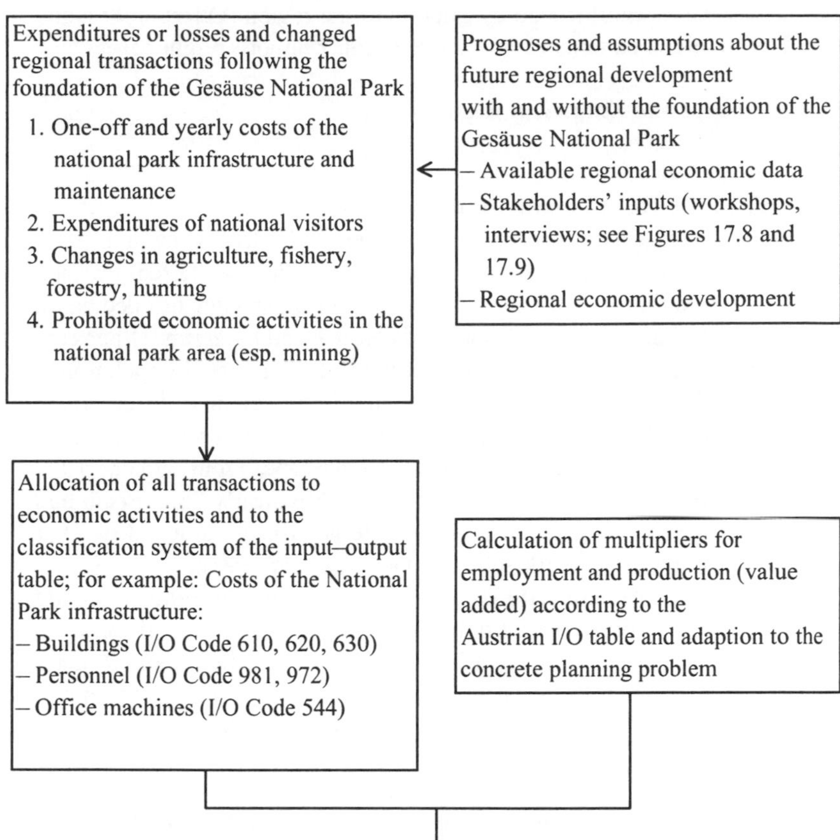

Depending on available data and assumptions:
Calculation of employment and production effects and allocation of effects to communities and regions
Primary effects split into:
- Direct effects on employment and production (regional effects)
- Indirect effects (intermediate goods and services produced within the region as well as outside)

Secondary effects
- Multiplier effects of additional income spent on consumer goods; average without regionality

Figure 17.2 Overview of the method of calculating the regional economic impact of the Gesäuse National Park

which themselves are influenced by imports to the region (Olfert and Stabler 1994). The smaller a particular region is, the higher imports might be.

3.2 Scenarios and Empirical Results

3.2.1 The regional economic status quo

The region of the district of Liezen faces problems of a decreasing number of inhabitants, an aging population and a continuous reduction of regional and local jobs. Within the last ten years, the number of inhabitants has decreased by 3 per cent, and the number of jobs has been reduced by around 4 per cent (for all figures see E.C.O. 1999). The education of the regional population is below the Austrian average. Prognoses of the future regional development predict continued loss of population. Furthermore, the region faces a continuing loss of tourists despite the unique landscape. From 1985 to 1997 the number of tourists staying overnight decreased by nearly 25 per cent and the capacities of the tourist sector (for example hotel beds) dropped by over 30 per cent (Amt der Steiermärkischen Landesregierung 1997).

The reasons for the continued loss of tourists are manifold. While there are 'external' reasons (global competition, low airfares, and so on), there are a number of circumstances that might be improved within the region. A main cause for decreasing numbers of tourists is the poor quality of tourist infrastructure like bed and breakfast accommodation, hotels, transport and outdoor activities. Furthermore, marketing efforts have been uncoordinated and not very effective (E.C.O. 1999).

The regional economic conditions led to an acknowledgement of the region of Liezen as an Objective 2 area (industrial regions in decline) of the European Regional Development Fund (ERDF), which is one of the European Union's four Structural Funds. Its aim is to support small and medium-sized enterprises, promote productive investment and improve infrastructure and local development. The ultimate aim of assistance from the ERDF is to create jobs by fostering competitive and sustainable development.

3.2.2 Building scenarios for the future regional development

As discussed above in section 3.2.1, the current economic state of the Gesäuse National Park region is rather poor. On the basis of this current state, a number of workshops and interviews were organised with stakeholders in the region. Extensive economic regional data do not exist because the statistical units of the official Austrian economic statistics are larger than small regions which include only a few communities. Furthermore, some data are based on the national census which is undertaken only every ten years (the last census took place in 1991). Thus, existing data are not completely adequate for building prognoses and scenarios.

The economic impact of founding the Gesäuse National Park is modelled within scenarios for several economic activities. In building the fundamentals of these scenarios stakeholders are crucial as information sources on past developments as well as (planned) future actions (the importance of stakeholders' involvement is discussed in Section 4). Without going too much into detail, the main arguments of the different scenarios are (all figures are based on a ten year planning period):

- Variants of the Gesäuse National Park itself (size, costs of infrastructure): In discussions with regional and federal government officials, two main variants were developed by the project team (a 'small' and a 'large' variant regarding the size of the proposed national park).
- The agricultural sector (small farms) may face an additional marketing opportunity if they choose to label their products as growing in or near a national park (ecologically grown products). That label might increase the farms' value added by an estimated 0.5 per cent per year.
- Scenarios regarding the number of future visitors to the national park: Information on past and current number of visitors is provided by tourist experts as well as by 'Stift Admont', a unique monastery with an old library, that records its visitors. Workshops with stakeholders, especially those from the tourist industries, yielded further information on future actions planned to improve the attractiveness of the region. As the tourist activities are extremely low in the region, an increase in the number of visitors by 2 per cent per year (tourist scenario 1) and of 5 per cent per year (tourist scenario 2) was estimated and agreed upon by participants in the workshop process (see section 4).

Besides these concrete scenarios a few assumptions have to be made. As concrete planning and implementation steps have not been undertaken, it is not completely clear which economic activities can be carried out in a national park that meet the international IUCN criteria. These activities are mainly mining and recreational hunting (see below).[8]

3.2.3 Building and maintaining the national park infrastructure

The establishment of a national park is linked to expenditures by government bodies. In the case of the Gesäuse National Park, the planning costs (and supposedly also the infrastructure costs of the national park itself) are borne by the Provincial Government of Styria (based in the City of Graz) and by the Federal Ministry of the Environment (Vienna). If those bodies spend a certain amount of money, this money can be considered as a flow into the Gesäuse

National Park region. These additional transactions in the region can only be considered as increasing production (value added) and employment if local or regional enterprises are employed in building the national park infrastructure. In this specific aspect there exists a crucial uncertainty. As the establishment of a national park is a public project, firms have to apply for contracts in a publicly announced invitation to tenders.[9] Thus, firms from outside the region might apply and win the contest. In that case, overall economic efficiency is guaranteed as the most competitive firm is awarded the contract, but the regional goals of promoting production and employment might not be fulfilled.

The preliminary one-off costs for founding the Gesäuse National Park are 73 million Austrian schilling (ATS) for variant 1 and an additional 54.5 million ATS for variant 2. The main investments include the building and renovation of buildings for the national park administration as well as a visitors' centre and a museum; plus costs of planning and management. The timeframe for establishing a national park is about two to three years.

The annual operating costs of the national park lie between 32 million ATS per year (variant 1) and an additional 25.25 million ATS (variant 2). The main expenditures are for personnel, administration, research and documentation.[10]

While one-off expenditures only yield a one-off effect on production and employment, annual expenditures lead to an enduring regional economic effect. Figure 17.3 shows effects on production, while 17.4 shows employment effects. Expenditures for building and maintaining the infrastructure of the national park can increase regional[11] annual production by 13 to 16.1 million ATS and regional employment by 18.2 to 23.1 full-time jobs per year. One-off effects are higher but they occur only in the first two years after the establishment of the national park.

3.2.4 Opportunities for the agricultural sector

The agricultural sector is, as noted above, facing a serious crisis. A significant loss of jobs in the agricultural sector in the last decades has led to high unemployment. However, the establishment of a national park can be considered partially as a chance for redevelopment of the agricultural sector. Agricultural products can, on the one hand, be sold to visitors. On the other hand, they might be exported. A cautious assumption is used in the calculation of the economic impacts. It is assumed that the local farmers manage to increase their sales (and thus their value added) by 0.5 per cent per year over a period of ten years. This leads to an increase of around 5 per cent within the planning period. The main precondition for that development is a consistent marketing strategy including an eco-label for products from the national park region.

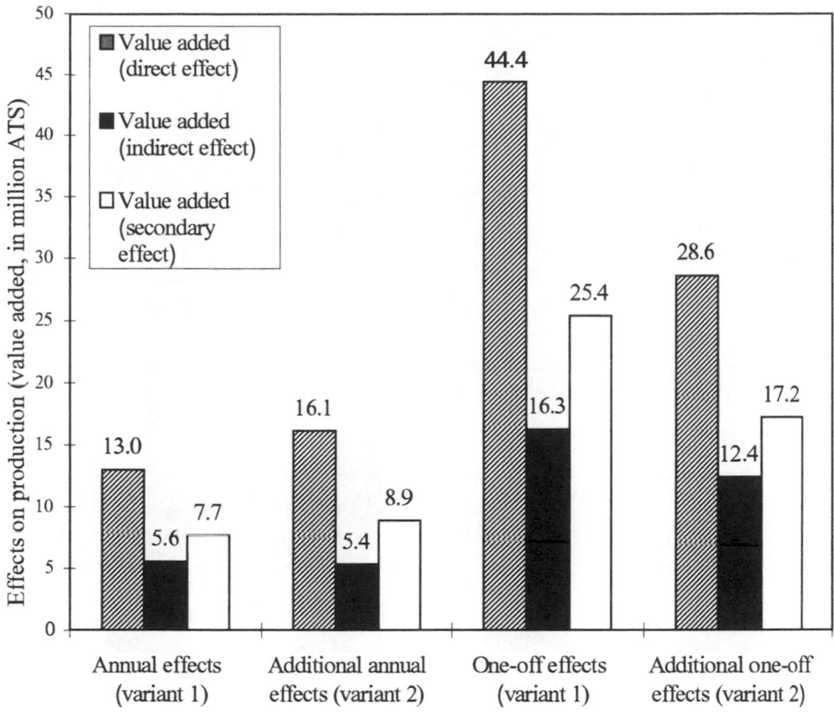

Figure 17.3 Production (value added) by one-off and annual expenditures for infrastructure of the Gesäuse National Park (in million ATS)

Figure 17.5 shows the value added and the employment effects of increased demand for ecologically produced agricultural products which might be realised due to eco-labelling. Twenty-one additional jobs in the regional agricultural sector can be expected directly. The way in which these additional jobs can be realised is open. As multipliers show only average effects on value added and employment, excess labour in farms might lower or even neutralise these potentially additional effects. It can be taken as granted that additional demand for eco-labelled products can be met by existing capacities (this assumption was also made by participants in the workshops). Thus, the specific regional situation gives only hope of a consolidation of employment in the agricultural sector.

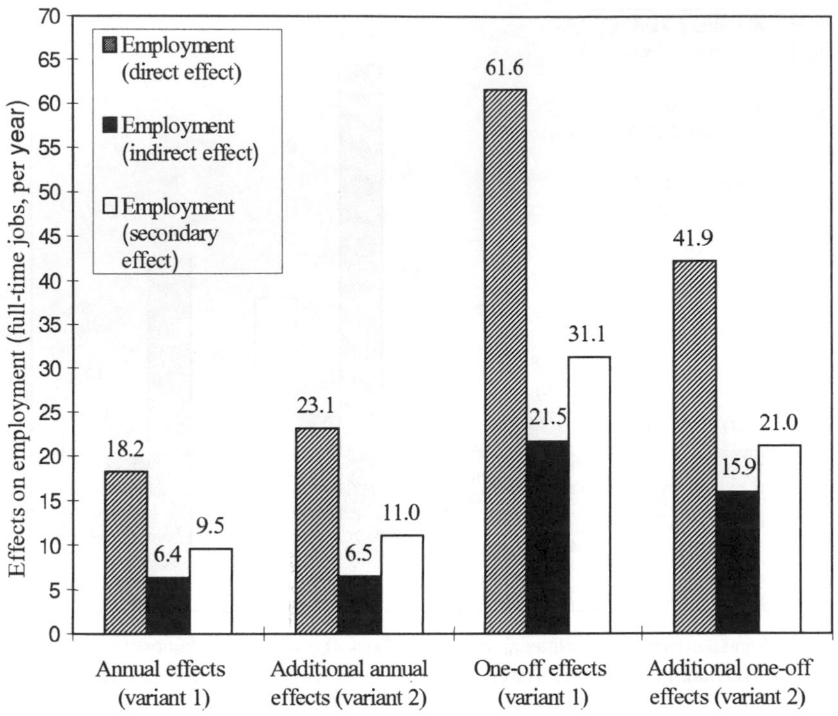

Figure 17.4 Employment by one-off and annual expenditures for infrastructure of the Gesäuse National Park (in years)

Figure 17.5 shows the value added and the employment effects of increased demand for ecologically produced agricultural products which might be realised due to eco-labelling. Twenty-one additional jobs in the regional agricultural sector can be expected directly. The way in which these additional jobs can be realised is open. As multipliers show only average effects on value added and employment, excess labour in farms might lower or even neutralise these potentially additional effects. It can be taken as granted that additional demand for eco-labelled products can be met by existing capacities (this assumption was also made by participants in the workshops). Thus, the specific regional situation gives only hope of a consolidation of employment in the agricultural sector.

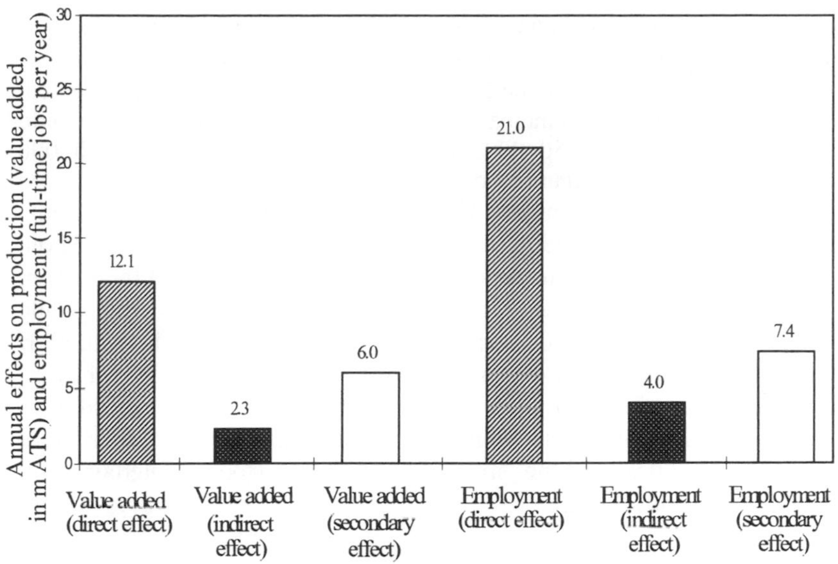

Figure 17.5 Production (value added, in ATS) and employment (in years) in the agricultural sector due to eco-labelling after the establishment of the Gesäuse National Park

3.2.5 Expenditures by additional tourists

National parks, according to the IUCN regulations, should not only be about protecting a unique landscape, endangered species or ecosystems. One of the main issues connected with the establishment of a national park is visitors' access to the area and education concerning the national park as well as other important aspects of ecology and the links to society. On the other hand, national parks are considered as a tool for regional development by means of promoting ecotourism (for example Sinclair 1998; Bergstrom et al. 1990; Child and Heath 1990).

As noted above, the number of visitors for a day as well as of those staying overnight has decreased over the years. Although the landscape is unique, the tourist infrastructure is unattractive. For calculating the possible effects of a national park on tourism, we have to make two assumptions. First, the tourist infrastructure will be improved to attract guests. Second, the Gesäuse National Park will be efficiently promoted by local tourist managers.

Tourists' expenditures depend on the season and on the duration of their stay. Currently, about 80 000 visitors come for just one day (about 72 000 in summer and 8 000 in winter), and another 30 000 visitors stay overnight which leads to about 97 000 overnight stays in total.[i] Assuming tourist scenario 1 (a plus of 2 per cent per year), an additional 17 000 tourists would stay for a day, and some 50 000 overnight stays could be expected. With tourist scenario 2 (an increase of 5 per cent per year) the region would encounter an additional 50 000 guests for one day and about 90 000 overnight stays[ii] (for all figures see E.C.O. 1999).

Money tourists spend on their holidays can be considered as additional transactions within the region, and as a flow of money into the region. Tourists' spending behaviour depends on their activities and on the season. During summer, they spend 451 ATS per day on average[iii] (this is the average of Styria), while they spend 716 ATS on average in winter. If guests stay overnight, their expenditures are about 400 to 500 ATS higher. To calculate the effects on production and employment these expenditures have to be broken down into single expenditures allocated to the different economic activities of the input–output table (food, entertainment, shopping, transport, skiing).

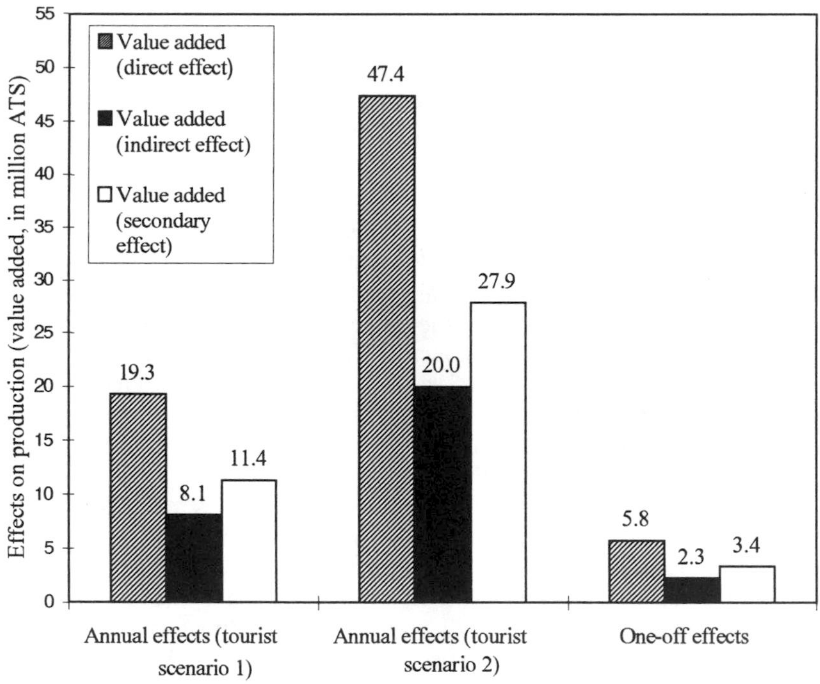

Figure 17.6 Production (value added) by one-off and annual expenditures by visitors to the Gesäuse National Park (in million ATS)

Figure 17.6 and Figure 17.7 show the results of the multiplier calculation. Additional annual expenditures of 30.5 million ATS (tourist scenario 1) and 75.1 million ATS (tourist scenario 2) lead to a significant increase in production and employment. The numbers for the direct effects (which can also be interpreted as being the *regional* effects) are 19.3 and 47.4 million ATS for production, and 27.1 and 66.5 full-time jobs per year. It must be stressed once more that these effects will not automatically occur when the national park is established. The establishment of the national park can be a precondition for the development of the tourist sector. That development needs much commitment by tourist managers, other stakeholders and the national park administration.

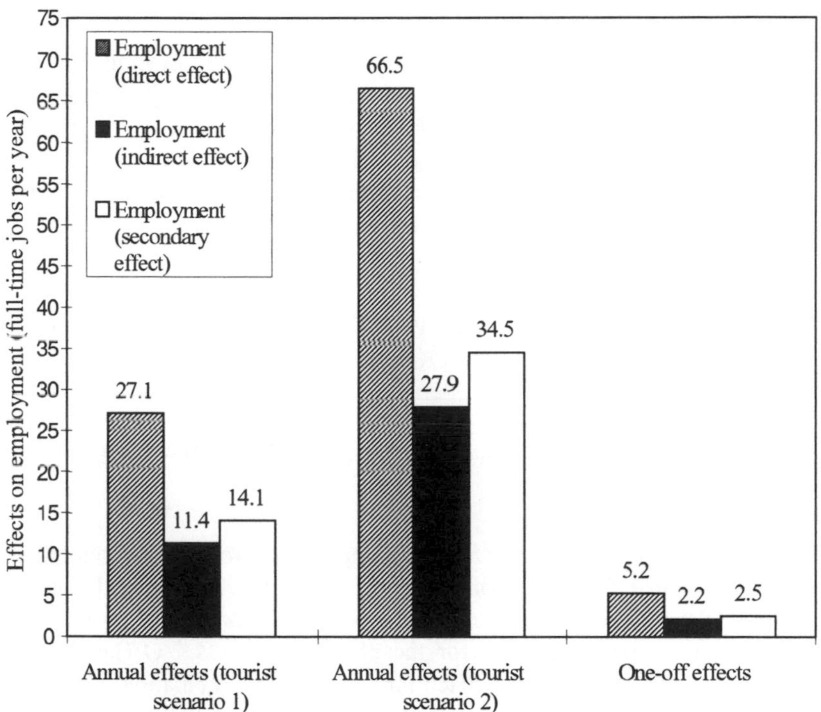

Figure 17.7 Employment by one-off and annual expenditures by visitors to the Gesäuse National Park (in years)

As the tourist infrastructure in bed and breakfast places as well as in hotels has to be improved, the figures also show one-off effects of improving the quality of tourist services (investments in existing and new tourist capacities).

3.2.6 Trade-offs in regional development: losses in economic activity

A number of sectors might face decreased economic activities after the establishment of the Gesäuse National Park. The establishment of a national park prohibits mining activities, which includes the mining of gypsum as well as gravel. Studies show the potential for mining gypsum at one site in the middle of the national park area. However, as the owner of the respective property has not agreed to mining on his property, the establishment of a national park will not cause additional economic costs. Mining for gravel in some parts of the area might have to be reduced. Some mining of gravel has to be carried out regardless of the establishment of the national park because infrastructures (roads) as well as houses have to be protected. (Gravel is transported down the mountains by wild creeks and deposited at three different sites in the national park area. It has to be removed to prevent dangerous landslides.)

In forestry and hunting, a number of activities might be lost in the national park due to changes in production. Those workers now employed in forestry and hunting and affected by the establishment of a national park could get new jobs in the national park administration. The value added will shift from the direct production of forest products and hunting services to activities conforming with the national park principles.

4 THE IMPORTANCE OF INVOLVING STAKEHOLDERS IN THE PLANNING PROCESS

4.1 Stakeholders' Involvement as a Precondition for Regional Development

The realisation of a national park is a complicated process that sometimes takes more than a decade.[15] While support from stakeholders and regional opinion leaders is crucial for the acceptance of a national park by the local population, it is also important for the planning process.[16] O'Hara (1996) discusses a discursive ethics approach for valuation and mediation in regional development projects. A similar approach was used to account for stakeholders' opinions and views. Stakeholders involved in the feasibility study on the Gesäuse National Park included not only businesses, citizens (residents), politicians, communities and the provincial and regional administration, but also non-profit organisations (for example the regional tourism agency and environmental groups). There is growing awareness in the scientific literature that institutional arrangements as well as the democratic involvement of stakeholders are crucially important for planning as well as for the economic outcome of decisions, and for the allocation of resources. Democratic and participatory decision processes shed light on different viewpoints of reality (Klein and Miller 1996). Thus, economic and planning decisions cannot merely be judged by the outcome – to fully understand the final allocation of resources one has to analyse the process of decision making (Getzner 1999b). The importance of involving stakeholders and local authorities is also stressed in the Agenda 21 approach to regional sustainable development (Bosworth 1993).

Developments in the tourism industries might particularly require stakeholders' involvement. The tourism industry has been called a 'community industry', reflecting the importance of local and regional stakeholders' involvement. Tourism is an industry that 'extends decision-making beyond the business sector to consider the long-term interests of the host community on which that industry is so dependent' (Murphy 1983, p. 181). The establishment of a national park and the subsequent regional economic development crucially depend on actions of all stakeholders and not merely on decisions by local or regional authorities and by the tourism sector.

Using workshops and interviews has, as mentioned above, two main objectives (see section 4.2). First, stakeholders are involved in the planning and valuation process, receive information and thus build or reformulate their opinion. This approach secures a transparent planning process. Involving stakeholders can also be considered as a precondition for accepting public projects.[17] Many ecologically sound and sustainable projects run aground due to lack of democratic participation and information.[18]

Second, besides the question of transparency and acceptance, the information input to the planning process is crucial. For example, regional development scenarios can only be formulated together with all stakeholders. On the one hand, workshops and interviews make tacit, unwritten knowledge available for consideration in the planning process and therefore increase the quality of the process.[19] Involvement of conservation organisations can also be considered as protecting potential investments because they can provide crucial information on environmentally harmful tourist developments (Giannecchini 1993). Much quantitative information for the calculation of the regional economic impact of the proposed national park stemmed from these 'soft' methods (a number of figures used in the feasibility study do not show up in the official statistics). Wagner (1997) used a set of structured interviews with 13 regional experts to close gaps in a regional SAM (social accounting matrix). Experts ranged from municipal officials with specific knowledge of local enterprises to state agencies and non-governmental organisations. In planning processes lack of information is often severe. Bodini and Giavelli (1992) used surveys of local people to assess and collect information for use in a multi-criteria analysis of tourism development on Salina Island (Italy).

On the other hand, the development of scenarios and realisation of regional economic benefits from the national park crucially depend on the involvement and activities of all stakeholders. Every assumption regarding future development depends on this involvement because the establishment of a national park cannot be considered as having a positive economic impact by itself. A national park in a particular region is an important precondition for sustainable regional development focusing on ecotourism. But nothing is automatic in regional development. As pointed out in section 3.2, the regional economic impact can be significant; but the mere establishment of a national park without any further regional development hardly leads to a noticeable economic development.

Regional economic development and the protection of environmental resources can be linked together. Regional 'environmental resources are more likely to be conserved when local residents participate in decision making, obtain a return from them and perceive the duration of the return to be linked to resource conservation' (Sinclair 1998, p. 41). Furthermore, the tourism development in the region depends on local stakeholders insofar as they can determine the desirable levels of development, the necessary control and the preferred direction of tourism. Ecotourism does not only include the educated tourist, but relies also on educating the host community, business sectors and government officials (Butler 1991, p. 204).

4.2 Stakeholders in the Feasibility Study on the Gesäuse National Park

Figure 17.8 presents a short overview of the different stakeholders that were involved in the feasibility study at various stages. The local and regional debate on the establishment of the Gesäuse National Park included as many groups as possible. The feasibility study on the Gesäuse National Park was written by an expert team of ecologists, sociologists, economists and regional planners. They had to rely on a network of stakeholders. Stakeholders in the debate were not only the local population (residents), but local communities, businesses and opinion leaders as well as the Provincial Government of Styria, the Ministry of the Environment and special interest groups (private hunters, single companies).

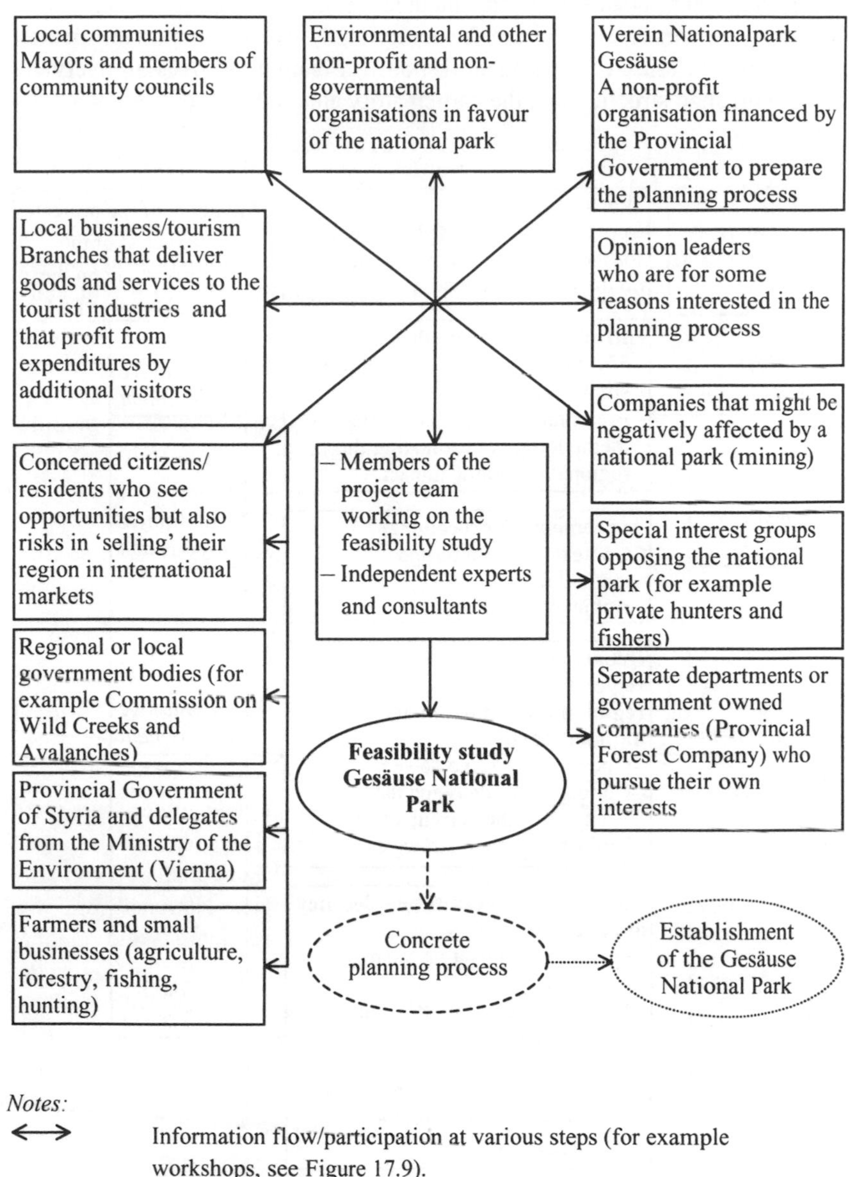

Notes:

⟷ Information flow/participation at various steps (for example workshops, see Figure 17.9).

- - -> After a positive result of the feasibility study the concrete planning process may start.

·········> Someday, the national park might be established.

Figure 17.8 Stakeholders of the Gesäuse National Park

More important, however, is the method of accounting for stakeholders' opinions and participation in the feasibility study. A very important method was the organisation of focused workshops.[20] Figure 17.9 gives an overview of the workshop structure and the participatory elements.[21]

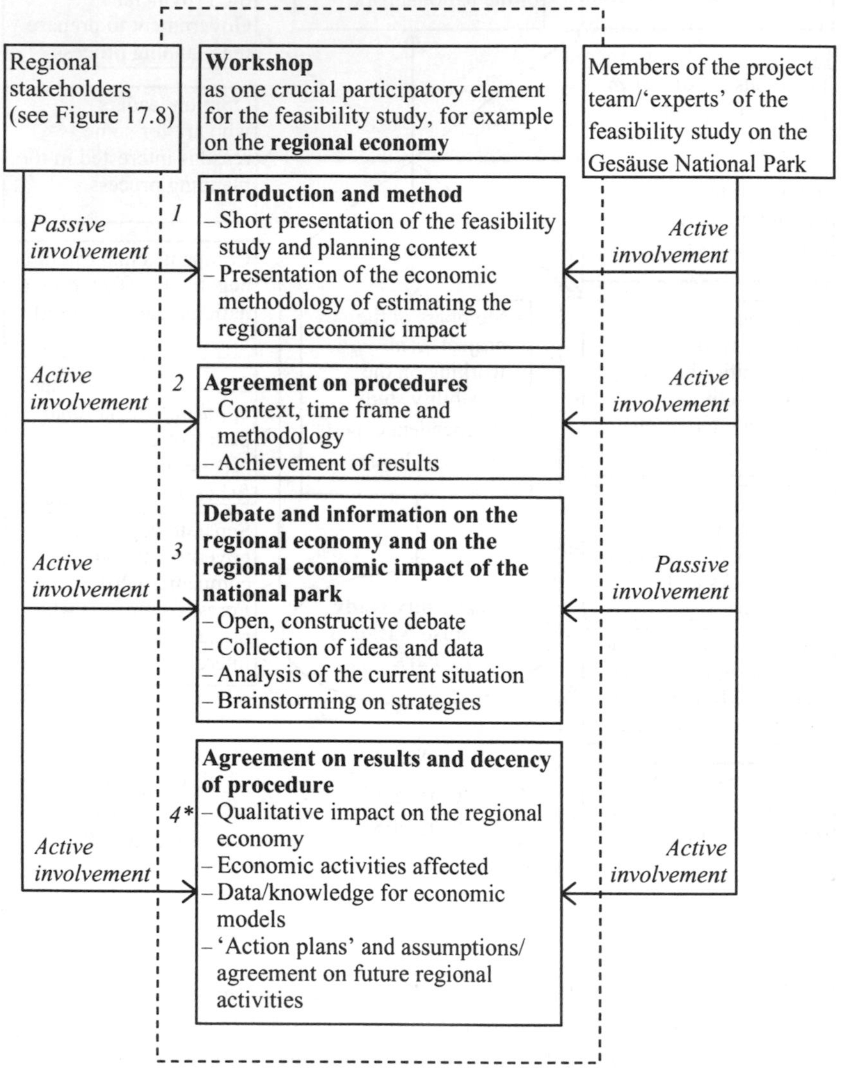

* 1–4 Steps of the workshop procedure

Figure 17.9 Stakeholders' involvement in participatory workshops on the regional economy

The decisive workshop for the current chapter was a workshop called 'Regional Economy', where stakeholders, particularly from the businesses and tourist industries, were included. Planning authorities and concerned citizens were invited as well. The first step of the workshop included a short presentation of the feasibility study in general and the methodology of the economic impact analysis to be carried out as part of the feasibility study. This first step was meant as a 'warm-up' round and information input to the workshop. The second explicit step consisted of agreeing on the procedures of the workshop.[22] Agreement on the time frame, on the questions to be answered, and on how results should be achieved, was reached among participants. Third, the debate on the regional economic impact and the different local and regional circumstances was the most important one in terms of data gathering. Fourth, the results of the workshop were summed up, and they were agreed upon almost unanimously. Concretely, the workshop yielded much uncodified knowledge held by various participants (for example regarding the causes of the decline in tourism). Furthermore, the workshop was important in order to reach agreement on concrete goals for future economic development, specifically regarding the marketing of tourism and agricultural products.

Summing up, the workshop

– yielded uncodified knowledge on various regional and local circumstances important for economic development,
– achieved agreement on future activities to promote regional development, particularly in the tourism industries, and
– provided a number of quantitative data that were used in the estimation of the regional economic impact by the multiplier model.

The experience shows that stakeholders' participation particularly rested on the agreement on the procedure of the workshop; in the end even those not agreeing upon the results were convinced that the results were achieved in a decent way through an open and constructive debate.

5 SUMMARY AND CONCLUSIONS

The Gesäuse National Park is located in a peripheral region enduring loss of population, jobs and development opportunities. Ecotourism can provide the foundation for regional sustainable development insofar as the ecological as well as the economic basis for development can be secured. The establishment of a national park can, on the one hand, protect a unique landscape and species, and secure ecosystem diversity. On the other hand, the

IUCN concept of national parks also promotes education and tourism, thus strengthening regional economic development.

The regional economic impact of a future Gesäuse National Park is calculated using a regional multiplier model. The results show that the establishment of the Gesäuse National Park could, in fact, increase employment significantly. About 50–100 additional full-time jobs could be created in the region. The unemployment rate of the region is currently at about 11 per cent; this rate could be reduced by about 10–25 per cent solely through the establishment of the Gesäuse National Park. These numbers show the importance of the establishment of a national park in such a peripheral region.

This hope for regional sustainable development rests on regional and local stakeholders. Not only are the results of the feasibility study built on stakeholders' information about past, current and future developments, but every future development crucially depends on the involvement of stakeholders. Thus there is nothing automatic in regional development following the establishment of a national park that can be considered as a precondition for a regional sustainable development. Furthermore, stakeholders' involvement provides a solid basis for the future acceptance of the national park.

NOTES

1. Some results presented in this chapter stem from the feasibility study of the Gesäuse National Park (E.C.O. 1999) that was financed by the Provincial Government of Styria (Graz) and the Federal Ministry of the Environment (Vienna). The author is indebted to Iris Velik, Michael Jungmeier and Dieter Weissensteiner for fruitful discussions, intensive co-operation and support. I also thank Karin Schönpflug and Christina Kopetzky for comments on an earlier draft of this chapter. Furthermore, I would like to thank a number of regional stakeholders who provided crucial information for the regional impact analysis. All remaining errors are, of course, the responsibility of the author.
2. The present author was part of the project team of the feasibility study on the Gesäuse National Park (see E.C.O. 1999).
3. See Jungmeier (1996) for a survey of national parks and their principles.
4. For a comprehensive analysis of the institutional framework regarding environmental decisions see Ostrom (1990).
5. This is also a main idea of the systems approach of 'Islands of Sustainability' discussed by Wallner et al. (1996).
6. This chapter only summarises the main characteristics of the model and the most important results. All underlying data as well as the structure of the multiplier model can be obtained from the author upon request.
7. This methodology is widely used in assessing the economic impacts of nature protection on a regional basis (for example US Department of the Interior, National Park Service 1995).

8. That uncertainty refers to different means of production. For instance, while ecological farming might be appropriate for a national park in certain areas, monocultural and intensive farming might not meet IUCN's criteria. However, the IUCN's criteria are certainly explicit in allowing only very few economic activities in a national park of category II.
9. The legal framework in Austria and within the European Union is not very clear on this point, and some government agencies do not publicly announce their invitations to tender in order to promote regional economic goals despite possibly contrary regulations.
10. All figures have been estimated by E.C.O. (1999) in cooperation with the Provincial Government of Styria and the Ministry of the Environment. The figures generally compare to those of national parks in Austria (see, for example, Schönbäck et al. 1997; Jungmeier 1996).
11. Under the assumption that mainly regional firms are contractors, the direct effects on production and employment are also the regional effects.
12. The numbers of visitors are rather vague. Furthermore, the issue of multiple destination trips could not be considered adequately in this study (for an appropriate methodology cf. Johnson and Moore 1993, p. 281).
13. An increase in the number of tourists in the Gesäuse National Park region clearly means that other national parks or recreation areas may face decreased numbers of visitors. However, as the study concentrates specifically on the *regional* effect on tourism demand, additional tourists in the Gesäuse National Park region lead to gains in tourism expenditures in that region. In order to show the impact on the Austrian tourism industries as a whole, we would have to account for all possible substitution effects (including net increases in the number of foreign tourists).
14. Figures of tourists' spending are taken from the Austrian Tourist Survey (documented in Lund-Durlacher 1998; Mazanec 1995), which is undertaken about every two years and shows tourists' behaviour, preferences and spending in all nine federal provinces of Austria.
15. In the case of the Donau-Auen National Park near Vienna the realisation took more than 23 years from the first plans to its establishment (see Schönbäck et al. 1997).
16. For the conceptual underpinning of stakeholders' involvement see Dryzek and Lester (1995).
17. In the cost–benefit literature, stakeholders' involvement is considered as 'implicit compensation' in order to avoid opposition stemming from a distribution of costs and benefits of a project perceived as 'unfair' (for example Cordes and Weisbrod 1985).
18. Even during the feasibility study process referred to in this chapter, that is, before concrete planning steps were undertaken, opposition to the foundation of a national park emerged due to lack of information and participation. Involvement of stakeholders generally complies with one important aspect of the concept of sustainable development, namely the social and democratic claim of many development concepts. Thus, 'empowering local communities to evaluate the trade-offs and strike this balance for themselves is at the heart of any successful ecotourism venture' (Theophile 1995).
19. Counsell (1998, p. 190) stresses this important issue by stating that development plan strategies can be seriously flawed 'if they are not based on sound facts about local environmental attributes'. Although regional or local data are often missing, conceptually sound data treatment can fill the gaps where no other data exist (Archer 1996).
20. Other methods included structured and unstructured interviews with stakeholders as well as opinion polls and the analysis of regional development concepts and local political decisions.
21. For procedures for stakeholders' involvement in environmental valuation and policy see Costanza and Folke (1996), and Toman (1999).

22. Procedural fairness is a major issue in environmental decision making and extends the framework of decisions processes based on instrumental rationality (Lawrence et al. 1997).

REFERENCES

Adensam, H. (1995), 'Konjunkturelle Auswirkungen des Kommunalen Energiekonzeptes Graz', Research Report 44, Department of Public Finance and Infrastructure Policy, University of Technology, Vienna.

Amt der Steiermärkischen Landesregierung (1997), 'Steirische Statistiken – Tourismus', *Steirische Statistiken*, **41** (7).

Archer, B. (1996), 'Economic Impact Analysis', *Annals of Tourism Research*, **23** (3), pp. 704–07.

Baud-Bovy, M. and F. Lawson (1998), *Tourism and Recreation Handbook of Planning and Design*, Oxford/Boston: Architectural Press.

Bergstrom, J.C., H.K. Cordell, G.A. Ashley and A.E. Watson (1990), 'Economic Impacts of Recreational Spending on Rural Areas: A Case Study', *Economic Development Quarterly*, **4** (1), pp. 29–39.

Blangy, S. and T. Nielsen (1994), 'Ecotourism and Minimum Impact Policy', *Annals of Tourism Research*, **20** (2), pp. 357–60.

Bodini, A. and G. Giavelli (1992), 'Multicriteria Analysis as a Tool to Investigate Compatibility between Conservation and Development on Salina Island, Aeolian Archipelago, Italy', *Environmental Management*, **16** (5), pp. 633–52.

Bosworth, T. (1993), 'Local Authorities and Sustainable Development', *European Environment*, **3** (1), pp. 13–17.

Butler, R.W. (1991), 'Tourism, Environment and Sustainable Development', *Environmental Conservation*, **18 (3)**, pp. 201–09.

Cable, T.T. and E. Udd (1990), 'Endangered Outdoor Recreation Experiences: Contextual Development and Lexicon', *Leisure Studies*, **9** (1), pp. 45–53.

Child, G.F.T. and R.A. Heath (1990), 'Underselling National Parks in Zimbabwe: The Implications for Rural Sustainability', *Society and Natural Resources*, **3** (3), pp. 215–27.

Cordes, J.J. and B.A. Weisbrod (1985), 'When Government Programs Create Inequities: A Guide to Compensation Policies', *Journal of Policy Analysis and Management*, **4** (2), pp. 344–54.

Costanza, R. and C. Folke (1996), 'Valuing Ecosystem Services with Efficiency, Fairness and Sustainability as Goals', in Daily, G.C. (ed.), *Nature's Services. Societal Dependence on Natural Ecosystems*, Washington (DC): Island Press, pp. 49–68.

Counsell, D. (1998), 'Sustainable Development and Structure Plans in England and Wales: A Review of Current Practice', *Journal of Environmental Planning and Management*, **2** (41), pp. 177–94.

Douglas, A.J. and D.A. Harpman (1995), 'Estimating Recreation Employment Effects with IMPLAN for the Glen Canyon Dam Region', *Journal of Environmental Management*, **44** (**2**), pp. 233–47.

Dryzek, J.S. and J.P. Lester (1995), 'Alternative Views of the Environmental Problematic', in Lester, J.P. (ed.), *Environmental Politics and Policy*. 2nd edition, Durham/London: Duke University Press, pp. 328–46.

E.C.O. (1999), 'Machbarkeitsstudie Nationalpark Gesäuse', Unpublished final report of a feasibility study (project heads M. Jungmeier and I. Velik) commissioned by the Ministry of Environment (Vienna) and the Provincial Government of Styria (Graz), E.C.O. Institute for Ecology, Klagenfurt.

Eichler, A. (1998), 'Methodische Grundlagen und praktische Anwendung der Wertschöpfungsrechnung auf Basis der Input–Output–Tabelle', *Der öffentliche Sektor*, **24** (2–3), pp. 78–89.

English, D.B.K. and J.C. Bergstrom (1994), 'The Conceptual Links Between Recreation Site Development and Regional Economic Impacts', *Journal of Regional Science*, **34** (4), pp. 599–611.

Farny, O., K. Kratena and B. Roßmann (1988), 'Beschäftigungswirkungen ausgewählter Staatsausgaben', *Wirtschaft und Gesellschaft*, **1**, pp. 65–94.

Fontanari, M. (1993), 'Umweltmanagement im Tourismus – Forschung und praktische Anwendung in einem Fremdenverkehrsort', in Wöhler, K. and W. Schertler (eds), *Touristisches Umweltmanagement*, Limburgerhof: FBV Medien-Verlag, pp. 219–48.

Frechtling, D.C. (1994), 'Assessing the Economic Impacts of Travel and Tourism – Introduction to Travel Economic Impact Estimation', in Ritchie, J.R.B. and C.R. Goeldner (eds), *Travel, Tourism, and Hospitality Research*, New York/Chichester: John Wiley, pp. 359–65.

Getzner, M. (1999a), 'Weak and Strong Sustainability Indicators, and Regional Environmental Resources', *Environmental Management and Health*, **10** (3), pp. 170–76.

Getzner, M. (1999b), 'Risk, Uncertainty and Discounting in Practical Environmental Decision Making', in Steininger, K. and F. Prettenthaler (eds), *Risk and Uncertainty in HD-Research. Proceedings of a Workshop of the Austrian Human Dimensions of Global Environmental Change Program,* Department of Economics, University of Graz.

Getzner, M. and M. Schneider (1999), 'Wertschöpfungs- und Beschäftigungsrechnung auf Basis der österreichischen Input–Output–Tabelle 1990', Unpublished Working Paper, Department of Economics, University of Klagenfurt.

Giannecchini, J. (1993), 'Ecotourism: New Partners, New Relationships', *Conservation Biology*, **7** (2) , pp. 429–32.

Inskeep, E. (1995), *National and Regional Tourism Planning: Methodologies and Case Studies*, London: Routledge.

Johnson, R.L. and E. Moore (1993), 'Tourism Impact Estimation', *Annals of Tourism Research*, **20** (2), pp. 279–88.

Jülg, F. (1993), 'Die Fremdenverkehrsgemeinde Heiligenblut als Fallbeispiel für das Ineinandergreifen ökologischer, ökonomischer und sozialer Probleme des Tourismus im Hochgebirge', in Jülg, F. and C. Staudacher (eds), *Tourismus im Hochgebirge – Die Region Großglockner: Symposium über ökologische, ökonomische und soziale Fragen*, Wiener Geographische Schriften 64, Vienna: Service Fachverlag, pp. 25–37.

Jungmeier, M. (1996), 'Ziele, Probleme und Strategien von Nationalparken – Ergebnisse einer internationalen Umfrage', UBA-Monographien, **77**, Vienna: Federal Environmental Protection Agency.

Klein, P.A. and E.S. Miller (1996), 'Concepts of Value, Efficiency, and Democracy in Institutional Economics', *Journal of Economic Issues*, **30** (1), pp. 267–77.

Kosz, M. (1996), 'Volkswirtschaftliche Effekte eines „Öko-Invest-Planes für Wien"', Research Report 54, Department of Public Finance and Infrastructure Policy, University of Technology, Vienna.

Lawrence, R.L., S.E. Daniels and G.H. Stankey (1997), 'Procedural Justice and Public Involvement in Natural Resources Decision Making', *Society & Natural Resources*, **10** (6), pp. 577–89.

Lund-Durlacher, D. (1998), 'Gästebefragung Österreich 1997/98, Steiermark-Bericht, Sommer 1997', Austrian Association for Applied Tourism Research, Vienna.

MacIntyre, G. (1998), *Sustainable Tourism Development: A Guide for Local Planners*, Madrid: World Tourism Organization.

Mazanec, J. (1995), 'Gästebefragung Österreich 1994/95, Österreich-Bericht, Winter 1994/95', Austrian Association for Applied Tourism Research, Vienna.

Murphy, P.E. (1983), 'Tourism as a Community Industry', *Tourism Management*, **4** (3), pp. 180–93.

Nationalparkplanung Donau-Auen (1994), 'Konzept für den Nationalpark Donau-Auen', Blaue Reihe, vol. 4, Ministry of the Environment, Vienna.

O'Hara, S. (1996), 'Discursive Ethics in Ecosystem Valuation and Environmental Policy', *Ecological Economics*, **16** (2), pp. 95–107.

Olfert, M.R. and J.C. Stabler (1994), 'Community Level Multipliers for Rural Development Initiatives', *Growth and Change*, **25** (3), pp. 467–86.

ÖSTAT (1994), 'Input–Output–Tabelle 1983, Band 2: Technologiematrizen', *Beiträge zur österreichischen Statistik*, Heft 1.138/2, Vienna.

Ostrom, E. (1990), *Governing the Commons. The Evolution of Institutions for Collective Action*, Cambridge: Cambridge University Press.

Perrings, C. (1995), 'Ecological Resilience in the Sustainability of Economic Development', *Economie Appliquée*, **48** (2), pp. 121–42.

Schönbäck, W., M. Kosz and T. Madreiter (1997), *Nationalpark Donauauen: Kosten-Nutzen-Analyse*, Vienna, New York: Springer.

Sinclair, M.T. (1998), 'Tourism and Economic Development: A Survey', *The Journal of Development Studies*, **34** (5), pp. 1–51.

Theophile, K. (1995), 'The Forest as a Business: Is Ecotourism the Answer?', *Journal of Forestry*, 9**3** (3), pp. 25–27.

Tiefenbach, M., G. Larndorfer and E. Weigand (1998), 'Naturschutz in Österreich', UBA-Monographien, vol. 91, Vienna: Federal Environmental Agency/Ministry of the Environment.

Toman, M.A. (1999), 'Sustainable Decision Making: The State of the Art from an Economics Perspective', in O'Connor, M. and C. Spash (eds), *Valuation and the Environment – Theory, Method and Practice*, Cheltenham UK and Northampton, MA, USA: Edward Elgar, pp. 59–72.

Ullmann, S. and B. Klauß (1993), 'Wettbewerbsvorteile durch eine umweltgerechte Unternehmensführung', in Wöhler, K. and W. Schertler (eds), *Touristisches Umweltmanagement*, Limburgerhof: FBV Medien-Verlag, pp. 191–218.

US Department of the Interior, National Park Service (1995), *Economic Impacts of Protecting Rivers, Trails, and Greenway Corridors*. Washington, DC: National Park Service Trails and Conservation Assistance.

Wagner, J.E. (1997), 'Estimating the Economic Impacts of Tourism', *Annals of Tourism Research*, **24** (39), pp. 592–608.

Wallner, H.P., M. Narodoslawsky and F. Moser (1996), 'Islands of Sustainability: A Bottom-up Approach towards Sustainable Development', *Environment and Planning*, **28** (10), pp. 1763–78.

WCED (1987), *Our Common Future*, Oxford: Oxford University Press.

Zhou, D., J.F. Yanagida, U. Chakravorty and P. Leung (1997), 'Estimating Economic Impacts from Tourism', *Annals of Tourism Research*, **24** (1), pp. 76–89.

Zimmermann, F.M. (1993), 'Trends und Szenarien für den Tourismus im Alpenraum', in Jülg, F. and C. Staudacher (eds), *Tourismus im Hochgebirge – Die Region Großglockner: Symposium über ökologische, ökonomische und soziale Fragen*, Wiener Geographische Schriften, 64, Vienna: Service Fachverlag, pp. 129–52.

PART VII

Promoting Environmental Protection by Co-operative Marketing of Food Products

18. The Marketing of Organic Food Products: the Case of Swedish Dairy Co-operatives

Erik Fahlbeck and Jerker Nilsson

1 BACKGROUND

During the last decade the sales of organic food products have expanded rapidly in many countries, and according to expectations in the food industry the demand may increase further in the years to come. The beginning of this market trend was, however, slow, for example ten years ago there was no more than a handful of organic food products, none of which was oriented towards the general consumer. Today some organic food products in for example Sweden have market shares of over 15 per cent (see Figure 18.1).

This sales success may seem remarkable, especially as the physical products most often do not differ from conventional products. Therefore, there may be problems when applying standard concepts, or traditional interpretation of food products. An episode in the early market development for organic milk in Sweden may serve as an illustration. When the pioneering dairy, Milko, was to introduce its first organic product on the market, an advertising agency worked out some proposals, none of which was accepted. At one stage the agency replied something like: 'It looks the same as conventional milk; it tastes the same; it has the same nutritional value. All we can say is that it costs more, but we can't claim it to be better in any sense. Sorry, we cannot do this job for you.' In retrospect it is obvious that the advertising agency did not grasp some of the most important dimensions of organic products.

In this chapter we take the approach that the market for organic food was established by producers and consumers with common, partly ideologically influenced, interests, as an alternative to conventional food. A number of co-operative institutional arrangements guide this market development, of which the Swedish non-profit private control organisation for organic products, KRAV, is the most crucial.

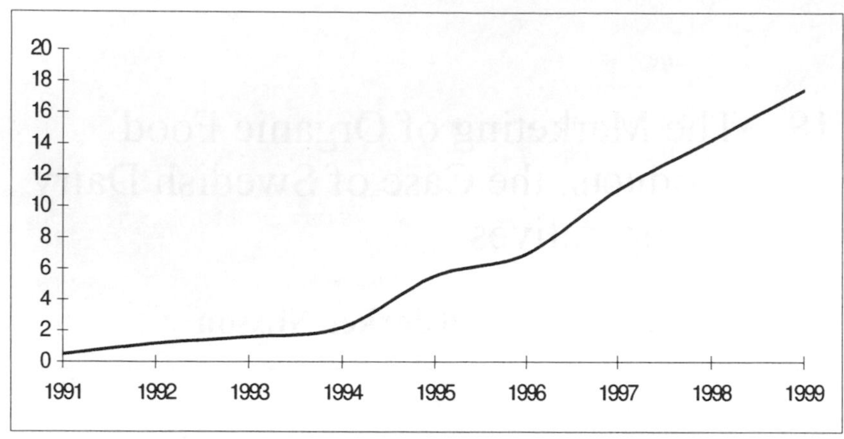

Note:
1. Figure for 1999 includes only January–May.

Source: Arla, personal communication.

Figure 18.1 Organic milk's share of the sales of fresh milk with medium fat content in Stockholm (in per cent)[1]

As in all cases in which a producer has similar items in his product mix, or items that are similar to those of his competitors, the various products must be differentiated from each other for the purpose of appealing to different market segments. Hence, the organic food producers must emphasise production methods and image building in their marketing efforts – changing the final physical products is not possible except for packaging. The summary concept for image building is the brand name. All values that the producer adds to the product should be incorporated in the brand name, as perceived by the consumer. Organic products should, from this perspective, be marketed under eco-brands.

As the most important difference between organic and conventional food is the production method, it is, from a consumer perspective, important that this difference is reliable. In Sweden many sellers have their own brands, but if so, they often also have the most common and widely accepted KRAV label. Since the KRAV control organisation is a non-profit organisation, incorporated as an open membership co-operative, and since the members represent a wide variety of producers and consumer organisations, its label brings neutral objectivity to the producers' brands.

Still, the expansion of the market share for organic food products is remarkable. The sales are, however, regionally unevenly spread. The Swedish dairy sector may serve as an example. A significant share of Arla's production consists of organic products. Arla is a dairy farmer co-operative, completely dominating the mid-Swedish market and with a strong position in the south of the country. In the southernmost province of the country, dominated by another dairy co-operative, organic products have a significantly lower market share. The same is true for the three co-operatives in the northern part of the country as well as for the three local ones. There is no dairy processing firm of significance in Sweden aside from these eight co-operatives.

2 PROBLEMS

This chapter intends to discuss the issues hinted at above, the basic one being: Which factors can explain the development of the organic food market? Considering the dominant position of co-operatives in the Swedish dairy sector, a more precise wording is: What role may the dairy co-operatives play to explain the slow start and the present rapid expansion? These questions have a number of components, all in relation to the development of the market for organic products:

- What are the characteristics of organic dairy products, as perceived by the consumers? What are the values that consumers prefer in organic products, and what are the values that the producer builds into the products? Which market segments exist within the organic food product market – for example from the ideologically convinced consumers and producers to those marginally involved, or totally different sub-groups?
- What role do the characteristics of the dairy processing firms play? Has the dominance of dairy co-operatives had a stimulating or an impeding effect on the dairy industry's propensity to develop and exploit the new market demand? Are farmer co-operatives better or worse suited for eco-brands compared to investor-owned firms, that is, are the trust-dependent organic products better suited for co-operatives, or has the co-operative business form been inhibiting, considering that co-operatives are generally viewed as conservative, with slow decision processes, equal member treatment, and so on?
- Why do different organic sub-markets exhibit such large differences in market share? Could it be due to the fact that one processor is

dominating in one region, or are the consumer preferences basically different? To the extent that the hypothesis of processor identity is correct, why are there differences between dairy processors? Could it be scarce resources of the firm in terms of production and marketing, a deliberate choice of market strategy to differentiate the firm from its competitors, or something else?

3 APPROACH

The questions above are subject to theoretical discussions. A variety of neo-institutional approaches, such as transaction cost theory, are applied. Theoretical considerations concerning the organisation of farmer co-operatives, the characteristics of the organic products, aspects of specific assets and so on are addressed.

The authors arrive at conclusions that have the character of hypotheses. The purpose of the study is to explore the subject and identify a number of hypotheses concerning the production and marketing of organic products. The resources available do not allow for a proper testing of the hypotheses within this chapter. Instead, the hypotheses are illustrated with the help of data acquired from a series of informal interviews with representatives from Swedish dairy processors and with farmers within and outside the organic farming societies, in addition to representatives from the control organisation for organic products, KRAV. Hence, the road is paved for a more focused in-depth study at a later stage.

One section each is devoted to the three main questions above, that is, Sections 5–7. The next section, on the Swedish dairy industry in general, serves as a background.

4 THE SWEDISH DAIRY INDUSTRY

Milk production is the most important branch in Swedish agriculture in relation to gross income, full-time employment and environmental and rural concern. The agricultural sector plays a minor role in the Swedish gross national product, 2.2 per cent. Milk production does, however, account for one-third of the gross income in Swedish agriculture. Dairy farming is essential, especially among full-time farmers. About two-thirds of the full-time farmers are milk producers. Part of the Swedish countryside is still dependent on milk production. Hence, in the north, 84 per cent of the full-time farmers are milk producers. Further, milking cows, heifers and calves have traditionally grazed large areas of the cultural landscape that is highly appreciated by Swedes in general (for example Drake 1992).

Almost all milk is processed by dairy co-operatives. The total number of dairy processors is 16, 8 of whom are co-operatives that process 99.7 per cent of the milk production. Arla, the largest farmer co-operative, strongly dominates the Swedish market with a share of about 65 per cent. The five largest farmer co-operatives have a market share of above 96 per cent. The Swedish market for raw milk has a Herfindahl index of slightly over 0.45.

There are at present (December 1999) two ongoing merger processes; the most spectacular between Arla and the Danish MD Foods which would result in Europe's largest dairy co-operative, and the other one between the two medium-sized processors, Milko and NNP, both with operations north of Arla.

The present structure of the Swedish dairy industry should be understood in the light of history. For decades it operated under a protectionist national policy oriented towards domestic self-sufficiency. Co-operatives, strong governmental influence and yearly cost compensation were important parts of the policy while competition was more or less prohibited at both ends of the value chain – no competition either for suppliers/members or for consumers/buyers. Hence, the dairy co-operatives had little reason to be very efficient, thus they were very production oriented. Traditional co-operative ideology played an important role.

The Swedish membership in the European Union in 1995 completely altered the conditions for the dairy industry. Now, there is competition on all markets, both from domestic and foreign firms. Imported products are constantly increasing their market shares. Hence, the Swedish dairy processors have been forced to conduct many, and radical, rationalisation measures.

Against this background it may be understood that the turmoil in the Swedish dairy industry during the course of the 1990s has caused considerable economic stress. For these and other reasons, the primary production and the processing industry have undergone a painful but necessary process of restructuring which is ongoing. Nevertheless, profitability is still poor. Therefore, there are good reasons for the dairy processors, as well as the farmers, to welcome a trend towards more organic products, since these face less price sensitivity on the part of the consumer and are therefore more profitable. Some ten years ago, under the rule of the national agricultural policy, the dairy industry had less reason to care about organic production or market orientation in general. In those days Swedish consumers also had less reason to care about the effects of their milk consumption patterns in relation to landscape, regional development and environmental concerns.

5 CHARACTERISTICS OF ORGANIC PRODUCTS AS PERCEIVED BY CONSUMERS

The development of organic food products in Sweden is an example of how consumer concerns and producer interests have manifested themselves in a growing market. Environmentally oriented consumption has increased steadily during the last decade, including food products. Solér (1997, pp. 215–16) characterises consumers buying 'ecologically friendly products' under four headings: (1) those who are convinced that their consumption choices have an influence on the environment, (2) those who find it important to be an ecologically friendly citizen, (3) those who believe it is good for their individual health, and (4) those who consider themselves to be part of nature. Similar results are found in a Danish study:

> Consumer motivation to buy organic food products depends primarily on the individual consumer's faith in the products being healthier and more environmentally friendly than conventional food products. Since these are far from indisputable scientific facts, this should come as no surprise. In fact, what is remarkable is that a large proportion of the population pays a premium price for organic food products in spite of the scientific uncertainty. (Thøgersen 1999, p. 18)

Consumers may obviously have many reasons to buy organic food products. One can speculate whether a number of generally valid characteristics may be found when it comes to the consumption of organic milk.

Over the last years milking production systems have changed. Even if animal friendly legislation requires cows in Sweden to be kept outdoors during the summer season, the high yielding cows can hardly graze on pastures, if they are to keep their production levels (with a national average of more than 8000 kg/cow and year). Therefore, calves, heifers and beef cattle have partly replaced the milking cows in the Swedish landscape.

The rules for organic milk production state that the cows should have their main roughage intake through grazing. When buying organic milk consumers can therefore be seen as consumers of a bundle of environmental services. Together with the milk, elements of biodiversity, open landscape, and generally environmentally friendly production systems are also being marketed. From a number of studies and the increasing sales of eco-label products, it is today obvious that people in general as well as many producers and politicians want to take part in this production and consumption. Even if the objectives for this interest may be unclear and even questionable, it is obvious that most of them are strongly related to trust, and therefore a trustworthy trading partner is needed.

Concerns about the environment in general and animal welfare in particular may be an important motive for many Swedish consumers. When the distance between producers and consumers is as large as in modern western societies, producers may have difficulties convincing consumers that they are trustworthy in these respects. A third party can, however, fill such a purpose, that is, it may reduce transaction costs significantly (Krashinsky 1986). When it comes to trustworthiness in relation to consumption, a non-profit organisation may be superior, since it has no conflict between profit maximising objectives and costly arrangements in trust building. Through a non-profit control organisation, KRAV, it has become possible for farmers to produce and consumers to buy so-called public goods, that is, non-excludable and non-rival products.

6 CHARACTERISTICS OF THE DAIRY PROCESSING FIRMS

A basic notion in modern organisational theory is that the organisational structure of a firm decides the type of business it conducts, and vice versa; the business conditions decide the organisational structure. For a business firm to be competitive and successful it is essential that it reflects the characteristics of its business environment on to its own organisational attributes. These two sets of attributes must be congruent.

Hence, it is relevant to scrutinise types of organisations – how will different organisational models handle the production and marketing of organic milk products? We can distinguish between co-operative dairies and IOF dairies (Investor-Owned Firm, or profit maximising firm). Governmental organisations can be disregarded in this context.

6.1 Investor-Owned Firms

As concerns the production and sales of organic milk products, IOFs are expected to be market oriented, selling whatever the consumer demands. Hence, a growing demand would probably be satisfied by IOF dairy processors, with a potential advantage in relation to milk consumers. On the other hand, IOFs may be less well suited in procuring access to the raw product (see, for example, Staatz 1989 and Sexton 1986).

One solution would be that IOF dairy processors buy milk from independent dairy farmers. In this case, the dairy farmers will face a risk as they have invested heavily in a herd, in machinery, in their own training, and so on, most of which constitute transaction specific investments. Thereby the milk farmer is vulnerable to eventual deceitful behaviour on the part of the dairy processor. For this reason, IOF dairy processors may have difficulties in acquiring raw products, especially when it concerns organic milk because in that case, the farmers' transaction specific investments are still higher than for conventional milk. Contributing to this is that, when it concerns a special and low volume product like organic food, the number of competing dairy processors would be extremely small (probably a monopsony) which further adds to the farmers' perception of risk.

There are, however, some possible exceptions to this statement. One is if the production of organic milk in the region is large enough to accommodate two or several IOF processors and there is well-functioning competition between them. In this case, the farmers will conceive of the risk for deceitful behaviour on the part of the processor to be smaller, perhaps even satisfactory. The other is if the IOF processor is a well-established, large and reputable firm. Such a firm could be expected to behave honestly and with long-term perspectives because a bad-will campaign would be harmful to its reputation. Hence, dishonest behaviour would be too costly, as long as farmers have other channels for selling their products.

If the IOF processor has difficulties in signing delivery contracts with milk farmers, it could establish its own milk production facilities, that is, integrate vertically. It is, though, unlikely that a food processing firm would want to invest in the primary production of milk. The profitability level is often too low, the investments per litre are too high, and not insignificantly, the agency costs are too high in monitoring a plant for biological production, such as milk production, with employed staff.

A similar solution, though on a smaller scale, is that a large farmer might go into the processing of the organic milk that he produces, especially if his normal buyer (one of the co-operatives in the Swedish case) is reluctant to enter the organic food market. A badly functioning market for raw milk is superseded by forward vertical integration. In this case other problems may, however, arise; for example, a single farmer may have limited resources for processing and marketing the products, especially as concerns his relations to the retail trade. Hence, good vertical co-ordination between primary production and processing may be reached at the price of poorer vertical co-ordination between processing and consumer distribution.

To overcome the above-mentioned obstacles a number of organic milk farmers may establish a jointly owned firm. By pooling their resources they may get lower unit costs and gain a stronger market position. Again, this is most likely if the normal buyer of the raw milk is not eager to enter the organic food market. In recent years a few Swedish organic farmers have tried to go into the business of processing of milk and sales to retailers, though these initiatives ended in bankruptcy. The average costs were so high that the financial problems became too large. During the last decade, Danish organic milk farmers have established new co-operative dairies several times on a rather small scale, after they have been disappointed with the major dairy co-operatives' limited interest in organic milk products. Only one of the newly established firms, ØkoMælk, has been successful.

However the IOF acquires the raw product, the IOF organisational model may be expected to be innovative when it comes to the production and marketing of organic milk products. In the Swedish case, considering the strong market dominance of co-operatives, the probability that an IOF would be an active innovator is, however, small, especially as the economies of scale are salient in the dairy industry and a new firm will, by necessity, be small.

Hypotheses:

- Large dairy processing IOFs may be innovative in marketing of organic products when there is a consumer demand for it, especially with expected possible larger gains in the future.
- A new IOF entrant into the organic dairy market would have difficulties in acquiring raw products, unless production (and consumption) is already sizeable.
- An established food processor would hardly invest in primary production in order to get access to raw products.
- If their traditional buyers are not keen on organic products, individual dairy farmers may themselves enter the market for organic food, but due to their limited resources the prognosis for long-term survival is not good.
- The chances for success increase if a number of farmers establish a firm together for processing and marketing organic milk products.

6.2 Dairy Co-operatives

During the last decade the concept of co-operative organisational models has become topical. An increasing number of agricultural co-operatives are now in a process of changing their organisational form, by far most often from a traditional model to various other organisational set-ups. The reason for this trend is, of course, the ongoing processes towards internationalisation, liberalisation and concentration in agribusiness.

The concept of co-operative organisational models is still so new that no unanimity has been reached. Here, the classes suggested in the book *Agricultural Co-operatives in the European Union* (van Bekkum and van Dijk 1997) are used. Except for traditional co-operatives, mentioned above, there are four other types, which together are called entrepreneurial co-operatives. The reason for this term is that these co-operatives may be expected to be more innovative, apply more aggressive marketing strategies, use more product differentiation and market segmentation, and so on – on the whole, these co-operatives are less production oriented and more market oriented and business-like than the traditional co-operatives. The reason is that, while the traditional co-operatives are predominantly collective organisations, the entrepreneurial co-operatives are financed with individually owned capital, whereby the incentive structure is altered. A stronger interest in consumer demand is manifest in these organisations.

The entrepreneurial co-operatives differ in two main respects, namely (1) whether the individual co-owners are external investors or patrons (suppliers, users), and (2) whether the business activities are conducted within the co-operative society itself or take place within a PLC (public limited company). Combining these two dimensions, the four classes presented in Table 18.1 are arrived at.

Table 18.1 Four classes of entrepreneurial co-operative models

Locus of business activities	Investors' identity	
	External investors	Member investors
Business in co-operative society	Participation share co-op	Proportional tradable share co-op
Business in subsidiary PLC	Co-operative subsidiaries	PLC co-operative

- Participation share co-operatives: Members or non-members have bought tradable shares in the co-operative society for the purpose of receiving a return on that investment. Thereby, the capital base of the co-operative increases and the board as well as the management have an incentive to be market oriented.
- Co-operative subsidiaries: The co-operative holds the majority of a subsidiary firm, while the rest of the shares are owned by outside investors (including members in their investor role). Thereby, capital can be substantially increased, especially as there is a possibility for a two- or multi-tier system of subsidiaries, all with external co-owners. With large capital input from external investors, the co-operative has to be as business oriented as IOFs.
- Proportional tradable share co-operative: This model is practically identical with the well-known New Generation Co-operative model, which expanded rapidly in the US Midwest during the 1990s. It implies that the membership is closed, all members have production contracts with the co-operative, the shares (that is, the delivery

contracts) are tradable at a market rate, and the members invest heavily in the co-operative. All this means that the co-operative becomes market oriented to an extreme degree. The very initiative to establish the co-operative takes its departure in the final consumer market.

– PLC co-operatives: PLC co-operatives may function in pretty much the same way as new generation co-operatives (proportional tradable shares) but the legal form is different. As the PLC form facilitates the sales of shares to non-patrons, there are often quite a few non-patron shareholders, though less than 50 per cent of the votes, otherwise the firm would not qualify as a co-operative.

The four entrepreneurial co-operative models as well as the traditional one should be interpreted as ideal types in the sense of Max Weber, that is, not all real-life co-operatives fit neatly into the structure. There are many variants within each class.

6.3 Organic Business Depending on Organisational Model

These co-operative models accounted for here have, as one may expect, considerable differences when it comes to the co-operatives' propensity to work with organic food products. Hence, traditional co-operatives could be expected to take a reluctant attitude towards organic products. This organisational model is constructed in order to operate at a very low cost level, and hence to be competitive through low consumer price. Therefore, homogeneity is a keyword for attaining economies of scale. The products delivered by members should be homogeneous, therefore the membership should be homogeneous, like the production processes. The amount of equity capital could, and should, be small, as the members are not willing to supply large amounts of capital and as the operations are of a very simple kind. Interest is also focused on existing members, rather than potential new members.

All this implies that the introduction of organic products into a traditional co-operative would cause a variety of problems. The membership becomes more heterogeneous whereby the members will have more difficulties controlling the firm. Resources for R&D as well as for marketing of the organic products would probably be paid by money earned from the conventional business. This implies cross-subsidisation between conventional producers and organic ones which may not only create conflicts but also hamper efficiency. All in all, traditional co-operatives cannot be expected to embark upon new business areas like organic milk. To the extent that the market demand turns out to be very strong and the consumers are willing to pay a very high price, such co-operatives may feel obliged to change their mind, though hesitantly.

Empirical observations support these statements; all the Swedish dairy co-operatives have, for a long time, been opposed to organic products, as have the Danish. All of these are traditionally organised co-operatives, with open memberships, delivery rights, equal voting rights, collective finance, and so on. In the debates within the memberships, frequently heard arguments were that the conventional producers did not want the co-operative to market any products that might challenge the existing product mix. At present, when the demand for organic products has proven itself to be large and stable, the attitudes have changed, though only in the largest co-operatives.

The probability for organic milk marketing is higher in the entrepreneurial co-operative forms, as here the co-operative firms do adopt many of the characteristics of IOFs. One may, however, expect the following differences between the various models:

The participation share co-operatives do not deviate very much from the traditional form and so they may still be expected to be fairly negative. The co-operative is still basically collectively organised like a traditional co-operative, the difference being that the external investors' claim for a good return on their investment will create a more aggressive, market-oriented attitude.

The opportunity for organic business increases dramatically when co-operatives run business activities within subsidiaries with external co-owners. Such a subsidiary may even be devoted specifically to organic products, and that subsidiary's ownership may consist of farmers producing organic milk. The problems of traditional co-operatives are solved to a large extent; all conventional products are in the co-operative society and all organic products are in the subsidiary. The smaller the co-operative's share in the subsidiary, the fewer the problems.

Likewise, organic milk seems to be a perfect market niche for both new generation co-operatives and PLC co-operatives. Especially in an early phase of market penetration, co-operatives applying these models may be expected to be active while some problems may appear if the demand turns out to be very large and rapidly expanding, thereby requiring a larger amount of capital than the farmers are able to raise. The first larger dairy to produce organic milk in Sweden, Milko, initially organised the production of organic milk in a separate economic organisation with the Milko co-operative as the dominant owner and where the individual organic producers owned the rest of the organisation and also controlled the management of the organisation. The one successful Danish co-operative for organic milk, ØkoMælk, is incorporated as a PLC with only farmers as shareholders.

Hypotheses:

- Traditionally organised co-operatives may be expected to take a reluctant attitude towards entering the organic food market. Normally, the same applies to participation share co-operatives.
- When, and if, a traditional co-operative starts the production and marketing of organic products it may safeguard its existing organisational form by separating this product line from the rest of the firm, for example by establishing a subsidiary and even more so by inviting the members who supply organic products to be shareholders of this subsidiary.
- After the demand for organic products is clearly established, and it is steady and growing, a traditional co-operative may be expected to embark on that market segment, though its traditional organisational form is threatened.
- The new generation co-operative model and the PLC co-operative model are perfectly suited for serving the organic food market.

7 DIFFERENT SUB-MARKETS EXHIBIT DIFFERENCES IN MARKET SHARE

While the co-operative organisational model is certainly crucial in explaining the organisational issues in connection with ecological milk products, other variables are important as well. As all Swedish dairy processors are co-operatives, organised according to the traditional model, the regional differences in organic milk products' market share must be for other reasons. Some potential reasons are discussed below.

7.1 Processing Firms

The size of the dairy processor can be expected to play a decisive role, since dairy processing is an industry characterised by considerable economies of scale. This applies equally to conventional and organic products. Hence, a small processor will have difficulties in becoming competitive, especially in the introductory phase of the product life cycle. In this phase it may be necessary to establish an exclusive position in the market, thereby earning monopoly rents to cover the initially high costs per unit.

Arla may serve as an example. Being the by far largest dairy processor in the Swedish market, it has advantages compared to all the competitors. The market share for organic milk products is significantly higher within Arla's geographical area than in any other part of the country. As Arla has reached such a dominant position, it will be difficult for other processors to get a strong enough foothold in the organic market. Rather, Arla has good chances of selling its organic products in the regions where other processors are dominating the market for conventional dairy products.

Different dairy processors apply different market strategies. It should be remembered that traditional dairy co-operatives are not in business in order to sell organic products, but in order to improve the economies of their members, regardless of their production method. Hence, the co-operative might settle for a marketing strategy that implies focusing on conventional milk, induced by its cost structure, its existing market position, problems in monitoring members, difficulties in matching demanded and supplied volume, unsatisfactory price level for organic products, logistics (transportation), and so on. There are many economically sound reasons for a traditional dairy processor not to get involved in organic products.

There are good reasons to assume that the largest dairy co-operative is the most advanced in terms of marketing. Economies of scale are significant in milk processing and it should be even more important for a low volume product such as organic milk. In order to be profitable under such conditions the producer must use some degree of monopoly pricing, that is, set prices above marginal costs, and it must be able to control the inflow of raw milk.

Also, marketing is characterised by economies of scale. Hence, it is natural that Arla is the one that developed a deliberate strategy for organic products. Expressed differently: there may exist positive feedback loops – due to its size, Arla can reap economies of scale, thereby paying the members a fairly high milk price. This causes an increased volume of milk as existing members expand their operations and new members are attracted. In order to market the increasing volumes, Arla is propelled to constantly develop new products and new markets. Once the production of organic milk is established, Arla's larger production volume will give it a cost advantage over any newcomer.

It is true that the first dairy processor to market organic products in Sweden was one of the medium-sized co-operatives, Milko. This launch was, however, not a full-hearted attempt to conquer the market. It was rather the result of interested farmers and enthusiastic employees who wanted to test the market for organic milk.

To the extent that the demand on a processor's 'domestic' market grows and especially if competitors are fulfilling that demand, a revised market strategy is likely. Similarly, if a group of ecologically oriented members put forward a serious threat of leaving the co-operative, either establishing a competing firm or entering a neighbouring co-operative, there may be good reasons to reconsider the strategy.

The Swedish organic farmers who have established their own processing plants for organic products failed because they could not find means to finance a firm that was sufficiently large to have low average costs. A plausible reason for the fact that no new co-operatives or no new organic milk processor has got a foothold in Sweden is that Arla, and previously Milko, were rather alert in the development of organic food interests. In Denmark, new farmer co-operatives for organic milk have been established several times, though all but one have been forced to cease their operations. Interesting to note is that the newcomers have caused the major co-operatives to put more efforts into the marketing of organic products.

7.2 Consumers

The demand for organic products is unevenly distributed. Large population conglomerates tend to exhibit more interest in environmental issues while the reverse may be true for rural areas. Hence, the processing firm that has a strong market position in the larger cities will have the greatest chance to succeed with the marketing of organic products, and ceteris paribus this processor is more likely to launch such products.

As a good example, Arla supplies the greater Stockholm area with milk products. Except for the Stockholm market, Arla's market coverage also comprises several university cities, where the sales of organic products are very high. Milko, as a comparison, is marketing its products mainly to smaller towns and to large rural areas.

In the phase before organic products have got a foothold in the markets, some pioneering farmers may be strongly involved in the production of organic products, selling them to local consumers. The reasons may be varied; traditions, social influences, regional chauvinism, and so on. To the extent that this happens, those farmers, and perhaps even more the consumers, are likely to create more or less informal groups that could act as pressure groups in relation to their regular processing firm, whether co-operative or investor-owned. Some kind of co-operative organisation or contract production may be introduced jointly by producers and consumers.

Hypotheses:

- The position of organic milk products may be weaker in regions dominated by small dairy processors, since these are likely to start the organic milk operations later and to put relatively less resources into the operations, because they may be more sensitive to the higher risks in organic milk, compared to conventional production.

- Likewise, the market is weaker if organic products do not fit into the marketing strategy of the dairy processor and the competitive threat is small.
- The consumer demand for organic milk products may be expected to be larger per capita in large cities.
- Regions with a tradition of organic production within other industries may be expected to be pioneering in the dairy operations.

8 CONCLUSIONS

This exploratory study investigates the introduction of a new line of food products, namely organic food, using milk as a typical case. Milk is an important food item in Sweden. Most people drink milk even as adults. Dairying is also important to the agricultural sector as a majority of the full-time farmers in Sweden produce milk. Milking cows graze large areas of pasture, important as recreation areas, biologically rich habitats and appreciated open landscape.

The strong expansion of organic milk products in Sweden may be explained by a number of factors, for example a general interest for the environment, a trend towards more ‘healthy’ products, a more heterogeneous food market, producer interests and political ambitions. When it comes to consumers, one can identify many interesting aspects in relation to organic milk. Biodiversity, open landscape and environmentally friendly production systems are products that individual farmers cannot easily market. The organic labels on food products enable a new development. These brands make it possible to sell goods including elements that are traditionally seen as non-excludable and non-rival, that is, so-called public goods. The eco-brand, therefore, links consumers with preferences for such goods to producers and enables a market for goods that partly work as intermediaries for these public goods. In this respect organic food is only one part of what is exchanged. Producers also sell other goods and consumers partly buy a lifestyle and a belonging to certain social groups.

Farmer co-operatives seem to be well suited for organic products. However, the well-established traditional farmer co-operatives are not the best. The best ones are rather what has become known as new generation co-operatives, or co-operative subsidiaries. These organisations may close their membership, focus on specific organic products and direct their sales to a certain group of consumers.

If farmers with common interests in organic production join together they may reap the traditional advantages in the co-operative organisation. By using an exclusive brand they can attract environmentally oriented consumers. The co-operative firm may also have an advantage in the eyes of the consumers – it may be seen as something other than a pure profit maximiser. This may particularly be the case if environmentally interested consumers share opinions such as the consumption of food as a meaning-building activity related to other activities that, taken together, influence the environment. Hence, a farmer co-operative may seem to be a more trustworthy partner than an IOF.

In the initial stage it may be an advantage if the new products are treated separately. For farmer co-operatives it may be problematic to mix a new product, which differs mainly in terms of production system, with the traditional products. Tension between producer groups may be problematic, especially in smaller co-operatives. On the other hand, smaller co-operatives, or smaller firms in general, may have problems raising resources for becoming established in new markets. Further, regional differences concerning market shares for organic milk may be due to the size of the dairy processor, that is, economies of scale in production, distribution and marketing.

REFERENCES

Bekkum, O.-F. van and G. van Dijk (eds) (1997), *Agricultural Co-operatives in the European Union. Trends and Issues on the Eve of the 21st Century*, Assen: van Gorcum.

Drake, L. (1992), 'The Non-market Value of Agricultural Landscape', *European Review of Agricultural Economics*, **19** (3), pp. 351–64.

Krashinsky, M. (1986), 'Transaction Costs and a Theory of the Non-profit Organization', in Rose-Ackerman, S. (ed.), *The Economics of Non-profit Institutions*, New York: Oxford University Press, pp. 113–42.

Sexton, R.J. (1986), 'The Formation of Co-operatives: A Game Theoretic Approach with Implications for Co-operative Finance, Decision Making, and Stability', *American Journal of Agricultural Economics*, **68** (2), pp. 214–25.

Solér, C. (1997), *Att köpa miljövänliga dagligvaror (Buying Environmentally Friendly Grocery Products, PhD thesis)*, Göteborg: Nerenius och Santérus.

Staatz, J.M. (1989), 'Farmer Co-operative Theory: Recent Developments', United States Department of Agriculture, Agricultural Co-operative Service, Report No. 84, June, Washington DC.

Thøgersen, J. (1999), 'Making Ends Meet: A Synthesis of Research on Consumer Behaviour and the Environment', Working Paper 99-1. Aarhus: The Aarhus School of Business.

19. Evaluating Small-Scale Collective Initiatives Producing and Marketing Environmentally Friendly Food Products

Guido Van Huylenbroeck and Ingrid Verhaegen

1 INTRODUCTION

Agri-environmental policies try to stimulate the provision of agri-environmental goods and services (EGS) through compensatory payments. However, EGS production is often a joint product of agricultural commodities produced through the application of specific agricultural practices. This opens, as demonstrated for example by Merlo, Milocco and Virgilietti (2000), the possibility for creating specific markets and remunerating farmers for their efforts through increased market prices (the beneficiary pays principle).

The creation of such a market is, however, not easy and often requires collective action because, in most cases, the produced agricultural commodities are not different in size, shape or form from the normal produce, but only in their intrinsic quality. Market separation must therefore be realised using specific marketing techniques (labels or brand names) or specific marketing channels (for example direct marketing). To be successful, these efforts need a certain scale, in particular when environmental efforts require a certain dimension to be effective. This scale is only possible when several farmers collaborate and when also other actors in the marketing channel are involved. In this chapter, the organisational form of six Belgian initiatives producing and marketing environmentally friendly produced agricultural commodities is analysed from a transaction cost theory perspective. In section 2 a theoretical frame is presented. In section 3 the initiatives are described and classified into three distinguishable models, and the three models are analysed by breaking down the transactions into their components. In section 4 some conclusions are drawn.

2 THE TRANSACTION COST THEORY AND THE ANALYSIS OF PRODUCTION AND MARKETING ORGANISATIONS

The archetypal question in transaction cost economics is the make-or-buy question. This question is answered by characterising the transactions and the alternative governance structures and then aligning those two in a cost economising manner. The attributes that differentiate the transactions in a transaction cost perspective are the frequency with which transactions recur, the uncertainty to which they are subject, and the asset specificity which is involved in the transaction. The governance structures can be distinguished by the following attributes: the instruments they use (price incentives or administrative control), the performance attributes (autonomous or co-operative adaptation) and the kind of contracts they use (classical, neoclassical or relational contracts). The theoretical alignment between transactions and governance structures to obtain a (mainly) transaction cost economising result is given in Table 19.1 (Williamson 1996).

Table 19.1 Transactions aligned with governance structures

Transactions	Governance structure		
	Market	Hybrid form	Firm/Hierarchy
Specificity			
non-specific	X		
mixed		X	
idiosyncratic		X	X
Uncertainty			
low		X	(X)
high		(X)	X
Frequency			
occasional		X	
recurrent		X	X

The link between a transaction and the governance structure that is best suited to the organisation of that transaction in a cost minimising way, is principally determined by the asset specificity involved in the transaction. This relation is represented in Figure 19.1. That asset specificity is the most important attribute is mostly explained by the fact that, in an environment with bounded rationality, opportunism and uncertainty (complexity), the actors who invest specific assets want some safeguards to guarantee the continuation of the transactions. Governance structures have different abilities to ensure these safeguards. Frequency and uncertainty play an important secondary role for specific transactions. The costs of specialised governance structures will be easier to recover for large transactions of a recurring kind. An increase of the exogenous uncertainty with specific transactions makes it more imperative that the parties devise a machinery to 'work things out', since contractual gaps will be larger and the occasions for sequential adaptations will increase in number and importance as the degree of uncertainty increases (Williamson 1985; Ménard 1997).

To reach predictive capacity, Williamson (1998) proposed four subsequent steps in the research: (1) dimensionalising transactions; (2) dimensionalising governance structures; (3) effecting a discriminating alignment between the two; and (4) empirical testing of this alignment. How this theoretical frame can be applied in practice has been shown in Verhaegen and Van Huylenbroeck (1999).

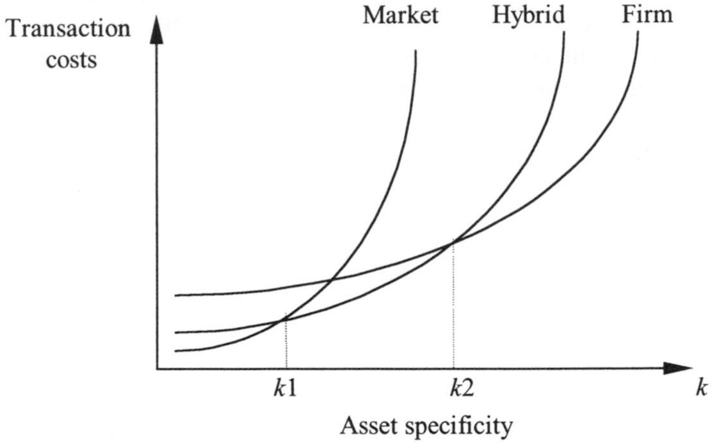

Source: Ménard (1997).

Figure 19.1 Asset specificity and transaction costs under different governance structures

In order to evaluate the net benefits of a participant in a specific marketing channel, the initiative must be compared with the normal market chain of their revenues, direct (production) costs and transaction costs. Suppose an initiative with a commercialisation chain wherein three actors are involved: the producer (p), the middleman (m) and the salesman (s). The profit functions can then be written for the situation with the initiative (index 1) and for the situation without the initiative (index 2).

Profit functions with the initiative:

$$\Pi_{p1} = P_{p1}Q_{p1} - r_{p1}I_{p1} - TC_{p1}$$
$$\Pi_{m1} = P_{m1}Q_{m1} - P_{p1}Q_{p1} - r_{m1}I_{m1} - TC_{m1}$$
$$\Pi_{s1} = P_{s1}Q_{s1} - P_{m1}Q_{m1} - r_{s1}I_{s1} - TC_{s1}$$

Profit functions without the initiative:

$$\Pi_{p2} = P_{p2}Q_{p2} - r_{p2}I_{p2} - TC_{p2}$$
$$\Pi_{m2} = P_{m2}Q_{m2} - P_{p2}Q_{p2} - r_{m2}I_{m2} - TC_{m2}$$
$$\Pi_{s2} = P_{s2}Q_{s2} - P_{m2}Q_{m2} - r_{s2}I_{s2} - TC_{s2}$$

With: P_p, P_m and P_s the product price received by the farmer, the middleman and the salesman respectively; Q_p, Q_m and Q_s the quantities sold by the farmer, the middleman and the salesman respectively; I_p, I_m and I_s the production factors and other inputs used by the farmer, the middleman and the salesman respectively; r_p, r_m and r_s the remuneration of the inputs paid by the farmer, the middleman and the salesman respectively; and TC_p, TC_m and TC_s the transaction costs borne by the farmer, the middleman and the salesman respectively.

So the profit (Π) is the difference between the revenues and the costs. The revenues depend on the price (P) and the quantity (Q) sold. The costs are threefold, namely the purchasing costs of the original product, the costs for the use of inputs (I) that have to be paid a remuneration (r) and the transaction costs (TC).

The model can be used to evaluate possible organisation models (see below). A first application of the model is to calculate the total profitability over all actors of a new commercialisation chain in comparison with the common chain. Working under the hypothesis that the actors in both chains use the same inputs against the same costs, the profit of the new commercialisation chain can be written as follows:

$$\Pi_{\text{chain}} = (P_{s1}Q_{s1} - P_{s2}Q_{s2}) - (TC_{p1} - TC_{p2}) - (TC_{h1} - TC_{h2}) - (TC_{e1} - TC_{e2}) \tag{19.1}$$

A second possible use of the model is to evaluate the effect when the new commercialisation chain has fewer actors than the common chain, which is the case when the farmer sells directly to the consumer, for example at a farmers' market. Then the profit of the chain can be written as:

$$\Pi_{\text{direct sales}} = \Pi_{p1} - (\Pi_{p2} + \Pi_{m2} + \Pi_{s2})$$
$$= (P_{p1}Q_{p1} - P_{s2}Q_{s2}) - (r_{p1}I_{p1} - r_{p2}I_{p2} - r_{m2}I_{m2} - r_{s2}I_{s2}) - (TC_{p1} - TC_{p2} - TC_{m2} - TC_{s2}) \quad (19.2)$$

This makes it possible to evaluate if the farmer has taken over the middleman's functions in a cost efficient way.

A third way to use the model is the one that will be used in this chapter, namely to evaluate the profitability of a new commercialisation chain for one actor in particular, in our case the farmer. For the farmer the following equation can be used:

$$\Pi_{p1} - \Pi_{p2} = (P_{p1}Q_{p1} - P_{p2}Q_{p2}) - (r_{p1}I_{p1} - r_{p2}I_{p2}) - (TC_{p1} - TC_{p2}) \quad (19.3)$$

The latter equation makes it possible to take into account trade-off effects between revenues, input costs and transaction costs.

3 DESCRIPTION OF THE INITIATIVES

In a 1996 countrywide inventory of innovative marketing channels for agricultural commodities, more than 100 initiatives were identified (Van Huylenbroeck et al. 1998). These initiatives were all involved in producing, transforming and selling farm products in a different way from the mainstream production. In most cases, differentiation of the products is based on the use of production practices respecting the environment, animal health, the local landscape, and so on. The production methods are in most cases described in a code of practice ('cahier de charge') stipulating what is allowed, obliged and/or defended.

Six of these initiatives have been studied in more detail. In Table 19.2 some characteristics of the organisations are described. As can be seen in all initiatives, several farmers are involved but also other actors in the marketing channel. In all the prescriptions for farmers to become members of the initiative, explicit environmental requirements are mentioned. In Fruitnet, an organisation promoting integrated pip fruit production, the central requirement is a ban of certain pesticides and the use of environmentally friendly insect control methods. In the beef co-operative ProQA, the use of grain produced at the farm, the minimum animal health prescriptions and the maximum number of animals per hectare are requirements which are also beneficial for the environment. Coprosain and Fermière de Méan have clear prescriptions as to the protection of the environment and the use of fertilisers, pesticides and other inputs.

Table 19.2 Characterisation of the transactions of six innovative marketing channels for environmentally friendly produced food products

	Fruitnet	ProQA	Coprosain	Fermière de Méan	Farmers' market	Food teams
Products sold	pip fruit	beef	meat and meat products	farm products	farm products	Farm products
Main activity of the organisation	co-ordination, control and promotion	co-ordination and promotion	co-ordination, processing, trade, promotion	co-ordination, processing, trade, promotion	co-ordination, control, promotion	co-ordination, promotion
Main actors involved in the chain	farmers, auctions, supermarket, fruitnet, controlling organisation	farmers, cattle-merchant, butchers, controlling organisation	farmers, coprosain, controlling organisations	farmers, fermière, consumers	farmers, consumers	farmers, consumers, two organisations
Environmental requirements	ban of certain pesticides and adoption of integrated control	extensive production methods (BBF requirements), minimum % of own feed	specific conditions on the use of sustainable agricultural practices	specific conditions on the use of sustainable agricultural practices	no formal rules, except only selling own produce and use of packing material which can be recycled	no general rules, but in each team consumers decide on acceptance of certain practices
Asset specificity	high (special production knowledge)	moderate (specific production practices)	high (production + transformation)	high (production + transformation)	high (production + transformation)	high (production + transformation)
Product specificity:						
– external	not	not	weak	weak	not or weak	not or weak
– quality	moderate	moderate	high	high	high	high
Uncertainty	low	high	high	moderate	moderate	moderate
Frequency	high	high	high	high	high	high

The last two initiatives (farmers' markets and food teams) are less formal with respect to applied practices, but both initiatives only accept farmers selling their own output (regional dimension). Further, at the farmers' markets only products sold in packages that can be recycled are accepted. In the food teams, also, no general rules are applied, but each team can, in negotiation with the farmers, require certain guarantees about the use of sustainable practices. Although not a formal requirement, it can be observed that most participants refer to environmentally friendly practices in their publicity to consumers and that a large part of them are organic producers.

In Table 19.2 also, the specificity of the produced commodities is indicated. In all marketing channels the transactions could be characterised as moderate to highly specific, with moderate to great uncertainty and high frequency. The specificity is mostly due to the specific investments (in assets and human capital) necessary for the production and sale of farm products. The products themselves are specific but only in intrinsic quality because they definitely carry the identity of the farmer-producer by taste, storage possibility, and so on. However, the products cannot really be distinguished from similar products on the basics of external signs such as form or shape and must be distinguished through packaging, and most of all by the information that accompanies them. The high uncertainty is due to a great vulnerability to sales variation and because of the great product risks due to a lack of craftsmanship and knowledge networks. The frequency is high, at least weekly. The characterisation of the transactions points out that, theoretically, the firm is the most appropriate governance structure, also because the best form of communication is direct contact between producers and consumers. This means that the farmers will integrate the production and commercialisation in their own agricultural enterprise. However, this is only possible when farmers are selling their own products directly and have labour in excess to do this (extra costs). But when this is not possible or when the scale is increased other forms of communication requiring a certain form of organisation are necessary in which case three approaches can be distinguished:

- The use of traditional marketing channels but market separation through certification and labelling (Fruitnet, ProQA).
- The construction of a separated marketing channel with own selling points (Coprosain, Fermière de Méan).
- The use of direct marketing channels but with a certain form of co-operation and central organisation (farmers' markets, food teams).

In the next section these three forms are further analysed and discussed from a transaction cost perspective.

4 ORGANISATION OF THE INITIATIVES

4.1 Product Specification through Certification

In the first model the farmer signs a contract with a central actor in the marketing channel (a wholesaler in the case of the beef co-operative ProQA; a central organisation linked to an auction in the case of Fruitnet) to produce according to the environmentally friendly standards of the label. The compliance with these rules is controlled by at least one of the parties, but in most cases also by a state recognised certification and control organism, which certifies when the products are delivered to the central organisation that the production standards are respected. This control is paid for by the farmer, who in return receives a higher price as long as consumers are willing to pay a higher price for the labelled product. In terms of the theoretical model (19.3) of section 2, the only differences for the farmer, if we assume that the specific environmental requirements have no influence on the quantity sold, are the higher price for the output (+), the eventual higher costs for the inputs caused by the environmental requirements (–) and the extra transaction costs because of the payment to the certification organism (–).

In the analysis for the labelled beef of ProQA in Verhaegen and Van Huylenbroeck (1999), it is shown that the higher prices are enough to compensate the higher costs, although the price advantage has decreased the last couple of years because of generally lower market prices and due to the inflation of labels in the meat sector after the hormone scandal and BSE crisis, which has diminished the specificity of existing labels and thus the benefit of participating farmers. Also for the integrated pip fruit, received prices at farm gate are on an average 10 per cent higher than for products not sold under the label. The increased success of this organisation is an indication that, in this case, the label is beneficial for participating farmers.

4.2 Own Marketing Channel

In the previous model each farmer remains independent and the normal marketing channel and actors are used. Contacts among farmers or between farmers and consumers are not previewed or necessary although in practice regular meetings between participants are organised to discuss the problems of the label. The second organisation model is more complex and based on closer collaboration between different partners. This model has its origin in the direct marketing of farm products.

At a certain moment, however, farmers producing specific environmental quality feel the need to increase their market possibilities and start a closer co-operation, mainly in the transformation of their products. In order to maintain the specificity of the products, their marketing chain is constructed selling these (transformed) products under a common name in own selling points which can be their own shops, a special car for selling at public markets or even their own or related restaurants. Such creation of a transformation and marketing channel requires, of course, a high internal organisation with agreements on delivery amounts and times, internal quality controls, monitoring systems for the compliance with the agreed production rules, extra administration and employment of qualified people. Although in this model the direct contact between the organisation and the consumers is maintained, the contact of consumers with the farm practices and production methods becomes less evident as professional selling people are employed. Another factor decreasing the specificity of the model is that in order to have a higher variety of products and a more constant supply and quality, more farmers are accepted into the group, automatically leading to less homogeneity.

In terms of the theoretical model of section 2, this organisational form for selling environmentally friendly produce causes bigger changes, as the price of the products must also include the organisation costs of the co-operative. As shown for example by Saccomandi (1998), such a co-operative will only be profitable for its members at a size where the increase in organisation costs is in equilibrium with the decrease of production and functioning costs due to economies of scale. In practice, this means that a tension will exist between the farmers willing to receive a higher price for their products and the co-operative trying to maximise the profit of the central organisation. Although it could be observed that for the two case studies the prices farmers receive are higher than under normal conditions, some farmers started to complain and were also selling part of their product through other chains (for example direct marketing), indicating that the cost–benefit ratio of the organisation is not always positive for the farmers.

4.3 Organised Direct Marketing

The third model has a more simple structure and seeks to preserve, as much as possible, the direct contact between farmers and consumers. The only objective of collaboration here is the creation of a 'meeting point' between consumers and farmers to make transactions easier and create a certain economy of scale. The meeting point can be physically through the organisation of a specific 'farm product' market on a specified day in the week or more 'organisational' through the creation of consumer groups placing global orders (for example weekly) to farmers, as is the case in the 'Food team' model. Although in comparison with direct selling at the farms, no extra 'production' costs are required, this organisational form also causes higher transaction costs for making the transactions possible. Going to a farm market or delivering at food teams requires extra time from the farmers, and also extra costs (organisational costs, market licence, transport, and so on). Participating farmers are therefore predominantly small-scale farmers producing under a certain agri-environmental programme (for example organic farmers), with an excess of labour which they can validate through this self-marketing. When this activity, however, increases, a choice has to be made between the production and the transformation and marketing activity.

Specific in this model is that the scale per market or team remains limited but that one seeks to realise the economies of scale by multiplying the model at different places. However, this requires a central organisation to manage the different teams or markets, causing in its turn extra transaction costs (costs of the central organism). The advantage is that the direct contact between producers and consumers is maintained, and thus no extra costs are required to specify the products. Another consequence of this close contact is that consumers are willing to voluntarily take up some part of the transaction costs, such as the handling of the orders, the distribution of the goods and the collection of the payments. The role of the central organisation is to protect the model, to control agreed upon production methods, to search for new markets or teams and to promote the existing markets or food teams. Further, local volunteers take care of the internal local organisation and control.

5 CONCLUSIONS

The six described cases clearly show that it is possible to make the beneficiary pay for the increased effort of environmental protection on the part of farmers through the selling of joint products (increased 'intrinsic' quality of products produced according to environmentally friendly practices). To do this at a certain scale, requires, however, co-operation between farmers and between farmers and actors in the market. Three different models of market organisation to increase the scale of such organisations have been described and analysed. Each of them requires extra transaction costs, mainly because environmentally friendly products can only be distinguished from the mainstream products through guaranteeing quality. The lower the direct contact between the farmers and consumers, the higher the need for formal guarantees of the specific quality.

The three models all have their advantages and disadvantages and the best form will depend on the product, farm and market size. Direct marketing co-operation, as in the case of farmers' markets and food teams, can be a solution for relatively small farmers having an excess of labour on their farm, producing non-transformed products with farm practices protecting local public goods. The second model seems to be a possibility for larger farms applying specific environmentally friendly practices and for products needing a transformation and for which the added value is lost if they are sold to the normal transformation channels. The use of a co-operative form with own selling points can guarantee the specificity of the produce.

Finally, the use of certificates and labels seems most appropriate for generic actions towards the environment in which the decrease or ban of certain inputs is the central issue, but for the rest the product quality remains the same. Here the normal market channels are used and farmers are not involved in the market organisation themselves but certification and labels are used as a market separation tool to obtain a higher price compensating the extra efforts or higher costs of the farmers (compare also the AOC model).

All three models, however, cause extra transaction and organisation costs decreasing the added value of the market chain. These costs must certainly be taken into account when setting up co-operative action. When this is not done and the extra costs are not remunerated, the initiative will not last long as proved by the relatively high number of failures that could be observed (for example the failure in Flanders to set up a chain of organic food shops). As indicated in Verhaegen and Van Huylenbroeck (1999) it is also very important to choose the correct organisational form. Transaction cost theory can be a helpful framework for this kind of analysis.

REFERENCES

Ménard, C. (1997), 'Le pilotage des formes organisationnelles hybrides', *Revue économique*, **48** (3), pp. 741–50.

Merlo, M., E. Milocco and P. Virgilietti (2000), 'Market Remuneration for Goods and Services Provided by Agriculture', in Brouwer F. (ed.), *CAP Regimes and the European Countryside*, Wallingford: CABI.

Saccomandi, V. (1998), *Agricultural Market Economics: a Neo-institutional Analysis of the Exchange, Circulation and Distribution*, Assen: van Gorcum.

Van Huylenbroeck, G., I. Verhaegen, E. Collet, M. Mormont, P. Stassart and J. Vannoppen (1998), 'An Inventory of Emerging Innovation Projects in Belgian Agriculture', in Arfini, F. and C. Mora (eds), *Typical and Traditional Products: Rural Effect and Agro-industrial Problems*, Proceedings of the 52nd Seminar of the European Association of Agricultural Economists (EAAE) on 'EU Typical and Traditional

Productions: Rural Effect and Agro-industrial Problems" June 19–22, 1997, Parma – Italy, Parma: Università di Parma, pp.169–86.

Verhaegen, I. and G. Van Huylenbroeck (1999a), 'A Transaction Cost Analysis of a Small Innovative Marketing Channel for Beef in Belgium', *Journal of International Food and Agribusiness Marketing*, **10** (3), pp. 1–17.

Verhaegen, I. and G. Van Huylenbroeck (1999b), 'Analysing the Governance of Innovative Local Marketing Channels in Belgian Agriculture with the Transaction Cost Theory', Paper presented at the IX EAAE-Congress 'European Agriculture Facing 21st Century in a Global Context', Warsaw.

Williamson, O.E. (1985), *The Economic Institutions of Capitalism*, New York: The Free Prcss.

Williamson, O.E. (1996), *The Mechanisms of Governance*, New York: Oxford University Press.

Williamson, O.E. (1998), 'Transaction Cost Economics: How it Works: Where it is Headed', *The Economist*, **146,** pp. 23–58.

Index